INTERDISCIPLINARY METHODS

This book is part of the Goodyear Series in Education,
Theodore W. Hipple, University of Florida, Editor

OTHER GOODYEAR BOOKS IN GENERAL METHODS AND CENTERS

AH HAH! The Inquiry Process of Generating and Testing Knowledge
    John McCollum

ART CORNER
    Bonnie Flint Striebel and Ruth Beazell Forgan

A CALENDER OF HOME/SCHOOL ACTIVITIES
    Jo Anne Patricia Brosnahan and Barbara Walters Milne

CHANGE FOR CHILDREN, Revised Edition
    Ideas and Activities for Individualizing Learning
    Sandra K. Kaplan, Jo Ann B. Kaplan, Sheila K. Madsen, Bette Gould

CREATING A LEARNING ENVIRONMENT A Learning Center Handbook
    Ethel Breyfogle, Susan Nelson, Carol Pitts, Pamela Santich

DRUGS, KIDS AND SCHOOLS
    Diane Tessler

GAMES CHILDREN SHOULD PLAY
Sequential Lessons For Teaching Communication Skills in Grades K–6
    Mary K. Cihak and Barbara Jackson-Heron

ONE AT A TIME ALL AT ONCE
The Creative Teacher's Guide to Individualized Instruction Without Anarchy
    Jack Blackburn and Conrad Powell

INFANT CURRICULUM Guide to the Care and Development of Infants in Groups
    Patricia Greenfield and Edward Tronick

THE OTHER SIDE OF THE REPORT CARD
A How-To-Do-It Program for Affective Education
    Larry Chase

RECIPES FOR LEARNING Exploring the Curriculum Through Cooking
    Gail Lewis and Jean Shaw

SECONDARY LEARNING CENTERS:
An Innovative Approach to Individualized Instruction
    Clifford Bee

SPECIAL THINGS FOR SPECIAL DAYS
    Pat Short and Billee Davidson

TEACHER-THERAPIST A Text-Handbook for Emotionally Impaired Children
    Doris B. Mosier and Ruth B. Park

THE TEACHER'S CHOICE Ideas and Activities for Teaching Basic Skills
    Sandra N. Kaplan, Sheila K. Madsen, Bette T. Gould

TEACHING FOR LEARNING Applying Educational Psychology in the Classroom
    Myron H. Dembo

T.V. TURN ON/OFF
    Ellen DeFranco

OTHER WAYS, OTHER MEANS Altered Awareness Activities for Receptive Learning
    Alton Harrison and Diann Musial

WILL THE REAL TEACHER PLEASE STAND UP?
A Primer in Humanistic Education, 2nd Edition
    Mary Greer and Bonnie Rubenstein

A YOUNG CHILD EXPERIENCES Activities for Teaching and Learning
    Sandra N. Kaplan, Jo Ann B. Kaplan, Sheila K. Madsen, Bette T. Gould

For information about these, or Goodyear books in Language Arts, Reading, Science, Math, and Social Studies, write to

                      Janet Jackson
                      Goodyear Publishing Company
                      1640 Fifth Street
                      Santa Monica, Ca 90401

INTERDISCIPLINARY METHODS

A Thematic Approach

Coauthored by:

Alan H. Humphreys

Thomas R. Post

Arthur K. Ellis

University of Minnesota
Minneapolis, Minnesota

GOODYEAR PUBLISHING COMPANY, INC.
SANTA MONICA, CALIFORNIA 90401

Library of Congress Cataloging in Publication Data

HUMPHREYS, ALAN H.
    Interdisciplinary methods, a thematic approach

    (Goodyear series in education)
    Includes index.
    1. Curriculum planning. 2. Interdisciplinary approach in education. I. Post, Thomas Richard. II. Ellis, Arthur K. III. Title. IV. Series.
    LB1570.H78   375'.001   81-2918
    ISBN 0-8302-4387-9   AACR2

Copyright © 1981 by Goodyear Publishing Company, Inc.
Santa Monica, California 90401

All rights reserved. No part of this book may be reproduced in any form or by any means, except those portions intended for reproduction by teachers for classroom use, without permission in writing from the publisher.

Y-4387-0

ISBN: 0-8302-4387-9

Current printing (last digit):

10   9   8   7   6   5   4   3   2   1

Production Editor: Susan Caney-Peterson
Copyeditor: Stacey Maxwell
Proofreader: Sheryl Rose
Art: Etc. Graphics
Cover Design: Curtis Cooper
Book Design: Linda Robertson
Composition: Computer Typesetting Services, Inc.

Printed in the United States of America

Contents

    Prologue   *xi*
    Acknowledgments   *xiii*

Chapter One   Why? A Rationale   1
    A Conversation   *1*
    The Teacher as Problem Finder   *4*
    From Problem Finding to Problem Solving   *6*
    Students as Problem Solvers   *7*
    You and Your Students As Problem Solvers   *7*
    A Few Activities to Get You Started   *8*
    Summing Up Problem Solving   *11*
    Integrated Studies—A Brief Overview   *11*
    Back or Forward to the Basics?   *14*
    Summary   *19*

Chapter Two   How? A Methodology of Thematics   21
    Integrated Teaching and Learning   *21*
    Developing Your Own Integrated Theme   *26*
    Questioning   *32*
    Reports and Displays of Children's Work   *39*
    Assessing Learning and Progress   *41*
    One Teacher's Theme: Peanut Butter   *52*
    Summary   *61*

Chapter Three   What? A Sampler of Thematic Units   63
    Introduction   *63*
    1. Parkland   *65*
    2. Flight   *70*
    3. Consumerism   *77*
    4. What Time Is It?   *90*

CONTENTS

    5. Sailboats *102*
    6. Energy *112*
    7. Cooperation/Competition *149*
    8. Environments *177*
    9. Growing and Using Plants *200*
   10. Read All About It! *217*
   11. Mnemonics *240*
   12. Patterns and Changes *260*
   13. Inventions *275*
   14. Go Fly a Kite! *290*

Epilogue   **303**

Appendix   Useful Instructional Resources   **305**

Photo Credits   **323**

Index   **325**

Some Interesting People

E. F. Schumacher *4*
Jean Piaget *8–9*
Zoltan P. Dienes *12*
Ivan Illich *14*
Jerome Bruner *16–17*
Hilda Taba *23*

Abraham Maslow *27*
Lev S. Vygotsky *31*
Maria Montessori *40*
Robert Gagne *42*
David Ausubel *49*

THEME	MAJOR AREAS OF EMPHASIS	APPROPRIATE GRADE*	PREFERRED SEASON	ALLOTTED TIME AT (1 Hr/Day)
Peanut Butter	Mathematics, Decision Making, Communication Skills	3–6	FWS	6 weeks
Parkland	Science, Mathematics	2–6	Spring	3 weeks (spread over 2 months)
Flight	Social Science, Science, Language Arts, Mathematics	6–8	Fall	3 weeks
Consumerism	Social Studies, Language Arts	4–6	FWS	2 weeks
What Time Is It?	Mathematics, Science, Archeology	3–6	Fall	1–2 weeks
Sailboats	Science, Social Studies, Language Arts	3–6	Spring	2 weeks
Energy	Science, Mathematics Social Science	4–6	Winter	3 weeks
Cooperation/Competition	Language Arts, Social Studies, Decision Making	3–6	Fall	3 weeks total (spread over 3 months)
Environments	Social Science, Science, Decision Making	3–6	FWS	3 weeks
Growing and Using Plants	Science, Mathematics	3–6	Spring	3 weeks (spread over 2 months)
Read All About It!	Social Science, Language Arts	4–6	FWS	2–4 weeks
Mnemonics	Psychology, Mathematics, Social Science	3–6	Fall	3 weeks (spread over 3 months)
Patterns and Changes	Science, Mathematics	3–6	FWS	2 weeks
Inventions	Science, Mathematics, Language Arts	3–6	FWS	2 weeks
Go Fly a Kite!	Science, Language Arts, Social Science	2–4	Spring	3 weeks

*Approximation: you may find that your students can become effectively involved at grades other than those indicated.

Prologue

> *The goal of education is not to increase the amount of knowledge, but to create possibilities for a child to invent and discover. When we teach too fast, we keep the child from inventing and discovering himself. Teaching means creating situations where structure can be discovered, it does not mean transmitting structure which may be assimilated at nothing other than a verbal level.*
>
> Jean Piaget

This book is about possibilities in teaching and learning. It is about the creation of effective learning situations for teachers and students. We have attempted to put together a number of themes that will allow you and your students to discover, explore, and experiment across the artificial boundaries of subject matter. In that respect, this book represents an attempt to integrate subjects. It is an attempt to create whole, rather than fragmented, patterns for learning. It offers you possibilities rather than finished products.

School subjects are typically taught as discrete entities. The teaching of math has nothing to do with the teaching of reading, which in turn has nothing to do with the teaching of science, and so on. There is little sense of "connectedness" among school subjects or among the parts of the day. Children, who come to school with an integrated view of life and of their world, are quickly dispelled of any notions of the connectedness of things. They are conditioned, in the name of learning, to the idea that knowledge and skills are conveyed through the means of separate subjects.

It is taken for granted, apparently, that in time students will see for themselves how things fit together. Unfortunately, the reality of the situation is that they tend to learn what we teach. If we teach connectedness and integration, they learn that. If we teach separation and discontinuity, that is what they learn. To suppose otherwise would be incongruous.

We propose in this book that you consider the idea of integrated teaching and learning. We have identified a number of themes that lend themselves to integration. In each instance, we have selected topics for the themes that incorporate the humanities and communications arts, the natural sciences, mathematics, and social studies. We have even suggested linkages with music and art.

We do not propose that everything can or ought to be taught to students in an integrated fashion. There are some mathematics skills, for example, that you will continue to teach formally and discretely. This holds true for other subjects as well. The value of the thematic or integrated approach lies partly in its function as a focus on the *application* of the knowledge, skills, and values that are learned in the various formal subjects.

Chapter Three contains fourteen themes to start you off in this integrated approach. You will find that the themes have differing emphases with respect to subject matter and academic disciplines, and we have scattered sketches of influential educators who have had a major impact on our thinking and our dream of assembling the ideas contained herein.

This book is a sampler, and that is our intent in selecting these themes. In addition to their subject matter variability, they will appeal to differing age ranges. We have attempted to sequence them from simplest to more difficult. It should be understood, however, that a good theme can be pursued at any level of sophistication.

In the spirit of thematic, integrated instruction, we challenge you to begin to develop your own units once you feel comfortable with those that we have provided. If you teach near a river, a prairie, a city, a swamp, an airport, a night sky, or a poet, you have the potential beginnings of an integrated unit. The rest is up to you and your students.

Acknowledgments

A manuscript such as this is, by its very nature, a melting pot of philosophies, ideas, and activities. As such, it represents both philosophical and tangible input from a variety of programs, projects, groups and individuals.

Initially, we would like to express our appreciation to the genius of individuals such as Jean Piaget, Jerome Bruner, Zoltan Dienes, and many others. Their writings have caused us to rethink, redefine, and redevelop our own philosophies of education and learning.

Next, we acknowledge the impact which the following projects have had upon our thinking: The Minnesota Mathematics and Science Teaching Project (MINNEMAST), The Unified Science and Mathematics Elementary School Project (USMES), and The Nuffield Mathematics and Science Curriculum Development Projects (English). We all have spent several years of our lives involved with these projects and have fond memories of the excitement and challenge of intellectual investigation and development.

We are indebted to our colleague in music therapy, Professor Judith Jellison, for her contributions to the mnemonics theme.

Last and certainly not least, we are grateful to our colleagues in the classroom, Robin Brown, René Macomber, Kathy Howe, Ann Friederich, Kathy McGree, and Patricia Sullivan, who shared with us their insights and so kindly have given their permission to adapt from their field tested materials. The authors accept full responsibility for any injustices that may have occurred to these materials during the adaptation process. Our special thanks is due to Cyndy Crist who edited the entire manuscript.

We hope that in some small way this work will assist the classroom teacher in making learning a more vibrant, a more stimulating, and a more meaningful experience for every student.

To the teacher interested in pursuing such a goal, we dedicate this book.

INTERDISCIPLINARY METHODS

CHAPTER ONE

Why? A Rationale

A CONVERSATION

ART: What we are advocating in this book is quite different from what often happens in classrooms. We are asking teachers to choose instructional themes in order to develop knowledge, skills, and values in a truly integrated fashion. Preservice and inservice teachers are going to want to know how all these bits and pieces fit together and how to manage the whole process. How do they get students to become effective problem solvers?

ALAN: You're talking about the exciting part of teaching. I would hope that whoever uses these materials will look at them as learning tools. We can't look ahead 20 years and know exactly where we're going to be. By the time the teacher reads this things will be happening that are not happening now. Before Sputnik, I wrote something that said *man may never get to the moon.* I looked at that sentence a dozen times and changed it to *he will get there.* In schools we need to open up all kinds of possibilities for kids. Our job is to provide tools that enable children, when they have an idea, to pursue that idea.

TOM: We don't know specifically where we want all children to end up and we don't always know the best way for them to get there. Too often we assume that all children need precisely the same competencies, and that we know exactly how best to teach them. This simply is not true. Activities are included in this book because they relate small pieces of knowledge to larger conceptual structures.

ART: I think a question that is going to arise in a teacher's mind is, "How are specific themes chosen?" There's so much to learn. Are learning themes completely negotiable or are there certain ones that are crucial? Are we going to have to assure teachers that we've chosen the ten or fifteen crucial things?

ALAN: I visualize two answers. There is a certain content accountability for which we're responsible. We should be able to lay out a content outline for language arts or social studies or science or math. Whatever is taught should constitute reasonably comprehensive content in the several disciplines. The other answer is that in this book we are taking this content and putting it together in a form in which the interdisciplinary connections are made clear for the kids. The more examples of interrelationships that kids see, the more likely they are to generate other connections. We believe it is those interdisciplinary connections that cause children to become problem finders and solvers. The knowledge and the skills today are the blocks on which children build tomorrow. We should ask ourselves, "Are we as teachers providing opportunities for children to create something new?"

ART: In that sense, I think we have chosen some themes that are both interesting and important. In all the themes we have chosen, there is good opportunity for the development of knowledge, skills, and values. Of course, we would be the first to admit that not everything can or should be taught using the thematic approach. This summer, in England, I spent considerable time looking at integrated themes, and visiting various schools that use them. Nowhere did I see a program that was entirely integrated. Schools still maintain separate components where mathematics, language arts, and science are taught. It is their way of addressing specific competencies which society demands of its educational system. There is always the integrated part of the day that some schools called "Project" or "Topic." These experiences develop new understandings of broad conceptual areas and use the specific knowledge and skills that are developed elsewhere in the school program.

ALAN: One of the primary roles of the teacher is to teach children the basic skills and understanding that will serve them throughout life. These are well defined and are referred to as the "3 Rs." This has been the traditionally defined role of the teacher and has been adequate in a world far less complex than the one in which we now live. The second role is to help children learn to build and develop new ideas and concepts from the existing foundation. We don't expect these ideas to be world shattering. But it is the very act of building and acting on these new ideas that is so important. The thematic approach makes this possible.

TOM: Exactly. Integrated study encourages children to develop new knowledge by putting ideas together in new and different ways.

ALAN: These inventions may not be new to us and they may not be new to the world, but they are new to the kids. That's the key.

TOM: That's quite different from presenting knowledge in its finished form to the child.

ALAN: We are not saying that children have to reinvent the wheel, but they do have to invent, or reinvent, a few things. The very act of invention, the very act of being creative, is one of the important things that can come out of the thematic approach.

ART: Teachers are asked to be accountable for developing a wide variety of skills. We have tried to illustrate how skills can be integrated so the child can see how they relate to each other. For example, mathematics is used in investigating social and natural systems.

TOM: I have found that an integrated study motivates children to master particular skills. Mathematics is necessary for a clear understanding of virtually every area or discipline. To the child, application is quite different from memorizing a specific procedure such as that used for adding two-digit numbers. The actual learning of the skill can take place within the context of an integrated study. Here the motivation to learn that particular skill comes from within. But I would not rely on an integrated study to teach children all the arithmetic skills that society will require. The motivation to learn such skills can arise through an integrated study, but there needs to be separate attention to skills outside of the limitations of the theme.

ART: So the integrated study, or the thematic approach, functions as a support system for learning basic skills. It gives children a chance to bring skills together, to see that they connect and reinforce one another. It provides meaning in the learning process.

ALAN: And it provides us with diagnostic, prescriptive, and evaluative opportunities. The teacher can observe students at work, interview them, and record progress on check lists, such as the one described in the evaluation section.

ART: Because of the very nature of a theme it is not only diagnostic, but it also provides a chance for the evaluation of what's gone on during the other parts of the day.

ALAN: Does it accomplish something beyond that?

ART: I think it does. I think it provides an opportunity during the day for attitudes toward learning to develop. I won't go so far as to say that it automatically develops positive attitudes toward learning, but it does provide the opportunity.

TOM: There really is no limit to the higher order objectives to which an integrated study can relate. Problem solving, inductive and deductive reasoning, drawing inferences, extrapolating, developing research skills, becoming familiar with the literature in the field, using a library adequately, and using the community as a resource, are all part of an integrated study. Such study can be a very natural learning extension and a means for the pursuit of high order objectives.

E. F. SCHUMACHER

E. F. Schumacher believes that the Western world is in a state of crisis and that something must be wrong with its education. Education is humanity's greatest resource. The task of education is not simply to transmit scientific and technological know-how but to convey ideas of value that allow people to discover meaning and purpose in their lives. Education should make us wise.

Schumacher makes an analogy between know-how to education and piano to music. Technology and science provide the tools that are instrumental in providing ultimate wisdom. However, these tools must not be mistaken for wisdom itself.

An economist by profession, Schumacher presents his philosophy of education in his book *Small is Beautiful: Economics as if People Mattered* (1973). Although he was a Rhodes Scholar, economic advisor to the British Control Commission in postwar Germany, top economist, and head of planning at the British Coal Board, Schumacher is a far cry from anyone's notion of the orthodox economist. His "other side" reveals intense interest in Gandhi, nonviolence, and ecology. He is a sponsor of the Fourth World Movement, a campaign that is devoted to political decentralization and regionalism.

In his writing, Schumacher identifies the faults of education as it exists today. He criticizes scientific pedagogy because of its failure to instill the significance of scientific laws and because it has divorced science from the cosmos of human thought. He writes that all subject matter should be connected at a common center. The center should consist of ideas that transcend the world of facts and be composed of basic connections, metaphysics, and ethics.

The truly educated person is not someone who knows a bit about everything or even one who knows the details of all subjects. The educated person may, in fact, have little specialized knowledge. The educated person is one who is not in doubt about his basic connections. He or she has achieved inner clarity about the purpose and meaning of his or her life.

And what is the role of the teacher in an educational system that values metaphysics and ethics? The teacher serves to clear the minds of the students, to clarify the large universal ideas in their minds. The way people experience and interpret the world depends on the ideas that fill their minds. "If they are mainly small, weak, superficial, and incoherent, life will appear insipid, uninteresting, petty and chaotic . . . the vacuum of our minds may only too easily be filled by some big, fanatic notion—political or otherwise—that suddenly seems to illuminate everything and give meaning or purpose to our existence. It needs no emphasis that herein lies one of the great dangers of our time" (*Small is Beautiful*, pg. 84).

Schumacher concludes that our civilization is in danger. Furthermore, education as it exists today may be an agent of its destruction. If education does not serve to make us wise, to provide ideas that will enable us to choose between one thing and another, living will become a meaningless tragedy.

THE TEACHER AS PROBLEM FINDER

Teachers involved in thematic curricula are naturally involved in ongoing problem-solving activity. What are the major problems that teachers face? What are some things that need to be resolved in order to make your teaching more effective? If several obstacles could be removed in order to make teaching simpler and more rewarding, what would they be? Take a few minutes to list in the space provided five problems that you face in teaching.

1. _____

2. _____

3. _____

4. _____

5. _____

If you've listed five problems, perhaps you're overwhelmed. This may be the first time you have ever brought some of teaching's major obstacles into focus. To simplify matters for our present purposes, go back to your list of five problems and choose one that you would like to solve. If you were unable to list even one problem, don't conclude they don't exist. All of us face problems; particularly those of us in the teaching profession. *Problem finding* is a little-recognized skill. As Albert Einstein once said, the solutions to certain problems are relatively simple once someone has found the problem. So force yourself to identify at least one problem you face as a teacher and write the problem down on paper.

All this may be somewhat abstract to you at this point. To bring a more concrete perspective to this matter of problem finding, consider this list of the five most common problems identified by seventy teachers who work with students from kindergarten through secondary levels, in regular classrooms as well as with learning disabled students. These seventy teachers do not represent a scientifically selected probability sample of any population. Rather, they were inservice teachers from a number of districts who enrolled in a course for using newspapers in education. Here, in order, are the problems identified by this group of teachers.

1. Lack of time for planning lessons and activities
2. Too many students to be given the individual attention they deserve
3. Too many meetings and distractions
4. Not enough really good material from which to teach
5. Too much time spent on discipline and not enough on instruction

Can you identify with one or more of these problems? Use the space provided to write as a statement the problem you have chosen either from the preceding list or from your own list.

A major problem I face in teaching is _____

_____

_____

FROM PROBLEM FINDING TO PROBLEM SOLVING

Having identified a problem, you are ready to begin work on its solution. While no magical sequence of steps exists for solving the problem you have identified, we can give you some general guidelines. Apply them to your problem and see if you can come up with a meaningful solution. Some suggested procedures for problem solving follow.

Possible Steps in Problem Solving

Identify the problem. Develop a written statement that gives an accurate description of the problem. Try to isolate the problem. Untangle it from other factors which may represent separate problems.

Determine causes of the problem. Try to find out the underlying reasons for the problem's existence. List as many possible causes as you can. Try to rank the causes in the order of their importance.

Think creatively about the problem. Conduct a brainstorming session in which you try to think about possible courses of action. Try to be open to all ideas and plans at this stage. If the problem is real, and worth solving, it probably demands a creative approach. Often, plans you may reject initially as being too far out of line are exactly what is ultimately needed to solve a problem.

Gather some information about the problem. At this stage you need to seek advice, do some reading, gather some data. The chances of solving a problem without gathering information from outside sources is usually very remote.

Sort the information. You will probably find it helpful to develop some quantitative display of your data. It is useful to make graphs, charts, and maps if possible. In addition, you need to analyze your findings qualitatively. The basic question is, "What does the information tell me?"

Make decisions based on your findings. Perfect solutions to real problems seldom exist. Therefore, you will have to decide which course of action seems best given the information and resources which you have.

STUDENTS AS PROBLEM FINDERS

In addition to asking teachers to identify problems that they face in the classroom, we asked the more than 1500 students of these teachers to identify some of their most urgent problems related to learning. Here, in order, are the five most common problems identified by the students. What problems would your students identify? Find out and compare their list to the one that follows.

FIVE MOST COMMON PROBLEMS IDENTIFIED BY 1500 STUDENTS
1. I don't always understand the work.
2. There is too much noise for me to think.
3. Sometimes the teachers aren't fair.
4. School is too boring.
5. There is too much homework.

YOU AND YOUR STUDENTS AS PROBLEM SOLVERS

Talk to students and develop a list of problems. Determine which one is the most common. Try applying the steps of problem solving to see what you and your students can do. The basic purpose of problem solving is to apply rational thought and action to an issue. Even in those cases where a problem is not "solved" (perhaps because of factors beyond your control), a valid experience in thinking and doing inevitably takes place.

The Interdisciplinary Nature of Problem Solving

The problems identified by the teachers and the students in our sample were problems of an interdisciplinary nature. That is, the problems could not be identified in the narrow sense of school subjects such as mathematics, science, social studies, or reading. True problems tend to be interdisciplinary in scope and the chances are good that the problems that you identified were interdisciplinary. The term merely refers to the combination of subject areas. Thus, interdisciplinary problem solving makes use of the skills of all curricular areas.

Interdisciplinary Problem-Solving Activities for the Classroom

In this book we will present a wide range of tested activities, most of an interdisciplinary problem-solving nature, for you to use with your students. Almost all of the activities will be designed to help you teach your students basic skills in the following areas:

JEAN PIAGET

The increasing complexity of our society requires that people be able to distinguish facts from myths, evaluate thoughtfully the choices available for them in life, and discover innovative ways to confront new and different situations or problems. The educational theorist Jean Piaget has forwarded ideas that promote the creation of an educational system that would nurture creative, inventive, and critical thought processes. Paramount to his philosophy is the argument for frequent use of activity sessions in our classrooms.

The foundation of Piaget's work lies in his view of intelligence developing through certain identifiable, ordered stages. In forming this educational theory, Piaget has examined the development of human intelligence from the state of a baby to that of an adult. The rate of this development depends on the child's level of physiological maturation, the degree of meaningful or educational transmission, and relevant intellectual and psychological experiences. A fourth factor in a child's progress is a concept termed equilibrium, which involves the processes of assimilation and accommodation. Assimilation is the application of a person's past knowledge or insights to new, yet familiar situations, while accommodation requires that the individual develop new concepts or schemes in order to confront a new dilemma successfully.

Piaget has identified five stages in this development. Individuals progress through these stages in the same order, although the rates may vary. The first of these stages is the *Sensorimotor Stage* (birth to eighteen months), which involves the intelligence of action since the child is incapable of complicated thought processes. Here the child develops the concept of object permanence and thereafter realizes that objects exist even when they are not within his or her immediate perceptual field.

The next stage is that of *Intuitive Thought* (ages two to four years). During this period, symbolic language development occurs, and thought and action are coordinated. This is followed by the *Preoperational Stage* (ages four to seven years), when additional mental operations evolve, although the child still lacks the understanding of conservation

---

1. Language development and communication skills
2. Mathematical functions and number concepts
3. Scientific reasoning and logical thinking
4. Social skills and research strategies

Some of the activities teach single concepts and are of short duration—perhaps one lesson. Others are designed as mini-units appropriate for use over time, as much as two or four weeks. We have called this book a sampler, and in that spirit we hope that you will use it as a starting place toward the collecting and development of problem-solving activities appropriate to the age level and situation in which you teach.

A FEW ACTIVITIES TO GET YOU STARTED

The psychologist J. W. Getzels writes about the power of insight and creativity in the problem-solving process. He suggests that imagination and a sense of

of matter. Up to this point, Piaget believes that the child, overwhelmed by his or her perceptions, makes many errors in thoughts, at least as judged by adult standards. For example, the child thinks the number of elements in a set changes when they are spread out, the volume of a liquid changes when poured into a container of a different shape, and so on. Piaget contends that children at this stage lack the ability to reverse an operation and also are mentally incapable of processing more than one variable at a time, that is, when poured into a thinner glass, the liquid is both higher and narrower at the same time.

The fourth stage is that of *Concrete Operations* (ages seven to eleven years). During this time, actions or the handling of objects are necessary in order for the child to develop logical thinking abilities. Here the child has generally developed the concepts of reversibility and of the conservation of length, number, weight, and volume.

Formal Operations (ages eleven to fifteen years) is the fifth and final stage. The individual now begins to think critically, using formal logic and abstract reasoning. He or she can reason scientifically and make conclusions regarding hypotheses that he or she has formulated.

The implications of Piaget's work for school instruction are many. First of all, teachers should develop a more refined sensitivity toward the child and the child's needs and unique learning patterns in contrast to those of adults. Secondly, teachers need to more actively involve students in the learning process by guiding them through sequences of concrete activities. Teachers also need to use instructional methods appropriate for each individual child, with new concepts developed from the concrete to the abstract. The need for teachers to give children ample opportunities to evaluate their own conclusions by being exposed to the thoughts of others, is a fourth implication of Piaget's works. Finally, teachers should build logical patterns of expression in children through questioning. There is ample evidence that indicates that speech is a child's way of organizing thoughts into logical structures. By encouraging children to answer carefully using temporal and causal conjunctions and operational definitions, speech, communication, and understanding are enhanced.

humor are integral factors that come into play in the effective solution of problems. Here are two examples of problems that will call on your powers of insight, creativity, imagination, and even your sense of humor, to solve.

The horse trading problem. A man bought a horse for $50. He then sold it for $60. After that he bought it back for $70. Deciding that he couldn't keep the horse, he again sold it—this time for $80. How much money did he lose or make altogether?

Of course, this problem can be solved with simple arithmetic. What makes it a true problem and not a mere exercise is the psychological dimension involved in which a horse keeps going back and forth. Here is one solution to the problem. Can you think of other ways to solve it?

Solution: The man paid $50 for the horse the first time and $70 the second time. Therefore, he paid a total of $120 for the horse. He received $60 the first time he sold the horse, $80 the second time *and so received a total of $140 for the horse. The answer is—he made $20 profit.*

$$\begin{array}{r} \$140 \text{ received} \\ -120 \text{ paid} \\ \hline \$\ 20 \text{ profit} \end{array}$$

A Teaching Strategy for the Horse Trading Problem

A useful approach to the horse trading problem is to first give students an opportunity to solve the problem alone and then place them into small groups of four to compare answers and methods of solution. Give students an opportunity to rework their individual answers after they have discussed the problem in small groups for ten minutes or so. Ask students if it helped them to share ideas in their groups. Did they gain new insights by listening and talking to others? The sharing and exchange of ideas is basic to integrated studies and to problem solving. Of course, you can return to the steps of problem solving presented a few pages earlier and note their application to this problem-solving process. But in another sense, a problem such as this illustrates the interdisciplinary concept of building language development, communications skills, number concepts, logical thinking, and social skills.

Here is another activity. This one involves students in creative writing. As students write or tell their story, encourage them to use their imagination.

The gasoline pump problem. Here is a picture of a person standing beside a car at a gasoline pump. Write a short story which tells what you think is happening in the picture.

Teaching Strategy for the Gasoline Pump Problem

This is basically an exercise in *problem finding*. Obviously there is no "correct" answer. However, in talking with students after they have developed their story, try to convey to them the difference between a *stimulus-bound* and a *stimulus-free* interpretation of the picture. A stimulus-bound interpretation is one in which the storyteller does not mentally leave the stimulus or picture. Here is an example:

> *The woman came to a self-service gas station. She is wondering how you make the gas go into the car. Now she thinks she knows how.*

A stimulus-free interpretation is one in which the storyteller uses the picture as a point of departure to let imagination roam freely. Here is an example:

> *This looks like a gas pump but it isn't. It's really a place for this woman to change her clothes so she can become Energy Woman and wage war on gas guzzlers.*

SUMMING UP PROBLEM SOLVING

Insight, creativity, sense of humor, and imagination are valuable learner attributes in problem solving. We have emphasized them here because they are often overlooked. Of course, basic skills from math, science, social studies, and communications are a necessary part of integrated studies and problem solving. Lastly, the steps of the problem-solving process are useful as a tool for helping students manage what often seems to be an overwhelming task, that of beginning with a question and ending with an answer.

In the pages to come, we will attempt to give you additional insights and examples of integrated themes, activities, and units.

INTEGRATED STUDIES—A BRIEF OVERVIEW

An integrated study is one in which children broadly explore knowledge in various subjects related to certain aspects of their environment. The introduction or focusing point of the study is, therefore, an environmental one. You will find it desirable to start with an educational visit, a film or a discussion, and selected readings. Such common experiences provide the nucleus from which the child's investigations arise. Select activities for the integrated study that are balanced in their educational content so that each child does some work within each broad subject domain. The children may work individually or as

ZOLTAN P. DIENES

Zoltan P. Dienes espouses an educational philosophy that encourages the provision of a mathematics laboratory. As a mathematician, philosopher, and educator he views mathematics as an art form to be studied for the intrinsic value of the subject itself. He feels that the establishment of learning situations in which students are self-motivated would create the most effective environment for mathematics learning. He also sees the learning of mathematics as an evolutionary process in which new and complex understandings develop from a base of existing, simpler ones.

Dienes's theory of mathematics learning consists of four major principles:

The dynamic principle. A student's understanding of a new concept progresses through three ordered stages, including a preliminary "play" stage, when students are involved with activities in a relatively unstructured setting and become familiar with the fundamentals of concepts in a very informal manner; a more structured activity stage, in which the children are given experiences structurally similar to the concepts to be learned; and a practice stage in which the student uses the concepts developed in the structured stage.

The perceptual variability principle. The second principle (sometimes called the multiple embodiment principle) suggests that conceptual learning is maximized when children are exposed to a concept in a variety of situations. For example, place value can be depicted using bundles of sticks, chips, an abacus, or any number of other embodiments. Dienes suggests implementation of instructional methods that, rather than promoting mere association, would promote abstraction, which he defines as the ability to perceive a concept without regard to its concrete embodiment.

The mathematical variability principle. If a mathematical concept is dependent upon a certain number of variables, then the variation of these is an important prerequisite for the effective learning of the concept.

The constructivity principle. The last principle asserts that children should be allowed to develop their concepts in an intuitive manner emanating from their own experiences, by having them act as constructive thinkers before they play the roles of analytic thinkers.

These four principles stress the importance of learning mathematics by direct interaction with the environment. Rather than merely learning techniques, students should be involved with understanding the ideas and developing the concepts of mathematics. It is also crucial that teachers provide for individualized learning rates and learning styles.

Dienes is critical of the present educational standard of grading when it is used to coerce students to learn. Students could be intrinsically motivated to learn mathematics in a way that would generate more interest and excitement about the subject. Another criticism about much of education today centers on its treatment of students as parts of a large group rather than individually. Since learning should be an individual matter, instruction to large groups usually proves to be inadequate.

Dienes suggests that mathematics learning should not be a spectator sport, but one in which children are actively involved as participants. No longer would the teacher be the main information source or director of the learning processes. Students would assume more responsibility for their own education and would work directly with physical materials and assignment cards. A mathematics laboratory with such a variety of materials would serve the purpose of creating an environment in which students and teacher could interact cooperatively to heighten student interest and achievement.

part of a larger group. Generally students will develop a wide variety of materials which depict various stages in their investigations. Encourage students to save this work as it will be useful later on for group presentations, classroom displays, and parent/teacher discussions.

Much of your success depends on your care in planning for the study. Collect books about the area, acquire films, slides, film loops, contact possible guest speakers and plan relevant field trips. Once the study is underway, play the role of facilitator. You are not expected to know answers to all questions students may initiate. Rather, your role is that of promoting student learning through encouragement and the establishment of appropriate learning conditions. This is a substantive departure from traditional views of the school curriculum and also of traditional expectations regarding appropriate teacher behavior. In some schools a single integrated study lasts five to seven weeks. These schools generally have teachers with highly developed, refined procedures for dealing with such an approach. It is more usual for such an investigation to last two or three weeks. This is especially true when trying it for the first time. The appropriate length of a single study should generally be based on four considerations: a) the age and developmental level of the children involved; b) the child's interest; c) your enthusiasm; and d) your initial preparations. Children can often be encouraged to pursue various aspects of a theme at home.

Divide children into work areas or groups. The groups invariably address different aspects of the problem under consideration. Of great importance is the fact that children of different abilities and attainment levels will work cooperatively on a common problem or theme. Cooperative learning is a necessary ingredient. You will find it useful to plan a number of assignments for each working group. These assignments can be designed in cooperation with students or they might be suggested by textbooks or other published materials. Such individualized assignments have many advantages, one of which is that resources are needed only for a small group of children rather than for an entire class. In time you will develop a wealth of classroom resources that can be kept and stored for the following year, resulting in substantial savings of limited school funds. Many of these resources can also be shared with other classrooms.

Upon completion of an integrated unit, the children's work should be displayed. The display can be undertaken for the benefit of other class members and also for the information of other children and teachers in the school. Such a display is an invaluable stimulus to worthwhile discussion at a parent/teacher meeting. As a general rule, children who have expressed themselves to the best of their ability on paper or through some other media should have their work displayed. These displays can then serve as motivators for additional investigations.

Generally, an integrated study is successful when the work is well prepared, assignments are ready and varied, and you are enthusiastic and willing to be very directive but able to sit back and "see what develops."

IVAN ILLICH

"A major illusion on which the school system rests is that most learning is the result of teaching."

With this statement Ivan Illich, reformer, educational philosopher and priest, challenges social and educational institutions.

From his residence at the Center for Intercultural Documentation, Cuernavaca, Mexico, and through *Deschooling Society*, Illich proposes a system of open access and universal, self-determined education. The system should be noninstitutional, appropriate to each learner and free, in that the learner repays his instructor by passing his knowledge on to others.

Often, Illich's writing style is in a question-answer format. "Why can't this be done?" he asks. Then he describes conspiracies designed to preserve institutional structures, including education, and outlines their carefully devised, self-perpetuating web of learner ensnarement; a web of technocracy, bureaucracy, and education governed by self-serving rules. He argues, for example, that economic drives to increase consumption can only be turned around through the commitment to production of a limited range of durable goods designed for utility, self-help, self-assembly, reuse and repair. Education is then refocused toward participation and self-support instead of mass production with the resulting loss of self-sufficiency and supportive skills.

Illich leaves few educational hallmarks untouched. Research, modern mathematics, and sensitivity fall prey to his logic. Only after using his straw man technique on the system does he proceed to the rebuilding.

According to Illich, the "four networks" thesis through which personalized life-learning can occur include (1) open and free access to the materials, systems, and agencies of learning; (2) a willing exchange of knowledge and skills at a person-to-person level; (3) a network, perhaps computerized, to facilitate access to sources of knowledge; and (4) an extension of the third, which is a reference service to people who have skills or knowledge and will share these with others.

Ivan Illich's revolutionary ideas suggest to the reader misgivings and reservations about the present education system, and the need for a deschooled social order.

BACK OR FORWARD TO THE BASICS?

Deciding what is basic in education is deceptive. The basics traditionally do not encompass the breadth of the school's curriculum, but only the "3 Rs." Various groups approach this issue in decidedly different ways. The traditionalists promote those things which are familiar and well understood. Other groups have come to a decidedly different consensus when asked to identify the basic skills. Parents, teachers, administrators, and university professors do not necessarily agree on exactly what the basic skills are or should be. This causes problems to the extent that these groups misunderstand and misrepresent one another.

At a recent conference in Euclid, Ohio (October, 1975), mathematics educators were asked to define the basic skills in mathematics. Their lists re-

WHY? A RATIONALE

veal a concern for issues beyond the development of simple arithmetic. Participants suggested that objectives such as estimation, approximation, collection and interpretation of data, rational decision making, generalization, and graph analysis techniques, along with appreciation for the sheer power of the subject, rates of change, measure, equilibrium, the use of the calculator and of course problem solving, are basic and should occupy the school mathematics agenda.

Implementing such objectives may require a redefinition of school mathematics. The same applies to science, social science, and language arts. The basic needs today are different than the basic needs of our parents. The school program should (must) reflect those differences. In many cases it does not.

Certain issues and needs must be addressed if school programs are to meet today's societal demands to become more relevant and to be more consistent with the psychological development of the child. Some of these issues and needs are:

- The need to redefine the utility of mathematics, science, and social science in light of developments in today's world, i.e., the calculator, nuclear energy, and the emergence of third world nations
- The need to discuss ways in which children learn and develop intellectually
- The need to provide educational programs at all levels that deal with both higher order and lower order objectives, such as specific factual knowledge and understanding of the manner in which knowledge is accessed and generated
- The need to consider the coordination of the various disciplines
- The need to identify program objectives that cannot be presented in the form of precisely defined curriculum
- The recognition that process skills and complex thinking cannot be adequately evaluated using traditional measures
- The need to develop new and more efficient ways to define the term "basic"
- The need to provide continuous, viable, and systematic procedures for teacher inservice
- The need to become more knowledgeable about the politics involved in institutional change. Too often well-meaning people forge ahead with essentially good ideas but neglect to consider the politics involved. When the suggested innovation "fails," it often has nothing to do with the qualitative nature of the idea but rather is due to the naïveté of the attempted approach.

On the other hand, the issues do not appear to be:

- Lack of developed curricular activities that are supplementary in nature—literally tens of thousands of ideas already exist. The task is to locate rather than develop.

JEROME BRUNER

In recent years, Jerome Bruner has become widely known in the field of curriculum development through his controversial elementary social studies program, *Man: A Course of Study* (MACOS).

MACOS brought Bruner's fundamental ideas about children's learning to public attention, and some of the activities became the center of the external curriculum debate. No single individual has had as much influence on social studies curriculum development in recent years. Alone among major cognitive psychologists, Bruner moved beyond a theory of learning to a theory of instruction.

Bruner's instructional model is based on four key concepts: structure, readiness, intuitive thinking, and motivation. These concepts are developed in detail in Bruner's classic book, *The Process of Education*.

Structure. The concept of the structure of a discipline is not new. It is certainly as old as Aristotle who made the case for learning significant ideas as opposed to mere facts. Bruner defines the structure of a discipline as its basic concepts and methods. The structure of anthropology, for example, is composed of its organizing concepts such as culture, beliefs, customs, and symbols, as well as its methods of investigation, for example, direct observation and case studies.

Bruner suggests that teaching students the structure of a discipline as they study particular content leads to greater active involvement on their part as they discover basic principles for themselves. This, of course, is very different from the learning model, which suggests that students be receivers rather than developers of information. Bruner states that learning the structure of knowledge facilitates comprehension, memory, and learning transfer.

The idea of structure in learning leads naturally to the process approach where the very process of learning (*how* one learns) becomes as important as the content of learning (*what* one learns). This position, misunderstood by many, has been the focus of considerable controversy. The important thing to keep in mind is that Bruner never said that content is unimportant.

Readiness. A key to readiness for learning is intellectual development, or how a child views the world. Here Bruner refers to the work of Piaget, stating that "what is most

- Lack of funds to purchase supplementary materials. Most activities require the germ of an idea, and a desire to carry it through, not expensive paraphernalia. Teachers will be amazed at what can be accomplished with "stuff" already on hand.
- A parent population opposed to a departure from basic skills. Most parents evaluate school programs in terms of what they remember and are relatively uninformed as to current developments and thinking regarding the learning of mathematical and other concepts. An informed parent population is generally supportive of innovation. It is, however, our responsibility to provide the needed background and rationale.
- An administration opposed to redefining the objectives, content and teaching procedures. Most administrators defer to the "experts" on these issues.

important for teaching basic concepts is that the child be helped to pass progressively from concrete thinking to the utilization of more conceptually adequate modes of thought."*

Bruner suggests three modes of representational thought. That is, an individual can think about a particular idea or concept at three different levels. *Enactive* learning involves "hands-on" or direct experience. The strength of enactive learning is its sense of immediacy. Evidence suggests that children's concepts basically evolve from direct interaction with the environment. This is equivalent to saying that children need a large variety of enactive experiences. Many school programs are low in both the quantity and quality of these experiences. The mode of learning which Bruner terms *iconic* is one based on the use of the visual medium: films, pictures, etc. *Symbolic* learning is that stage in which one uses abstract symbols to represent reality.

Bruner feels that readiness depends more upon an effective mix of these three learning modes than upon waiting until some imagined time when children are capable of learning certain ideas. Throughout his writing is the notion that the key to readiness is a rich and meaningful learning environment coupled with an exciting teacher who involves children in learning as a process that creates its own excitement.

Intuitive thinking. Bruner takes issue with the typical school pattern of formalized instruction, particularly with regard to the memorizing and reproducing of verbal and numerical exercises. He clearly values intuitive thinking as a learning style and feels that it has been generally overlooked and undervalued as a legitimate tool for learning in classrooms. Real problems, particularly those with an interdisciplinary focus, seldom lend themselves to the neat, lock-step approach found in textbooks.

Motivation. Intrinsic *motivation* is an essential key to effective learning. John Dewey wrote about "the teachable moment" when motivation and information come together. A teacher who is curious, who values reflective thinking, and who accepts students' childlike attempts at intellectual reaching out will be a motivating presence.

Bruner clings to the idea of intrinsic motivation—learning as its own reward. It's a refreshing thought.

---

*Jerome Bruner, *The Process of Education* (New York: Vintage Books, 1963), p. 38.

Again, teachers do need to provide appropriate information and rationale for proposed changes.

One could argue that much of the school curricula exists now because it has always been there and not because it is the most important or the most relevant to the child's life and future needs. The amount of time devoted to the development of speed and accuracy in the mathematics program is a case in point here. Never again will individuals be employed to do long complicated problems by hand. So to argue that speed and absolute accuracy in hand calculation is all (or most) of what an individual must know to survive in tomorrow's world is simply not true. Why then do most schools spend all this time on the development and maintenance of these skills?

It seems more reasonable to devote at least a portion of the child's time to things such as estimation, approximation, interpreting, hypothesizing, and classifying, to name but a few. These are the things that are more likely to serve our students well in tomorrow's world. These, incidentally, are also the types of skills which can best be developed through an interdisciplinary approach.

Bertrand Russell in his Law of Rational Skepticism stated that, "When the experts are agreed the opposite opinion cannot be held to be certain." Although this sounds like a reasonable proposition, education is currently involved in precisely this issue. If you will allow us to define expert as the Ph.D. who always works within a closely defined area, then it can be said that the experts are agreed as to the nature of the basic skills. These skills, however, are not the same ones suggested by the people who advocate a return to the basics. In fact, the two views are very much in opposition.

Clearly we need to rethink this issue and attempt again to answer the question, "What really are the basics?" This discussion should involve people from all educational strata who have a basic interest in this issue. The fact that the answers will not be the same ones that would have evolved a generation ago is to be expected. The world and its demands are not the same as then and never will be again.

One attempt to redefine the basics recently resulted in the development of the following four categories:

1. Coping skills (includes various academic disciplines and their interrelationships)
2. Social and character development
3. Citizenship and social responsibility
4. Private realization skills

What is your reaction to such a list? Does your school curricula consciously address each of these areas? Before leaving this topic, answer the following question: What do you want your child to be like at age twenty? List five to ten desirable characteristics in their order of importance.

1. _____

2. _____

3. _____

4. _____

WHY? A RATIONALE   19

5. _____

6. _____

7. _____

8. _____

9. _____

10. _____

How well does the school program contribute to the development of the items on your list?

In conclusion, we would like to suggest that a thematic approach has the potential of addressing not only the basic skills as traditionally defined but also the more open ended process objectives that are often ignored. Such a curricula invariably relates the basics to contemporary interests and problematic situations that naturally arise in the course of events.

SUMMARY

A school day is often divided into reading time, recess, more reading, spelling, lunch, arithmetic, recess, clean up, and go home. A child's day may be made up of thoughts of play, conversations, pretending, watching the custodian or the painter, constructing forts or making cookies, and looking forward to family sharing time. The former seems efficient and logical, the latter disorganized and illogical.

The heretical thesis of this book is that the latter day, the child's day, may be a better model on which to develop thinking abilities, problem solving abilities, and conceptual structures. If children are to learn how their world works, they must interact with it. And their world is not like an assembly line. An integrated theme begins within the child's environment and expands to include elements of reading, arithmetic, science, social studies, and many others. You, the teacher, build the theme around the child's interests and slowly facilitate conceptual development through the challenges you offer, the questions you pose and the investigations you initiate.

CHAPTER TWO

How? A Methodology of Thematics

INTEGRATED TEACHING AND LEARNING

The notion of an integrated approach to curriculum springs back from tenets of modern cognitive psychology and philosophy, developed by John Dewey, Jean Piaget, Zoltan Dienes, Jerome Bruner, and others. These individuals have adopted a holistic view of the learning process and have been concerned with children acquiring an understanding of fundamental structures. Integrated studies, also known as thematic curricula, offers variation in the teaching and learning process that is probably not attainable under normal classroom procedures.

One of the differences is the nature of the objectives these activities are designed to promote. Discipline-centered teaching places major emphasis on specific predetermined knowledge, the expository teacher role, and individual seat work. Integrated teaching is usually process oriented and is not concerned principally with the transmission of specific information. Instead students become involved in a wide variety of large and small group situations designed to develop processes, skills, concepts, and affective outcomes. Some examples of appropriate outcomes by category are reflected in the following chart. (Note that the dividing line between processes and skills is necessarily indistinct.)

PROCESSES	SKILLS	CONCEPTS	AFFECTIVE OUTCOMES
problem solving	map, picture reading	measurement	motivation
observing, recording & describing	indexing	pattern	self concept
	library skills	influence	respect for self & others
classifying	calculation	communication	
		structure	enthusiasm

21

PROCESSES	SKILLS	CONCEPTS	AFFECTIVE OUTCOMES
social interaction	question asking	cause & effect	sharing
data gathering & analysis	outlining	balance	cooperation
hypothesis	summarizing	energy	
synthesis	understanding sequence		
decision making	following directions		

Notice that these outcomes are not only appropriate to an integrated approach, but also relevant to conventional classroom instruction. The difference, however, lies in the fact that these skills become the primary, rather than the secondary, emphasis. Thematic units do not focus primarily on content objectives such as "the student will solve ten two-digit addition problems with eighty percent accuracy in fifteen minutes."

As a result of the differing objectives and the different nature of student activities implied by those objectives, it seems unrealistic to assume that a thematic approach will result in higher levels of specific skill development when contrasted to the usual school curricula.

Schools today are largely concerned with basic skills. The assumption is implicit that at some future time basic skills will be useful in resolving real world problems. The difficulty with this line of thinking arises from the fact that many children never adequately master these basic skills, and, therefore, never get involved in applying this knowledge to the real world. The idea suggested here is that one should involve children in the solution of real world problems even before they have mastered the skills that might be necessary for the problem's complete solution. Under such conditions, we expect attitude improvement and renewed motivation that will in turn promote involvement in the development of basic skills. The authors' involvements with the British primary schools and with American undergraduate and graduate students in education have supported this position. Often, undergraduate students and practicing teachers come to methods classes as "mathephobes."[1] They often undergo an attitudinal change once the application of the subject matter is demonstrated through real world activities and through their personal involvement with relevant problems.

Integrated Studies: When and What Level of Involvement:

It would be foolhardy to suggest that schools abandon the traditional educational structures and in their place develop a totally integrated curriculum. The problems in such a move could prove to be enormous and overwhelming. We suggest that such an approach to teaching and learning be accorded a portion of the school day. It is simply not true that basic skills will be all that

HILDA TABA

Although Hilda Taba (1902-1967) was not a native American, she devoted her life to improving the American educational system as a researcher, professor of education, and consultant to schools. Taba studied under John Dewey at Columbia University where she received her Ph.D. Her interest in progressive education and curriculum grew out of years of making careful observations of teachers and students.

Taba's research interests included relations between ethnic groups, curriculum processes, instructional techniques, and the development of cognitive processes in children. She was critical of the application of the scientific method of research to the study of learning and teaching. Taba argued that because the humanistic sciences are by nature unlike the exact sciences, they demand a different set of concepts and categories of thinking. Different methods of obtaining data and different techniques of formulating problems are necessary if scientists are ever to realize a comprehensive understanding of the social sciences and their applications for education.

Because the scientific method is characterized by an emphasis on atomism, separation, and fixed one-to-one relationships of cause and effect, it is unsuited for the study of vital phenomena. Taba observed that much of educational practice was suffering from theories based on information gathered exclusively by the scientific method.

The world, according to Taba, is in the process of continuous and cumulative change. Behavior should be regarded as a passing moment in the never static course of events rather than the outcome of a more permanent state. Any act may be explained by what happened before it, by the nature of the processes involved in it, by the state of the world at that given moment, and by the purpose for it. Taba's work in curriculum planning, social sensitivity, evaluation, and theory of education had its roots in her beliefs about the dynamic nature of the world.

A prolific writer, Taba's work can be found in numerous professional journals and books. She served as director of curriculum in Dalton, Ohio, professor of education at Ohio State University and the University of Chicago. Shortly before her death, she had been appointed professor of educational administration at San Francisco State University.

---

individuals will need to prepare them for a very uncertain future. The individuals who are successful in coping with tomorrow's society and its problems will be those who can cope with new and unfamiliar situations in an understanding and creative manner. What better preparation for such future citizens than to involve them in such activity during the formal school day? One or two afternoons a week is a reasonable goal in the beginning. More time is appropriate as the teacher and child become more familiar with the new organizational format.

Once you accept this premise, the next problem becomes "What do you teach in this time block?" One begins by asking questions from the real world. The initial question posed is often not oriented to a particular discipline. Sometimes the questions will come from students and other times they will come from some other source such as the teacher, learning materials, television, books, or random observation. For example, if you were asked to design a bus route from point A to point B, you would need to consider a wide variety of information, such as existing roads, population density, and costs. This in turn would involve map reading, exploration of population statistics, and a variety of calculations. Problems of this nature are usually not well defined and require initial discussions with students as to problem delimitation, identification of relevant variables, type and amount of data to be collected, data analysis procedures, formulation of conclusions, and the development of recommendations that are based on the information gathered. Other areas that might be explored are "identify the major sources of pollution in your town and propose a plan to help alleviate the problem," or "design a recreational facility for your local community or school." The list could go on forever.

The attempted solution of such problems requires an interdisciplinary approach. Such an effort will involve one or more of the process-oriented objectives referred to earlier. Note that the individual designing a bus route may have to add a long series of one- or two-digit numbers on several different occasions in order to determine the length of the various routes suggested. This is not the major objective of the stated problem. Here the basic skill of addition is of secondary concern, but still necessary to the problem's solution. Many times such an approach will motivate students to learn to add numbers so as to enable them to deal with the larger concern.

The remainder of this chapter contains examples of sketches of thematic and integrated studies that have been classroom tested in the past. The general nature of such themes is intended to accommodate a wide diversity of interpretation and allow individual teachers to modify them as seems appropriate. Teachers do, in fact, make many crucial decisions as to the direction these themes take; such a role is most appropriate for a true professional.

How does an integrated study develop? How is the classroom organized? What can one expect of students? The following quote from a letter received from a British headmaster (principal) whose school is heavily involved in such a curriculum illustrates one school's answer.[2]

> *We believe that education (certainly for children of the age range we cater for, eight to twelve) should not be broken up into subject compartments. Our children learn from their experiences, those encountered at random and those to which we introduce them deliberately; but these experiences are all-embracing and involve all aspects of knowledge at once. We believe that it is artificial to attempt to provide separate experiences for each subject.*
>
> *Every effort is made to show the underlying unity of all knowledge. Math assignments are planned to involve other subjects, naturally and without rigid demarcation lines appearing. For example, when initially planning a unit on Swedish immigration, I found myself thinking that we might first have introduced this idea by making a register of all the names in the school, grouping them (work on "sets"), and noting those which indicated a Swedish origin (origins of surnames?). This would lead to such ideas as "why did they immigrate?" (history)—the geography of the Baltic area—*

methods of travel, then and now—distances by sea and air—speeds of sailing ships, steam ships, and aircraft—courses (angles), headings and fixing positions (latitude and longitude, coordinates, bearings and distances)—the development of the steam engine—science work on transmission of heat—sources of fuel—causes of wind—meteorology—salt water—flotation—specific gravity—areas of sails—food kept fresh for long sea voyages?—bacteria—Pasteur and his work—refrigeration—canning—pickling foods?—how does the diet of various countries differ?—why?—what weights of food would be required—how have the sizes of ships increased?—convert the measurements of Noah's ark into modern day units—compare it with a modern ship of comparable size—the animals in the Ark—and back to "sets" again. I set down all of these ideas without any pre-thought, just as they came into my mind and as fast as my typing skills would allow. They would now need ordering and development before I would start using them. The point I am trying to make is how completely, from one given idea, you can involve work in all the subjects—though, as you can see my mind tends towards my own interests of maths and science. All children would cover all of this work—though a slow child might be content with working on straight-forward speeds and distances, while a more able child would be relating fuel consumption to different speeds, having obtained help by writing to an airline, or shipping company.

The work of each study is dealt with by the children in a series of graded assignments, prepared and presented by each teacher. The manner and order in which they are presented is entirely the responsibility of the teacher in charge of a class. Assignments presented on illustrated cards are almost standard, but whilst some teachers present several weeks' work at a time, others (myself included) prefer to work from a weekly pattern of assignments. Children are given their week's work on Monday and arrange their own pattern and sequence of working. When they arrive each morning (often well before the required time) they continue with whatever work they are engaged in throughout the day, without interruption. A time-table is only used to indicate periods used, for there are no "lesson times." Teachers, having provided the starting experiences and presented their choice of assignments, spend their days directing, discussing and helping on an individual or small-group basis. Each child is encouraged to deal with every assignment as fully as individual ability will allow—the "high-flyer" producing work in great depth, whilst the child of lesser ability will produce work at a lower level, yet dealing with the same overall study.

The "bitter test" of any system is simply, whether it works. We can say, most emphatically, that it does. Our experience is that every child works throughout every day with eager interest, and without any of the problems of inattention or lack of interest which some schools may encounter. Our brightest children reach an outstandingly high standard, whilst our less able children no longer feel themselves struggling to keep up with a "lesson", and develop at their own speeds to a level which is as gratifying as it is surprising.

Impressive? Undoubtedly, but such an approach is not without its pitfalls. First and perhaps most importantly, such an approach requires a capable and industrious teacher who is willing to expend the additional effort required of such an approach. Secondly, integrated curricula are not sufficiently developed nor are they intended to ensure student involvement in all of those areas that are considered crucial to the literate individual. This is especially true if one considers the problems of logical sequence within a discipline such as mathematics. Finally, within such a program, all students will gravitate (with the help of the teacher) to activities that are in keeping with their interests and abilities. All students will not have the same experiences and, in fact, certain students may spend the majority of their time within different subject domains. It will, therefore, not be possible to fairly evaluate student progress using group administered or standardized achievement tests.

Happily the decision to involve students in integrated studies or thematic curriculum is not an either/or situation. The appropriate question is not whether such an approach should totally replace the more structured curriculum, but rather, is student involvement therein educationally justifiable and if so, can such an approach be used to enrich the total experiences provided for children? If these two questions can be answered in the affirmative, then it seems appropriate to include such activities as one of many viable components in the student's overall educational experience.

DEVELOPING YOUR OWN INTEGRATED THEME

Integrated studies take on a variety of forms. They may be of brief duration or extend over several weeks. They might center about a narrow theme such as kites or a broad one such as flying. In the past decade themes have been generated by curriculum development groups including ESS (Elementary Science Study), Minnemast (Minnesota Mathematics and Science Teaching Project), USMES (Unified Science and Mathematics for Elementary Schools), and extensively by offshoots of the British Nuffield projects and within many British primary schools. Teachers have found that as they help children plan and work their way through integrated studies, they all become more and more skilled in identifying and developing their own themes.

Once the theme has been identified, related ideas are generated using a brainstorming process. Generally, other curricular areas and disciplines are quickly tied to the identified themes. Specific lessons then evolve from the

ABRAHAM MASLOW

Abraham Maslow (1908–1970) is credited with founding the third main branch of the general field of psychology termed humanistic psychology. (The other two branches are psychoanalytic and behavioristic.) He is best known for his hierarchical theory of motivation. During his career as a psychologist Maslow taught and conducted research at Brooklyn College, Brandeis University, and just prior to his death had been appointed Resident Fellow at the W. P. Charitable Foundation in Menlo Park, California. Maslow served as president of the American Psychological Association in 1967–68.

Dissatisfied with psychology's preoccupation with physiological drives as the explanation of motivation, Maslow set out to study human motives. As a result of this study, he proposed in 1943 a *holistic-dynamic* theory of motivation that was based on a hierarchy of human needs. The hierarchy's most basic need is that of physiological necessities (food, air, water, etc.). After these needs are satisfied, humans seek safety, followed by the higher needs of belonging, love, and self-esteem. Upon satisfaction of these needs, the individual seeks feelings of adequacy and self-confidence. The final need to be realized is the need of self-actualization.

Self-actualization, a term coined by Kurt Goldstein, is described by Maslow as "the tendency for (the individual) to become actualized in what he is potentially. This tendency might be phrased as the desire to become more and more what one is, to become everything that one is capable of becoming" (Maslow, 1954).

Maslow proceeded to study the attributes of people who he felt were self-actualized. Among these were Abraham Lincoln, Eleanor Roosevelt, Beethoven, and Albert Schweitzer. He analyzed fifteen characteristics that distinguished the self-actualized from more ordinary people. The most discriminating criterion was "full use and exploitation of talents, capacities, potentialities, etc. These people are doing the best that they are capable of doing" (Maslow, 1954).

In his work, Maslow stressed the positive, optimistic aspects of the study of human psychology. He criticized conventional psychology for concentrating on human shortcomings, for ignoring the aspirations, virtues, and potentialities of humanity. Maslow proposed that the study of self-actualized populations would contribute greatly to a more universal science of psychology. As unhealthy and immature specimens were traditionally the focus of psychological research, there is little doubt that the field was suffering from this restricted scope.

Neurosis was viewed by Maslow as a blocking of self-actualization, a failure of personal growth. He viewed mental health as contingent upon introspychic strength versus extrapsychic success. The task of the clinical therapist is to help his client get to know himself.

Abraham Maslow's work has greatly influenced American psychology and related fields. It is probably impossible to measure to what degree he has positively affected the lives of the people upon whom his humanistic psychology is based.

---

brainstormed topics. The example given in this chapter has been developed in precisely this way. At first this procedure seems very complex. However, with a small amount of experience you will be able to make mathematics, science, social science, as well as the language arts, a meaningful part of almost any integrated study. Once the general outline has been identified, it is then appro-

28   HOW? A METHODOLOGY OF THEMATICS

priate to continue brainstorming with students. Such experiences give them control over their own destiny and encourage them to utilize their awareness of the related nature of the world around them. In addition, such student involvement will help to develop a sense of self-direction.

To convince yourself that this is not an impossibly difficult task, try your hand by beginning a theme at this time. "Trees" has been selected for this purpose, although others would be just as appropriate.

The first step is to list topics or ideas that relate to the theme Trees, for example, wood, circumference, houses, leaf growth, and economic importance.

After a few minutes of such brainstorming you should have twenty to thirty items on your list. The next step is to impose some type of structure on the items generated. No one structure is recommended. Various examples are: easy to hard, ideas separated by discipline area, ideas separated by physical limitations such as outdoor and indoor, or ideas of current and historical interest. The list can be extended almost indefinitely. It is important to understand that there is no *right* list of topics and/or ideas. Many different lists will result from different persons working from the same theme. Each person's view of the world is unique. Each arrangement will have special significance for the person or group suggesting it. The individual teacher should, therefore, begin with the ideas generated and coordinate children's suggestions so that they impose some type of structure on the ideas.

Place the word *Trees* in the middle of the page.

TREES

Surround the central idea with concentric circles, each of which represents some span of time, that is, 3 days, 1 week, and so on.

Then place the various activities within the concentric circles. Activities that are physically closest to the center are viewed as the most important and will, therefore, be completed by most (or all) of the students. As one proceeds outward (in time as well as space) the activities become more diversified (as depicted by the larger amount of space available) and, therefore, are more capable of accommodating several student interests and abilities. It is reasonable to assume that only one or two individuals or small groups will actually complete those activities that appear in the outermost circle or periphery. It can be seen from this diagram that the longer the time spent on the theme, the larger the number of student options available.

The major objective is often process-oriented and can be loosely described as getting the student involved in relevant, worthwhile explorations, developing problem solving, social, general, and intellectual communication and research skills, as well as promoting a sense of responsibility and self-worth. These global objectives are not tied to any particular piece of content. It is therefore appropriate that students become involved in projects of their choice as the theme progresses. Specific skills and knowledges for all students are addressed in the inner circles of the diagram. Activities that offer choices fall on the outer circles.

If it is decided that the topic activities need to be directly relatable to the individual disciplines, the previous diagram can be further subdivided by adding horizontal, vertical and/or diagonal lines, each of which passes through the center. Each "slice" then is labeled with the name of a particular discipline.

The number and designation of the subdivisions will be determined by the interests and abilities of the students and by the innate expansion potential of the topic or theme. Such an organizational format provides further structuring and may prove to be quite useful in both the design and selection of appropriate activities.

One word of caution regarding this diagram: If taken literally, the diagram implies that there is no overlap among the disciplines. Such is not the case! A certain measurement activity, for example, might be placed in either the mathematics, the science, or the social studies portion of the diagram. You should also realize that such interdisciplinary activities might more correctly be placed on the line separating mathematics and science or between reading and music, so as to indicate their interdisciplinary nature. Early activities (those nearest the center) will generally have a single discipline orientation; later activities will exhibit typical interdisciplinary development.

Schematics such as this can also be used to provide feedback to both pupil and parent as to the nature and quality of the work accomplished. More detail on the nature of appropriate evaluation and assessment techniques is provided in the next section.

The next and final stage in the development of an integrated theme is the identification of specific student activities that are related to and suggested by the various subclusters of ideas, topics, and disciplines. Textbooks, library books, newspapers, magazines, and encyclopedias will all be useful in the gen-

HOW? A METHODOLOGY OF THEMATICS

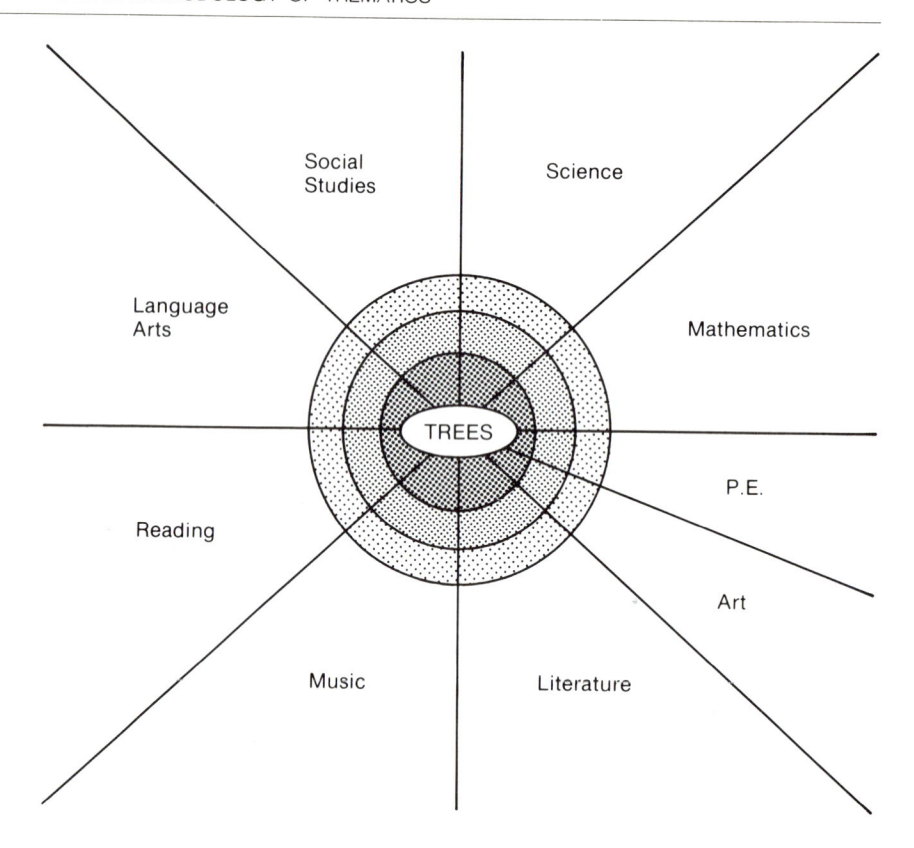

```
         Social        Science
         Studies
 Language                          Mathematics
 Arts
                    TREES
                                        P.E.
 Reading
                                      Art
         Music        Literature
```

eration of such activities. Since one important objective of such activities for the students is the development of research and library skills, it is most appropriate to assign the task of theme clarification to the students. Of course, it will be desirable for the teacher to have an idea or two in readiness and several examples of related materials available.

Let's return to the generation of an integrated plan. The first step is to divide the diagram into a number of appropriate "slices." Next, place important, or basic, activities nearest the center. Continue with this process until the theme begins to take shape in your own mind. Do not turn the page until your thoughts begin to gel.

Now compare your diagram with one on page 32 that was competed on the same topic by the Nuffield Junior Science Project.[3]

Do you notice differences and similarities? Similarities exist because of the common ideas that most persons associate with trees. The differences are there because of the infinite variety of ways in which people view the world around them.

It is useful to view another conceptualization of a particular theme, but keep in mind that the one developed by you is the most relevant for you. Also keep in mind that any theme can be improved upon and that one should con-

LEV S. VYGOTSKY

Lev Semenovich Vygotsky (1896-1934) was a Russian psychologist who, in the last ten years of his life, formulated a theory dealing with the parallel development of language and thought. Of his eighty research manuscripts, only a few have been translated. *Thought and Language*, a later work, was first published in English in 1962. Though controversial and incomplete, he brilliantly portrays the child's interdevelopment of prelanguage and language with his growing ability to interact meaningfully with his world. Words and language, according to Vygotsky, coevolve with social needs, and school instruction and understanding comes from internalized verbal thought.

He describes the states in the coevolution of language and thought that in many respects parallel Piaget's description of stages of logical thought, and neurologists' descriptions of the physical development of intrahemispheric connections in the brain. The stages, labeled syncretic, complex, preconceptual, and conceptual are characterized by recognizable speech patterns and evidence of concept formation.

Causality, in particular, illustrates the stages. Nonlogical linking of words and events is followed by speech that reflects and anticipates, and finally speech that orders, relates, analyzes, synthesizes, and values accurately and independently. Of importance to educators is the evidence from Vygotsky's research that indicates carefully structured investigations and teacher interactions are essential in developing the child's causal and temporal language. In turn, this "conceptual" language enables the child to further synthesize into concepts the essence of the real systems with which the child systematically interacts.

In one study, Vygotsky reports that children are able to use the causal conjunctions (because and although) correctly more often in scientific than everyday situations. He interprets this within the framework of his language-thought theory by saying:

The child must find it hard to solve problems involving life situations because he lacks awareness of his concepts and, therefore, cannot operate with them at will as the task demands....Why is he capable of performing the operations in this social science case? Because the teacher, working with the pupil, has explained, supplied information, questioned, corrected and made the pupil explain.

Clearly, as more and more of Vygotsky's manuscripts are translated, the rich, logical structure of his theories can be expected to add additional substance to our understanding of how thought and language constitute the formative substrata of understanding and intelligence.

tinually strive to bring in more relevant and useful ideas. This invariably happens once the theme is underway with children in the classroom setting.

The students' involvement is gradual. First, they will explore and utilize components of a particular discipline related to the problem under consideration. Later, they treat interdisciplinary topics, and finally become involved in tangential explorations resulting from detailed investigations.

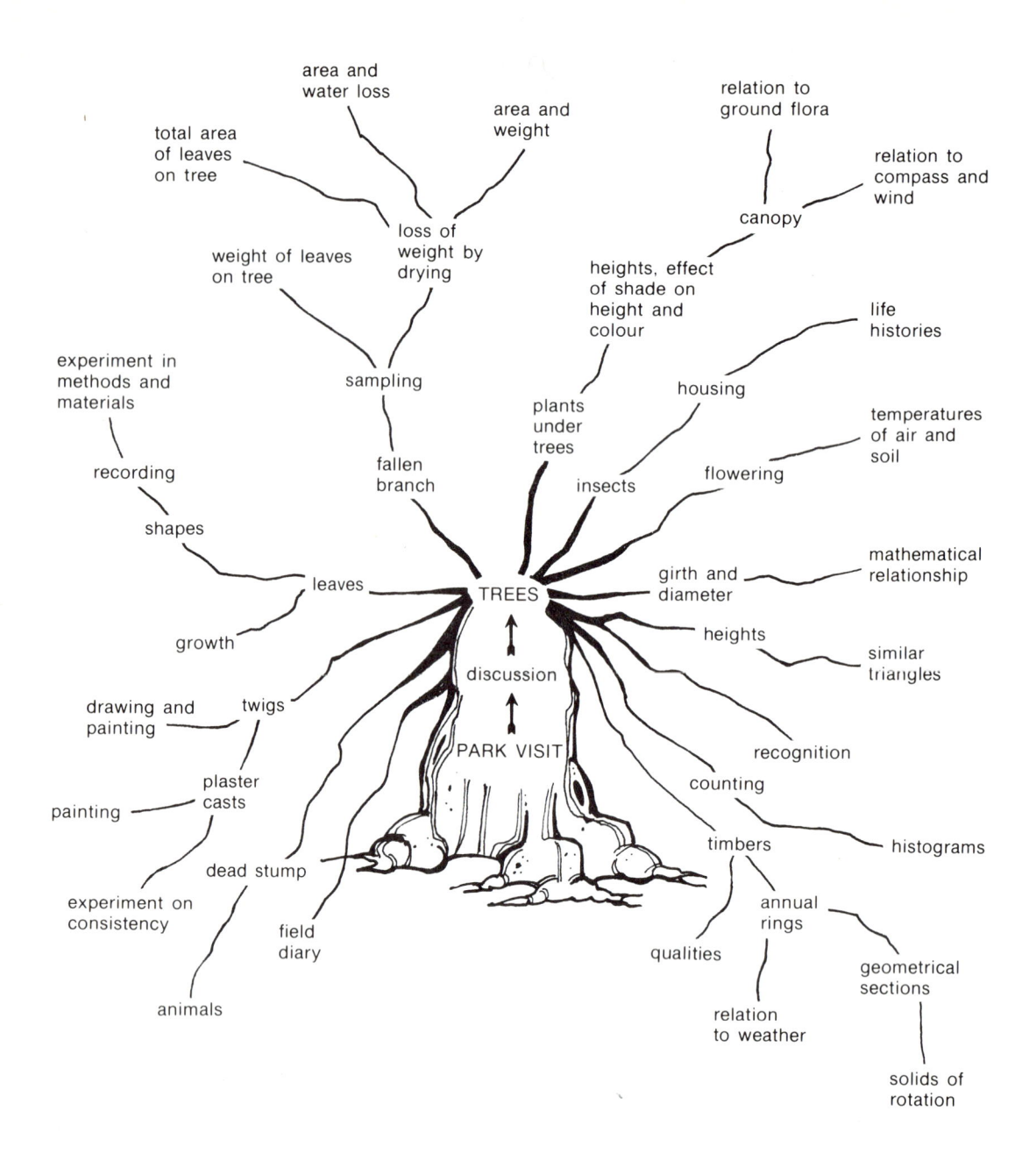

A concept web centered on **TREES** with branches radiating out from a **PARK VISIT** through **discussion**:

- **sampling**
  - total area of leaves on tree
  - area and water loss
  - area and weight
  - weight of leaves on tree
  - loss of weight by drying
- **fallen branch**
- **leaves**
  - experiment in methods and materials
  - recording
  - shapes
  - growth
- **twigs**
  - drawing and painting
- **plaster casts**
  - painting
- **dead stump**
  - experiment on consistency
  - animals
- **field diary**
- **plants under trees**
  - heights, effect of shade on height and colour
- **insects**
- **housing**
  - canopy
    - relation to ground flora
    - relation to compass and wind
  - life histories
  - temperatures of air and soil
- **flowering**
- **girth and diameter**
  - mathematical relationship
- **heights**
  - similar triangles
- **recognition**
- **counting**
  - histograms
- **timbers**
  - qualities
  - annual rings
    - relation to weather
    - geometrical sections
    - solids of rotation

QUESTIONING

Once the integrated unit is underway, you shift your role from director of theme development to that of facilitator. Questions facilitate information sharing. As a teacher, you want information about the thinking that children are doing, the conclusions they are making, and the logical mental structures they are building. Children, in turn, want to know when, why, and where.

To understand the art of question asking, a bit of situational classification helps. What kind of an answer are you expecting? Questions often divide into two categories: those which can and those which can't be answered. If children have never seen nor eaten asparagus, it is not useful to ask what asparagus tastes like! If they are not familiar with a thermometer, little value comes from asking what the name of the red liquid is.

Questions that can be answered fall into two subgroups: those designed to elicit a desired answer and those that are genuine information seekers or sharers. The former may go like this: "What is the name of the state north of Florida?" Child: "South Carolina." Teacher: "Wrong!" or "Try another." The teacher desired the answer, Georgia; the child remembered that South Carolina was north of Florida. Once the desired response is elicited, the teacher goes on to another line of questioning.

If our questioning strategy can begin as one that frames questions intended to assess a child's understanding of a particular idea or concept, questions become a powerful methodological adjunct. Inquiry, investigation, and discovery, all contemporary instructional methods, require that the teacher ask many questions. In the following situation, the use of questions as an instructional and diagnostic tool is illustrated. The teacher is at a developmental point where children are investigating electrical connections and circuits using "Bulbs and Batteries" as the curriculum resource. The teacher has identified a set of processes, skills, understandings, and concepts that are to be developed. After several lessons in which children have investigated connections, the teacher checks the list of hoped-for outcomes (lesson objectives). Questions alternated with further investigations serve to focus and move the activities toward desired understanding. This does not negate the possibility of many unexpected learnings along the way: it serves to assess the central efficacy of the lessons and to help children arrive at a particular stage in the learning process. Your objectives serve as organizers for your questions. This will help you avoid subjective, impressionistic, off-target assessments. Begin by locating the child within a frame. The child will normally display some of the desired behaviors, but lack others. You may wish to explore those areas where understandings seem thin or confused. Finally, test the child's state in concept development by posing questions requiring application of information, calling for a pulling together of data, or assessing how firmly the concept is held. Some of the questions are verbal, some augmented with manipulation of apparatus.

Consider this situation in which you have observed the group. The children began with bulbs, wires, and batteries. They not only found out how to get the bulb to light but discovered how important it was that electrical connections were secure and contact surfaces were clean. They made switches from paper clips and brass fasteners. They wound wire on nails and discovered that they could make an electromagnet. They set up several simple circuits on a piece of cardboard. From their discussions, you knew that some of the intended objectives of the activity were being accomplished. Here are a few of the stated objectives to which you might refer when asking questions:

HOW? A METHODOLOGY OF THEMATICS

- Describe and explain the use of several of the parts in a circuit.
- Display "trouble-shooting" strategies when faced with a circuit that seemingly does not work.
- Carry out a one-part-at-a-time substitution procedure in order to discover which part of the circuit is faulty.
- Demonstrate a beginning understanding of the (+) and (−) marks on a battery.
- Apply knowledge gained from one circuit to a second, and different, circuit.

Here is a transcript of the questions related to the electricity unit. Relate parts of the conversation to the accomplishment of the objectives stated above.

	T: Tell me what this is for?
	S: This is a bulb holder, this is a bulb.
Identification of the parts of the system	*T*: Are there other pieces?
	S: There is a switch, this is a lightbulb.
	T: How could you tell if this is a switch or if it is a bulb holder?
	S: The switch would push down, like this.
	T: Are the two pieces in the switch touching?
	S: No, they're not.
Knowledge of the function of the parts	*T*: Not touching, so would it work as a switch?
	S: Yes.
	T: What else could it be used for?
	S: As a bulb holder.
	T: And what do you think this is?
	S: A battery holder.
	T: How does it work?
	S: You'd put this in here and to complete the circuit you would have a wire going out.
Ability to assemble the parts	*T*: Can you show me how to make the bulb light using these pieces?
	S: (unsuccessful attempt)
	T: You said this would work like a switch.
	S: (more manipulation)
Understanding of how the parts go together to make a circuit	*T*: Does it work?
	S: No.
	T: What's the trouble?
	S: Battery is dead—or something.
	T: Can you think of a way of troubleshooting?
	S: Uh-huh (thirty seconds of puzzled manipulation)

Lack of clarity about testing parts, one at a time	*T*: Are you going to try a new battery? *S*: Uh-huh (puts in a new battery, removes switch) *T*: What happened? *S*: The bulb lit. *T*: Why didn't it light before? *S*: —the switch. *T*: or the battery—Which? *S*: (puts switch back in circuit, bulb won't light)
Understanding of the need for clean connections (corrosion acts as an insulator)	*T*: Good guess! Is something wrong with the switch? *S*: It's got brown stuff. It's blocking the electricity. *T*: So it may be corroded. (gives student another switch) Do you see any corrosion? *S*: No. (connects switch in circuit) *T*: Do you think the bulb will light this time? *S*: Gee, it doesn't light, how come? (pause) I didn't press the switch. (presses)
Emerging understanding of troubleshooting one part at a time	*T*: Now it works. How did you know if it was the battery or the switch that was the problem? *S*: Change them—substitute. *T*: Look at your working circuit carefully. Can you tell me how the wires must be connected to get the bulb to light? *S*: They have to have something that joins.
Explanation of simple circuit concept—parts connected form an unbroken pathway	*T*: Are the wires part of the joining? *S*: Yes. *T*: How is it joined in the bulb? *S*: (looks at bulb) There must be something. *T*: (picks up flashlight) Can you get the flashlight to work? *S*: (assembles flashlight)
Not clear on what (+) and (−) ends connote	*T*: Does it make any difference which way you put them (the batteries) in? *S*: Not really. *T*: How does the red button work? *S*: Same as this. (points to switch) (slides switch—bulb lights)
Can transfer concept to a new system	*T*: What do you think will happen if I take the bottom off? (unscrews bottom flashlight cap) *S*: The light will go off. (takes flashlight, unscrews bottom) It did! *T*: Remember how we had to have a wire connected to the top and bottom of the battery? *S*: (nods)

Discrepant idea tests security of concept	T: I didn't see any wires touching the battery in the flashlight. I don't see one going to the switch. Do you?
	S: No.
	T: How can it work without a wire from the battery to the switch? (points to previous bulb-battery system)
Answer indicates concept secure	S: The flashlight is made of metal. The electricity goes right through the flashlight.

Occasionally, the child will answer in the following way.

Child reverts to a "commonsense" answer that seems to satisfy the "new" situation. This suggests that the concept is not understood or firmly internalized.	S: You don't always need a connection. You don't have a connection in the flashlight so the electricity must go through just one wire.

Questions can focus on understandings that children have. The following categories suggest possible kinds of information-eliciting or triggering questions.

Information questions:
What antecedent information do you have? These deal with facts, relationships and skills. Can you relate these to the task at hand?

Purpose questions:
What is the purpose of the task? What is the student's perception of the purpose? If the student is off-task, how can questions effect refocusing? Such questions frequently deal with component parts, definitions, and parameters.

Outcome questions:
What are some possible outcomes? What sort of guesses, inferences, projections, or hypotheses is the child developing? Understanding the regular nature of a system will enable the child to make fairly good outcome guesses.

Relationship questions:
How does this fit with other things the child knows? What have you done before that is somewhat like this? Did what you learned about that system help you understand this one?

Definition questions:
How can we define what we mean or what we do in operational terms? Often children can learn to use a known situation and extract a basic principle from it that is useful. "How could the kite's shadow help you find out how high up in the air your kite is?"

Synthesis questions:
If you know these things, how can you put them together to help you understand this?

Analysis questions:
Can you break this problem into two or more simpler parts?

Application questions:
Could you use this sampling procedure to find out how many grasshoppers are in the field?

Try your hand at framing questions. Here are six situations. Think of one or more questions for each. Try to include at least one type from each of the preceding categories.

1. A child planted several items to see if they would grow. One piece of candy apparently sprouted.
2. A toy train going around a track jumps the track at the turn. A child wants to know why the train won't stay on the track.
3. One youngster brought some minnows left over from a fishing expedition to class. The teacher put them in an aquarium and added water. The next day most of the minnows were dead. The children want to know why the minnows died.
4. A child receives a water-propelled rocket and brings it to school. The children are excited and the teacher lets the child fire the rocket on the playground. Children discuss how high the rocket goes. One asks if there is any way to tell.
5. A child punches 1, 2, 3, 4, 5, 6, 7, 8 into his hand-held calculator. He then punches the divide button and punches 11. The answer reads out 11223344. He punches the same numbers and then divides by 111. The answer reads out 111222333. He asks, "Why are the first numbers of the answer always the same as the divisor?" (Note: Variations in the answers will occur depending on the calculator rounding-off functions. This does not interfere with the situation presented here.)
6. A child notices that a plastic bag stretched over a geranium plant is soon coated on the inside with tiny drops of water. He asks where the water came from.

The last section introduced you to several hypothetical children's questions. Before going further, it is important to note that children are not very good at framing questions, and the teacher may need to help the child clarify meaning before proceeding. Once clear, questions can be divided into two kinds: those which seek needed information and those which are off-target. Some off-target questions are asked to gain attention, and even upset the classroom order. You may find it wise to pretend you didn't hear the question. Some, perhaps innocent, may be so timed that they sidetrack a critical activity nearing closure. If you choose to deal with them, you should make it a point to get the activity back on-target as soon as possible. Some children have mastered, with a loaded comment, the technique of "blowing away" a moment where understanding is at stake.

With sensitivity and care, you will have to sort questions and provide useful responses. Sometimes this calls for refraining from reinforcing disruptive behavior; sometimes you must painstakingly pick up the pieces and try to restructure the learning.

You need to consider at least three possible kinds of answers to information-seeking questions.

1. Direct answers
2. Reference to a source of information
3. A possible procedure to find a useful answer

1. Direct answers are appropriate for questions calling for specific facts and data, specific procedures, precautionary measures, and explanations when such information is not quickly available or when the act of finding such information might well lead a child's task focus astray. If, for example, a child asks how long the pendulum string should be to measure one-second durations, it might be better to say twenty-six centimeters than suggest that he experiment and find out, especially if an activity requiring duration measurements is in progress.

2. A recommendation to consult a source is appropriate in other cases. If a child has a collection of shells and wants to know their names, far more attention to detail and variation is possible if you send the child to the resource center for a copy of one of several excellent guides to shells.

Often several answers are appropriate. For example, a child might want to know how to find out how fast she can go on her new bicycle. In this case, especially if some measuring skills have been developed, you might want to direct the question to the class. "Nancy wants to know how fast she can go on her bicycle. Does anyone know how to find out?" Suggestions such as (a) install a speedometer, (b) ride your bicycle beside your dad's car and have him watch the car speedometer, or (c) measure off a 100-meter course on the playground and then use a pendulum (or a watch with a second hand) to see how long it takes to go 100 meters, are written on the chalkboard. Nancy can select a procedure and recruit helpers if needed. You may find that several children would like to lay out a course and time their bicycles over it.

3. Finally, some questions are best answered by, "I don't know but here is a way we can find out." Suppose a child asks, "I wonder who invented peanut butter?" You might well say, "I don't know, but here are some ways we can find out." These, too, can be written on the chalkboard.

1. Consult reference books—list books such as encyclopedia, dictionary, Department of Agriculture yearbooks.
2. Invite the librarian to the class to explain how to find answers to historical questions.
3. Telephone or write to the local library and ask the reference librarian for help.
4. Check the card catalog under such titles as peanuts, peanut butter, and food products.
5. Write to the country agricultural agent, the county homemaking agent, or the state or federal departments of agriculture.

Even though you might be quite sure that it was George Washington Carver who invented peanut butter, you might wish to hold back the answer in order to deal with the general question of information retrieval.

We can unconsciously condition children to expect a teacher to always provide "correct" answers. Yet, when dealing with investigations and processes common to mathematics, science, and social studies, meaningful answers may require considerable investigation by the child.

Both process and content objectives are vital components of problem solving. A good example comes from a child's need to measure the volume of a rock. A *process* for measuring the volume of irregular objects involves submerging the object in water. If this is done in a container, such as a graduated cylinder, the displaced volume is equal to the upper reading on the cylinder minus the lower reading. At this point arithmetic skills (*content*) are needed, for even if the process is understood a subtraction error will yield useless numbers.

Questioning develops a child's understanding of relationships. The child becomes aware of the *order of happenings* (temporal, before and after relationships). We learn to describe related happenings in *causal terms*. (When I do this, this happens; or, if you pour into this, this will happen; or, the light bulb lit because I connected it to the battery.) Children learn the utility of an *operational definition*. In defining length, for example, the child can operationally hold two pieces of wire next to each other and say, "This one is longer than this one because when I line up these ends, this end sticks out further."

Question asking and answer framing is the way much of everyday conversation takes place. You can sharpen the child's listening skills and help the child build understanding through the asking of carefully framed questions.

REPORTS AND DISPLAYS OF CHILDREN'S WORK

It will be comforting for you to know that, aside from movable desks or tables, there are really no absolute prerequisites for a whole classroom approach to an integrated study. In most cases the study will take the students beyond the

MARIA MONTESSORI

It is not true that I invented what is called the Montessori Method. I have studied the child, I have taken what the child has given me and expressed it, and that is what is called the Montessori Method.

Dr. Maria Montessori opened the first Casa de Bambini (House of Children) in Rome in 1907. Her professional contact with retarded children, while working as an intern in an insane asylum, sparked her intense interest in the development of normal children under the age of five. As a medical student, Montessori had the opportunity to study Jean Itard's attempts to educate the "wild boy" of Aveyron and to analyze the methods of Edouard Seguin.

What are the theoretical underpinnings of the Montessori Method? First of all, Montessori believed that school experience for three and four year olds can significantly affect the children's later development. Second is the notion that intelligence is not as fixed as was believed in the early 1900s, and that the retarded can be educated. Montessori argued that development is not predetermined and that education should be based on "children's spontaneous interest in learning." Furthermore, the materials with which children interact should be intrinsically motivating. Finally, the role of the teacher in the Montessori Method is to observe and help as the children work with didactic materials.

Although Maria Montessori is applauded today as a pioneer in early childhood education, there was a time when her work was not accepted enthusiastically in the United States. In the introduction to Montessori's *The Montessori Method* (1971), J. McV. Hunt discloses that Montessori's views of development were opposed to the popular theories of her day. In the early 1900s Montessori's belief in children's natural interest in learning conflicted with the drive theory in vogue at that time. Her emphasis on sensory training was opposed to the popular support for behavioralism and motor response. Also, the function of the teacher as helper/observer was counter to the teacher-directed classroom environment that was typical of that time.

During her life, Dr. Montessori traveled all over the world, including two trips to the United States, lecturing about her observations of early development and about her method of education. The Association Montessori Internationale was founded in 1929 and Maria Montessori remained president until her death at the age of eighty-one. At that time her son, Mario, became director general. More than twenty of Montessori's pamphlets and books and more than sixty professional journal articles have been published in English.

In the United States today, Montessori preschools abound. Most of these schools have developed their own philosophy and curriculum based on their interpretation of Montessori's teachings. Fundamental to all of the various programs, however, is the belief that education should be in tune with the child's inner drives and that the goal of education is individuals in control of themselves and their environment. Montessori's followers envision a world improved by young people who are confident, competent, self-disciplined, spiritually strong, and able to work cooperatively for a better society.

---

four walls to the school library or resource center, to the gymnasium, to the school grounds, and even off campus to gather needed information. The classroom itself, therefore, is rarely an inhibiting factor restricting student progress.

Since the products of student work are normally reported on and otherwise shared as part of the theme, bulletin boards or display space will be necessary for exhibiting written and pictorial works. It is not unusual for students to design and develop projects that, because of their size, cannot be exhibited within the classroom boundaries. In this event a central hallway, vacant room, or corner of a large meeting or lunch room can be used for display on a short-term basis. This expands the opportunity for other children and teachers to observe the results of such an effort.

Integrated studies demand a variety of summarizing procedures designed so that groups of children can tell the others working on related parts of the study what they are doing and what they have found out. During the peanut butter study, Kathy McGree, the originator, gathered children around her each morning; Robin Brown, who developed the kite unit, had children put their work on display and scheduled time for all children to study the displays. John Stangl, whose children studied chemicals, asked them to prepare written reports, which he bound into booklets and made a part of the classroom resource center. Dick Johnson's children studied animals. They published a research report that contained summaries of the activities of individuals and participating groups. In every case, the reports, displays, and booklets were accepted by the teachers only if judged to be of good quality and representative of careful thought and effort. You may wish to try any one of these reporting techniques. Regardless of what is selected, you will discover that the quality of children's work and the learning progress they make is closely correlated with your expectations for careful, neat, quality products representing the best (in your judgement) that the child or group of children can deliver. The following relates to displays of projects but could equally apply to other information-sharing procedures.

Display develops pride and self-assurance on the part of the students involved as well as providing information for the observer. It follows that materials displayed should be judged to be among the best work produced. If anything the child produces is displayed without consideration of quality, the whole procedure loses credibility and validity in the eyes of the children and they will be less likely to put forth their best effort in the future. You should encourage recopying, emphasizing the need for clear sentences and legible writing. You will find that planning for a formal display of the results of student investigations is an important factor in motivation.

ASSESSING LEARNING AND PROGRESS

Let us now consider the test trap. It goes like this: *We* want to know if children are learning. *Parents* want to know if their children are learning. *Children* want to know if they are learning. So we sample parts of the unit and write some test items or some desired behaviors. Then we give the test or make the observations. If children miss certain items, we feel duty bound to go back and review that section of the unit. Then it occurs to us that we can avoid the review altogether if we use the test items or desired behaviors to suggest where

ROBERT GAGNE

Robert Gagne represents an interpretation of the learning process quite different from those already discussed. As a neobehaviorist, Gagne is concerned primarily with the end product of learning. He is most concerned with "what" the individual knows or has learned, and less concerned with "how" or the method used. Thus his philosophy asserts that the efficacy of a school's curriculum should be based on the degree to which the actual terminal student behavior corresponds to the desired end result.

A major component of this theory is the requirement that such an end result or desired behavior be task analyzed. In other words, a learning hierarchy, which will systematically arrange the prerequisite behaviors for the desired result, must be constructed. A close examination of these prerequisite learnings involves the determination of whether or not the learner possesses necessary background skills. When a student suffers from a lack of one or more of these skills, it is the teacher's role to instruct the student in those weak areas. If the student's ability includes mastery of the prerequisites, the teacher may move directly to the instruction regarding the next desired skill.

In forming the hierarchy of necessary skill development, the desired capability is placed at the top, with branches spreading out in a tree diagram arrangement so that the most fundamental and basic skills are located at the lowest points of the framework. A teacher may then look more analytically at the sequence of skills that must be included in instruction in order to properly prepare students to master a desired capability.

Since Gagne is primarily concerned with the specific outcomes of the learning process, any number of teaching methods including lecture, discussion, and guided or true discovery techniques, may be used. A teaching strategy is deemed successful if the learner masters the desired skill. Any other considerations, such as student motivation and teacher-student interaction, are viewed as less important than the final result of the learning. The only reason for regarding these issues at all is in their being the means to an end, namely specific achievement.

It is thus assumed that when the student is capable of performing all prerequisite tasks for a required skill, it will be possible to achieve mastery of that capability. Mathematics curricula are developed through the construction of learning hierarchies and the subsequent writing of specific behavioral objectives to correspond to the various subtasks or skills. In that way, academic activities are programmed to be directly applicable to the stated goals and objectives. Such a situation can become somewhat inflexible if all informal activities that may have value are disregarded. Thus, while students may be active participants in the learning process at varying rates of development, all activities are directed toward specific objectives or outcomes.

Gagne's views will continue to have a significant impact on school curriculum development. His position can perhaps be best summarized by his own words. ". . . there are many, many specific sets of readinesses to learn. If these are present, learning is at least highly probable. If they are absent, learning is impossible. So if we wish to find out how learning takes place, we must address ourselves to these specific readinesses."*

*Gagne, R.N. "Learning and Proficiency in Mathematics," *The Mathematics Teacher*, December 1973, p. 626.

we should place the teaching emphasis. We are now focusing our teaching on the test, and it works! It works so well that we may forget how important *all* of the activities are in the unit for concept formation. Some curriculum developers have tried to solve the test trap problem by eliminating testing as a part of the instructional process.[4]

We are all under pressure to rank children and compare their learning accomplishments. In doing this we sometimes forget that (1) children are different; and (2) lesson quality from day to day varies considerably.

Administrators, parents, and teachers view testing differently. Teachers are concerned with learning differences and individual progress among children in their room. Administrators may be more interested in mean score differences from room to room and building to building. Parents hold a dual view, one focusing on the needs of a single child, the other seeing the school as a low budget conveyor of basic skills.

The most important thing a teacher can do to affect learning is to recognize and teach to the abilities and needs of each child. This implies that minimum outcomes are expected and that differences in abilities within classrooms call for a variety of teaching styles and learning tasks.

If you develop a variety of activities to challenge the more able children into side explorations while keeping the seemingly less able children involved, all children will accomplish the minimum desired objectives. Some will complete the minimum task and will branch out into self-selected investigations. Such individualization demands flexible teacher evaluation procedures.

The evaluation procedures that follow are based on a theme called, "GO FLY A KITE!", which is included in the next section. You may wish to look over the kite theme before continuing reading.

"GO FLY A KITE!" encourages children to notice weather and wind conditions; to follow, modify, or invent plans for kites; to apply arithmetic facts and measuring skills; to investigate kite behavior and the effect of design modifications on this behavior; to explore the history of kites; and to creatively express ideas and feelings about kites through art work, poetry, prose, and song.

You can stimulate interest and involvement during the development of the kite theme by combining skills and concepts from several disciplines. Explore the many possible avenues for individual and group investigation. Such a diversified approach can develop interest in and motivation for reading, foster a need for developing planning skills, and provide an opportunity to associate sounds and music with the excitement of a kite first floating freely in the breeze. An equally important lesson is the value of personal success through planning and cooperative activities.

You will be faced with the task of evaluation. It would be wrong to award a blue ribbon for the best kite. Each kite may be the product of the best skills children can muster. A badge for each kite day participant would make more sense. You can't deduct points for spilled glue or broken or miscut sticks for the very acts of manipulation, participation, and enthusiasm are valued and are basic to learning. Children will learn many facts, skills, and concepts.

They may learn:

- something of the history of kites and the part they play in Eastern culture
- something of the arrangement of sticks, string, and paper to form a rigid structure
- many manipulative skills
- how to scale and read plans
- something of the nature of the forces acting on an airfoil
- something about center of gravity
- how to determine the cost of constructing a kite
- how to sample opinion relative to preferred kite design
- how to plan and organize a kite flying day
- how to work cooperatively, share ideas, and resolve conflict
- perhaps even learn how to start a small kite manufacturing business

The foregoing list may appear to be nothing more than many discrete bits of information, skills, and inquiry abilities. Yet, this list, and lists of accomplishments for other themes, fits into a global learning pattern. In each case you are asking children to:

- gain basic knowledge
- learn to make judgments and choices
- sense the values that come from active learning
- be able to extract from a learning activity useful, lifelong skills, concepts, and values
- inquire into problems, social systems, and natural patterns
- learn the need for patience, care, and repetition
- build a willingness to take risks that carry with them the chance of failure
- generate from one system, a set of principles, rules, and concepts that have multiple applications

Global goals are very difficult to assess. The small steps in the direction of these goals can be measured. The next three parts of this chapter deal with questions of pupil progress measurement, lesson quality assessment, and a procedure for collecting and analyzing information during the course of instruction to assess these goals.

Assessing Pupil Progress

The development of thematic units, the assessment of pupil progress, and the measurement of effectiveness of the parts of the thematic unit are illustrated in this simplified flow chart.

HOW? A METHODOLOGY OF THEMATICS

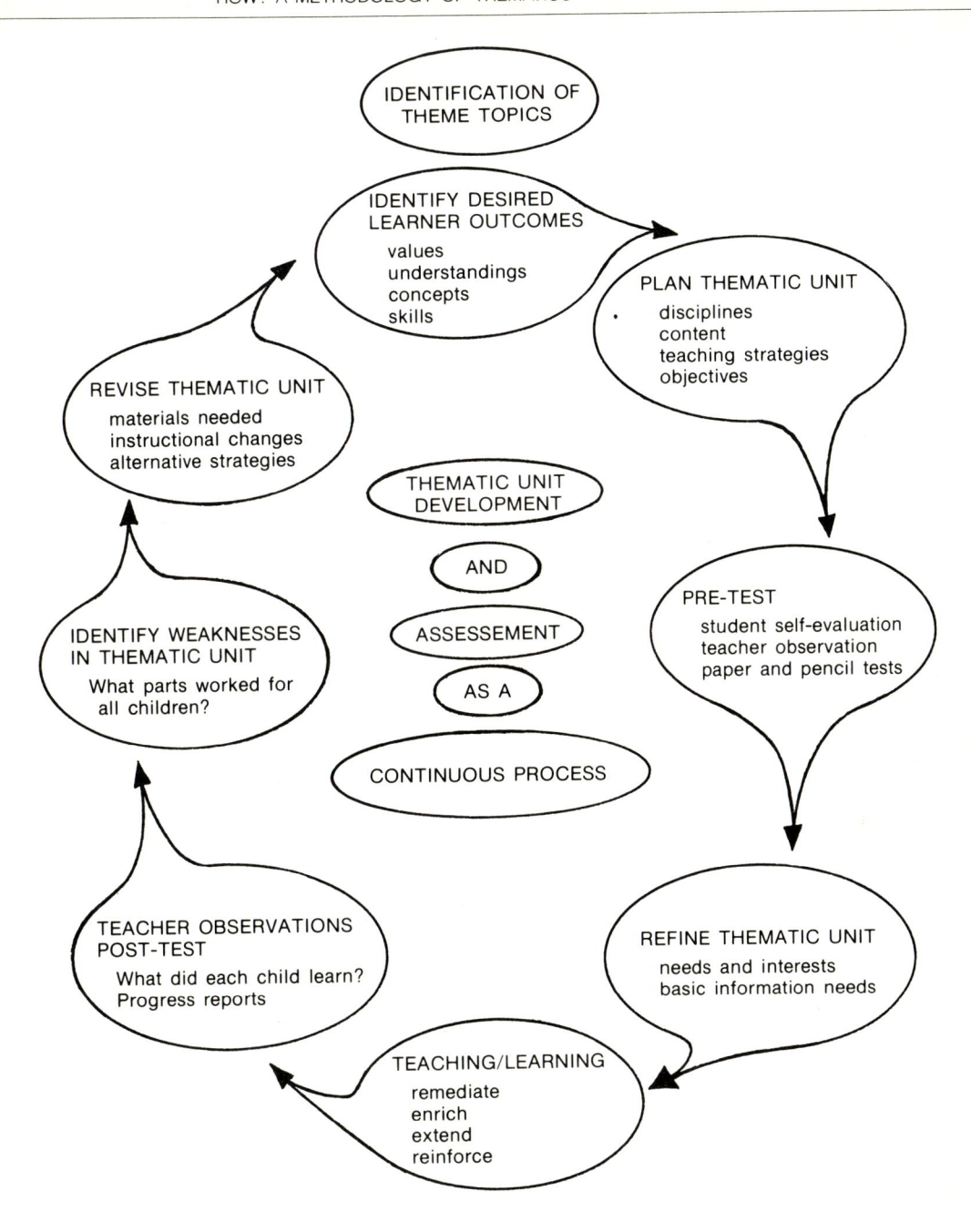

THEMATIC UNIT DEVELOPMENT AND ASSESSMENT AS A CONTINUOUS PROCESS

- IDENTIFICATION OF THEME TOPICS
- IDENTIFY DESIRED LEARNER OUTCOMES
  - values
  - understandings
  - concepts
  - skills
- PLAN THEMATIC UNIT
  - disciplines
  - content
  - teaching strategies
  - objectives
- PRE-TEST
  - student self-evaluation
  - teacher observation
  - paper and pencil tests
- REFINE THEMATIC UNIT
  - needs and interests
  - basic information needs
- TEACHING/LEARNING
  - remediate
  - enrich
  - extend
  - reinforce
- TEACHER OBSERVATIONS POST-TEST
  - What did each child learn?
  - Progress reports
- IDENTIFY WEAKNESSES IN THEMATIC UNIT
  - What parts worked for all children?
- REVISE THEMATIC UNIT
  - materials needed
  - instructional changes
  - alternative strategies

We need to find out what children know at the beginning of a thematic unit. We need this information so (1) we don't lose valuable instructional time; and (2) we can incorporate activities for all children, small groups, or even a single child being assured that needed prerequisite skills are present. We then need to find out what children have learned as the unit is being taught and when the unit is complete.

Since children are not always able to express what they know through language, it is useful to behavioralize desired learning outcomes. Vygotsky's studies tell us that language may pose problems for children. Language coupled with activity enhances both language skills and the child's acquisition of concepts. It becomes important to ask children to explain and at the same time to demonstrate understandings through showing, manipulating, and drawing pictures. Test items and behavior statements get at the same information. Suppose the child's kite is unstable. It swoops, dips and frequently crashes.

WRITTEN ITEM

The balance of a kite is most closely related to:
a. size of the kite
b. location of kite's center of gravity
c. bridle attachment angle
d. wind velocity

BEHAVIORAL STATEMENT

When assembling and flying a kite a child will be able to make adjustments so that the kite will fly in a stable, well-balanced way. You say to the child: "What can you do to your kite so it will fly without tipping and crashing?" or "Notice Mary's kite, it doesn't wobble and crash. What's different about Mary's kite? What can you do to your kite?"

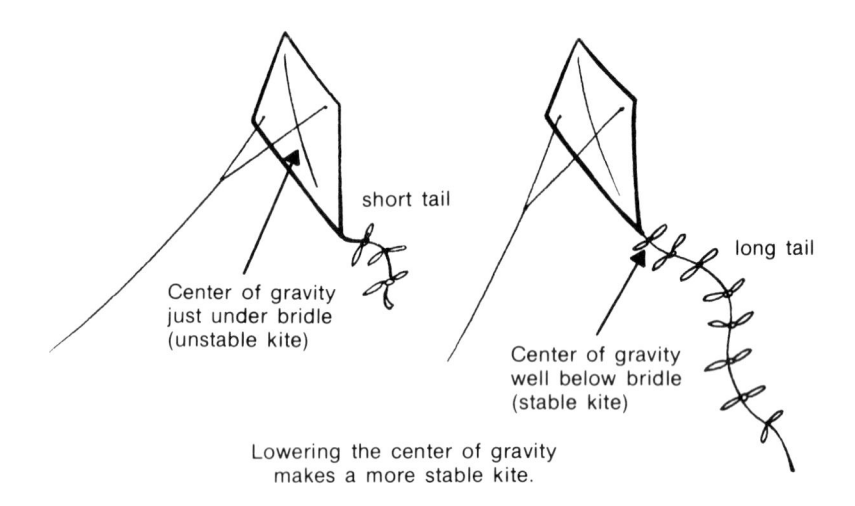

Center of gravity just under bridle (unstable kite) — short tail

Center of gravity well below bridle (stable kite) — long tail

Lowering the center of gravity makes a more stable kite.

Both testing procedures are equally effective *providing* the child does not miss the written item because of language misunderstanding. You will need to write behavioral statements following the objectives of the thematic unit.

The following is a hypothetical year's plan for concept development. It has been shortened to serve as a better example. Each intersection represents an objective to be gained in one subject area. The kite unit focuses on several of the intersections. Even though only five have been sampled, it would not be difficult to write one or more activities for most of the intersections on the chart. The teacher must decide which objectives are stressed in a particular thematic unit and how many will be used to assess the progress of each child.

A GENERALIZED MASTER PLAN* MATRIX

COGNITIVE DOMAIN OBJECTIVES†	LANGUAGE ARTS	SCIENCE	SOCIAL STUDIES	MATHEMATICS	OTHERS
1. Observing	X				
2. Recording		X			
3. Describing					
4. Defining					
5. Measuring					
6. Posing questions					
7. Synthesizing					
8. Hypothesizing			X		
9. Inferring					
10. Predicting				X	
11. Generalizing					
12. Evaluating					
13. Verifying					
AFFECTIVE DOMAIN OBJECTIVES†					
1. Functioning independently					
2. Functioning effectively with others					X
3. Developing and holding a set of values					

*The five marked intersections are used to illustrate the development of desired behavior statements.

†These objectives are general; there is no list of subparts.

Writing Behavior Statements

Five intersections on the matrix have been marked. These five will be used to illustrate the development of *desired behavior* statements. Begin with: The child will be able to __1__, __2__. On line 1 insert a verb such as tell, write, explain, point to, connect, reverse, sort and so on. On line 2 describe what you expect the child to do to satisfy the objective. For example:

1. Intersection of Observing and Language Arts
   Write a description of the shapes of three different kites.
2. Science—Recording
   Make three changes in the kite bridle.
   Record the performance of the kite with each change.
3. Intersection of Hypothesizing and Social Studies
   Make three guesses as to why Asian kites are often shaped like dragons, birds, and fish.
4. Intersection of Predicting and Mathematics
   Several children have attached a spring scale to their kite string. At the same time they have set up a device to measure wind speed. They have plotted kite string pull versus wind speed. From your data, predict what the pull on the kite would be if the wind speed was thirty kilometers per hour.
5. Intersection of Functioning effectively with others and Music
   Sing with a choral group as part of the kite day festivities.

Diagnosing Learning Needs

As a teacher you need a variety of diagnostic tools. Learning needs fall in the motor, cognitive, and affective domains. The following collection is intended to suggest a number of ways you can gather information.

Peer perception statements. Sociograms can promote effective social interrelationships and help to identify those needing intervention. If each child is asked to supply the names of two other children with whom he would like to build a kite, the number of times each child is selected gives some information about peer perception and insight into effective grouping. If you use a roster and tally the number of times each child is selected this will give you a quick ranking of children in terms of peer perception specific to the task.

A somewhat more elaborate space-diagram can be developed that will identify natural, cooperative working groups.

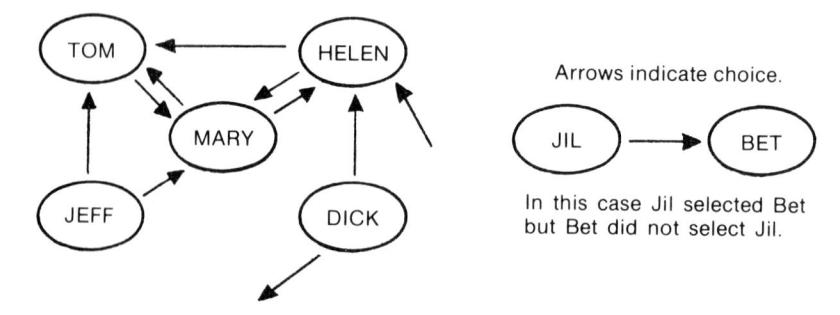

Arrows indicate choice.

In this case Jil selected Bet but Bet did not select Jil.

Such a diagram will help to identify potential leaders and children who are frequently excluded.

Priority statements. The children's ranking by preference of subjects will help you choose interesting instructional activities, and will measurably aid in

DAVID AUSUBEL

Ausubel distinguishes between reception and discovery learning. In reception learning, students learn content as product. Students are required to internalize material so that they can give it back (e.g., on a test) at a later date. Discovery learning is based on the idea that content is not given to learners in finished form; rather, it is discovered by learners before they can internalize it. Thus, in discovery learning, the learner's major task is to discover something and not merely to learn some content. Put rather simply, the difference lies in emphasizing *product* in learning versus emphasizing *process* in learning.

Ausubel points out that the distinction between reception and discovery is not identical to the distinction between triviality and meaningfulness. This is a misconception often conveyed by well-intentioned advocates of discovery learning. Ausubel writes:

Actually, each distinction constitutes an entirely independent dimension of learning. Thus reception and discovery can each be rote or meaningful, depending on the conditions under which learning occurs. In both instances meaningful learning takes place if the learning task is related in a nonarbitrary and nonverbatim fashion to the learner's existing structure of knowledge. This presupposes (1) that the learner manifests a meaningful learning set, that is, a disposition to relate the new learning task nonarbitrarily and substantively to what he already knows, and (2) that the learning task is potentially meaningful to him, namely relatable to his structure of knowledge on a nonarbitrary and nonverbatim basis.*

Ausubel contends that the best balance between reception and discovery learning is one that favors more reception than discovery. Of course, such a balance presupposes meaningfulness of instruction regardless of the method used. The power of discovery learning lies in the fact that the learner actually generates the knowledge to be learned and is thus able to see how information comes into existence. The limiting factor in the discovery approach is that it is an inefficient means of delivering large bodies of subject matter knowledge.

*David P. Ausubel, "The Facilitation of Meaningful Verbal Learning In The Classroom," *Educational Psychologist*, vol. 12, 1977, pp. 162–163.

grouping children for different thematic investigations. A sample priority list follows.

Mark 1 by the thing you would choose first. Mark the other items 2, 3, 4, and so on showing your second, third, and fourth choices.

____ Looking at pictures of kites

____ Visiting a kite shop

____ Listening to stories about kites

____ Writing a poem about a kite

____ Drawing pictures of kites

____ Watching movies of kites

____ Flying kites

____ Measuring how high your kite flies

HOW? A METHODOLOGY OF THEMATICS

Feeling statements. You can gather *information that will help you understand emotional problems about children's feelings* by asking children to complete statements such as:

When I work with my kite building team I _____

When someone does all the talking I _____

I wish the group leader would _____

Sometimes I feel unhappy because _____

The information you gain is valid only if you have established a sound level of trust with the children. Interest, feelings, and understandings can also be understood through the use of a variety of mini-tests, which can be given at regular intervals.

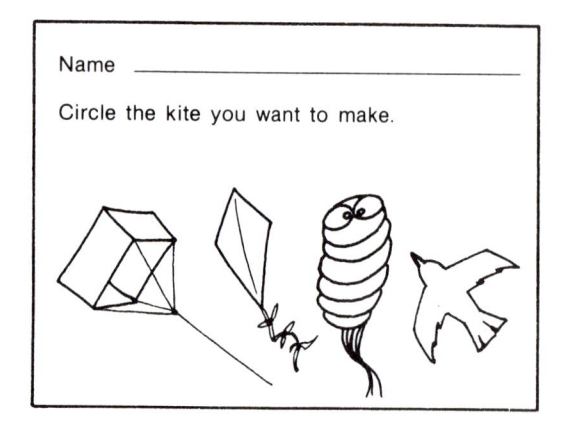

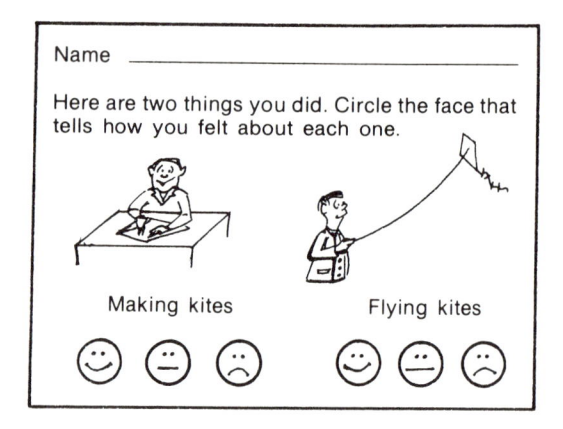

Name _____
Circle the kite you want to make.

Name _____
Here are two things you did. Circle the face that tells how you felt about each one.

Making kites   Flying kites

Awareness statements. These can help you identify children who never grasp directions, know what is supposed to be happening, or know the nature of the task at hand. This information will help you get children involved and reduce classroom confusion.

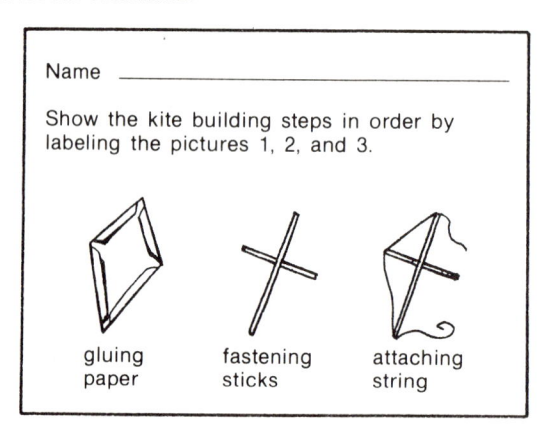

Name _____
Show the kite building steps in order by labeling the pictures 1, 2, and 3.

gluing paper   fastening sticks   attaching string

HOW? A METHODOLOGY OF THEMATICS **51**

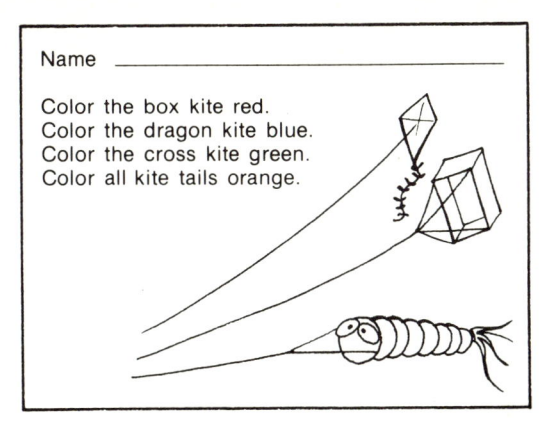

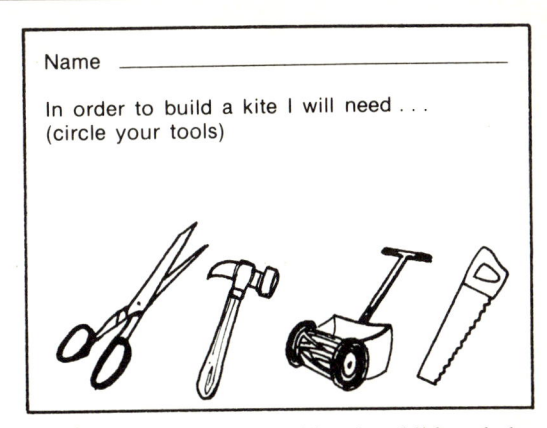

```
Name _____
Color the box kite red.
Color the dragon kite blue.
Color the cross kite green.
Color all kite tails orange.
```

```
Name _____
In order to build a kite I will need . . .
(circle your tools)
```

"I learned" statements. A list of learned items created by the children helps you assess their understanding of the purposes and objectives of the theme.

```
Name _____
When I was flying the kite in the air, I learned:
```

Using Behavior Statements

Many teachers have found that a two-way chart is a simple way to keep records of pupil progress. It will provide you with daily information on (1) how each child is progressing; and (2) how well each part of the lesson is working. You will notice that previous behavioral statements are repeated. As the thematic unit progresses, you can add additional behaviors or you can start a new chart. Teachers have found that the chart can be cumbersome if too many behaviors are used at one time. In practice you will find that if you select two or three behaviors and about one-third of the children per day to observe, the chart won't interfere with your work with children. In fact, some teachers have observed that it helps them in framing questions and keeping children on-task.

When the unit is complete you can convert the blanks, lines, and crosses into numbers and can generate progress estimates of the performance of each child in the class. In addition, the two-way chart is a useful tool when reporting to parents during conferences. The chart enables you to indicate the positive accomplishments of the child and those which will require additional effort. In fact, the chart might suggest ways that parents can work with their children and thus help you in accomplishing objectives.

The marks in the boxes enable you to indicate improvement as the child approaches and accomplishes the objective.

If you do not see any evidence of the desired behavior ☐

If you see some, but not adequate, evidence ◸

If the child's behavior indicates satisfactory accomplishments ⊠

The numbers at the right side are generated by assigning and adding the separate numbers.

☐ = 0   ◸ = 1   ⊠ = 2

When you add the columns vertically, you are able to assess the entire class's progress on each of the desired behaviors. Low numbers indicate that a review or a revision may be in order. High numbers indicate that your teaching and the lessons are accomplishing the objectives.

The sample two-way chart could be interpreted as follows:

1. Bill, Tommy, and Bette seem to be working and accomplishing in a satisfactory way.

2. Mary and Beth are doing above average work; you may want to direct them to more complex investigations of their choice.

3. Greg is having trouble. You may wish to make some careful observations and ask some questions to find out where the problems are. You may have to develop some specific remedial assignments.

4. There is something wrong with the activity intended to develop the first objective. The activity may not have been presented effectively, it may be too difficult or needed antecedent skills may be lacking. In any event, a review or additional activities are in order.

Teaching is a complex art form and the teacher, with the children, attempt to create the best learning environment possible. In order to do this well, the progress of each child must be continuously assessed and those lessons or instructional procedures which are ineffective must be replaced with better ones. Learning environments are only improved through careful, systematic evaluation.

Thematic units are challenging, difficult, and often complex. But they do exploit knowledge connections that are natural to children, and they do offer alternatives to a compartmentalized approach. The bridges often prompt new learnings and expand the child's understanding of the interconnections of the elements of the theme.

ONE TEACHER'S THEME: PEANUT BUTTER

This unit represents a documentation of some thoughts and reactions of Kathy McGree, who, together with her children, explored an unlikely subject.* The

---

*The authors are indebted to Ms. Kathy McGree of Bethune Elementary School, Minneapolis, Minnesota, for her permission to include an overview of this theme.

HOW? A METHODOLOGY OF THEMATICS

TWO-WAY CHART

	CAN EXPLAIN WHY KITES FLY	CAN CALCULATE STICK LENGTHS	CAN DEFINE LIFT, DRAG AND BRIDLE	INDIVIDUAL TOTALS
Billie A.	⊠	⊠	⊠	4
Tommy B.		⊠	⊠	3
Bette G.		⊠	⊠	3
Mary J.	⊠	⊠	⊠	5
Beth M.	⊠	⊠	⊠	5
Greg R.		⊠		1
Julie G.				
Cathy J.				
Rick L.				
Noah M.				
Julie N.				
Jack N.				
Mary O.				
Dana P.				
Mike R.				
Lorie R.				
Jason R.				
Pat S.				
Gail T.				
Robert T.				
Sheri W.				
Class Total	2	10	9	

No evidence ☐ 0 points   Some evidence ⊘ 1 point
Good evidence ⊠ 2 points

topic was peanut butter. It was developed and implemented with primary-age children in an inner-city setting. The following section tells you why and how Ms. McGree tried this theme.

The Need for an Alternative

The need for an alternative became apparent to me because of numerous observations made over a period of time, of children in my school, Bethune Elementary. I saw that many were being encompassed by what I call the 3 Fs, that is, feeling Fragmented, Frustrated, and Failure-oriented. This was brought especially to my attention by the Title I children I work with in a math lab program. I was feeling quite good about what was happening in the lab concerning individuals' progress in attitudes toward math as well as growth in basic skills. The children were verbalizing similar feelings. However, math was divided in their minds. Sid verbalized it one day when he said, "Math in the math lab is fun; math in homeroom is ugly." My question then was why? The children could not tell me what made math different in the lab.

Upon investigation of the classroom situations, several interesting things were evident. The seemingly disconnected components of the school day were difficult for many children. They were fragmented into parts here, parts there, and so was their learning. Math was here, language there, with little attempt to show how they correlate. Everything was pushed into its isolated academic area, which was then confined to a defined time slot.

Scheduling existed on a half-hour basis and caused great frustration at times in terms of completion of projects. In the math lab very little direct teaching went on; each concept was taught through experience-oriented activities that included some decision making. Concepts were introduced according to the level of the individual child. I had done this because of exposure to Bruner's and Piaget's ideas on how children learn. The children reacted much more favorably to activities studied along these lines than to their normal classroom instruction. The difference must have been in the way these activities were designed.

Four concepts seemed important to me and were kept in mind during the theme's development; these were progress, relevance, freedom, and integration. I found a definition of progress that coincides with my own: "To progress means to advance. Unless every child is advancing (i.e., going forward, making improvements when measured by his own performance in the past), he is not progressing. That progress is measured, not against an arbitrary 'class' standard, but against his own past attainment and involvement, is the essence of the meaning of the term individual. But, it does not mean that everything a child does must be done alone."[5] It also seemed reasonable that children need to be involved in and see the relevance of their learning.

The concept of freedom also seemed important for me to consider when planning and developing this theme. Again, I agreed with Sybil Marshall's ideas on freedom: "Freedom does not indicate a complete absence of advice or guidance—or even of rules. It *may* in some cases imply 'do what you want to do when you like,' it *never* implies 'don't ever do what you do not wish to do, or what others (including the teacher) may require you to do.' If the teacher has understood his task, no child in his charge is ever 'free' to regress or to stop advancing. He is only 'free' to progress according to his ability and aptitude, and with as much pleasure and meaning in the process as possible.[6]

Finally, the concept of integration: "Integration is, essentially, a form of organization in which the *child* exercises a greater degree of choice about what he is going to do and when he is going to do it, and the teacher helps to guide his or her daily program so that learning and progress take place."[7] Integration also includes the fusing of subjects and interrelating them as is present in real life. I felt the skills learned through this kind of an approach would be more beneficial for these children than the memorizing of irrelevant and isolated facts.

I chose the theme of peanut butter because all children would be familiar with it and because the implications for activities in all curricular areas seemed somewhat clear to me. I also felt that it easily could lead into a large variety of action-oriented projects. Although I had certain preconceived ideas as to the theme's design, the children were quick to modify these, expanding some, eliminating others, and suggesting new ones as well. In general, the final activities were a result of student and teacher development. A schematic diagram on the following page depicts an overview of the theme.

Along with the diagram is a list of specific activities in which the various groups participated.

The following are the children's projects according to group sizes:

Individual projects
- peanut books: facts, pictures
- report on uses of peanuts, and chalk drawings illustrating uses
- changes that occur when peanut butter is left on a knife for many days
- report and picture of Carver
- painted pictures of peanut plants
- book about Peanuts characters (Charles Schultz)
- pictures using peanuts
- peanut cartoons
- clay model of a peanut
- letters to places asking for information, i.e., Skippy Peanut Butter Company and Agricultural Department of Georgia
- map of United States colored in where peanuts grow
- dittos of Alabama/Georgia and information about peanuts and how they grow there

Small groups
- paper mosaics of animals that eat peanuts (4' × 4')
- recipe books containing the recipes we used in class plus some others

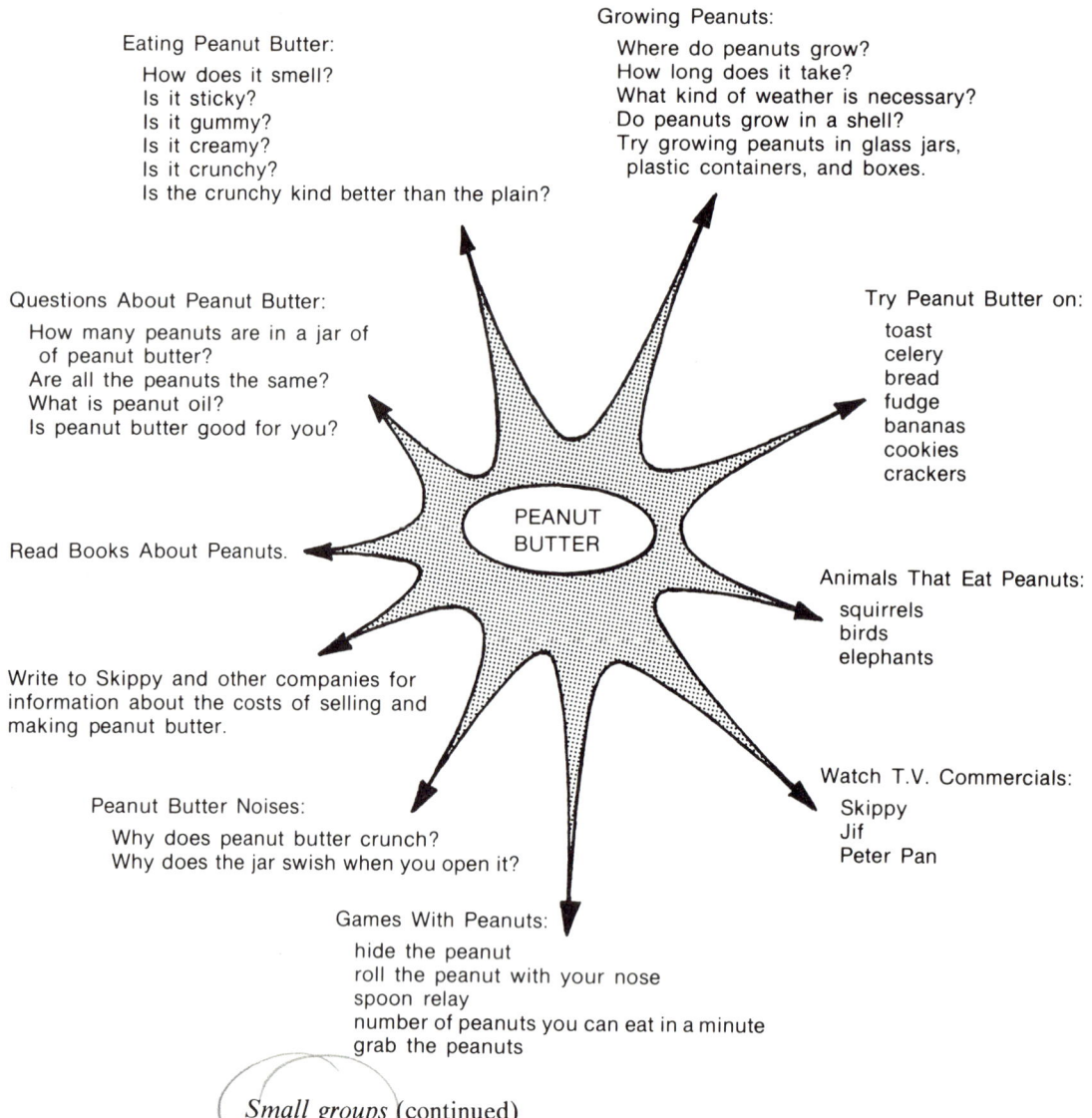

Eating Peanut Butter:
 How does it smell?
 Is it sticky?
 Is it gummy?
 Is it creamy?
 Is it crunchy?
 Is the crunchy kind better than the plain?

Growing Peanuts:
 Where do peanuts grow?
 How long does it take?
 What kind of weather is necessary?
 Do peanuts grow in a shell?
 Try growing peanuts in glass jars, plastic containers, and boxes.

Questions About Peanut Butter:
 How many peanuts are in a jar of of peanut butter?
 Are all the peanuts the same?
 What is peanut oil?
 Is peanut butter good for you?

Try Peanut Butter on:
 toast
 celery
 bread
 fudge
 bananas
 cookies
 crackers

PEANUT BUTTER

Read Books About Peanuts.

Animals That Eat Peanuts:
 squirrels
 birds
 elephants

Write to Skippy and other companies for information about the costs of selling and making peanut butter.

Watch T.V. Commercials:
 Skippy
 Jif
 Peter Pan

Peanut Butter Noises:
 Why does peanut butter crunch?
 Why does the jar swish when you open it?

Games With Peanuts:
 hide the peanut
 roll the peanut with your nose
 spoon relay
 number of peanuts you can eat in a minute
 grab the peanuts

Small groups (continued)

- cooking things, i.e., pudding, cookies, crispies, bars, cake, sandwiches, peanut brittle, peanut butter
- learn to count by 2s
- bird feeders: oral report on results
- painted mural 8' × 4' of peanuts growing and an explanation next to it
- T.V. commercials videotaped and shared with whole unit
- peanuts used as counters in math
- peanut animals using shells

- surveys of 4 classes who liked peanut butter–favorite kinds
- graphs of results of a couple surveys and of how many peanuts we could grab in one hand—lead to contests
- estimating number of peanuts in jars—set up a booth in front of office and results were kept, tabulated, and sent out with winners getting prizes
- estimating number of peanuts that can be grabbed in one hand—discussed possible reasons why
- sorting nuts into sets by size, kind, shape
- read plant stories
- measured the size of a lot of peanuts to see how long they usually are

Large groups

- songs like "Found a Peanut"
- games: relay push, carry peanut on spoons by noses, hide the peanut, etc.
- tasting party
- graph on feelings about theme learning—taped discussion after doing graph
- growing peanut plants and taking care of them
- going to store to buy ingredients for cooking; comparing prices of brands and sizes
- reading book *PEANUTS,* by Millicent Selsam

Objectives and Evaluation

In order to effectively evaluate my thematic teaching experience, objectives had to be set; objectives for me as well as for the children. My objectives were to try it and, if possible, to emphasize math in an application format. I wanted the chance to pick a theme, set it up, and try it with a group of children. I did not self-choose an evaluation process other than periodic mental reviews of each child's progress.

On the other hand, specific evaluation methods and procedures were established for the children. Five objectives were established:

1. children would gain skills in decision making;
2. they would gain skills in gathering, recording, and reporting learning experiences;
3. they would gain skills in becoming independent workers;
4. they would work across curriculum areas; and
5. they would gain some factual knowledge of the theme.

Evaluation of the objectives set for the children would be accomplished mainly through observation. It would be done by watching and recording the observations made of each child daily or weekly and through examining their projects. I would look to see if changes occurred in their decision-making ability. Was it easier for them to choose a new project to work on? Could they choose someone to work with faster or without hassles and were their coworkers only friends, or did they change because of interests? If none of these things occurred, then my judgement would be that thematic teaching was not effective in this area.

In the area of gathering skills, could the children gather some data, record it and report on their results? What were the ways they did it; did they change as they did new projects; were the projects more precise, were the children using new places to find information? If I perceived no change in their methods, I would conclude thematic teaching was not accomplishing this goal.

Success of independence could be seen by the students not requiring my help as much. Initiating projects on their own and settling down to work in a room filled with other people doing other things would be other ways. No change seen here would point towards failure of this objective, that of gaining independence.

Integration of curriculum areas would be most visible in observing children doing research and in the completed projects. By looking at a project, one can see if language skills were used, or if math computations or measurement skills were used, to mention two possibilities. If at least two academic areas were not found within the student's project, I would have to judge failure as far as this area was concerned.

Finally, through observing children working, talking together, and by talking to each child either formally or informally about what he or she was doing, I could learn if they were gaining any knowledge about the topic. If a child could not tell or show me about the project, what he or she was learning from it or other people's projects, then I would conclude that no skill was attained through this alternative.

Another method of evaluation would be through five-minute, structured, oral interviews with children at the end of the theme and again at the end of the school term.

Observations and Results

As the theme progressed, most of the children were able to make decisions more easily. When first confronted with what each of them might want to learn about, or what project they might want to start, I was faced with eighteen blank faces. The whole class just sat and looked at me. The common answer that started to appear after the shock had worn off was, "I don't know." The next response to come was, "Mrs. McGree, what should I do?" Some children needed a bit more structure. In these cases, I gave them two or three ideas they could choose from. This seemed to really help some students.

The best example was Laural, since growth in several areas could easily be seen. The first project decision was impossible for Laural. I finally gave him two alternatives from which to choose. Laural decided to work on a peanut picture with his friend, Leon. However, when Laural and Leon were finished, Laural made the decision to make something about peanuts out of clay. Laural's biggest decision came when he decided he wanted to make a clay model of a peanut by himself. First, the project was his own idea, and second, the decision to work alone was something new for Laural. He often relied on others to complete his work. Working alone would not allow this to happen. Laural completed his project and wrote a short explanation to accompany it. The explanation was nicely matted on construction paper and the clay peanut had been carefully carved so that it could be opened and the inside examined. It was the nicest work I had seen him do. Difficulty in making decisions and completing projects well was common to a lot of the children. But like Laural, most children found it easier as they were involved in more experiences. It should be understood that Laural's progress was greater than that of some of the others.

Growth in independence was seen in Laural's case as well as others'. Small group work was new for several children. They were used to being told to do their own work and not to talk to others. By the end of the school term, I could actually sit and observe five or more groups working intently within the same room on different projects without too many hassles. It was great!

By looking at the projects, it was evident that curriculum areas were being integrated and that the children were gathering, recording, and reporting data. For instance, Tammy chose to learn about George Washington Carver. Her final project was a picture she drew of him using chalk, a short story pasted next to his picture, and an oral sharing of her findings with us at sharing time. Another project that expressed curriculum integration was the television commercials some children made and videotaped for the rest of us to see. Two of the boys worked up a commercial during their time with the speech clinician. This project resulted in two parents visiting us to find out what was going on. Each project took language skills, socializing skills, and art skills, to enumerate a few areas that were covered.

Another activity required children to survey, record, and write about the findings of the group. This, in turn, led to an estimating project in which children set up a booth outside the principal's office. As people went by they were asked to estimate the number of peanuts in jars A, B, and C. Each guess was kept along with the person's name and room number. At the end of two weeks, the children announced the names of the people that were the closest and awarded a prize to the winners. The prize was a jar of peanuts.

Integration of curriculum was present much more than originally anticipated. Unfortunately it was not possible to extend this throughout the day. It, by necessity, was limited to thirty to forty-five minutes daily. I would have liked more. When possible we did use peanuts during other parts of the day. For instance, peanuts were our counters in math, and in reading, many of our language art exercises, such as our creative writing books, were in the shape of peanuts or peanut butter jars. Some children even made pictures using peanut shells and wrote stories to go with them.

The results of the interviews showed growth mainly in attitudes and retention of factual knowledge. Statistically, the 100% positive attitudes of the children towards thematic teaching was great. It shows they really enjoyed it.

Afterthoughts and Cautions

Problems arose in my experience which I feel need to be expressed. They seemed to fall into one of two categories: problems encountered by the children or by the teacher. One of the hardest things throughout the six weeks for the children was to understand their new role. There was a need for "instant" training for the children. The first week was unbelievable for all concerned. The children weren't sure of what was going on and, this being my first real experience, neither was I. However, we quickly got it together by setting up some routines for consistency and some rules. I set up a daily routine for the purpose of having some structure. We always then started project time on the rug in a circle. Here we would share what we were doing, anything new we had learned, or something about our projects. After sharing, children that had a project going were free to leave and get started, whereas anyone entering into a new project or needing help remained on the rug to see me.

Rules were set up by the children and they were enforced by them. They set up special areas for messy art projects and one for NO noise. They also assigned people to be in charge of cleanup on a rotating basis. As a result, very few discipline problems arose that had to be handled by me alone. As the routine became set and people got into projects, fewer and fewer problems arose. However, it wasn't easy in the beginning!

Another problem for the children was completing a project to the extent I expected. I was trying to stress doing a project so that they would be proud of it. I was finding that things were done any old way in order just to get them done so they could go on to something else. I must admit, in the beginning I accepted everything as it came in, but slowly I tried to illustrate how much better, for instance, a picture looked if matted before it was put up for display. I stressed this several times in sharing time. I did see quite a bit of improvement with some children. As my expectations went up, so did the quality of their work.

Time was a problem for everybody. A time problem arose because thirty to forty-five minutes was not enough time to have sharing, go get materials, work with them, and clean up. Two problems resulted because of it. One was that the children never got time to really get into their work and, as a result, projects were drawn out, causing interest to dwindle at times. Also the shortage of time caused a lot of frustration and tears for some children. John actually tore his project up one day. It was also very frustrating for me since I never seemed to get around to everyone I wanted to see. Next time I will definitely try for an hour block of time or more.

My first problem was trying to be on top of everything that was going on and to follow through with things that had been started. Wow! I didn't think I was going to make it those first few weeks. With the starting of a definite sharing time, I found things began to straighten out a bit. I used sharing time to find out more about what the children were doing and to record it in my daily log. As I wandered around the room, I also wrote short notes in the log. It was my way of keeping records on each child. Their projects were also entered in the back next to their names.

The next problem was how to keep up with setting up materials and activities in interesting ways. Slow readers and younger children needed more activities than the children who were older and had better reading skills. A lot of my time was spent tape recording articles so the children could read along for information. It was definitely time consuming.

Two other problems need to be looked at. One, because the theme involved cooking experiences and no school funds were provided, it became quite expensive for me. We had quite a few cook-ins, and every time anyone made something they would make enough for the whole group. Needless to say it added up. The greatest expense was incurred at our tasting party. We decided to have a peanut butter tasting party and include five kinds. It all started because Randall and Jeff were going to make peanut butter as a project, and we were wondering if we would like it as well as others. We planned a party and invited everyone on our team to join us, including Mr. McDonough, our principal. At the end of the party we had everyone vote for their favorite kind. Banana Koogle won, and Randall and Jeff's peanut butter came in second. Buying enough of all five kinds of peanut butter along with the ingredients for Jeff and Randall and the crackers to put it on was quite an expense. It was worth it though. You may want to consider this when choosing a theme.

Taking everything into consideration, including how time consuming it was for me, I think thematic teaching is definitely a valuable enough experience to do again. The gains I saw in the children in terms of decision making, learning to put things together, and in their ability to generalize by far outweighed any disadvantages or complications I experienced.

SUMMARY

- When you use a thematic unit as your instructional guide, you must follow a clear set of operations.
- The theme must come out of joint teacher/pupil planning.
- Guidance, direction, and suggestion come from the teacher.
- The teacher's role shifts from dispenser of information to facilitator of learning.
- The teacher must identify appropriate and desired learning outcomes and must assess the children's progress against them.
- The teacher must provide many opportunities for children to succeed, to

report, to display work, and at the same time must set and maintain quality standards to the end that children take pride in their accomplishments.

- Lastly, you must be patient and have faith. Anyone can teach a child to recite a nursery rhyme. A master teacher helps children build concepts, learn to solve problems, generate new ideas and create new knowledge. Unfortunately, if one is to judge from tests, we often place more credence in the teacher's worth if children get high scores on standardized tests than if they are creative problem solvers and idea generators.

NOTES

1. A person who openly admits disliking mathematics and cannot see any use for its study. One source estimates that half the lay population are mathephobes. We suspect there are also science and social science "phobes."
2. STEVEN BERRY, Deputy Head, Hollybrook Middle School, South Hampton, England.
3. E. R. WASTNEDGE, ed., Nuffield Junior Science Project, Teachers' Guide 2 (London and Glasgow: Collins Publishing Company, 1967), p. 79.
4. An example of eliminating test traps is Elementary Science Study Materials (ESS).
5. SYBIL MARSHALL, *An Experiment in Education* (Cambridge: Cambridge University Press, 1970).
6. Ibid.
7. Ibid.

CHAPTER THREE

What? A Sampler of Thematic Units

INTRODUCTION

By now, you have a basic understanding of what we mean by interdisciplinary education. You have seen how this style of teaching overcomes the artificial barriers between subject areas imposed by a traditional school curriculum, and how a "connectedness" can be fostered in children's awareness and understanding of their world by integrating these subject areas.

You have also learned strategies for implementing interdisciplinary units, from the planning stage through the display and evaluation of student products. More specifically, techniques have been presented for unit theme identification and development, classroom organization, questioning techniques, student expectations, and assessment and evaluation. Finally, you have shared one teacher's experiences in putting these theories and techniques into practice in her own classroom.

At this point, your head may be filled with ideas, both those that you have read and the countless others that undoubtedly popped into your mind as you considered the contents of this book. At the same time, many questions may be clouding a clear understanding of how specifically to plan and implement your own thematic units.

Each of the units in this chapter opens with a webbing diagram showing some of the general areas and specific topics and activities that can be pursued as part of the unit. This is followed by an introduction to the unit, unit objectives, and suggested appropriate grade levels. Most units then go on to describe a number of activities, each containing objectives and materials lists, teaching procedures, brief evaluations, and additional activities and related resources as appropriate.

There are two notable exceptions to this format, and they open Chapter Three. The first of these is "Parkland." This is a narrative account of the implementation of such a unit in an elementary school in England. It is included to provide a kind of transition for you from the explanations of Chapters One and Two into a more activity-oriented set of unit outlines and materials. It may also help you see how a thematic unit develops as it is implemented, and the involvement of students in this process. The second exception is the "Flight" unit. The body of this unit consists of a student contract outlining projects for individual choice and completion. It serves as an example of one way in which interdisciplinary units can be handled in a largely individualized format.

You will note, in glancing through the units that follow, that some contain pages intended for duplication. Such pages are designated within the activity plans, and are separated from the teacher's directions for easy reproduction. These pages can also be modified to better fit the skills and/or interests of your class. What we have given you here are examples of what can be, or have been, done with students.

It is important once again to note that good themes can be adapted for use with any age group. The classroom teacher knows best the ways in which each group of children, even at the same grade level, differ in interests, skills, and abilities. You are urged to examine these units as jumping-off points for your own curriculum development. It is our hope that the ideas and materials presented in the following fourteen units will stimulate you to both develop and implement some integrated units in your classroom. As in the case of Kathy McGree, we think you and your students will be pleased with the results!

PARKLAND

Parkland: A trip to the park resulted in an incredible variety of student generated investigations. A British teacher describes, with clarity, insight, and sensitivity, an illustrative sample of those investigations.

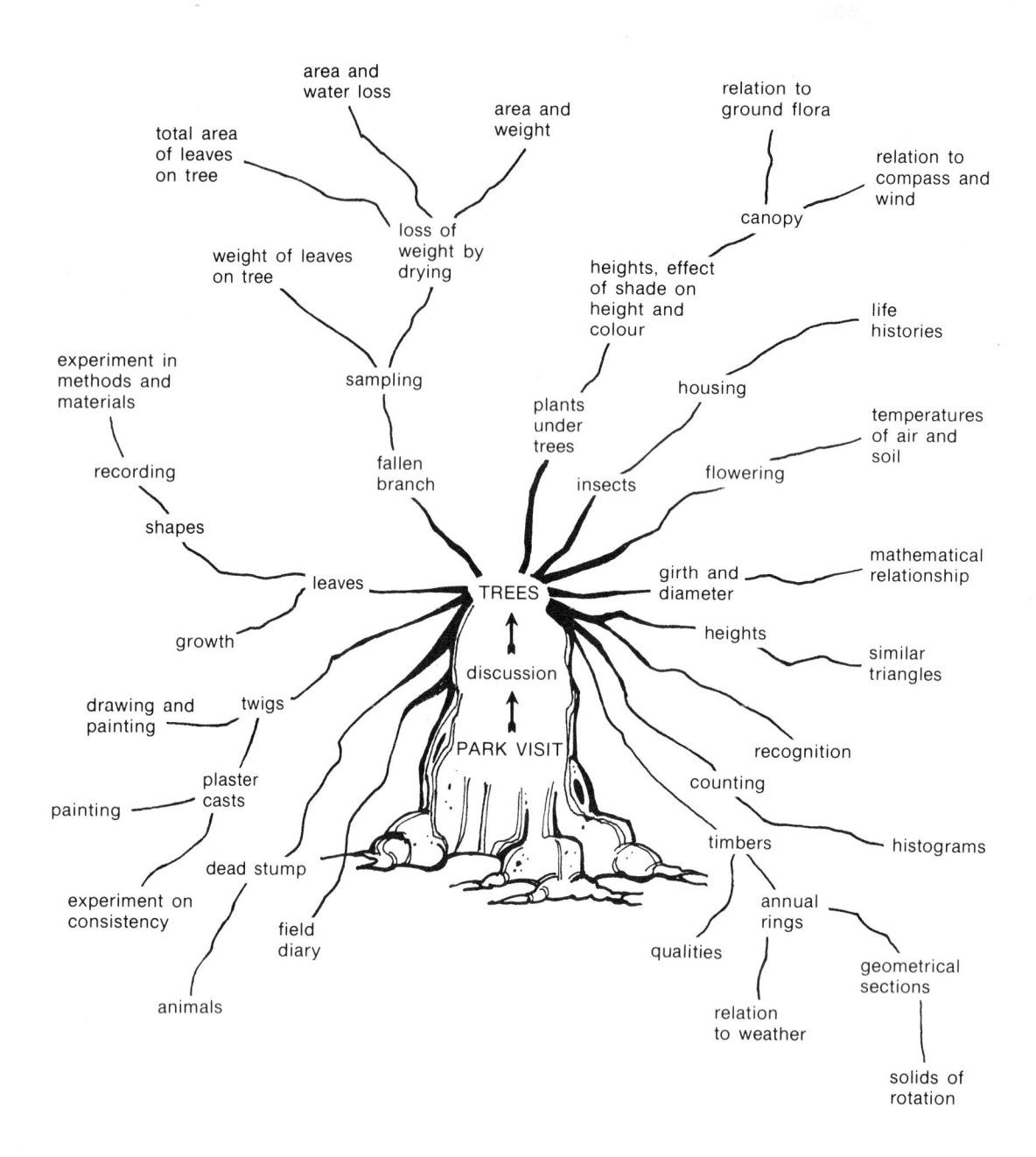

Concept map surrounding a tree illustration, with branches labeled:

- area and water loss
- area and weight
- total area of leaves on tree
- loss of weight by drying
- weight of leaves on tree
- relation to ground flora
- relation to compass and wind
- canopy
- heights, effect of shade on height and colour
- life histories
- temperatures of air and soil
- experiment in methods and materials
- recording
- shapes
- sampling
- plants under trees
- housing
- flowering
- fallen branch
- insects
- mathematical relationship
- leaves
- TREES
- girth and diameter
- similar triangles
- growth
- heights
- discussion
- PARK VISIT
- drawing and painting
- twigs
- recognition
- painting
- plaster casts
- counting
- histograms
- dead stump
- timbers
- experiment on consistency
- field diary
- annual rings
- qualities
- geometrical sections
- animals
- relation to weather
- solids of rotation

Introduction

Parkland was a thematic unit conducted during the spring and summer months in an English country school in the mid-1960s. Twenty-six children, aged seven to eleven, participated in its development. The teacher's log has been reproduced here.* It provides keen insight into the malleable nature of a

---

*Reprinted from *Nuffield Junior Science Project, Teacher's Guide 2*, E.R. Wastnedge, ed., Collins Publishing Co. (London and Glasgow, 1967), pp. 74–79. Copyright owned by Nuffield-Chelsea Curriculum Trust.

theme, ever growing, contracting, and extending into new and different areas of interest and appeal.

Procedure:

The first visit to the park was by the whole class and was used to decide what should be studied. They quickly concluded that there was far more material than they could deal with, and that it would be better to restrict their attention to trees. The first task was to count and identify the trees, as far as they were able. In fact, they had doubts about the identities of only two trees, and their suspicion that these were Norway Maple and Turkey Oak proved to be correct. This visit also led to the decision to keep field diaries and to draw block graphs showing the numbers of trees.

Back in the classroom, the children argued out how to make a start on the problem, and they determined to work in small groups, each group including children of various ages. This decision was based on the belief that the older children would be able to help the younger ones, whereas a group made up entirely of young children would be faced with too many obstacles.

Some of the children started to collect twigs, but when they felt that the twigs themselves were not a satisfactory form of recording, they decided to make plaster casts. This was not without its problems, with early mixes being too wet and later ones setting too quickly, and one boy was deputed to find out what proportions of plaster and water gave the most satisfactory consistency.

Records took the form of plaster casts, drawings, and paintings. The children used reference books extensively to discover the names of detailed structures.

Work continued during the Easter holiday when a large proportion of the class visited the park. Attention was now focused on seeds found under the trees, and back at school a selection of seeds was planted in pots and boxes and allowed to germinate. This was to determine what kinds of seeds they were and what proportion of them was capable of germination.

At the beginning of the summer term, several children were surprised to see that some of the trees were flowering, even though they had no leaves. They were now keeping field diaries, and began to compile progress reports on foliage to enter in these. The facts were assembled formally at a certain time each week, but the entries were written freely by the children.

It was at this point that two boys who were studying ash trees in widely different positions in the park realized that one tree had flowered two weeks before the other. Tommy thought that it was related somehow to temperature and that it would be useful to know something about ground and air temperatures. These were measured.

By now, the leaves were opening and there was a general interest in the changes occurring during growth. Leaf shape and details of veins and margins were examined. The class as a whole decided to keep a record of the leaves, but one group in particular was dissatisfied with the method of pressing or of sticking leaves on cards, since the results were fragile and short-lived.

This group investigated the relative values of different materials and methods of recording. They were given a free hand and a wide range of materials in their efforts to find the best way of taking permanent leaf impressions. These included rubbings, pressings, and spatter prints.

At about this time, there was a period of strong winds, and during one of their visits to the park the children found a branch lying on the ground under the tree. Interest was high. Why had it broken off? Examination showed that it was not rotten. Could it be the wind? They were not very convinced of this. The most popular idea was that the weight of leaves had caused it to fall.

What was the weight of leaves? Indeed, what was the weight of leaves on the whole tree? The children decided to count the leaves on one section of the branch, and weigh them. Then, by estimating how many similar sections there were, they could calculate the total weight.

The leaves from the broken branch were tied into a bundle for weighing, and it was a matter of interest that when they were weighed again, they had lost weight. By now, several new lines of investigation had been opened up. The children had determined the weights of equal numbers of leaves from different kinds of trees, and drawn graphs of their findings.

There were also graphs showing the relationship between leaf size and weight, and between size and kind of tree. Other graphs showed rate of loss of weight due to drying. All these graphs were compared.

Finally, one boy calculated the total leaf area on a tree. To do this, he used 0.1" squared paper, thus getting his introduction to decimals.

There were other measurements being made, too. The children had decided to measure the height of each tree, first using a stick placed against the tree and estimating how many times it would go into the height. They measured girths and also diameters, noting the simple relationship. The girth at different heights was related to the height of the measurement from the ground, and hence indirectly to the vertical growth of the tree.

The group noticed the vegetation under the tree and compared it with that under others but, unfortunately, this study ended when the farmer applied weedkiller. It was noted, however, that nettles and chickweed grew under the trees, but not in the open; and that there were bare uneven patches under the conifers, and that these were related to the varying extent of the canopy which in turn depended on the prevailing wind.

One group collected insects from the foliage by rapping a branch smartly with a stick, or by shaking. These had to be housed and this meant making cages from cardboard boxes, muslin, and cellophane. The children learned to recognize the creatures they collected and compared them with those they found on a dead tree stump. The eggs collected from the stump were kept and eventually proved to be those of a spider. From these collections, the children were able to observe life cycles in a number of cases.

Stephen collected insects from the trunk and branches. David became interested in timbers and collected and compared twigs from the trees. He also corresponded with the Forestry Commission, and started to enquire into the properties of different woods. For example, he investigated hardness by seeing how many strokes of the hammer were needed to knock a large nail into different kinds. He learned to tell the age of twigs by counting rings. To do this more efficiently, he decided to saw a twig at an angle. He then discovered that the cross-section was elliptical instead of circular. The teacher used this as the basis for a general class discussion on shapes, especially those obtained by sectioning and also by rotating common objects such as pennies, books, and cards. David also noticed that the distance between rings varied from year to year and wrote away for details of weather records over the years to see if there were any connection.

The study had now reached a stage where it had a bearing on all parts of the school curriculum. The children did a great deal of computation and making graphs, and learned numerous new words. Philippa compiled a dictionary. Another group collected poems about trees and then took to writing their own. Art work grew out of the twig and leaf records. Leaves provided stencils for patterns and the children made leaf and bark rubbings. The teacher brought into the classroom a fantastically shaped piece of wood that he had found and they used their imaginations about it eagerly, discovering weird monsters in the shapes. The study also gave rise to geography and added to the children's interest in the history of their village.

Sometimes the children made tape recordings describing the work they were doing. They exchanged these with tapes made by a similar school some thirty miles away, and this led to one school visiting the other.

FLIGHT

Flight: Birds, airports, people, careers, and flying machines all play an important role in this theme that is rich in the diversity of possible extensions. An example of a student's performance contract is included.

FLYING MACHINES
    helicopters
    rockets (e.g., Apollo 11)
    flying saucers
    UFO's

BIRDS
    flight patterns
    bone structure
    feathers
    wings
    other animals with wings

PEOPLE IN FLIGHT
    Leonardo Da Vinci
    Wright brothers
    Icarus and Dedalus
    Superman
    Pegasus
    "Star Wars"

NONMOTORIZED FLYING VEHICLES
    gliders
    balloons
    hang gliders
    parachutes
    kites
    boomerangs
    paper airplanes

AIRPLANES
    history and development
    aircraft wars
    airplane parts
    biplanes

FLIGHT

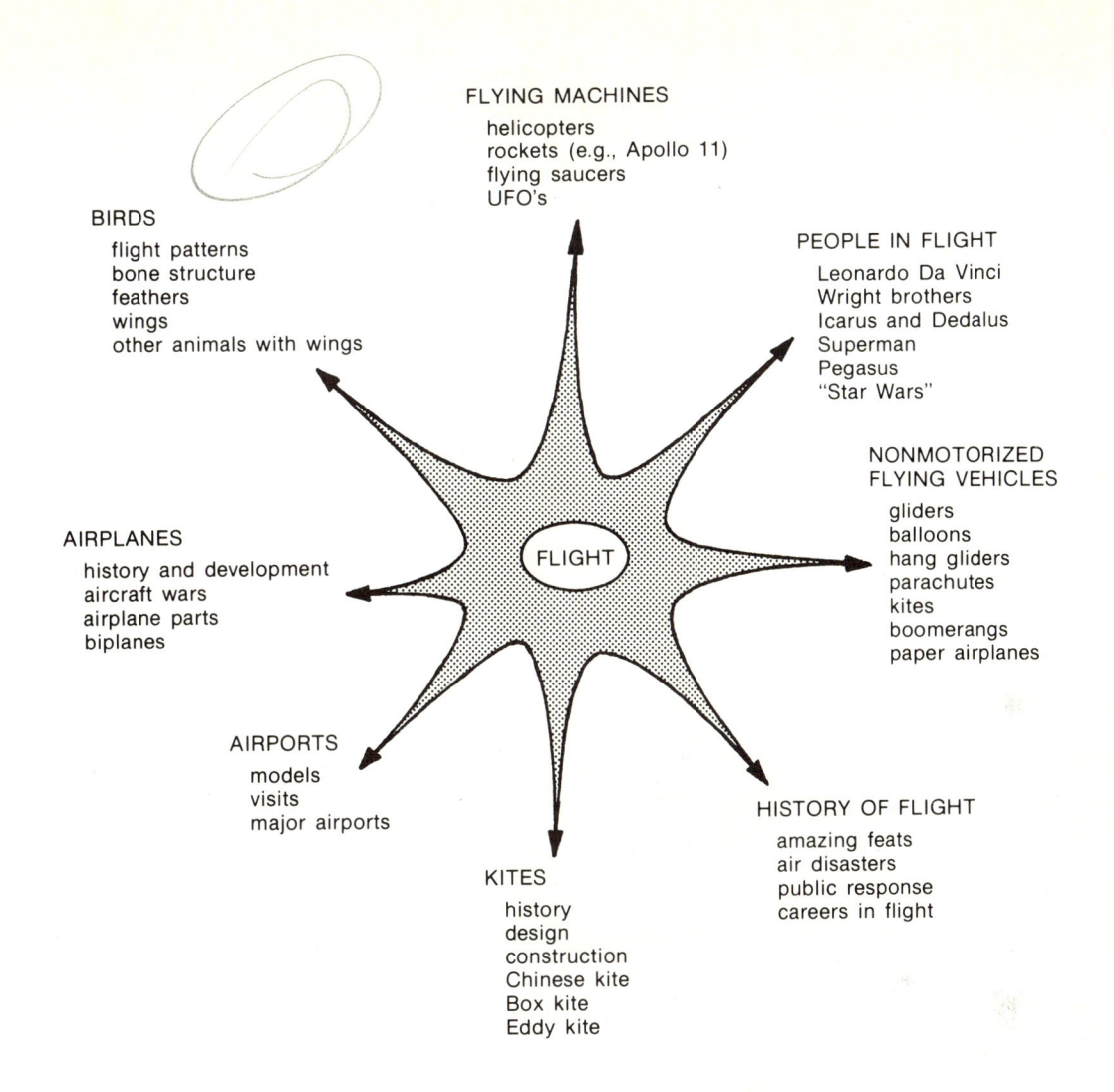

AIRPORTS
    models
    visits
    major airports

HISTORY OF FLIGHT
    amazing feats
    air disasters
    public response
    careers in flight

KITES
    history
    design
    construction
    Chinese kite
    Box kite
    Eddy kite

Introduction

The following unit on flight deviates from the standard format used in most of the units in Chapter Three. It consists of a brief overview, by curricular area, of some of the potential activities that can be pursued within the unit. Some of these are intended to be carried out with the whole class as part of your instruction concerning basic principles of flight.

The remainder of the activities presented in the overview are among those found within the individual Flight Contract, which you may wish to reproduce for use in your classroom. These activities are intended for the most part to be completed by individual students. You should find the contract system to be helpful in providing some basic structure for student use of class time, setting standards for acceptable work, and evaluating performance. At the same time, however, it allows for flexibility and tends to encourage the production of high quality work because of the high degree of individualization provided.

Resources and materials are easily obtainable and inexpensive. Those materials that will be used extensively include paper, cardboard, wire, sticks, and cloth. Guest speakers and field trips can also be an important part of the classroom activities, but films and filmstrips can be substituted if necessary. You might also be lucky enough to find TV documentaries on the air that can provide a kind of out-of-the-classroom experience. Other supplementary materials should be readily available through various local and school libraries.

Unit Objectives:

The students will:

1. learn some basic principles of flight.
2. complete at least one project outlined in the Flight Contract.
3. gain skills relative to independent goal setting and work completion.

Appropriate Grade Levels:

Six–Eight

SUGGESTED ACTIVITIES BY DISCIPLINE

LITERATURE AND LANGUAGE ARTS

1. Read *The 21 Balloons* by William Père BuBois.
2. Fly a helium balloon. Send a message or self-addressed postcard.
3. Read flight-related poetry.
4. Read "A Bridle for Pegasus" by K. Shippen, out loud.
5. Write a description of an aerial view.
6. See Walt Disney's *Man in Flight*.
7. Read about famous flight contributors such as Lindbergh, Earhart, and Wright.
8. Write flight-related short stories.

MUSIC AND DRAMA

1. Sing "Up, Up and Away," "Fly Me To the Moon," and "Leaving On a Jet Plane."
2. Put on a dramatic skit of the life of a famous flight person.

MATH

1. Measure the distance of a flight with paper planes by calculating time and distance.
2. Figure the cost of airline tickets.
3. Design flight plans and routes.
4. Build models of famous planes and airports using ratio and proportion.

FIELD TRIPS AND GUEST

1. Visit an airport.
2. Invite a pilot to speak.
3. Invite a hang gliding expert to speak.
4. Visit a science museum.

SOCIAL STUDIES

1. Learn the history of flight. See *Man in Flight*.
2. Research famous people in the field of flight.
3. Study countries producing contributions to flight.
4. Study how aircraft changed wars and developed military warfare.
5. Study how aircraft changed people, politics, etc.
6. Research how airports are organized and built.
7. Explore careers related to flight, ornithology, and engineering.
8. Write to NASA about its history and future work.

SCIENCE

1. Develop a basic understanding of the principles of flight by using paper airplanes in simple experiments.
2. Name the parts of a plane.
3. Name the parts of a rocket.
4. Compare the parts of a bird to the parts of a plane.
5. Build kites.
6. Complete the science contract.
7. Study flying machines—both current and early.
8. Study the parts of an insect and how flight is a part of its lifestyle.
9. Research rockets, satellites, and space exploration.

ART

1. Display the best plane design.
2. Build and design kits.
3. Display research information with posters.
4. Draw a map from an aerial photograph.

CONTRACT FOR FLIGHT UNIT

NAME _____

You will have class time to work on this contract from _____ to _____. (approximately 2½ weeks). Reporting time will be every Friday.

Minimum Requirements (C)

- Know the basic principles of flight we worked on together in class
- Be able to pass the test on flight
- Complete one of the following projects listed below

Above Average Work (B)

- Know basic flight principles
- Be able to pass the test on flight
- Complete two of the activities listed below

Top Quality Work (A)

- Know basic flight principles
- Be able to pass the test on flight
- Complete three of the projects listed below

Projects:

1. Read about the flight of the Double Eagle II (balloon). Write a one-page report summarizing its flight and problems. Draw a map of where it was launched and where it landed. (See *National Geographic* magazine.)
2. Research how the invention of the airplane affected wars, particularly World War I. Starting points might be to find out something about Count Zeppelin and his invention and how it was used in the war. Other pilots might be Anthony Fokker or a flying "ace" such as Oswald Boelcke. Two pages.
3. Do a paper on the flying ace of World War I—Baron von Richthofen—the "Red Baron." Report on his role in World War I. Maps or drawings can be included.
4. Research planes of World War II. Present pictures or drawings of each with their names. This can be done on a poster.
5. Research the life of Orville and Wilbur Wright. Two pages. Include information about where and when they lived and worked, and the problems they overcame in order to build the first successful plane. Build a model of their first plane.

6. Make a booklet of early flying machines or inventions. Include at least five. Explain when they were invented, by whom, where. Draw a good picture of each. Examples might be Montgolfier, Da Vinci, Lillienthal, Cayley, or any of the names from the list given in class.

7. Make a study of birds' anatomy (body structure) and make drawings showing the parts of birds, particularly the wings. Explain in your report how a bird's design is similar to an airplane and also how birds control their flight pattern. Gather feathers of different birds.

8. Find out the history of the parachute. In a one- to two-page report tell who invented it, when, and how they were perfected. Explain how it works today. Build a simplified model to explain what you learned and demonstrate this in class.

9. Make a poster or bulletin board of how aircraft has changed and developed in recent years. Include pictures or drawings of each type of aircraft and a paragraph about each.

10. Research the history of gliders. Who invented and perfected the first successful gliders? Build a cardboard glider with essential parts.

11. Read the book *Five Weeks in a Balloon* by Jules Verne. Report to the class about it. Use a visual means such as a poster or diorama as part of your report. Discuss with teacher.

12. Learn more about how airports are designed. Write to airports and airport designers to obtain information and report your findings. One page. Build a model of an airport.

13. Write about the history of ballooning—both hot air and gas. Include the inventors and be able to explain how balloons work. Design a hot air balloon of your own on a poster and label parts, or build a hot air balloon and we'll attempt to fly it. (Difficult)

14. Make a large time line, to be put up in the room, of the most significant events in the history of flight since the time the Montgolfiers invented ballooning.

15. Research the history of rocketry beginning in America with Robert Goddard. Explain in your report how rockets work and include a diagram with parts labeled. You can demonstrate simple experiments or build a model. (There are kits for this but they cost money.)

16. Research the history of helicopters in a report and build a simple model to demonstrate (not paper).

17. Explain the principles of kite flight. Make a kite to demonstrate (not from a kit unless it's unique).

18. Research the space race between the United States and the Soviet Union. Include information about Sputnik I and II. Discuss United States achievements in the early 1960s.

19. Report about Apollo II landing on the moon: who the astronauts were, how they accomplished their mission. Interview three people who watched it on TV and write about their reaction at the time. Or make a poster or bulletin board about how people felt about the space race.
20. Write a complete biography of Charles Lindbergh or Amelia Earhart. Be sure to explain their greatest feats in flight history.
21. Get background information about any person(s) connected with flight and write a dramatic skit about them to be presented to the class. Minimum time: five minutes. (four people may work on this)
22. Read the short story by Edgar Allen Poe, "The Unparalleled Adventure of One Hans Pfaall." Write your own short story concerning flight and illustrate it. Be ready to read it to the class.
23. Research and gather any songs that have to do with flying. Get the lyrics, titles, copyrights, and a recording if the library has it. Perform one for the group. (for three people)
24. If there is another project you are interested in you may discuss it with your teacher.
25. Conduct an interview with a pilot, flight attendant, or any other person whose career is associated with flight and report to class.

I WILL COMMIT MYSELF TO DOING THE LEVEL OF WORK CHECKED.

____MINIMUM   ____ABOVE AVERAGE   ____TOP QUALITY

DATE_____   SIGNATURE_____

CONSUMERISM

Consumerism: Using concepts such as supply and demand, economic stability, advertising, and product promotion, students critically examine and evaluate TV and newspaper advertisements, systematically collecting various types of data in the process.

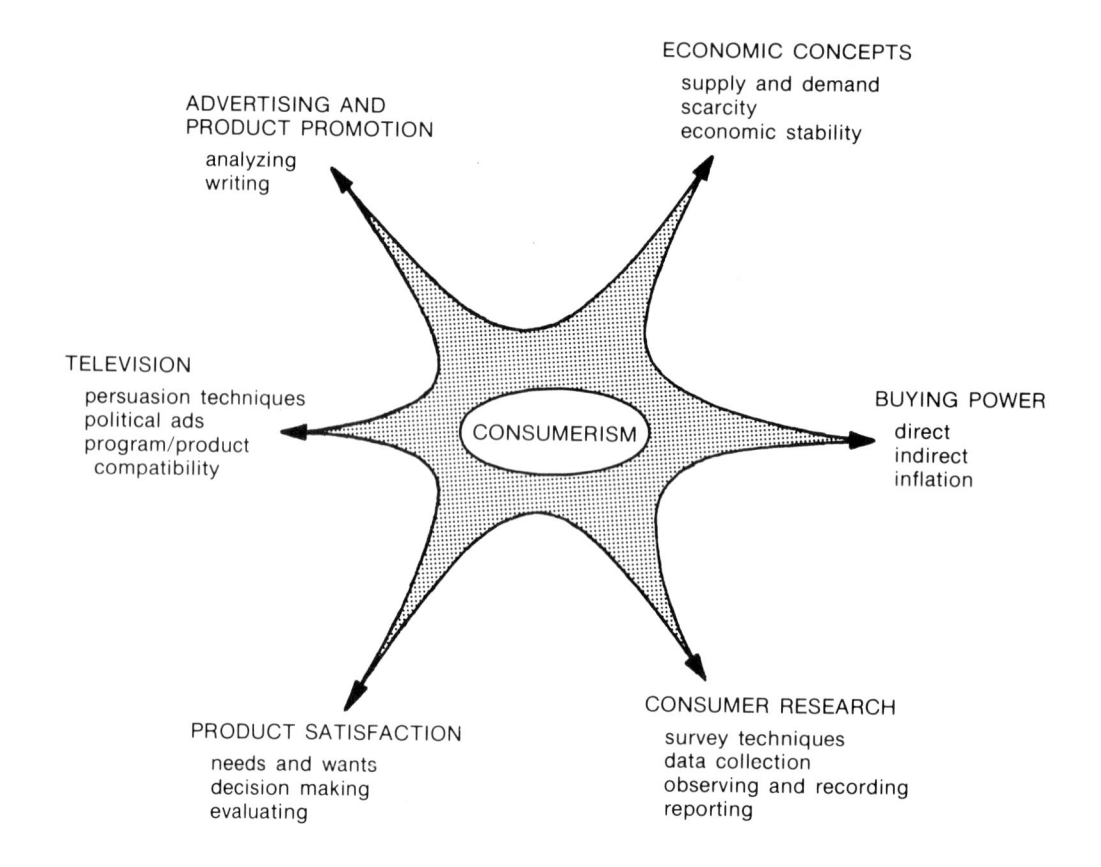

```
                              ECONOMIC CONCEPTS
                                supply and demand
        ADVERTISING AND         scarcity
        PRODUCT PROMOTION       economic stability
          analyzing
          writing


    TELEVISION
      persuasion techniques                    BUYING POWER
      political ads              CONSUMERISM     direct
      program/product                            indirect
      compatibility                              inflation




            PRODUCT SATISFACTION      CONSUMER RESEARCH
              needs and wants           survey techniques
              decision making           data collection
              evaluating                observing and recording
                                        reporting
```

Introduction

An integrated unit on the topic of consumerism need not be a fabricated, contrived set of exercises for students. Students are themselves consumers of a wide range of products and ideas. Toys, foods, clothing, records, sports and leisure equipment, and television programs are just a few of the things that students consume.

Of course, students are both direct and indirect consumers of goods and services. Some things they buy themselves. In many cases, goods and services are purchased for them by their parents. Like all of us, students in our society are continually bombarded with messages designed to make them want to purchase something. The various forms of coercion they are subjected to include radio and television advertising (probably the most pervasive form of advertising to this age group), messages in newspapers and magazines, and even messages printed on cereal boxes. All of these messages are then compounded by the pressure of the peer group.

What can be done from an educational point of view to make students more aware of the nature of advertising and the worth of the products that they consume? How can a study of consumerism lead to a conceptual frame of reference for students in which they begin to develop basic economic concepts such as *supply and demand, scarcity,* and *needs and wants*? How can a consumerism unit help students develop such skills as data gathering, observing and recording, decision making, and reporting?

Questions of *value, concepts,* and *skills* are fundamental to the purpose of any interdisciplinary unit. In the consumerism activities that follow, provision is made for the development of all three of these essential concerns.

Unit Objectives:

The students will:

1. be introduced to such broad concepts as supply and demand and scarcity.
2. demonstrate an awareness of the persuasive messages to which they are subjected.
3. learn to visualize their own roles as consumers.
4. make more effective decisions about the consumption of goods and services.

Appropriate Grade Levels:

Four–Six

ACTIVITY ONE: SURVEY RESEARCH

Objective:	to conduct a consumer research survey, using as an example the survey conducted by Dawn Kurth*
Materials:	paper and pencil
Procedure:	Using the following example of a consumerism survey, ask your students to design surveys that can be used with other students in the school or in the neighborhood. While your students need not sample 1500 children, as Dawn Kurth did, they can perform a valuable service by asking questions about consumer awareness, buying power, satisfaction with products, and sources of persuasion. 　　An eleven-year-old girl named Dawn Ann Kurth from Melbourne, Florida, became interested in advertising for children because of her younger sister.

*From *The Family Guide to Children's Television,* by Evelyn Kaye (New York: © Random House, Inc., 1974), pp. 104–105.

My sister Martha, who is 7, had asked my mother to buy a box of Post Raisin Bran so that she could get the free record that was on the back of the box. It had been advertised several times on Saturday morning cartoon shows. My mother bought the cereal, and we all (there are four children in our family) helped Martha eat it so she could get the record.

It was after the cereal was eaten and she had the record that the crisis occurred. There was no way the record would work.

Martha was very upset and began crying and I was angry too. It just didn't seem right to me that something could be shown on TV that worked fine and people were listening and dancing to the record and when you bought the cereal, instead of laughing and dancing, we were crying and angry.

Dawn had been chosen with thirty-five other students at Meadowland Elementary School to do a project in any field they wanted. She decided to find out how other children felt about deceptive advertising. She began by watching television one Saturday morning, and clocked twenty-five commercial messages during one hour, 8:00 to 9:00, not counting ads for shows coming up or public service announcements. She also discovered that during shows her parents like to watch there were only ten to twelve commercials each hour, which surprised her.

Dawn devised a questionnaire and asked 1,538 children the following questions:

Quiz:

1. Do you ask your mother to buy products you see advertised on TV?

    ____yes ____no

2. Did you ever buy a product to get the free bonus gift inside?

    ____yes ____no

3. Were you satisfied?

    ____yes ____no

4. Write down an example.

    _____

    _____

5. Do you believe that certain products you see advertised on TV make you happier or have more friends?

    ____yes ____no

6. Please write an example.

    _____

    _____

    _____

7. Did you ever feel out of it because your mother wouldn't buy a certain product?

    ____yes ____no

8. Did you ever feel your mother was mean because she wouldn't buy the product you wanted?

    ____yes ____no

Answer these questions yourself.

Dawn got the following responses to her questionnaire:
1. Yes 1,203, no 330.
2. Yes 1,120, no 413.
3. Yes 668, no 873.
5. Yes 1,113, no 420.
7. Yes 802, no 735.
8. Yes 918, no 620.

Some adults concerned with advertising for children heard about Dawn's study, and Senator Frank E. Moss invited her to appear before the Senate Subcommittee for Consumers at special hearings on May 31, 1972. Dawn's testimony explained her concerns and outlined the survey she had carried out. Her testimony is now part of the Senate record of the hearings.

Evaluation: teacher observation of successfully carried out and completed survey

ACTIVITY TWO:
AN INQUIRY INTO TELEVISION ADVERTISING

Objective: to analyze the uses, appeals, and effects of television advertisements

Materials: none required

Procedure: This activity includes several parts. To carry out all of these parts will require more than one day's time. How many you choose to do, and how much time you choose to allocate to each, will determine the total length of time required for this second activity.

Television Commercial Analysis
To help students see more clearly the "commercial" aspects of the television industry and the strong connection between individual TV programs and the products that are advertised during them, a series of activities can be conducted.

1. Working with a teacher-made list of every product advertised during particular popular TV programs, have the class discuss what the nature of these products indicates about the intended audience for the programs. (What age group? What educational level? What socioeconomic level? What values or life style? What ethnic group?)

2. Have the class participate in a matching exercise in which a number of different products and a variety of TV programs are listed, with the stu-

dents determining which programs would be appropriate to carry ads for those products. Conclusions can be verified by watching the particular shows or types of shows included in the matching exercise.

3. As a homework assignment, have the students conduct an ad analysis of a show of their choice, noting the products advertised and drawing conclusions about how they reveal and/or coincide with the intended audience for the program.

Unmarketable Programs
Have the students brainstorm the kinds of shows that are not on TV because they would appeal mainly to people who do not have the money to buy the products the sponsors want to sell, and therefore no sponsors for these shows can be found. These shows demonstrate how the consumer population determines the types of programs that are on TV.

TV Advertising Appeals Analysis
Have the students analyze the different advertising "appeals" used in television commercials, with the objective of determining the assumed values and needs of TV viewers (need for ego-enhancement, security, status). Note how the programs themselves also reinforce these values and needs through the characters and situations they portray, and have the students discuss how they feel about being viewed this way (students should realize that their age group is one of the prime targets for TV ads and programs).

Whom Do You Believe?
To explore how much our buying habits are influenced by TV and other advertising, have students:

1. look through kitchen, bathroom, and hallway closets and find manufactured products that they have *never* seen advertised. It's one way to see whose ad messages they believe; and

2. note how many selling messages (communications and advertisements of any brand name) they are exposed to each day through TV, radio, billboards, newspapers, matchbook covers, and cereal boxes

Political Images Through Advertising
Develop mock political campaigns with media managers and with tactics students have observed on television, and have them role play TV spots, short documentaries, and interviews with potential voters. Encourage your students to develop a case "for" as well as "against" TV advertising in political campaigns. Have them decide if our democratic process is helped or damaged by the increasing use of political advertising on television.

Evaluation: completion of discussions and analyses of the outlined activities (subjectively based on teacher observation)

WHAT? A SAMPLER OF THEMATIC UNITS

ACTIVITY THREE:
THE NEWSPAPER: WHO CONSUMES WHAT?

Objective: to survey and evaluate the contents of a newspaper

Materials: paper and pencil

a duplicated list of the fourteen categories can be used as desired, either by reproducing the list supplied here or by making a different copy

Procedure: This activity is designed to (1) make students aware of the various parts of a newspaper; (2) help students think about their own reading preferences; and (3) give them an opportunity to communicate in a small group setting.

1. Give each student a list of the fourteen categories of information in a newspaper. Ask your students to rank (on their own) the categories in order of their importance. If, for example, a student felt sports was most important, he/she would place a number "1" beside that category.
2. When students have finished their individual rankings, place them in groups of five and ask them to come up with a group ranking of the categories. In order to do this, everyone will need to express an opinion, and a great many points of view will have to be exchanged.
3. When the groups have finished their rankings, share the results of the polls of actual editors and readers of newspapers.

Evaluation: successful completion of both individual and small group rankings

ACTIVITY FOUR:
CONSUMER RESEARCH

Objective: to actively participate in, and complete in small groups, the researching of a particular product

Materials:
five rolls of different brands of paper towels
measuring instruments, such as rulers and cups
vegetable oil
eye droppers
graph paper

Procedure: In our society, a particular product usually appears in a variety of forms under a variety of brand names. In some cases the various forms of that product are

WHAT DO NEWSPAPER READERS WANT?

	INDIVIDUAL	GROUP	PRESS*	PUBLIC†
Energy News			4	4
Sports News			2	8
Fashion News			9	13
Local News			1	1
Food News			6	5
Government News			10	6
International News			12	7
Science News			11	9
Commentary			8	12
Trade Association News			14	14
Entertainment / Arts			3	10
State News			7	2
National News			5	3
Financial News			13	11

*Results of Harris Poll of newspaper editors

†Results of Harris Poll of newspaper readers

actually different with respect to quality. In other cases, the success of one brand over another may be more closely related to the amount and type of advertising used to convince consumers to buy the product.

In this activity, students will be given the opportunity to test several brands of a particular product. There are many possible products that students might test, such as toothpaste, writing tablets, pencils, felt pens, breakfast cereals, peanut butter, and toys. To get you started with product testing, we suggest you have your students test paper towels.

Bring about five rolls of different brands of paper towels to class. Remove the wrappers so students won't know what the brands are. Tell the students that their challenge is to test and rank in order the five brands from "best" to "worst" buy.

Divide the class into small groups of about five students per group. Explain to the groups that they need to devise and carry out several tests to determine the relative worth of the towels. Perhaps a discussion of types of appropriate test will help students at this point. Examples of tests are *dry strength, wet strength,* and *absorption.*

Once the groups are ready to begin testing hand out the materials needed. Tell the students they have about forty-five minutes in which to complete their testing. When testing is underway, place a chart on the board that gives information about the towels.

COLOR	PRICE	NUMBER OF TOWELS PER ROLL	NUMBER OF SQUARE FEET PER ROLL
Blue	79¢	124	100
White	59¢	100	85
Red and White	79¢	120	85
Floral	79¢	100	100
Yellow	73¢	125	100

Some students in each group may wish to do a cost analysis while others will proceed with the actual product testing. Encourage students to develop graphs and charts of their results.

When the testing is completed, ask each group to report its results. Not all groups will agree on the rank ordering of the paper towels. Take time to examine both the tests and the reliability of the tests used by various groups. After each group has presented its results, tell the class the name brand of each roll of towels.

Evaluation: successful completion of small group research as presented in final written or oral format

ACTIVITY FIVE:
WRITE AN ADVERTISEMENT

Objective: to create an advertisement designed to promote a particular product

Materials: paper and drawing or writing instruments (pencils, markers, crayons)

Procedure: Because your students have been involved in actually testing a product, they may now wish to have an opportunity to promote one. Ask students to develop an advertisement for the paper towel they felt was the best product or, ask them to develop an advertisement for an imaginary product, such as a toy or movie.

Here is an example of a student's advertisement:

> BUY FLUFFO PAPER TOWELS!
> THEY'RE THE HOUSEWIFE'S FRIEND!
> THEY'RE THE MECHANIC'S HELPER!
> WITH FLUFFO, SPILLS AND MESSES
> ARE NO PROBLEM!
> BE SMART, GET FLUFFO TODAY
> AND DO YOURSELF A FAVOR!

Evaluation: successful creation of an advertisement to share with the class

ACTIVITY SIX:
ADVERTISING APPEALS

Objectives: to identify examples of a variety of advertising appeals in television, radio, or printed ads, and to rewrite an advertisement by replacing advertising appeals with more factual information

Materials: student-provided example of one or more advertisements, or printed ads from magazines and newspapers

paper and pencil

Procedure: When goods and services are advertised, certain appeals are made to the consumer. Challenge your students to:

1. Find an example of television, radio, magazine, newspaper or billboard ads which use the appeals listed below.
2. Rewrite an advertisement using more factual information than appeals in a given ad.

Advertising Appeals

1. *Brand loyalty:* The advertiser wants you to continue buying the established brands, especially those from older, well-established businesses.
2. *Conformity:* The "bandwagon" approach. "Everybody" is buying this particular brand or item.
3. *Hero worship:* Endorsement of a product by a big name in entertainment or sports.
4. *Status:* An appeal to the buyer's class-consciousness.
5. *Humor:* Entertaining, but deceptive; says little about the product.
6. *Feminine attractiveness:* A wishful-thinking ad, appealing to those girls or women who wish to be more beautiful, sexy, and alluring.
7. *Masculine attractiveness:* Same kind of appeal as number six; an appeal to the he-man image.
8. *Style changes:* The buyer is asked to keep up with the times. This may include fad items.
9. *Vanity:* This kind of ad appeals to the buyer's self-image; ego gratification. The buyer's happiness is placed first in importance.
10. *Economy:* Everyone likes to think he or she can economize while spending.
11. *Luxury:* Symbols of wealth and excess.
12. *Convenience:* Work-saver and time-saver devices.
13. *Creativity:* Buyer can add personal touch to product's use.
14. *Security:* This covers many kinds of security—emotional, social, or financial.
15. *Sex:* The ad appeals to the lure of sex. It is very similar to the appeals of numbers six and seven.

There are also combinations of appeals, and more than one appeal may appear in an ad.

Analysis of Advertising

1. How does the ad explain the real features or advantages of the product?
2. Does the ad compare with that of a competitive item?

3. Are there any meaningless or "puff" words added?
4. What specific appeals to the buyer does the ad make?

Evaluation: correct identification of a variety of advertising appeals from verbally or visually presented ads; completion of rewritten advertisement; correct answers to four questions under "analysis of advertising"

Additional Activities:

1. Have students do some comparison shopping. Collect copies of newspapers from the day your area grocery stores run their large store ads. Instruct each student to choose a single food item, and find the "best buy" price and where it can be found. Be sure students consider the unit price rather than just the list price of the item.

2. Since a large part of being a consumer involves spending money, it might be appropriate to include activities concerned with identification of coins, making change, and writing checks during this unit. Skills with decimal computation could also be taught or reviewed.

3. Build reading skills in skimming and finding details through the use of classified ads. Assign specific or general features to be identified, and instruct students to find these by skimming through the ads. You might then encourage them to write their own ads including these details or features.

4. Several resources contain ad-related units and activities. Two examples of these are the "TV Center" from *Change for Children,* Revised Edition, by Kaplan, et. al., and "Roatsy Oatsies" from Forte, Pangle, and Typa's *Center Stuff for Nooks, Crannies and Corners.* Reproducible worksheets and a variety of materials and activities are included in these two units.

WHAT TIME IS IT?

What Time Is It? The concept of time is presented in a broader context than usually found in school curricula. The earth's rotation, pendula, sundials, and the clocks are all used to measure the passage of time.

MEASURING TIME DURATIONS
   car racing
   fizzies

MEASURING EVENTS OF GREAT DURATION
   wastebasket archeology
   tree rings
   rock layers

TIME
"what time is it?"
record events in chronological order
measure time durations
read clock faces
calendars as extensions of clocks

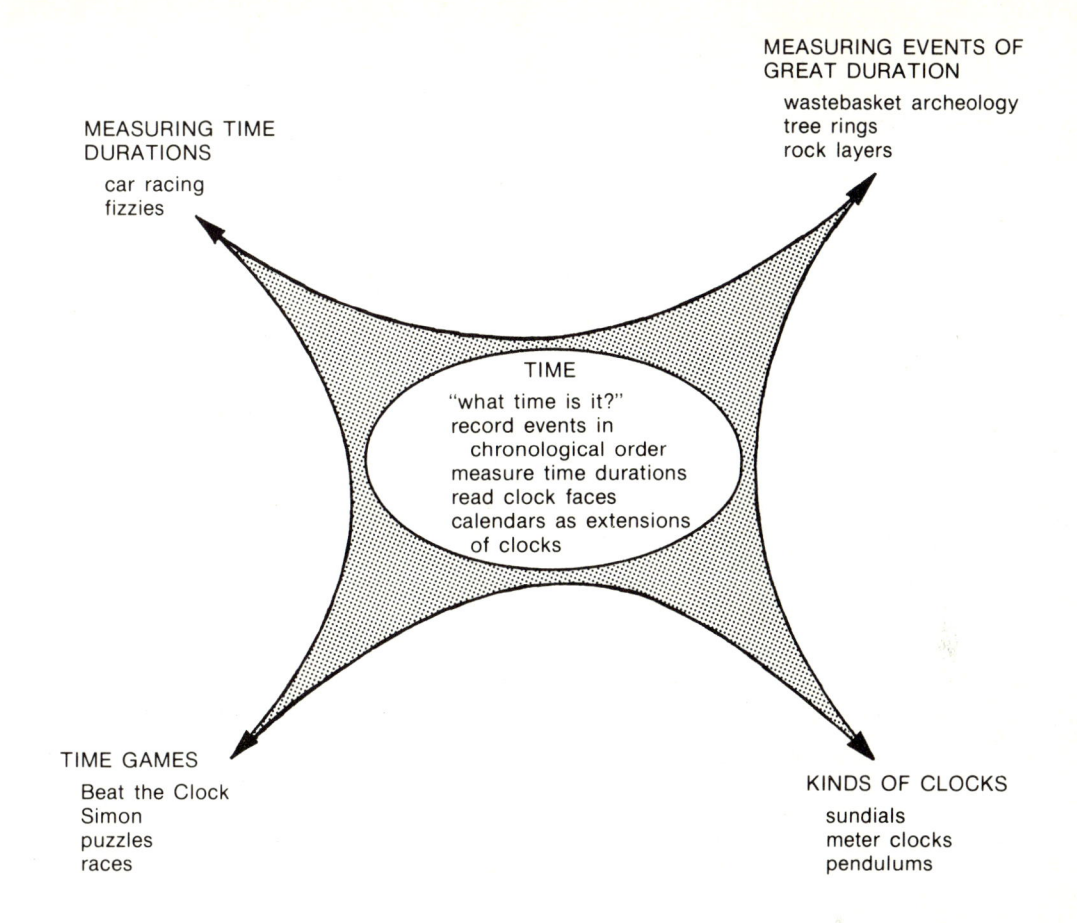

TIME GAMES
   Beat the Clock
   Simon
   puzzles
   races

KINDS OF CLOCKS
   sundials
   meter clocks
   pendulums

Introduction

Time has been described as a flowing river, or as a fixed set of points through which we pass. Whatever it is, it plays an important part in everyone's life. This thematic unit centers about time, its measurement, and its application to simple situations that are familiar to children. The unit includes science, social science, mathematics, and language arts activities.

Although there are several ways that this unit could be followed, we would suggest the following sequencing. Following the pretest and the presentation of some introductory information are seven activities, which are presented in a logical sequence. You may wish to combine two activities together or extend one over several days. As children evidence interest, you will want to direct them to some of the independent investigations.

Unit Objectives:

The students will:

1. demonstrate an understanding of sun time
2. demonstrate an understanding of how early clocks were synchronized with the sun.

3. become familiar with other time-measuring devices (candles, water clocks, pendulums).
4. correctly calculate lapsed time.
5. correctly order events according to time sequence.
6. demonstrate a preliminary "feel" for very short and very great time durations.
7. be able to recognize anachronisms.

Appropriate Grade Levels:

Three–Six (some activities also usable or adaptable to grades one–two).

ACTIVITY ONE:
SUGGESTED PRETEST

Objective: to measure time concepts before unit implementation

Materials: paper and pencil

Procedure: Have your class read the following story, or read it to them, and have them answer the questions that follow it. This will serve as a standard by which you can later measure the learning that has occurred through completion of the unit.

> *The station wagon stopped at the fishing pier. Nancy, Bill, and their dad got out. The children took their fishing poles and ran on the noisy boards to the end of the pier. Dad brought the bucket of worms with him. As he set it down he said, "I will be back to get you at 3 o'clock this afternoon." "What time is it now?" asked Nancy. "It's 10 o'clock in the morning."*

1. For how many hours can Nancy and Bill fish?
2. Will it be dark when their dad picks them up?
3. They don't have a watch. How could they tell when it is about 3 o'clock?
4. Their fishing box contains hooks, sinkers, lines, shiny little spoons, and artificial worms. Which of these could be used to make a time-measuring device? Draw a picture showing how you would make it.

Evaluation: correct answers given to the four questions

ACTIVITY TWO:
INTRODUCTION

Objective: to present preliminary information concerning time and time measurement

Materials: none required, although examples of a variety of time measurement devices may be useful

Procedure: In a discussion, or by the use of a film, present some of the ideas that follow. Eliciting as many as possible from students' acquired knowledge will generally be preferable to "lecturing" to them. It is important that students are exposed to this information during the course of the introductory discussion.

Time Information

People began developing time units and measuring durations by making comparisons with the position and (apparent) movement of the sun across the sky. When the sun was visible, it was daytime; after the sun set it became night. Later people watched shadows move, constructed sundials, and noted that the shadows were the shortest when the sun was overhead. They also noticed that at noon, winter shadows were much longer than at noon during the summer. Morning, noon, end-of-day, and seasons were "invented." Sundials were refined with markings so that the passage of an hour could be measured. Later, mechanical devices (candles, water clocks, and mechanical clocks) were invented. They "ran" at the same speed as the sundial, and had the added advantage of "telling time" on cloudy days and at night. History records the development of astronomical instruments, refined clocks, and watches, the discovery of the pendulum and an increasing ability to measure the duration of events with precision.

Over the years sundials and water clocks were replaced by clocks with escapements (the ticking devices) and pendulums. These are being replaced today with electronic devices containing a tiny crystal of vibrating quartz, printed circuits, and light-emitting numerical readouts.

We can relate to events that have durations of seconds, minutes, hours, days, months, and quite a few years. It is easier to relate to shorter events measured in seconds, minutes, and sometimes hours. The ability to conceive of duration decreases as we deal with events of great duration such as geological eras, which may extend over millions of years, and events of very short duration, such as the single vibration of the quartz crystal, or the duration of a single computer calculation measured in nanoseconds (millionths).

Time-measuring devices provide two distinct kinds of information. First, the device shows what time it is at that moment. Second, it can tell us the length or duration of an event. To measure such a duration, one records the time at the beginning and at the ending of an event and then subtracts. If, for example, Jim started to mow the lawn at 2:00 P.M. and finished at 3:30 P.M., the duration would be: 3:30 − 2:00 = 1:30. To avoid the subtraction step, we could wait until the hands are at zero (12 o'clock) and then start the event. Stop watches work this way; when you press the button, the hands instantly move to zero.

Note: You may wish to check and see that all children understand how to read clock faces. If children have problems, use a take-apart clock face and begin with the hour hand, then the minute hand, and then a combination.

Evaluation: none needed directly, except perhaps relative to the final note concerning clock-reading skills

ACTIVITY THREE: "BUILT-IN" CLOCKS

Objective: to present the concept of "built-in" time, and to provide opportunities to measure individual accuracy of such

Materials: a watch or small clock

slips of paper and pencils

Procedure: Begin by covering the face of a clock. Select one child to be clock watcher. Set the clock at zero (12:00) and begin reading a short story. The clock watcher should have small slips of paper and a pencil. Tell the children to listen to the story and not look at the clock. When they think five minutes have elapsed, they should raise a hand. Have the clock watcher give a card to each child as hands go up. On the card the clock watcher writes the elapsed time in minutes (2, 3, 4, etc.). When all children have a card, have all the children with the lowest number form a line. Do the same in succession for the other numbers. With the children in lines, explain how they form a graph. Then draw a grid on the chalkboard. Enter the number of children guessing two, three, and so on. Call the children's attention to the most guessed time, shortest guessed time, number of people guessing five minutes, etc.

Help children read the graph by asking questions such as the following:

1. How many guessed two minutes? How many minutes "off" were they?
2. How many minutes was the longest time duration guess?

Number of children guessing

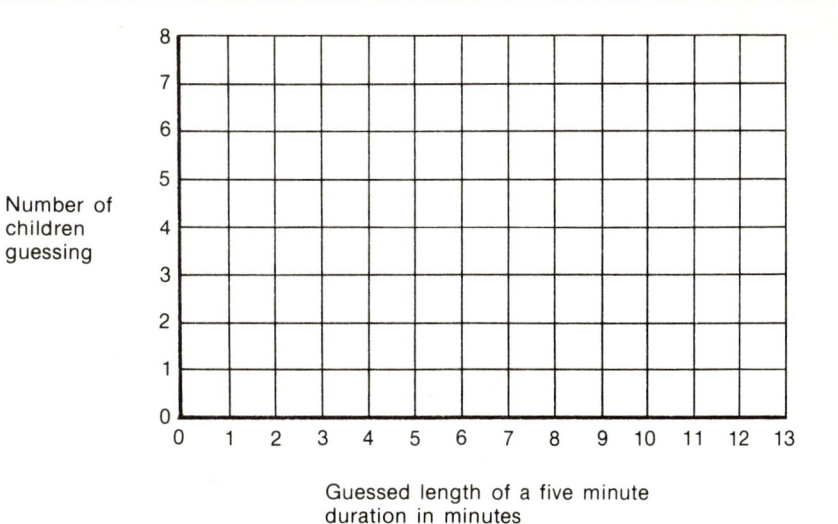

Guessed length of a five minute duration in minutes

3. Did anyone guess (pick one that no one guessed) twelve minutes?
4. If we used Mary for our clock (Mary guessed three minutes) would we go to lunch early or late?
5. If we used John (suppose John raised his hand at seven minutes) as our clock and we agreed that he told the right time, would the real clock be said to run fast or slow?

Encourage children to work in pairs. Have them practice guessing one-, two-, and even three-minute intervals. Have them do this by having one child guess with eyes closed while the other watches the clock. If time allows, bring children together and repeat the first activity. Compare the two graphs. Have children discuss whether or not the practice of guessing elapsed time improves the accuracy of the guess.

Evaluation: completion of graphs, active participation in guessing activities

ACTIVITY FOUR: MAKING AND USING CLOCKS

Objective: to identify daily events according to time of occurrence

Materials: paper plates and brads, or prepared plate clocks (one per child)

Procedure: Children rarely know when events in their lives occur. Poll the class to find out when they think they do the following:

- get up in the morning
- leave home for school (or to catch the school bus)
- start the school day (bell rings, buzzer sounds, etc.)
- go to lunch
- leave school in the afternoon
- have the evening meal with their family
- go to bed on school nights

For each question, have children set clocks. Have them do so by using paper plate clocks they have made themselves or that have been prepared for them. You may wish to have one row of children per question line up from earliest to latest time for each of the events.

Pick out one of the questions that many children seem to be uncertain about. If it is "go to bed," have the children ask their parents when they, the children, go to bed. The next day, compare the early responses of the children with their new responses.

Note: At this point, you may wish to use the clocks for some skills practice in translating spoken time to a clock face configuration and vice versa. This will give you an opportunity to do some diagnostic work and assign additional practice as needed by individual students.

Evaluation: ability to identify accurate or near-accurate times for daily events, completion of take home activity and class time-telling activities; correct completion of paper plate clock if assigned

ACTIVITY FIVE:
MAKING A PENDULUM

Objective: to create and use a pendulum

Materials:
    string
    washers
    clay balls or other weights
    twigs or sticks
    masking tape

Procedure: Help children construct a pendulum from string, washers, and clay balls or other weights for bobs. Supply each child with a short piece of twig or stick and some masking tape. Show them how to fasten the stick under a chair or desk after fastening the weight-tied string to the stick. Explore the operations of a pendulum, and relate these as much as possible to the various aspects of time explored in this unit.

For more specific suggestions for using pendulums, you may wish to refer to the "Patterns and Changes" unit in this book, or to the books *The Great Perpetual Learning Machine* by Jim Blake and Barbara Ernst, or *The Whole Cosmos Catalog of Science Activities* by Joe Abruscato and Jack Hassard.

Evaluation: completion of pendulum and related activities as directed

ACTIVITY SIX: DAY AND NIGHT

Objective: to understand how day and night are caused by the rotation of the earth

Materials:
globe and/or white ball
clay
small stick
direct light source (flashlight, lamp, etc.)

Procedure: If children have not done globe and map work, begin by holding up a globe and explaining how, each day, the earth makes one full turn or rotation on its axis. Turn off all but one light or close all but one shade. Slowly rotate the globe. Ask where it is day and where it is night. Locate your city (or state) on the globe. Identify it with a lump of clay. Turn the globe so that the "sun" is directly over the clay. Rotate the globe so the sun appears to set in the west. Continue rotating the globe until the sun appears to rise in the east. Have children guess what time it is when the sun is in various positions in relationship to the lump of clay.

A second and similar activity works best if you have a white ball. Again, fasten a lump of clay to the ball or globe and repeat the rotation. Then fasten a vertical stick about 5 cm. long into the clay. Have children watch the shadow of the stick as the globe or ball is turned. Through questions, relate the position of the shadow to the time of day. Then relate the globe or ball to the earth and the clay to the region where the school and the playground is located. Ask, "What would happen if, instead of erecting the stick on the globe, we erected a pole on the playground?" Finish by explaining to the class that their next-day activity will be to find out the answer to this question.

Evaluation: ability to correctly answer questions, either verbally or in writing, concerning the causes of day and night and how shadows are changed or affected by the earth's rotation

ACTIVITY SEVEN:
SHADOW MOVEMENT

Objective: to watch and record the movement of shadows

Materials:
- stick or pole, about one meter long
- ten rocks
- marker
- camera and film (optional)

Procedure: State this activity first thing in the morning. After briefly reviewing the findings and explorations of Activity Six, have children erect a pole about one meter high on a sunny spot on the playground. Have other children collect about ten fist-sized rocks (if you wish, these can be painted white). At exactly 9:00 A.M., place one rock at the tip of the shadow of the pole. Have a student write the number 9 on the rock. Plan your schedule so that each hour, a small group of children can go the the playground to place and label a new stone.

Shortly before dismissal time, have all children visit their sundial, noting the positions of the rocks. You may wish to climb a stepladder and take a picture of the pole and the rocks, so that further discussion and examination of the experience can be carried on.

Evaluation: completion of group activity, ability to verbally relate findings to the passage and measurement of time

ACTIVITY EIGHT:
RECORDING CLOCK TIMES

Objective: to teach skills relative to the recording of clock time and of time durations

Materials:
- paper plate clocks
- worksheets or paper for recording times

Procedure: This activity is designed to introduce clock recording skills and duration measurement skills. Children will need previously made paper plate clock faces and worksheets for recording.

  Begin with a clock face with an hour hand only. Have children record various face configurations on the worksheet. Remove the hour hand and put on a minute hand. Have children, again, record various configurations. Some time must be spent explaining the two number lines on the clock's face. Then combine the two hands and show children that recording time is a matter of recording the two hand positions separately. Point out that when the hour hand is between two numbers, the smaller number is recorded. Ask if there is an exception to this rule. If no answer is given by a student, point out that, when the hand is between 12 and 1, the 12 is recorded.

  This is a good time to compare clock faces with digital clock faces. Children will recognize that a digital readout eliminates the conversion from hand configuration to number.

  When measuring time durations, children record the time on the worksheet at the beginning and at the end of the event. So that the subtraction process is simplified, the ending time is recorded in the top box and the beginning time is recorded under it.

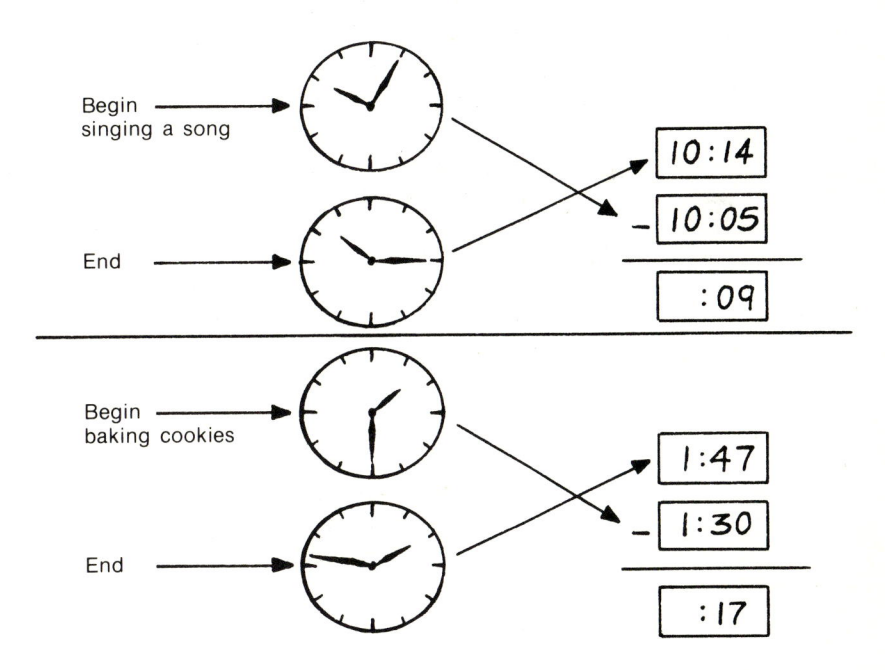

Begin singing a song → [clock]
End → [clock]

$$\begin{array}{r} 10:14 \\ -\ 10:05 \\ \hline :09 \end{array}$$

Begin baking cookies → [clock]
End → [clock]

$$\begin{array}{r} 1:47 \\ -\ 1:30 \\ \hline :17 \end{array}$$

Evaluation: correct identification and recording of clock times and correct calculation of elapsed times

ACTIVITY NINE: CALENDAR TIME

Objective: to relate clock time to calendar time, and to build skills and awarenesses of the concepts and identification of *week* and *month*

Materials:
- large calendars
- seven-day strips

Procedure: Bring several large calendars to class. Begin by asking questions about days. For example, you might ask:

1. How long is a day?
2. When does a day start? End?
3. Why are days given seven different names? (You may wish to point out the seven-day sequence of names, and the religious origins of this seven-day unit.)
4. What part of the calendar represents a day?
5. How can we tell the name of any particular day?

Make up a number of seven-day strips. Explain how the strip represents a week; how it begins with Sunday and ends with Saturday. Perhaps some children would like to find out about the origins of the names given to days. Assemble the seven-day strips to form a month of four weeks. Ask children to name some months. Ask them to name the month of their birthday and lay out a large calendar with class birthdays. If desired, you may relate various holidays to the calendar as well.

Evaluation: active participation in group activity, subsequent ability to identify, verbally or in writing, days of the week, number of days in a week, number of weeks in a month, names of some months of the year, month of his/her birthday

Additional Activities:

1. *Battery, spring, or fly-wheel driven cars* can be raced along a marked track. Floor tiles provide convenient distance marks. Encourage children to run one car at a time over a uniform distance. The lapsed time, which can be measured with a one-second pendulum, allows children to report their car's speed. Children can redesign cars for increased speed or distance.

2. *Fizzies or Alka Seltzer* tablets, when dropped in water, release bubbles of carbon dioxide. The tablets contain a dry mixture of sodium bicarbonate and citric acid plus other ingredients for flavor and digestive aid. The

rate at which they react is related to the temperature of the water. Children can measure the "fizz time" in water of various temperatures.

3. *Beat the Clock* was a popular television game in which contestants were challenged to perform certain tasks in a given time. Points were gained for early completion and lost if contestants were unable to beat the clock. Children can come up with a variety of "Beat the Clock" contests. For example, you might try nail driving, card sorting, transferring liquid from one jar to another with a spoon, blowing up balloons, threading several needles or beads, or stacking dominos, blocks, or Tinkertoy connecters.

4. *Early time-keeping devices* can be researched by children. Man has developed many ingenious devices to determine time of day, day of the month, and month of the year. The following words can be used as keys for dictionary, encyclopedia, and reference book research.

sundial	escapement	zodiacal constellations
water clock	sidereal time	pole star
pendulum	horology	big dipper
	observatory	

5. *Wastebasket archeology* simulates the procedures used by archeologists in excavating "digs." The concept of sequential deposition applies to trash thrown in a wastebasket, to artifacts thrown onto garbage dumps, and to stratas of sediment deposited by water that has eroded and transported rocks, sand, and soil. Wastebaskets can be secured from several places such as other classrooms, secretaries' offices, stores, and professional offices.

Encourage children to lay out a table top into four areas and remove about one-quarter of the contents of the basket at a time. The first pile is labeled "late afternoon," the next "early afternoon," then "late morning," and finally "early morning." Rummaging for interesting items and clues will not interfere too seriously with the development of a chart representing items and order of deposition. Have the children reconstruct a scenario describing the source of the basket, the habits of the people using it, and a chronology of their activities during the day.

Other systems made up of layers deposited over time include tree rings, rock layers, rust and corrosion on metals, barnacles encrusted on sunken ships and snow and dirt layers that can be detected by cutting through banks or drifts of snow with a shovel. These can also be examined and used to develop concepts of time passage.

SAILBOATS

Sailboats: Children design, construct and test various types of wind-driven craft with activities encompassing science, mathematics, language arts, and literature.

A SAILOR'S GEOGRAPHY
  major ports of call
  trade routes
  trade winds
  great circle routes

SPECIAL LANGUAGE OF SAILBOATS
  sails
  masts
  booms
  rigging

MAKING SAILBOATS
  testing boats

SAILBOATS

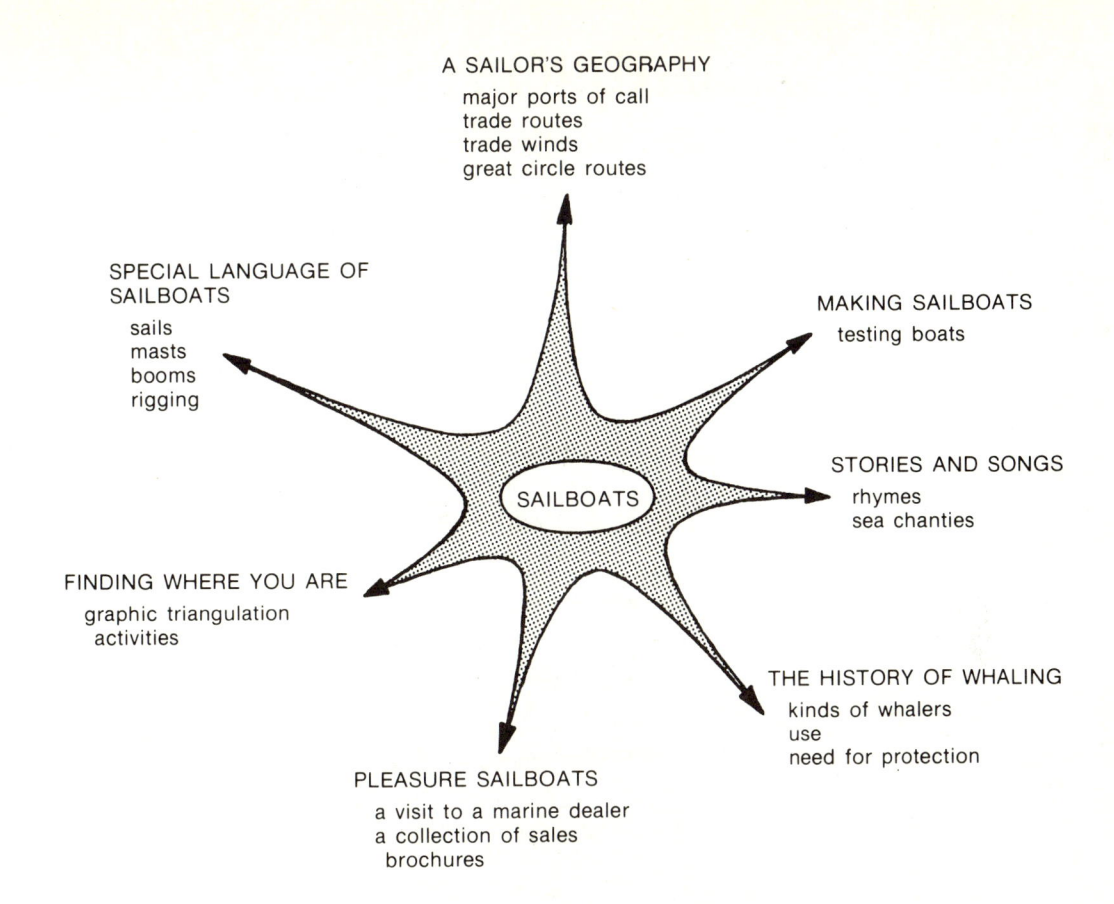

STORIES AND SONGS
  rhymes
  sea chanties

FINDING WHERE YOU ARE
  graphic triangulation
  activities

THE HISTORY OF WHALING
  kinds of whalers
  use
  need for protection

PLEASURE SAILBOATS
  a visit to a marine dealer
  a collection of sales brochures

Introduction

Boats have played a major role in the discovery of new ideas, new languages, and new peoples, for boats were the connecting link between ports and continents. They are mentioned in many of our earliest writings. The great forests of Lebanon were slowly depleted and destroyed by man's need for strong, straight trees for masts, spars, and planking.

Each nation developed its special kind of boat. The Chinese junk, the Phoenician galley, the Egyptian kuffa and the Boston whaler are examples of special boats, constructed from native materials and developed for a specific purpose. Before the steam engine was invented, boats were propelled by oars or sails.

This unit gives children a chance to explore the wonderful, exciting, adventurous world of sailboats. Sailboats had their heroes and villains: Jason of the *Argonaut*, Captain Bligh of the *Bounty*, Captain Ahab of the *Pequoit*, and Captain Horatio Hornblower of *Saturday Evening Post* fame in the fifties and sixties.

Sailboats evolved from simple boats with a single mast and sail to fast clipper ships of the early nineteenth century with four masts and as many as twenty sails. Once again, sailboats are becoming popular. They require no gasoline and glide through the water with no more than a whisper. Moreover, they are a challenge to the sailor's skills to sail in a particular direction. Each direction sailed requires both a specific rudder angle and a set of the sails.

Sailboats illustrate most graphically vector forces. One can sail a sailboat almost into the wind by taking advantage of the rudder and the angular force of the wind against the sails.

The sequence of activities in this unit is for your guidance and should be varied according to the special interests of your children. You may wish to begin the unit with a daily reading from any sea story, such as *Treasure Island, Peter Pan, Moby Dick,* or *Kon Tiki.* Once interest has been stimulated, work with the children and develop a thematic web, similar perhaps to the one that begins this unit. Then, you and your class will be ready to delve into the fascinating world of sailboats!

Unit Objectives:

The students will:

1. read or listen to several stories whose settings are on lakes, rivers and oceans.
2. learn, from their readings, about various aspects of life aboard a ship, including procedures for storing food and water, the social organization of ships, and the various duties of sailors.
3. learn and listen to traditional songs of the sea.
4. design and decorate one or more ships.
5. be able to tell how the various parts of a sailboat work together to redirect the force of the wind so the boat can sail in many directions.
6. gain knowledge concerning ports-of-call and their inhabitants, naval history and early attempts at describing and mapping the surface of the globe.

Appropriate Grade Levels:

Three–Six (some activities could be used at the junior high level as well)

ACTIVITY ONE: SAILBOAT FILM

Objective: to introduce the class to the unit topic

Materials: a film depicting sailboat races (consult your school or public library listings for an appropriate film)

Procedure: This first activity is designed to introduce the sailboat unit to your class. This can be done by showing the class one or more films or filmstrips, or by reading to them one or more storybooks about sailing if you are unable to obtain or show a film. After viewing the film, or whatever you have chosen, lead the class in a discussion, leading ultimately to the need to know more about the structure and the parts of sailboats. This might be a good time as well to refer to the web provided, and to expand it by adding other items of interest to individual children of your class. You might also begin to keep a list of questions to be answered or words to be defined.

Evaluation: active participation in the discussion following viewing of the film or listening to the story

ACTIVITY TWO:
RESEARCH CENTER SEARCH

Objective: to help each student locate, and provide time for the reading of, books related to boats and sailing.

Materials: library books

Procedure: Help your children find books about boats, sailing, racing, and the history of boats. Allow time for each child to read the chosen book(s), and to look at pictures, consult tables, and look at diagrams and plans provided in the resources. Let them know that they will later be asked to discuss what they have learned from the books they have each chosen.

In order to save time, you may wish to check ahead with your librarian or media specialist and have him or her locate a large selection of appropriate books. Another possibility would be to spend a little time compiling a list of available resources to be found in the school library, or at least to provide your students with the call numbers of sections of the library containing related literature.

Evaluation: can be based on observation of the location and use of subject-related book(s) by each student

ACTIVITY THREE:
DISCUSSION

Objective: to carry on a discussion of individual reading and research completed in Activity Two, and to begin planning subsequent activities

Materials: paper and drawing instruments
book, poem, or song as desired

Procedure: Lead your students in a discussion of their first-hand information and what they have discovered about boats through their readings. Through this discussion, lead them to consider the possibilities of taking a boat trip, constructing model boats, and holding a model boat regatta and race.

You may wish to read a short excerpt or a poem, or to teach the children a song about boats. Finally, ask each child to draw a picture showing what his or her boat for the regatta will look like.

Evaluation: participation in class discussion including the subjects of Activity Two, completion of drawing as assigned

ACTIVITY FOUR:
TESTING HULL DESIGNS

Objective: to view and test various hull (body of boat) designs, to record the results of these tests, and to learn about the factors influencing these test results

Materials: precut soft wood blocks

string

spring scale

tank table (illustration follows)

Procedure: Supply your class with the materials listed above. You should also set up a test tank using a sturdy table, 2 × 6 lumber, and polyethelene sheeting.

Display and describe the three hull shapes illustrated on the next page. Attach string to each shape. Have your children test the several hull designs by pulling the blocks through the tank and recording the spring scale reading.

Finally, hold a short discussion and record the results of the boat tests on the chalkboard. It is expected that the results will not show any clear pattern because the children will have pulled the boats through the water at different speeds. Lead the discussion towards the consideration of how the activity can be redesigned so that the results of different groups using the same blocks will be compatible. Make sure the children understand that the boat's resistance depends on its speed and the force applied in pulling. Point out that they must pull the boats at the same speed and measure the force, or pull with the same force and measure the speed.

Evaluation: successful completion and recording of test results, participation in discussions

WHAT? A SAMPLER OF THEMATIC UNITS

Block shapes for testing resistance in water

A table supports the lined box. Boats are pulled through tank by the children.

Mast

Sail

Starboard

Boom

Adjustable boom line

Port

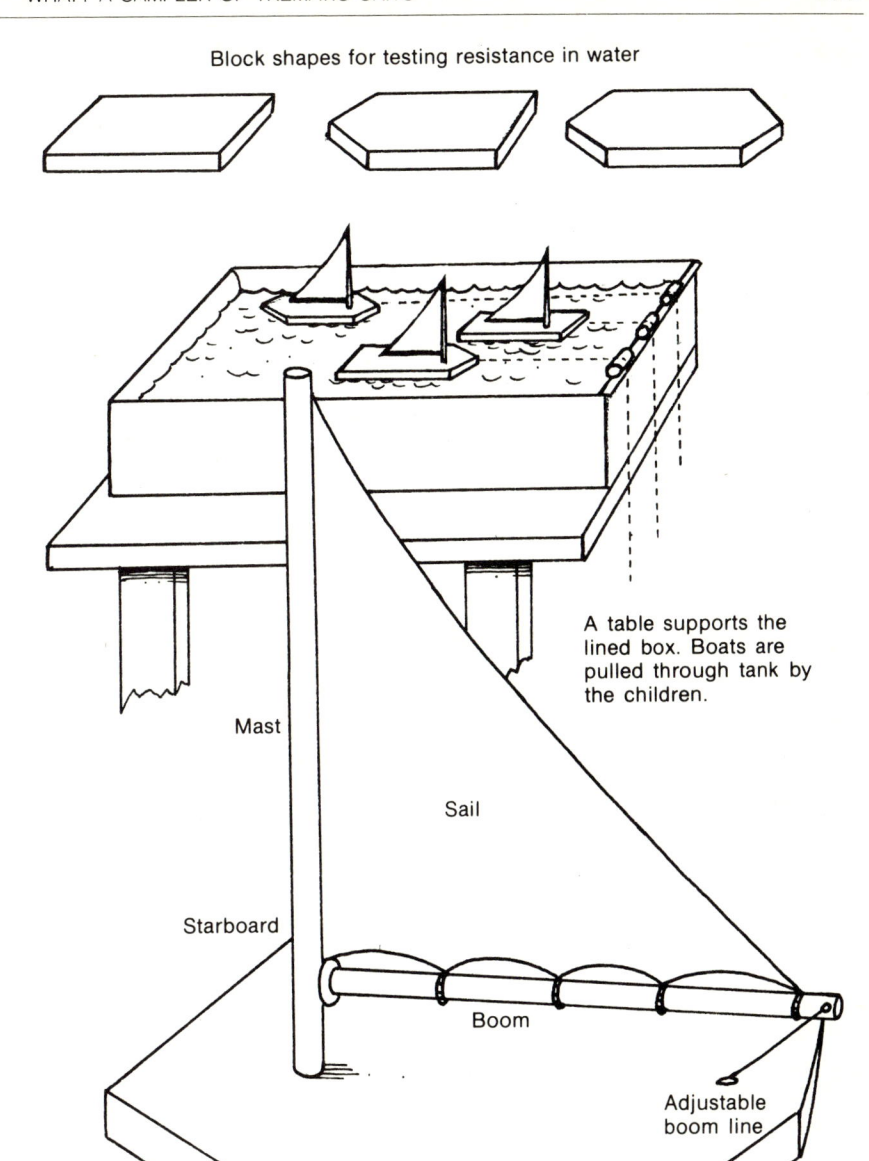

ACTIVITY FIVE: MEASURING SPEED

Objective: to learn how to measure speed and test for relative resistance, and to mount a mast and attach a sail and boom to a model boat

Materials:
- tank table (see Activity Four)
- pendulum
- wooden block, dowel, sail, and boom for each student

Procedure: The tank set up for Activity Four should be equipped with thread spools so that applied force can be held constant. Demonstrate to the class how speed can be measured in two ways (by comparing two boats or by setting up a pendulum and measuring the time duration of a boat over a measured course). Then demonstrate how hull shapes can be tested for relative resistance.

When the class understands this information, have them collect data using the pulley, pendulum system. Supply each child with a piece of ¼" dowel stick. Show the children first how to mount the mast in a drilled hole in the hull, and then how to attach a sail and boom. Carefully store these simple boats, labeled with names, for use in the next activity.

Evaluation: successful mounting of mast to hull and attachment of sail and boom to the mast, participation in class discussion

ACTIVITY SIX: COMPLETE BOATS

Objective: to complete and test individual sailboats

Materials:
- all of those listed for Activities Four and Five
- 2 electric fans

Procedure: This activity should involve providing time for the children to work individually on their sailboats. You should set up two electric fans by the tank so that, when boats are completed, their sails can be tested. Problems that arise should be noted and discussed.

While this seems like a simple activity, it will probably require a full class period. You should be free to move throughout your class, giving individual help and advice as it is needed. It would be helpful if you could have

WHAT? A SAMPLER OF THEMATIC UNITS

several good resource books for students to refer to while they are waiting for your personal attention.

Evaluation: successful completion of individual sailboats, and testing of those boats through the use of the fans

ACTIVITY SEVEN:
BOAT MODIFICATIONS

Objective: to modify boats as needed, to plan the regatta

Materials: no new materials required, unless to provide such items as paint, sandpaper, etc.

Procedure: Children should be given time to modify and test their sailboats based on the results of Activity Six. Discuss with the children plans for holding a regatta on an outdoor lake or pond or on an indoor pool. Committees should be set up to work out details for the regatta, including activities, races, rules, and allowable boat modifications (smooth hulls, paint, maximum sail area).
Your role during this activity will again be to move freely around the classroom, answering questions as they come up and guiding children to the materials needed and modifications desired or required for a successful sailboat. Your aid will also be needed by the committees responsible for setting up the regatta and related events.

Evaluation: successful completion of all boat modifications, completion of plans for the regatta

ACTIVITY EIGHT:
MORE ON SAILBOATS AND EVALUATION

Objective: to provide further information of interest on the subject of sailboats and to test attainment of basic concepts taught during the unit

Materials:
    filmstrips, films, or drawings as desired
    paper and pencils, or printed evaluation sheet

Procedure: To provide your class with further information on the subject, you may choose to use enlarged drawings, film strips, or a film to present and discuss the changes that have been made over time in sailboats, the uses of sailboats, and classes of racing sailboats. Ask each child to make a drawing of a sailboat, to label its parts, and to show length (boat, mast) and sail area. This will provide a measure of the knowledge gained by each student over the course of this unit. Be sure that any specific information presented to be learned is included in the evaluation you use. If little specific information was required to be learned, the evaluation should be correspondingly general.

Evaluation: successful completion of evaluation sheet or activity

ACTIVITY NINE:
REGATTA AND DISPLAY OF BOATS

Objective: to provide a recreational chance for students to sail their boats and compete in one or more races with them

Materials: awards as desired (ribbons, certificates, etc.)

Procedure: The final activity in this unit is the carrying out of a regatta using the model boats created in class. This should be carried out based on the committee work done within the student groups.

Thought may be given to choosing to award all boats a commemorative sail emblem, or you may wish to develop ribbons for many categories (enough so that each boat will have a display ribbon). Categories might be run winners, race winners, hull design, art work, craftsmanship, and first boat to tip.

Keep in mind that the main objective of this final activity is a recreational one. Make sure that each child in your class enjoys the regatta, and finishes the unit feeling good about his or her participation in it.

Evaluation: participation in the regatta

Additional Activities:
1. One child may know someone who is an ardent sailor and could serve as a resource person. There may be nautical exhibits or marine museums in your area. There may be harbor facilities that could be visited. A local ROTC Naval officer could be asked to discuss the history of naval craft and answer children's questions. These are all examples of how the small-scale activities of this unit can be expanded to experiences involving full-size sailboats.
2. Point out to your students that locating a position on land is not difficult. Street names, addresses, and road numbers define intersections where specific buildings, lots, or farms are located. Explain that locating a posi-

WHAT? A SAMPLER OF THEMATIC UNITS   **111**

tion on water, especially when out of sight of land, is a bit more difficult. Provide the class with information concerning the history and development of sea navigation, focusing specifically on latitude and longitude and devices used to measure them.

3. Today ship captains use several electronic locating devices. Have your children find out about LORAN (Long Range Navigation), radio compasses, and the satellites that send signals to help ships instantly locate their position. Children can locate their position on a state map if the location of two radio station transmitting towers are known. Using the map, circle two radio tower locations. Lay the map flat and turn it so north on the map points north. Set a small transistor radio on the map and tune in a station. Rotate the radio and when the signal is strongest, draw a line from the center of the radio across the map in line with the radio. Repeat this for the second radio station. Extend the two lines until they cross. The crossing should be at, or very close to, the point where you are located.

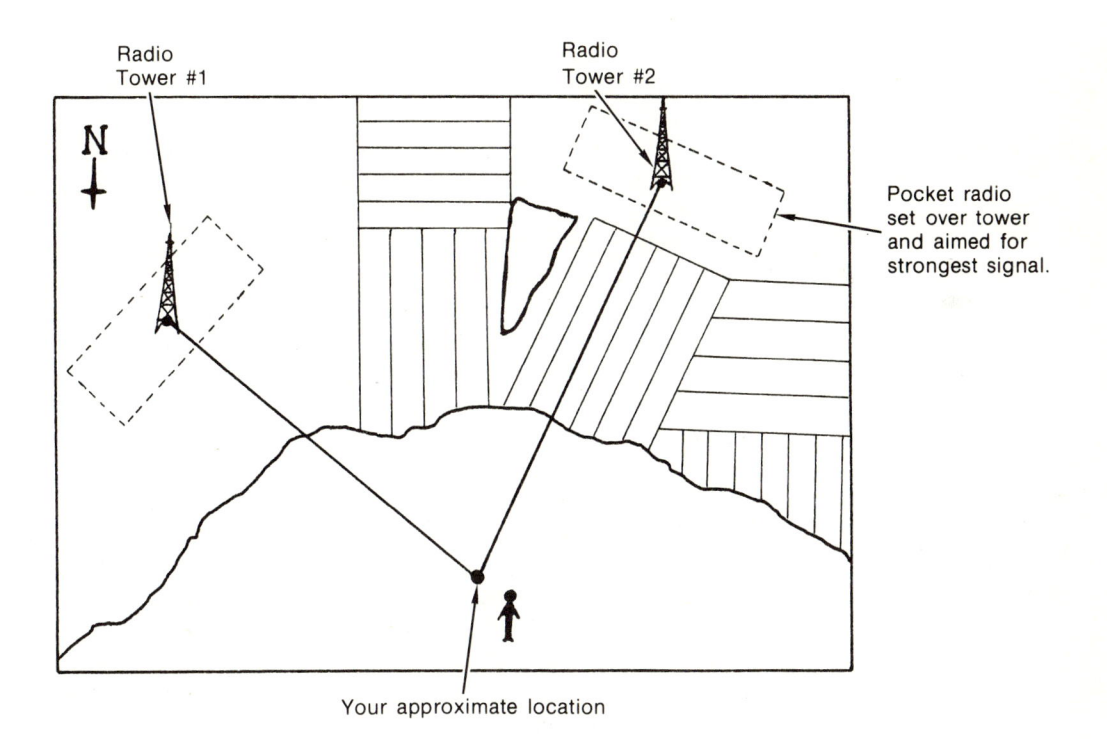

ENERGY

Energy: These activities emphasize measurement of energy consumption, methods of energy conservation, and related data collection techniques. Heat, solar, mechanical, and electrical energy are considered.

CONSERVATION
  insulators
  containment of heat
  color and heat loss
  heat loss and house drafts

CONSUMPTION
  data collection and
    comparisions
  patterns
  calculating costs

ENERGY

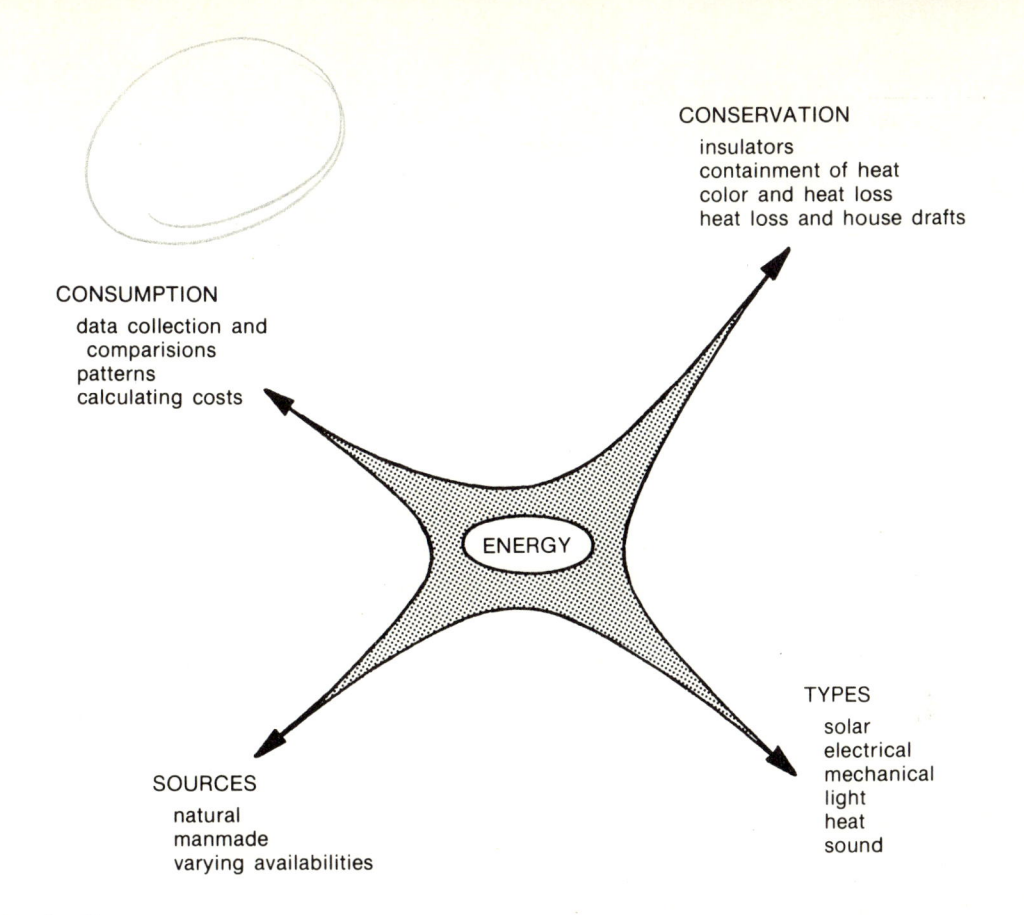

SOURCES
  natural
  manmade
  varying availabilities

TYPES
  solar
  electrical
  mechanical
  light
  heat
  sound

Introduction

The energy crisis, expected by some segments of our society for several years, has arrived. It is having profound effects on many aspects of our economy as well as on our environment. Some of these effects may be positive in nature. For example, expanded use of smaller, more economical automobiles, renewed efforts to locate and develop additional sources of energy, and the evolvement of a more energy-conscious citizenry are likely to result.

Classroom teachers throughout the nation will no doubt encourage students to discuss and research various ramifications of the shortage and begin to detail the implications for each of us. Mathematics can provide an added dimension to such activities, for only through a quantitative analysis of the current situation can one begin to understand both the extent of the shortage and the magnitude of the energy-reducing measures required to counteract it. For example, school children can be asked to determine the level of energy consumption in their own homes. Such an activity will also provide valuable experience with the collection and manipulation of gathered data.

For comparison purposes, it is necessary for students to have access to baseline data. Local electrical power and gas companies regularly compile data on the amounts of gas and electricity used and the costs to the consumer. The companies will supply this data to interested persons on request. Energy usage is a function of climate and so varies from place to place, but Table 1 provides examples of the kinds of data available from utility companies.

Many activities can result from classroom energy-related discussions and subsequent analysis of data collected. The variety of activities is limited only by the originality of the students and teachers involved.

The ultimate benefit in such activities lies not in getting the right answer but in sensitizing students to the implications that a major national crisis has for a concerned citizenry. In addition, these activities provide meaningful opportunities to use basic skills and arithmetic techniques. Students also will be using data collection techniques, sampling and estimative procedures, and analytic techniques in a manner that is both useful and significant.

Because this is a rather extensive unit, the activities have been divided into two large groups. The first of these are energy conservation activities, and may be carried out on separate days or may be combined for completion. The first eight of these are explained for general classroom use. The following seven activities are presented in the form of reproducible worksheets for individual or small group use.

Activities Sixteen–Twenty-four deal with solar, mechanical, and electrical energy. The required materials are readily available. An important component of these lessons is the student discussion that should follow the actual activities. Whenever possible, encourage students to deal with the social aspects of energy consumption and the role and responsibility of each individual and household if we as a nation are to deal realistically with the energy shortage.

Remember that the specific individual activities in and of themselves are less important than the total concept that the child will develop. You should be more concerned that children develop an energy consciousness than with the mastery of any particular subconcept.

Unit Objectives:

The students will:

1. learn techniques related to surveying, measuring, and recording energy consumption.
2. learn ways to lessen energy consumption.
3. be able to calculate the costs of energy consumption and the savings of conserving energy.
4. create a display of what they have learned and what they recommend about energy.
5. learn about varying kinds and sources of energy, and will produce some kinds of energy themselves (electrical, solar, etc.).

Appropriate Grade Levels:

Four–Six (some activities could be very usable at junior high level as well)

ACTIVITY ONE:
INDIVIDUAL SURVEYS

Objective: to complete individual home energy use surveys and share these surveys with the class

Materials: paper and pencils

Procedure: Ask individual students to survey the energy consumption of their own homes. They should be sure to note the kind of energy used as well as the amount consumed. Students should either be provided with a printed form for recording the results of their survey, or a general format should be discussed in class.

    Once surveys are completed, make a class graph of the average yearly (or monthly, or weekly) levels of energy consumption. Use group data to determine whether levels of consumption are less than, equal to, or greater than large group averages quoted in tables. Discuss practical methods of curtailing energy consumption.

Evaluation: successful completion of both individual surveys and the class graph

ACTIVITY TWO:
MEASURING CONSERVATION

Objective: to measure energy savings resulting from conservation efforts, both in amounts consumed and cost

Materials: paper and pencils

Procedure: Tell your students to pretend that they have each turned off unneeded lights in their homes. They should then estimate the number of kilowatts saved each month:

1. by each individual residence
2. by the entire class

Determine the number of homes that could be powered each year by such savings. Note that this problem will require more precise definition before it is solvable. Your class would need to know the wattage of various bulbs in individual homes, how many of each kind are being used, and how many are likely to be turned on at a given time.

116   WHAT? A SAMPLER OF THEMATIC UNITS

A possible follow-up to this activity would be to have students put the conservation techniques discussed into actual practice. At the end of one month's time, they could compare the two month's energy bills to measure actual savings. If this activity is carried out, be sure to point out to students that the results are not entirely accurate, since a variety of variables in home consumption were not controlled.

Evaluation: successful completion of activities described

ACTIVITY THREE:
ANNUAL ENERGY CONSUMPTION

Objective: to measure annual energy consumption, and to construct problems relative to that consumption

Materials: paper and pencils

Procedure: Before pursuing this activity, it will be necessary to consult appropriate tables of data. To do so, you may use the tables that follow this activity, or obtain your own from your local library or energy companies.

Once data has been obtained, ask students to use them to find the answers to the following questions:

1. How many kilowatt hours of electricity are consumed annually by:
   a. residences?
   b. small commercial and industrial companies?
2. How many cubic feet of natural gas are consumed annually by:
   a. residences using gas for heating?
   b. commercial establishments?

These are just two examples of the kinds of questions you may wish to present to your students. Once questions have been answered and students have become comfortable with the tables being used, have them make up problems that can be answered by using the tables and exchange these with other students for solving.

Evaluation: correct answers given for questions posed, and student-constructed problems

TABLE 1   ANNUAL USE OF ELECTRICITY

ANNUAL USE OF ELECTRICITY IN KILOWATT HOURS (A 100-WATT BULB BURNING 10 HOURS EQUALS 1 KILOWATT HOUR).

Annual Northern States Power Output—25,059,000,000 Kilowatt Hours.*

Percentages Used by Various Customers:

Residences	32.8
Small commercial and industrial	14.1
Large commercial and industrial	42.1
Street lighting and others	3.2
Municipalities	3.6
Rural electrical cooperative	0.3
Other electric companies	3.9

AVERAGE ANNUAL USE OF ELECTRICITY BY 1 RESIDENCE—7,049 KILOWATT HOURS.

Average Annual Use of Electricity, Expressed in Kilowatt Hours, by Various Appliances:

Vacuum cleaner (used 1 hour a week)	48
Radio	96
Coffee maker (used twice a day)	96
Washing machine (used 12 hours a month)	108
Iron (used 16 hours a month)	156
Dishwasher	360
Black and white television	600
Conventional refrigerator	796
Clothes dryer (used 16 hours a month)	960
Range (for family of 4)	1,200
Color television	1,200
Frostless refrigerator freezer	2,000

*Lighting a home in winter time figures out to about 10 kilowatt hours per month a room (50 for a 5-room house); in the summer, with longer daylight hours the use of electricity for lighting would be less.

Figures from the Northern States Power Company, appliance figures based on average use of electricity in the Twin Cities metropolitan area.

TABLE 2   ANNUAL USE OF GAS

TOTAL ANNUAL DISTRIBUTION OF GAS BY MINNEGASCO IN MINNEAPOLIS AND SUBURBS (INCLUDING ALL OF HENNEPIN COUNTY AND PARTS OF WRIGHT, ANOKA AND DAKOTA COUNTIES)—107 BILLION CUBIC FEET.*

Percentages of Output Used by Various Customers:

Residences using gas for heating	.43
Commercial establishments using gas including heating	14
Commercial establishments using gas, but not for heating	1
Industrial use of gas, including heating	2
Industrial use of gas, but not for heating	1
Part time industrial and commercial (interruptable)	.39

The percentage figures are rounded out; use of gas by residences which do not heat by gas accounts for a fractional use too small to be taken into account.

Cubic Feet

Average annual use of gas for heating by one residence (3 bedroom rambler)	147,000
Average annual use of gas in 1 residence for water heating	29,000
Average annual use of gas in 1 residence for cooking	14,000
Average annual use of gas in 1 residence for drying clothes	5,500
Average annual use of gas by 1 yard light (figured at 2 cubic feet an hour over 365 days)	17,520

*Figures, but not percentages, from Minnegasco.

TABLE 3   COST TO THE CONSUMER

PER KILOWATT—COST OF RESIDENTIAL ELECTRICITY CONSUMED:

Amount	Rate
October through May	
1st 1,000 Kilowatts (kw)	3.82 cents per Kilowatt Hour (kwh)
Anything after	2.26 cents per Kilowatt Hour (kwh)
June to September	4.21 cents per Kilowatt Hour (kwh)

TABLE 4   PER KILOWATT COST OF COMMERCIAL ELECTRICITY CONSUMED

Amount	Rate
October through May	
Ist 1,000 Kilowatts (kw)	4.04 cents per Kilowatt Hour (kwh)
Everything over 1,000 kw	3.70 cents per Kilowatt Hour (kwh)
June through September	4.42 cents per Kilowatt Hour (kwh)

TABLE 5   NATURAL GAS RATES FOR RESIDENTIAL AND COMMERCIAL CONSUMPTION

Amount	Rate
1st 5,000 cubic feet	26.96 cents per 100 cubic feet
Next 45,000 cubic feet	26.54 cents per 100 cubic feet
Over 45,000 cubic feet	26.54 cents per 100 cubic feet

ACTIVITY FOUR: ENERGY SURVEY

Objective: to conduct neighborhood energy consumption surveys

Materials: paper and pencils, or preconstructed forms for recording data if desired

Procedure: Have class members conduct an energy consumption survey of the homes on their blocks or in their immediate neighborhood. Afterward, statistically analyze group results. It will be necessary to estimate certain aspects of this survey, such as the number of 100-watt, 75-watt, 50-watt, and 40-watt bulbs in a given house.

A preconstructed, standardized form on which data will be recorded will greatly simplify data collection and subsequent analysis. It will be important to determine precisely what kinds of data are to be collected. Children should develop the form ultimately used on the basis of class discussions.

Evaluation: successful completion of surveys

ACTIVITY FIVE: ENERGY COSTS

Objective: to measure and calculate energy costs

Materials: paper, pencils, and calculators

Procedure: At this point, your students have completed a number of activities concerning the measurement of energy consumption and the cost of that consumption. They should be familiar with the kinds of data used to record and calculate such information.

It should now be possible to relate this once again to family energy consumption by having students calculate the cost of heating or electrifying their individual homes. Instruct them to find out how much money could be saved if energy conservation measures were implemented by each member of their families. You might even encourage your students to share their results with their families for possible implementation of various conservation techniques.

Evaluation: correct calculations of energy costs

WHAT? A SAMPLER OF THEMATIC UNITS

Home Energy Costs

Survey Sheet

Use this survey sheet and Table 6 to calculate the cost of next month's electric bill.

Check your estimate with the actual bill when it comes.

CHECK THOSE APPLIANCES FOUND IN YOUR HOME

Yes	No	Appliance	Average Annual Kilowatt Hours Used	My House	Monthly Cost
___	___	Vacuum cleaner	48	___	___
___	___	Radio	96	___	___
___	___	Coffee maker	96	___	___
•	•	•	•		
•	•	•	•		
•	•	•	•		
___	___	Frostless refrigerator/freezer	2004	___	___
		Other (i.e., electrical lights)	___	___	___
		Totals	___	___	___

1. Is your total electrical consumption higher or lower than the average?

   _____Higher   _____Lower

2. By how much?_____

3. How could energy consumption in your home be reduced?

TABLE 6 CONSUMPTION AND COST PER MONTH FOR ELECTRICITY

		KILOWATTS*
HEATING, AIR CONDITIONING	Home heating	1,930†
	Oil burner	50
	Furnace fan	100
	Room air conditioner	300
	Dehumidifier	67
	Humidifier	60
LIGHTING	5-room house (winter)	50
	6-room house (winter)	60
	8-room house (winter)	80
	Christmas lights	120
COOKING, REFRIGERATING	Freezer (14 cu. ft.)	140
	Oven (microwave)	25
	Oven (self-cleaning)	96
	Range	100
	Refrigerator	83
	Refrigerator/freezer (frostfree)	167
LAUNDRY, HOT WATER	Dryer	80
	Iron	13
	Washer	9
	Water heater (quick recovery)	183
TV, RADIO, HI-FI	Hi-Fi	9
	Radio	8
	TV (b & w)	50
	TV (color)	100
KITCHEN	Blender	1.25
	Broiler	8
	Carving knife	.66

TABLE 6 (CONTINUED)

		KILOWATTS*
KITCHEN	Coffeemaker	8
	Deep fryer	7
	Dishwasher	30
	Frying pan	15
	Hot plate	7.5
	Mixer	1
	Toaster	3
	Trash compacter	4
	Waffle iron	2
	Waste disposer	2.5
HEALTH, BEAUTY	Hair dryer	1
	Heat lamp	1
	Shaver	.15
	Sun lamp	1.33
	Toothbrush	.04
OTHER	Battery charger	1
	Blanket	22
	Clocks (4)	6
	Fan (circulating)	3.5
	Fan (window)	14
	Heating pad	1
	Power tools (drill, sander)	3
	Vacuum	4
	Well pump (¾ h.p.)	20

*One kilowatt equals 1,000 watts. A 100-watt electrical item consumes 1 kilowatt in 10 hours.

†Based on 1,300 square feet: 5-room house, with a year-round budget payment. Figures from Northern States Power Company and Electric Energy Association.

ACTIVITY SIX:
SCHOOL SURVEY

Objective: to complete a school energy survey, and make recommendations concerning future conservation

Materials: paper, pencils, and calculators

Procedure: Have the class conduct a school-wide "energy survey" detailing fuel oil, electrical, and natural gas usage per day, week, month, and so on. Small groups could be assigned to survey different sections of the school building, or to look into the various kinds of energy consumed. As in the case of previous surveys conducted, you should either present the students with a form to be used or help them devise one themselves.

Following the completion of the survey, the class might be asked to develop a school-wide plan for further energy conservation. As part of this activity, you might wish to involve the school principal, custodial engineers, and any other members of the school's personnel who might be involved in the use of energy.

Evaluation: successful completion of the survey, and participation in group discussion to make recommendations for future conservation efforts

ACTIVITY SEVEN:
PRO-RATING AND ENERGY COSTS

Objective: to further explore and calculate the costs of energy use

Materials: paper, pencils, and calculators

Procedure: At present, in many utility companies, energy costs are pro-rated on a gradually declining scale. That is, the more energy consumed, the cheaper the per-unit cost. Have the class discuss this policy, noting its implications for the average consumer. If one of your students doesn't point it out, mention that such a policy can serve to encourage, rather than discourage, high levels of energy consumption.

After the discussion, have students answer the following questions individually or in small groups:

1. What is the monthly cost for a residence averaging 400 kilowatts of electricity?
2. What will be the average monthly bill for a home that annually consumes an average amount of electricity and natural gas? How much would be saved if energy consumption were reduced by 20 percent?
3. On the average, who pays more for electricity, residential or commercial users? Why?

Evaluation: correct answers given for the questions and problems posed during the activity

ACTIVITY EIGHT:
ENERGY DISPLAY

Objective: to complete a display of products of the energy conservation activities (see note following the procedure section)

Materials: varied, depending upon decisions as to the best ways to display activity results and findings

Procedure: Have the class develop an energy display that includes the results of their investigations, conclusions, and recommendations. Such a display could be made available to the general school population, community groups, or the PTA.

If this display is to be used as a major project, you may wish to expand somewhat on each of the preceding activities in terms of having the class produce lasting and attractive exhibits of their findings. On the other hand, if this display is for your room only, less time will be needed in putting together final products.

Note: You may wish to hold this display until completion of the entire unit. The following activities, while often pursued on an independent basis, will produce projects suitable for an interesting display.

Evaluation: completion and display of all related products

ACTIVITIES NINE TO TWENTY-FOUR:
A GENERAL OVERVIEW*

As explained in the introduction to this unit, Activities Nine through Twenty-four are in the form of reproducible worksheets. On each, the objective of the exercise and the materials are outlined for the student. In each case, evaluation involves simply the correct completion of the worksheet and the activities it describes. You may use them either as individualized assignments or in small group settings. In some cases, tables or diagrams accompany or follow the worksheets to which they are related.

It is very likely that you will not choose to have students complete all of these worksheets. One is not dependent upon another, and so you are free to pick and choose any which seem important or appropriate for your class to use.

---

*Activities nine to twenty-four have been adapted in part from materials produced by the American Museum of Science and Energy, Oak Ridge Associated Universities, U.S. Department of Energy, Office of Consumer Affairs, Washington, D.C. 20585.

ACTIVITY NINE:
HOW MUCH ELECTRICITY DOES YOUR HOUSEHOLD USE AT HOME IN 1 DAY?

Objective: to calculate daily home electrical use

Materials: kwh meter at home (kwh: kilowatt hour)

Procedure: Learn how to read a kilowatt meter, then find one in your home. Ask your mom or dad for help. Record the readings for two days. How many kilowatt hours did you use? How does your use compare with that of other families in your classroom?

Ask your mom or dad to let you see last month's electric bill. How much does 1 kwh cost?

Keep track of your family's electric use for one week. How much did each day's electricity cost?

	S	M	T	W	TH	F	S	WEEKLY TOTALS
# of kwh								
cost per kwh								
TOTAL COST								

ACTIVITY TEN:
HOW MUCH ENERGY DO APPLIANCES USE?

Objective: to determine how much energy is used by various electrical appliances

Materials:
    kwh meter at home
    several small electrical appliances

Procedure:

You will need to complete this activity at home with a partner. Be sure to have your parents' permission before starting any of these activities!

1. Decide on five appliances whose electrical energy consumption you will measure.
2. Observe the kilowatt meter without any of these appliances in operation. Note particularly the change in the reading of the small wheel which revolves continuously after two minutes. This change indicates the number of watts used in the two-minute period of time. Keep a record of this amount.

Now suppose you picked a toaster, an iron, a clothes dryer, an electric range, and a radio as your five appliances.

3. Ask your friend at a given signal to plug in the toaster for two minutes. Notice the change in the meter's reading during this time. The *difference* between this amount and the one you recorded in step 2 above is the amount of energy consumed by the toaster.
4. Repeat this process for the remaining four appliances. Record all of your results in column one of the table that follows. Complete the other four columns before you discuss your results with other students. Were your results similar? What was the difference between the largest and the smallest estimates? What was the average estimate? Develop a plan to reduce the number of kilowatts by ten percent.

APPLIANCE	# WATTS USED IN 2 MINUTES	# KW USED IN 1 HOUR	ESTIMATE # KW USED PER MONTH	COST PER KWH	ESTIMATED COST PER MONTH
Toaster					
Iron					
Clothes Dryer					
Electric Range					
Radio					

WHAT? A SAMPLER OF THEMATIC UNITS

129

ACTIVITY ELEVEN:
HEAT LOSS AND HOUSE DRAFTS

Objective: to measure house drafts and calculate resulting heat losses

Materials:
- pencil
- tape
- plastic food wrap

Procedure: Make a draftometer by following these directions: Cut a 10cm by 20cm strip of plastic food wrap. Tape it to the pencil. Your draftometer should respond to the slightest movement of air. Try it. Note: Forced air furnaces must not be in operation when using your draftometer!

Windows account for about twenty-five percent of heat loss. Test your windows and doors, electrical outlets, etc., for air leakage by holding the draftometer near them, especially by the cracks. Do the same for your fireplace, if you have one. What makes the plastic wrap move? List the three places where it moves the most.

1. _____

2. _____

3. _____

Ask your mom or dad to help you fix these spots.

ACTIVITY TWELVE:
HOW MUCH ENERGY CAN BE SAVED BY BOILING WATER IN A COVERED PAN?

Objective: to measure the energy saved by covering pans while cooking in them

Materials:
- hot plate
- pan with lid
- watch
- water
- styrofoam cups

Procedure: Pour two cups of water into the pan. Place it on the hot plate and turn the hot plate on. Be careful not to touch the hot plate or pan while they are hot! Begin timing when the pan is placed on the hot plate. Record the number of minutes required for the water to boil vigorously.

Now empty the pan and rinse it under cold water until it is thoroughly cooled. Add two more cups of water and cover the pan. Begin timing again when you place it on the hot plate. How long does it take for it to boil this time?

Now answer these questions:

1. How did you know when the water was boiling?
2. Did covering the pan save energy?
3. Assuming that the hot plate used 1,000 watts per hour (1 kilowatt), how much money would be saved if a household heated all its water in a covered pan?

ACTIVITY THIRTEEN:
TYPES OF INSULATORS

Objective: to measure the effectiveness of a variety of insulators

Materials:
- 40-watt bulb in ceramic socket
- a variety of insulating and noninsulating materials (wood, aluminum foil, fiberglass, glass, metal, newspaper, heavy cloth, and others)
- four thermometers
- cardboard box
- watch
- masking tape

Procedure: Set up the box as shown below. Be sure to place the light in the *center* of the box! When all is set up, turn the lamp on and leave it on for three minutes. Record the temperature on the outside of the box for each material. Which is the best insulator? How do you know?

Record your results on a chart like the one on the following page.

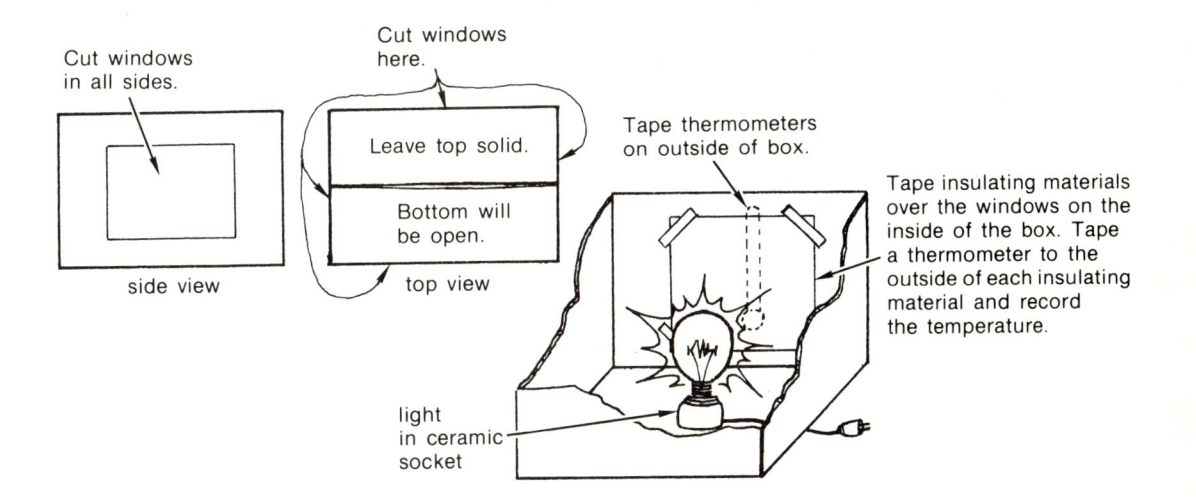

Cut windows in all sides.

side view

Cut windows here.

Leave top solid.

Bottom will be open.

top view

Tape thermometers on outside of box.

Tape insulating materials over the windows on the inside of the box. Tape a thermometer to the outside of each insulating material and record the temperature.

light in ceramic socket

TEMPERATURE

MATERIAL:	BEFORE	AFTER	DIFFERENCE
wood			
aluminum foil			
fiberglass			
glass			
metal			
newspaper			
cloth			

ACTIVITY FOURTEEN:
THE CONTAINMENT OF HEAT

Objective: to measure the containment of heat under varying conditions

Materials:
- tall cardboard box
- 40-watt bulb in ceramic socket
- thermometer
- watch
- knife

Procedure: Follow these steps:

1. Place the bulb inside the box.
2. Cut a small hole in the bottom of the box for the cord of the lamp.
3. Cut out flaps on one side of the box at both the top and at the bottom.
4. Make a small hole in the top of the box for the thermometer—do not put it directly over the lamp!
5. Fill in the temperature readings with the flaps open and closed on the chart below.

TEMPERATURE READINGS

	1 MIN.	2 MIN.	3 MIN.	4 MIN.	5 MIN.
Both flaps closed					
Top open, bottom closed					
Bottom open, top closed					
Both flaps open					

ACTIVITY FIFTEEN:
COLOR AND HEAT LOSS

Objective: to determine the effect of color on heat loss

Materials:
- four juice cans
- poster paint (white, black, green, red)
- hot water
- four thermometers
- food colors

Procedure: Paint each can a different color, then fill each with the same amount of hot water. Add food color to the hot water, adding all colors together to get black.

Put a thermometer in each cup. Record the temperature every three minutes until the water cools. Make a graph of the results. The graph will be more dramatic if the five points associated with each color are connected with a pencil of the same color. You will then have four separate graphs on the same grid. The graphs can now easily be contrasted and discussed.

After you complete your graph, answer these questions:

1. Which color held heat best?
2. What is the best color to paint a house to keep it warm in winter?
3. Why aren't all houses painted this color?

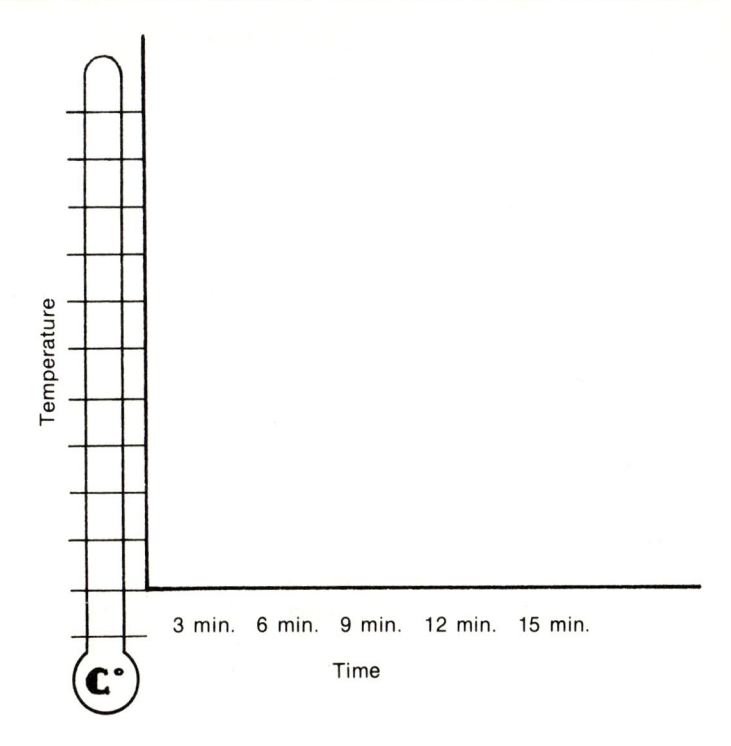

Temperature

3 min. 6 min. 9 min. 12 min. 15 min.

Time

C°

ACTIVITY SIXTEEN: TEMPERATURE DIFFERENCES IN SUN AND SHADE

Objective: to measure the differences of water temperature in sun and shade

Materials:
- two styrofoam cups
- two thermometers
- watch or clock

Procedure: Pour the same amount of very cold water into each of the styrofoam cups. After placing a thermometer in each cup, place one in the sun and the other in the shade. Measure the temperature and record after five, ten, and fifteen minutes.

Other ideas:

1. Try this experiment with different colored cans. Which color absorbs the most heat?
2. Attempt this experiment with different starting temperatures, such as 35°, 50°, and 65°. Are the differences between beginning and ending temperatures the same for each starting temperature? Set up a chart to record your results.

ELAPSED TIME

*	5 MIN.	10 MIN.	15 MIN.

*Use this column to give location or starting temperatures

ACTIVITY SEVENTEEN:
MAGNIFYING GLASSES AND SUN SPOTS

Objective: to determine the complications of using reflectors and lenses to collect solar energy

Materials:
- magnifying glass
- chair or stool
- masking tape
- watch with second hand

Procedure: Focus the lens on a piece of white paper or cardboard. Mark its position at 1 P.M. by making a circle around the light. Measure the time it takes for the light to leave the entire circle. Why does this happen? How do results of this experiment show how complicated it is to use reflectors and lenses for the collection of solar energy?

Here are some other ideas to explore:

1. Will the time it takes for the spot of light to move from the circle be the same if you try the experiment at 9 A.M.? How about 3 P.M.?
2. Now try it and see what happens. Can you explain the results?

ACTIVITY EIGHTEEN: HEAT COLLECTING IN PIE PLATES

Objective: to measure the heat collected in water-filled pie plates, and to explore factors influencing that heat collection

Materials:
- two disposable pie plates, different sizes
- black paint (not water soluble)
- candle
- thermometer
- measuring cup
- clear plastic food wrap
- newspapers, styrofoam cups
- masking tape

Procedure: Follow these steps:

1. Paint both pie plates black.
2. When the paint dries, add 100 cc of water to each pie plate and wrap plastic wrap tightly around them. Tape in place.
3. Place each on a stack of newspapers in the sun for ten minutes. Newspapers act as insulation. Is this important? Why?
4. Now pour the water into styrofoam cups and measure the temperatures. Note: The same amount of water in each plate serves as a "reservoir" for the heat collected by the two plates. The final temperature is an index of the amount of heat collected.

Now you may like to try this:

1. Refill the large pan. Heat to the same temperature as before, using a candle.
2. How much did the candle cost? How much did the solar energy cost? What are the advantages of each?

ACTIVITY NINETEEN:
DOES THE SIZE OF A MAGNIFYING GLASS AFFECT ITS HEAT-PRODUCING POTENTIAL?

Objective: to measure the effect of size on the heat-producing potential of a magnifying glass

Materials:
one six cm (or larger) magnifier
paper and scissors
watch
one sheet heavy black construction paper
one sheet dark or black lightweight paper

Procedure: Position the magnifying glass so the sun's rays focus the smallest amount of light on a piece of dark or black lightweight paper. How many seconds does it take before the paper starts to smoke? (Be *careful*—it gets *hot*!)

Now cover the lens with a piece of black construction paper that has a three cm hole cut in the center. How long does it take this time? Now try the same procedure with different colors of construction paper.

See if you can find out how a magnifying glass works. (Hint: It has something to do with the refraction of light as it passes through a convex lens.) Now can you explain why the paper burns?

Here's another idea to explore. Find out how much more sunlight a six cm lens lets in than a three cm lens. Draw one circle that is six cm wide and another that is three cm wide on a sheet of graph paper. Count the approximate number of squares that each circle covers. What's the total for each? Does this explain your results? Would this exercise be more accurate if your grid was on a half-cm scale?

ACTIVITY TWENTY: STORING SOLAR ENERGY

Objective: to measure and compare the ability to collect solar energy of a variety of materials

Materials:
- cardboard box
- black paint
- four small metal cans of equal size
- four thermometers
- sand, salt, water, and torn-up paper

Procedure: Fill each can with a different material and place a thermometer in each. Get a cardboard box and paint it black. Put the cans in the box and place it in the sun for half an hour. Now remove the cans and watch the temperatures fall.

Stir occasionally. Take a reading every three minutes. Which temperature falls the slowest? Which stores solar heat best? Make a graph of your results. Be sure to use a different color pencil for each material.

WHAT? A SAMPLER OF THEMATIC UNITS

thermometers

SAND SALT WATER PAPER

Temperature

3 min. 6 min. 9 min. 12 min. 15 min.

Time

ACTIVITY TWENTY-ONE: ENERGY AS FORCE

Objective: to measure the varying force of mechanical energy

Materials:
- lunch room trays, shoe boxes, or other containers
- pencils
- book or other weights
- rubber bands (medium weight)

Procedure: Attach the rubber band to the lunch tray so that it can be pulled along a table top for two feet. Measure how long the rubber band will stretch with the tray empty.

Now place several pounds of books or other weights on the tray and repeat the experiment. Repeat once more, doubling the amount of weight added to the tray. How far does the rubber band stretch this time?

Put three or more equally spaced round pencils or dowels under the box. Now try pulling it. How far does the rubber band stretch this time? Graph your results using the chart below. Then try to answer these questions:

1. What do you notice from your graph? Why?
2. Could you do the same experiment with a toy wagon? What do you think would happen? Try it.
3. Why do heavy cars use more gasoline than light cars?

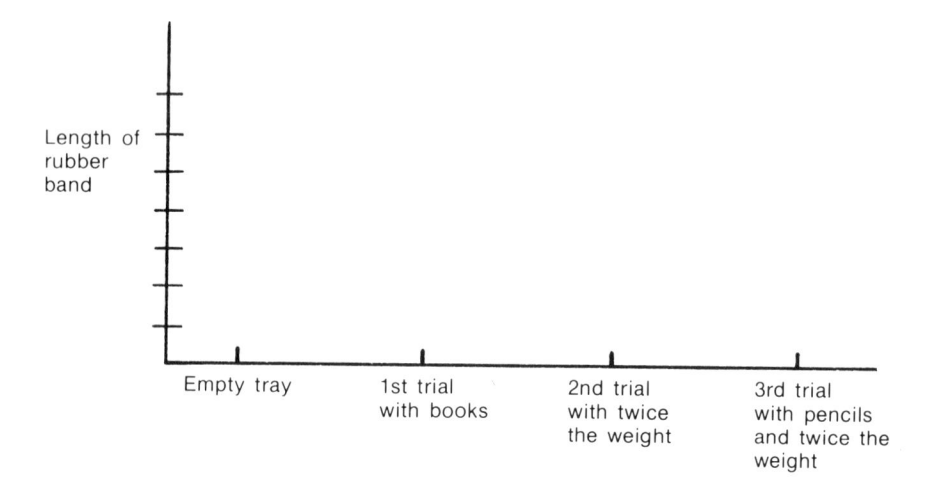

[Graph with y-axis labeled "Length of rubber band" and x-axis with categories: Empty tray, 1st trial with books, 2nd trial with twice the weight, 3rd trial with pencils and twice the weight]

ACTIVITY TWENTY-TWO:
HOW CAN YOU MAKE A BULB LIGHT?

Objective: to complete an electrical circuit between one or two batteries and a lightbulb

Materials:
- three size "D" flashlight batteries
- wires
- small bulb
- flashlight

Procedure:

1. Experiment with two wires and a battery and a bulb. See if you can make the bulb light. Note the strength of the light when it does appear.

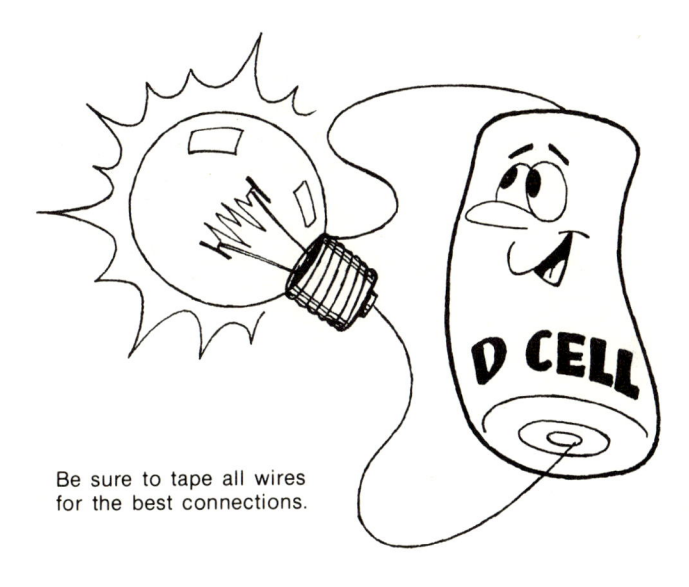

Be sure to tape all wires for the best connections.

2. Try connecting two cells to the bulb. You will need two more wires. What do you notice about the amount of light now?

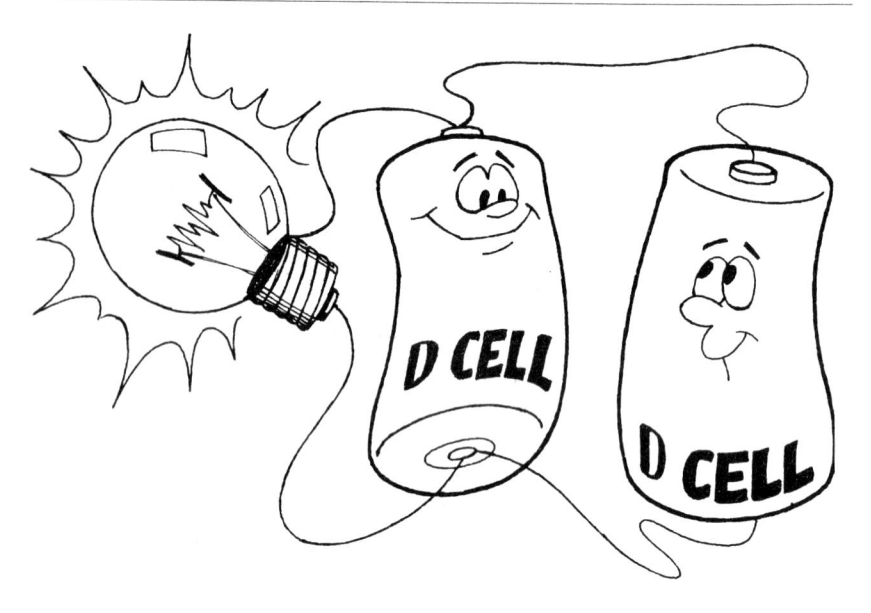

3. What would happen if you used three or more batteries? Try it.
4. Take a flashlight apart and see if you can figure out how it works. How is it the same as your homemade flashlight made only of batteries, a bulb and wires?

ACTIVITY TWENTY-THREE: CAN A SMALL LAMP CHANGE THE TEMPERATURE OF WATER?

Objective: to measure the heating effect of a lightbulb on the temperature of water

Materials:
- small cup
- six-volt battery
- bulb
- tape
- wire
- two thermometers (Fahrenheit and Celsius)

Procedure: Fill the cup with cold water, and measure its temperature with both thermometers. Record the temperatures on the chart below.

Now connect the battery wires to the light bulb so that the bulb lights. Place the bulb in the water. *CAUTION*: Do not attempt this experiment with any electrical source other than a battery.

Record the temperature after three minutes, and again after another three minutes (six minutes). Fill these temperatures in on the chart below as well. Now graph your results, and compare the graphs. What do you notice? Can you explain this?

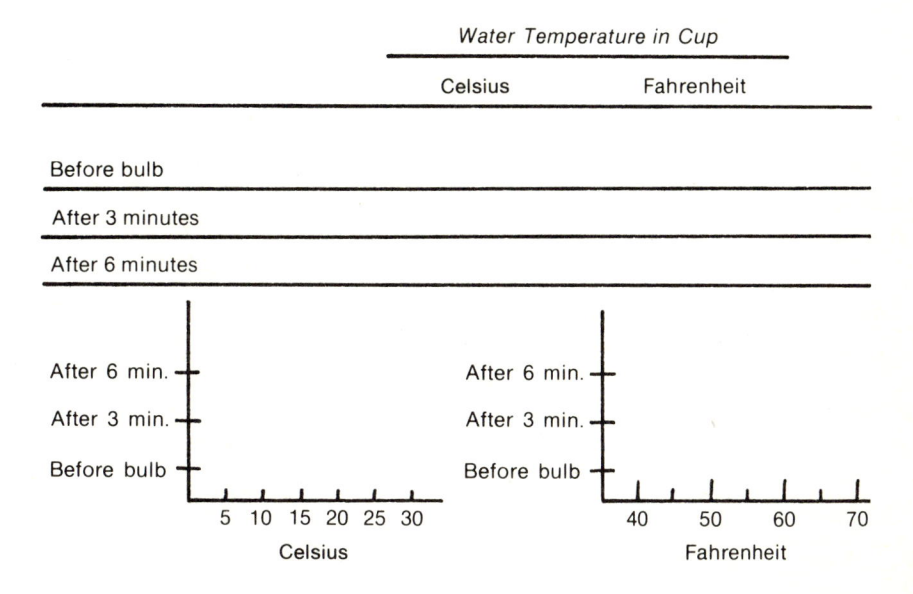

| | Water Temperature in Cup ||
	Celsius	Fahrenheit
Before bulb		
After 3 minutes		
After 6 minutes		

ACTIVITY TWENTY-FOUR:
GENERATE YOUR OWN ELECTRICITY

Objective: to generate electricity using a small motor and a bicycle

Materials:
- ten-speed bicycle
- small D.C. motor
- wires
- bulb
- masking tape

Procedure: Connect the bulb to the motor with the two wires. Build up the shaft of the motor with masking tape to about half the thickness of your little finger.

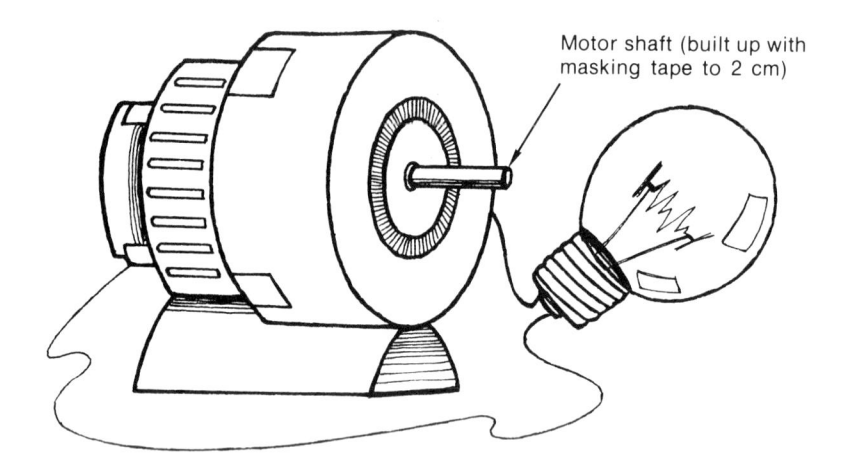

Motor shaft (built up with masking tape to 2 cm)

Turn the bicycle upside down. Hold the shaft of the motor next to the tire and turn the pedals with your hands. Turn the pedals slowly at first and then increase your speed. What do you notice about the light? Now shift gears and repeat the experiment. Do you notice any difference? Why or why not?

At this point, gather your data and fill it in on the chart that follows. When all the information is charted, compare the results across the different gears. What do you notice? Discuss your results with someone else who has completed the same experiment. Then transfer the information onto the graph.

BICYCLE-GENERATED ELECTRICITY CHART

Indicate the brightness of the light bulb generated in each gear (low, medium, or bright).

NUMBER OF REVOLUTIONS OF THE PEDAL PER 30 SECONDS

	5	15	25
1ST GEAR			
5TH GEAR			
10TH GEAR			

    Start your graph by placing a dot on the graph for each measurement. Use a black pen to represent first gear, a blue pen to represent fifth gear, and a red pen to represent tenth gear.

    Now connect dots of the same color. What do you notice? Are your results different from those discussed earlier? How does a chart differ from a graph? Do you prefer to make conclusions from the chart or from the graph? Why?

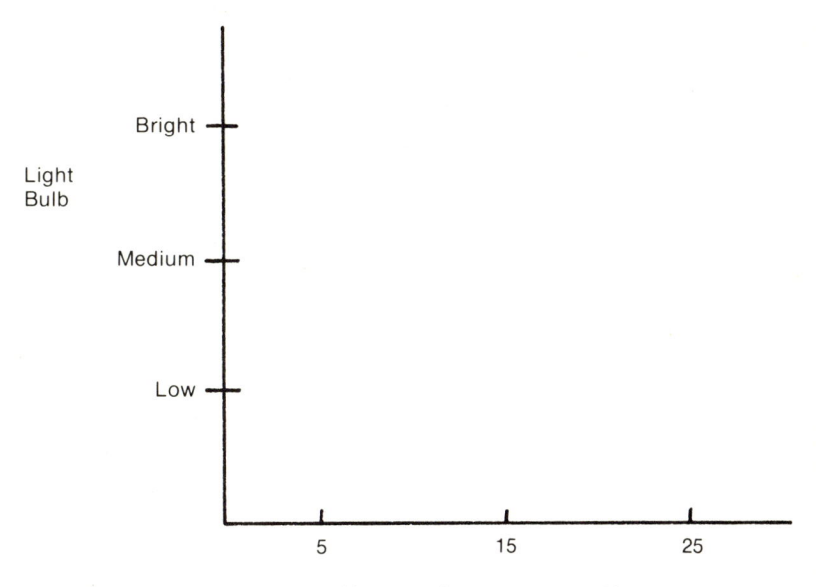

Number of revolutions per 30 seconds

Additional Activities: A variety of additional activities involving electricity, heat, light, sound, and mechanical energy can be found in two excellent resources. These are *The Whole Cosmos Catalog of Science Activities* by Joe Abruscato and Jack Hassard (Santa Monica, Calif.: Goodyear Publishing Co., Inc., 1977) and *The Great Perpetual Learning Machine* by Jim Blake and Barbara Ernst (Boston: Little, Brown & Co., 1976). In addition, most local utility companies and several United States agencies provide free materials and resources for classroom activities upon written or telephone request. Listings and addresses for such agencies can be found in the telephone book or at your local library.

COOPERATION/COMPETITION:

Cooperation/Competition: The examination of personal reactions to cooperative and competitive experiences through simulation games used to highlight important aspects of human behavior.

```
              GAMES      CONTESTS

      GRADES                          VALUES
                                      CLARIFICATION
                  COMPETITION
  DECISION MAKING         COOPERATION
  forced choices
  activities

       FEELINGS AND                SOCIOGRAMS
       ATTITUDES

          BLINDFOLD    GROUP ACTIVITIES
          GAME         art projects
                       problem solving
```

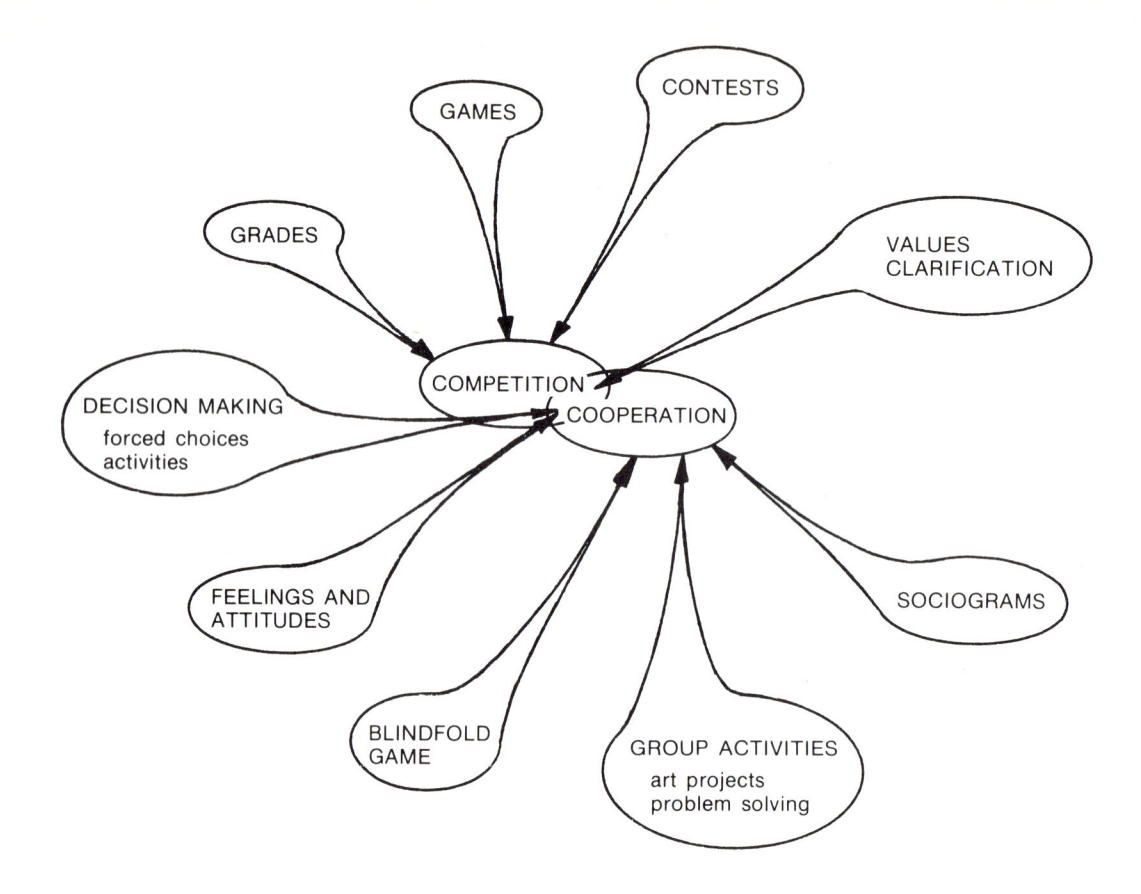

Introduction*

For students, competition is an almost daily fact of life. Cooperation is a word they have heard, but really haven't had much experience in understanding.

Students encounter competition in almost every facet of life: school, home, and on the playground. They compete with others in games, in choosing friends, in the clothes they wear, in obtaining grades, etc. Children learn early in life that our society values "getting on top" much more than trying to get along with others.

The lessons in this unit present two concepts: cooperation and competition. Through the implementation of the activities, students will come to question competitive behavior and will understand that working to improve oneself is a more reasonable goal.

It is also hoped that the students will gain new insight into how their behavior affects others in a group problem-solving situation, and that they will show an improvement in attitude towards working together with others. These goals could be evaluated very simply in the following manner:

*The authors are indebted to Ms. Kathy Howe, St. Paul, MN.

1. How did you feel about the activity? Indicate your feelings by underlining one of the following:

   ☺ 😐 ☹

2. How do you feel about the way your group worked together?

   ☺ 😐 ☹

3. How do you think the other people in your group felt about working with you?

   ☺ 😐 ☹

To begin with, you might like to administer a simple sociometric test that will give you some indication of an individual child's group status. Have the children answer these statements:

1. Name *three* children with whom you would like to work.
2. Name *three* children with whom you would like to play.
3. Name *three* children you would like to sit next to.

The child's group status is determined by the number of choices he or she receives from his peers. A test such as this could also be used as an evaluative instrument for the ten activities. It could be given after the activities have been completed in order to determine whether a child's group status has changed or improved.

The lessons are designed so that they can be used in a random fashion. They are independent of each other, but are unified by the concepts with which they are concerned. Most of the lessons require a great deal of interaction, which will produce a climate of acceptance and cooperation.

The activities also incorporate many of the inquiry processes. The three different surveys allow the child to "generate new knowledge." The child becomes a data gatherer, then is asked to classify the information and make inferences from it.

The "Eight Forced Choices" activity is a values clarification exercise which forces a child to make a decision on feelings in eight different competitive/cooperative situations. In the process, it is hoped children will become more aware of their values and more accepting of others.

"The Poster Contest" is a behavior specimen that gives the children an opportunity to become social scientists, as they observe the competitive behavior of two boys. This lesson also affords students an opportunity to make inferences about behavior.

The remaining five lessons have the children working together to solve a problem (Bean Jar Problem) or a puzzle (Cooperation Squares), win some money (Win as Much Money as Possible), perform an experiment (Blindfold Activity), and create an object of beauty. When you have completed this unit, you will have a room full of students who are able to get along with each other better. What could be a better goal in our schools today!

Unit Objectives:

The students will:

1. learn how their own behavior affects others in a group.
2. improve skills relative to working within groups to solve problems and create products.
3. begin to question competitive behavior.
4. learn to make decisions based on their values and feelings.

Appropriate Grade Levels:

Three to Six

ACTIVITY ONE: SOCIOMETRIC SURVEY

Objective: to conduct a survey to measure classmates' feelings about one another

Materials: survey sheets and pencils for each child

Procedure: The purpose of this activity is to take an introductory measure of attitudes of classmates towards each other and general class cooperation. It should be completed independently by students after you have ascertained that they understand the directions on the survey sheet. It is suggested that you reproduce the survey sheet provided.

Evaluation: completion of survey by each child, and participation in any additional activities assigned.

How Do You And Your Classmates Get Along?

Survey Sheet

We would like to find out how you feel the kids in your class get along with each other. Your name will not be used in our report, and we are not trying to decide what is good or bad. We are trying to get a scientific record.

1. I am a _____ boy _____ girl.
2. I am in _____ grade.
3. Most of the children in my class get along with each other

    _____ very well _____ fairly well _____ O.K. _____ terrible
4. In my class we usually pick on one or two people.

    _____ yes _____ no
5. There are certain people in my class who are not usually included in activities.

    _____ yes _____ no
6. We argue with each other a lot in this class.

    _____ yes _____ no
7. Most people in this class would be willing to stand up for a classmate who they felt was being treated unfairly.

    _____ yes _____ no
8. I enjoy working with my classmates in small groups.

    _____ yes _____ no
9. I get more work done in this class when I am

    _____ alone

    _____ with one or two people

    _____ with many people
10. I think learning to cooperate is one of the most important things to learn in school.

    _____ agree _____ disagree

Additional Activities:

1. Administer this survey in other classes in your school. This will yield a comparison of attitudes in different rooms and at different grade levels.

2. Save the results of the survey. After several months, have the children in your class complete the questionnaire again. Compare these answers with the previous results. Have attitudes changed?

3. If survey results show negative feelings about the classroom climate from class members, have the children brainstorm ways in which the classroom atmosphere could be improved so that individual members will feel happier. Attempt to implement the suggestions.

4. Sponsor a "Cooperation Day" in your classroom. The children can create slogans for ways to cooperate or posters demonstrating examples of cooperation. Play cooperative games. Work cooperatively, sharing materials, to create a class mural. The children can be urged to try especially hard on this day to eliminate name-calling, avoid arguments, and play fairly. A discussion and perhaps a cooperatively planned party can conclude the day.

ACTIVITY TWO: CREATING A THING OF BEAUTY

Objective: to create "things of beauty" by small groups

Materials: varied, dependent upon the nature of objects to be created by each group

Procedure: Before you begin this activity, prepare instruction sheets and gather the materials you will use in this exercise. Any materials you have available will be adequate. These might include construction paper, paper plates, straws, magazines, newspapers, tissue or crepe paper, scissors, paste or glue.

Divide your class into groups of three to four members. Retain three members of the class to assist you in judging the finished products, or, better yet, have the class elect the judges. Explain to them that today they are going to participate in a "beauty contest." Each group will create, with the materials you provide, a thing of beauty. Tell them that they all have the same materials from which to make something. They may use all the materials or just the ones they choose. Instruct them that you will put the paste or glue in a central location, in order that all groups may share it as needed. The groups may use pencils but not crayons or paints.

Explain that the individual creations will be judged on their attractiveness, use of materials, originality of idea, and neatness. Hand out a copy of the provided instruction sheet to each person. Read over it together so that the activity will be clearly understood. Emphasize the time limits of the planning and building period. The students are not told whether to compete or cooperate.

During the planning and building periods, you should supervise the groups, watch the time limits (you might announce "ten minutes left," etc.), and instruct the judges as to the qualities in the creations for which to look. The judges could also act as observers of cooperative/competitive behavior in the groups, which they could later report to the class.

After the projects are completed, you might wish to follow up with a few of these questions:

1. Did everyone in your group have something to do?
2. Did everyone feel that their ideas were listened to as to how to use the materials for the creation?
3. Did anyone feel left out of the decision making? If so, what behaviors or procedures could be changed so that group members might feel more satisfied?
4. Did any groups or group members feel as though they were competing with each other? How?
5. Did this affect the work on your creation in any way? Explain.
6. Did the silent period have any effect on how group members worked with each other? Explain.
7. Are there things about this activity you wish could have been different?
8. How must group members act towards each other to do an activity like this?
9. Do you see any similarities between this activity and the ways in which we behave from day to day?
10. Could we learn anything from this exercise?
11. Make a check on the continuum as to how you felt while you were working with your group on this activity.

INSTRUCTIONS FOR CREATING A THING OF BEAUTY

Planning Period (ten minutes)

1. During this time, decide with other members of your group what kind of creation you are going to design and what materials you will need.

2. You should draw plans or write down instructions to the steps you are going to take, since there will be no talking with your partners during the building period.

3. Decide who in your group is going to do each job. Have each person do something. A person should be appointed who will pick up the glue or paste in the central location, and who will hand in the creation when it is completed.

4. You may not start building your creation or using the paste or glue until the teacher announces the planning period is over.

Building Period (fifteen minutes)

1. Complete your creation as decided in the planning period. There is *no* talking or writing notes during the building period. Each person should do his/her own job during this time.

2. Your group will be disqualified if you are talking. You may raise your hand to have the teacher clarify instructions for you.

Evaluation

After your creations are completed and you have had a discussion, you will be asked to mark the following continuum.

```
   1    2    3    4    5    6    7
Very                              Very
Unhappy                           Happy
```

WHAT? A SAMPLER OF THEMATIC UNITS　　　　　　　　　　　　　　　**157**

Evaluation: completion of a "thing of beauty" by each group, with participation of each student in the process

Additional Activities:
1. This activity could be modified in many different ways. For example, the children could be instructed to make one specific thing (example: a bridge or a building) using specified materials. Likewise, instead of a "beauty" contest, structures could be judged on height, stability, arrangement, or abstractness.

2. Split the class into groups of four or five members. Give each group a ball (or a pair of dice, a jump rope). Instruct them to invent a game with the ball. Give them ten minutes in which to plan a game, then five minutes in which to demonstrate it to the class. A group discussion or an individual evaluation of the activity could precede the demonstration period, focusing on the following questions:

- What part of the game do you feel was your contribution?
- Did you feel free to contribute your ideas?
- How satisfied are you with the final plan? (Circle below.)

$$\begin{array}{ccccccc} 1 & 2 & 3 & 4 & 5 & 6 & 7 \end{array}$$
Completely　　　　　　　　　　　　　Completely
Dissatisfied　　　　　　　　　　　　　Satisfied

- Could you have made up a better game alone?
- Was your game designed to emphasize competition?
- Was there any emphasis on cooperation among the team members?

ACTIVITY THREE:
THE BLINDFOLD ACTIVITY

Objective: to cooperate with classmates to complete tasks

Materials:　　slips of paper, marked as directed below
　　　　　　　　blindfolds
　　　　　　　　pencils

Procedure: Give each child a slip of paper on which is drawn four identical squares about one inch on each side. Have each child choose a partner with whom to work, or designate partners yourself. One of the partners should put on a blindfold. Each set of partners should also have a pencil.

With the help of the partner, the blindfolded person should place the tip of the pencil in the center of the square. He or she should then try to color in the first square. The seeing partner cannot say anything to help.

When the blindfolded person has completed coloring the square, he or she should say, "I'm finished." If desired, he or she can lift up the blindfold and take a look at the results. Then the blindfold should be reapplied, and the same steps repeated, with the seeing partner again helping only to put the pencil in the middle of the square.

When the second square is completed, the blindfolded person labels the tries "without help." Then the partner does the same experiment on a separate piece of paper, and when finished, labels the results in the same way.

Now, have your students repeat the experiment. This time, however, the blindfolded person will be helped by the partner. While the blindfolded person is attempting to shade the third square, the partner will be giving directions, such as "more to the right," "shade in more to the left," etc. The partner will also tell the blindfolded student when the square is finished. The fourth square will be done in similar fashion. When these squares are finished, they are labeled, "with help," and the blindfolded person assists the partner in the same way he or she was helped.

When all four squares are completed by each team, carry on a follow-up discussion using questions such as the following:

1. How did your squares "with help" compare with those drawn "without help"?

2. How did the two squares drawn "with help" compare with each other?

3. What were your feelings as you were attempting this exercise blindfolded? In what ways did you depend on your partner?

4. What did you have to do in order to color a square the correct shape?

5. Could this experiment be related in any way to how we might behave with each other from day to day?

Evaluation: completion of four squares by each person

Additional Activities:

1. An alternative way of doing this experiment is to have the children attempt to draw a solid line that is four inches long up the paper from a designated point or line at the bottom. This is repeated three times, with partners only assisting in putting the pencil at the line at the bottom of the paper to start.

2. When this experiment is repeated the second time, the partner uses a ruler to measure each line. Directions will then be something like, "too long," "just too short," etc. The blindfolded person uses this information to guide the next three tries.

WHAT? A SAMPLER OF THEMATIC UNITS

ACTIVITY FOUR:
EIGHT FORCED CHOICES

Objective: to make forced choices and to evaluate and discuss them with the class

Materials: prepared worksheet for each student
pencils

Procedure: Prepare a sheet for each child including the eight choices as well as the feelings grid. Such a page is included in this activity for you to reproduce if you choose.

A possible way of introducing the activity would be to say, "Today we're going to look at some situations. I want you to force yourself to make a decision as to how strong or weak your feelings are towards these incidents." Explain the feelings grid, on which the students are to rank the eight choices according to how strongly they feel about them. Number one will be the example they feel strongest about (pro or con) and number eight will be the one they care about least. Suggestion: Try this exercise on yourself first!

After the students have completed the ranking, you could choose two possible means of discussion. First, you could have the students choose partners. They would then be instructed to share with each other the situation they have the strongest feelings about and the ones they care about least. Tell them to explain to each other *why* they feel this way.

A second possibility for discussion would be to call on individuals who share their strongest and weakest feelings and ask them to explain their reasons to the rest of the class. Of course, you won't want to force a student to share feelings. Also, avoid discussion as to whose choices are right or wrong. There are no "right" answers in this activity.

After the discussion, you could have the children make "I learned" statements, describing what they learned or relearned about themselves from this activity. Then, those who care to, could share their statements with the rest of the group. You could also alternate or substitute the following for "I learned":

- I noticed that . . .
- I realized that . . .
- I relearned that . . .
- I was pleased that . . .
- I discovered that . . .
- I was surprised that . . .

Evaluation: completion of worksheet by each student

Additional Activities:

1. Conduct a brainstorming session on different aspects of cooperation/competition. For example:

- How many ways can you think of to make this class a happier, more enjoyable place to be?
- Think of some ways in which we can cut down on the arguments during our playground games.
- Think of as many ways as you can to react when someone begins calling you names—instead of calling that person names back or starting a fight with that person.
- Think of as many ways as you can of helping a teammate who displays a bad temper whenever losing a game.

Remember during brainstorming that quantity is encouraged over quality and that no evaluation of the ideas should be allowed during the "thinking-up" session. This can inhibit a free flow of ideas.

2. Conduct a public interview using different questions concerning cooperation/competition. Ask for volunteers who are willing to be interviewed about their feelings or beliefs. Questions must be answered honestly by the student, but the student is also free to pass on a question if he or she does not wish to answer it. A time limit can be placed on the interview, or the student can end the interview at any time by saying, "Thank you for the interview." Just a few examples of possible questions that might be asked are:

- Did you ever cheat on a test? Why?
- Who is your best friend?
- What do you like about your best friend? What do you dislike?
- Do you compete in sports? If so, which ones?
- How do you feel about people who cheat just to get a better grade?
- Do you ever feel left out in this class? When?
- How do you feel about being in this class?
- Are you ever afraid in this class? If so, what about?
- What is your idea of a "perfect teammate"?
- Do you ever get angry about losing a game? What makes you most angry?

Eight Forced Choices

Worksheet

1. How do you feel about a classmate who fools around when you're supposed to be working together to complete a group project?
2. How do you feel about a person who pouts if he does not get his own way in a group?
3. How do you feel about a person who won't share or loan his belongings?
4. How do you feel about an opponent in a team game who is constantly calling the other side names?
5. How do you feel about a classmate who gets higher grades than you, but who you've witnessed cheating several times?
6. How would you feel if after your team lost a game, one of your teammates walked up to the first opponent he met and socked him?
7. How do you feel about a person who thinks *he* is the only one who can do the work the "right way" in a group?
8. How do you feel about a classmate who always has to be first or "tops" in everything?

FEELINGS

VERY STRONG	STRONG	MILD	LITTLE FEELING
1	3	5	7
2	4	6	8

ACTIVITY FIVE:
COOPERATION SQUARES GAME

Objective: to cooperate within small groups to solve puzzles

Materials: five sets of envelopes, each containing puzzle pieces as described under Procedure

Procedure: Before class, prepare a set of squares and an instruction sheet for each group of five students. A set consists of five envelopes containing pieces of stiff paper cut into patterns that will form five 6" × 6" squares as shown in the diagram provided for this activity. Several individual combinations will be possible, but only one total combination.

Cut each square into the parts a–j and lightly pencil in the letters. Then mark the envelopes A–E and place the pieces in them in this way: Envelope A, pieces i,h,e; B, pieces a,a,a,c; C, pieces a,j; D, pieces d,f; and E, pieces g,b,f,c.

In class, divide the students into groups of five (extra people can be used as observers of cooperative behavior in the groups). Each group should be given a set of envelopes and an instruction sheet. The envelopes are not to be opened until signaled to do so.

Begin the exercise by asking what cooperation means. List on the board the behaviors required in cooperation that are mentioned by the children. Describe the activity as a puzzle that requires cooperation. Read the instructions together. They are as follows:

1. Each person should have an envelope containing pieces for forming squares.
2. At the signal, the task of the group is to form five squares of equal size. The work is not completed until everyone has a perfect square, all the squares being of equal size.
3. Members *may not* speak to each other.
4. No member may ask for a card or in any way signal that he or she wants one.
5. Members *may* give cards to others.

When directions have been given, give the signal to begin. Wait until all or most of the groups have finished before calling time. A follow-up discussion might include questions such as these:

1. How did you feel when someone held a piece and did not see the solution?
2. What was your reaction when someone finished the square and then sat back without seeing whether his or her solution prevented others from solving the problem?

WHAT? A SAMPLER OF THEMATIC UNITS

3. What were your feelings if you finished your square and then began to realize you would have to break it up and give away a piece?
4. How did you feel about the person who was slow at seeing the solution?
5. If you were that person, how did you feel?
6. Did you feel as if the members of your group were thinking of others during the activity?
7. Did you feel as if your group helped or hindered individuals solving the puzzle?
8. Does this game relate to the way our class works from day to day? How?

Evaluation: successful completion of the puzzles by each group, with the active participation of all group members

Additional Activities:

1. As a follow-up, try this activity which requires cooperative effort. Show a picture which has the potential of eliciting many different stories from the children. Have each child write his story about the picture. Then divide the class into groups of four or five. Have the groups then try to agree on the best story about the picture. It might be interesting to appoint an observer for each group to report on cooperative or uncooperative behavior within the group. Each group would end by sharing its story with the rest of the class.
2. Another way of doing the same activity is to have the group members together write *one* joint story for the group. Instruct the groups that each person should have a contribution to the story.

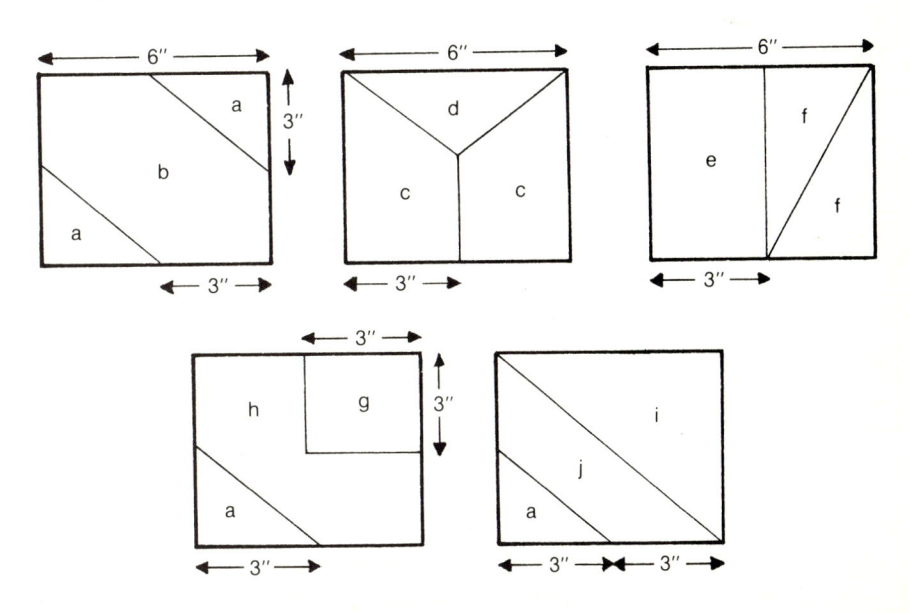

Adapted from *NEA JOURNAL*, October, 1969.

ACTIVITY SIX:
THE BEAN JAR PROBLEM

Objective: to cooperate within small groups to complete an assigned task

Materials: jars containing identical numbers of beans (one jar for each group set up)

paper and pencils

Procedure: Divide the class into random groups of four or five each. Give the groups identical jars, containing an identical number of beans. The jars should have been previously filled. Instruct the students that they are to invent as many ways as possible of estimating the number of beans in the jar (without opening it). They will be selecting only one way of making the estimate.

Ask each group to name a recorder to compile a list of ways to solve the problem, as suggested by the group members. Encourage groups to record all suggestions without evaluating them. An alternate way is to have each individual write down as many ways as he or she can think of to solve the problem and then come together to compile a joint list with the other members of the group. In any case, allow ten to fifteen minutes for this brainstorming period.

Ask each group to select the method it wants to use and then estimate the number of beans in its jar. The jars of beans may be handled but not opened. Allow about ten minutes for this part of the activity. When the time is up, tabulate on the board the number of inventions in each group and each group's estimate. Then give the actual number of beans.

Bring out in follow-up questioning how and if the groups cooperated and if this helped in getting a closer estimate. Elicit this and other information by asking some or all of the following questions:

1. Did ways of estimating come easily in the groups?
2. What happened in the group that helped or prevented cooperation?
3. Did everyone feel that his or her way of estimating was heard and accepted?
4. How did the groups decide what method to use?
5. Did anyone in the group dominate the decision making or argue that his or her invention was the "best way"? How did other members of the group react to this?
6. Did the groups arrive at more accurate estimates as they worked on the problem together?
7. Did the groups reject a more accurate estimate than the one they chose? If so, why?

WHAT? A SAMPLER OF THEMATIC UNITS **165**

        8. Do you think you could have come up with just as accurate or a better estimate working by yourself rather than with others?

Evaluation: completion, recording, and reporting of estimated counts

Additional Activity: Pretend your class is a group of people lost in a big, dark forest. First, have your students write down on a paper any ways they can think of that might help their group to know where it is and find its way out. Then have them get together as a group to suggest ideas and share plans. When the time period is up (about fifteen minutes) and each group is declared "safe" and "out," see how many ideas were suggested by each group that were not on individual papers.

Adapted from Today's Education, October, 1970.

ACTIVITY SEVEN: "WIN AS MUCH MONEY AS POSSIBLE"*

Objective: to play a group game and evaluate the results of that game

Materials: directions and score sheets

Procedure: Divide your class into groups of eight and position them in circles in chairs, on the floor, or in desks. Extra people can be used as scorekeepers, judges, or timekeepers. Within each group there should be four sets of partners. Each group operates independently of each other group. There is no cooperation between the separate groups.

    Explain to the children that they are going to play a game called "Win as Much Money as Possible." Pass out the score sheets for the game, one to each set of partners. The groups can either study the direction sheet to figure out how to play, or you can read through the sheet together. However directions are presented, be sure to mention the title of the game out loud. However, do not tell the partners whether they are to compete with each other in the group or to cooperate; they are left to assume which is correct. In most games, they will assume they are to compete, but in this game, they will only score successfully if they cooperate with their group members.

    After directions are clear, begin playing the game. Each set of partners should fill in the score sheet as the game progresses. You should conduct each round, keep time, inform the groups when they can consult and when choices

*Adapted from "Score as Much as Possible" in *Teaching Human Beings: 101 Subversive Activities for the Classroom* by Jeffrey Schrank (Boston: Beacon Press, 1972), pp. 39–42.

must be made, and make sure that everyone is following the rules. As an added factor of interest, you can pass out play money to the people who have won it during the rounds if you wish.

After round ten, each group of eight should figure out its total score. Here is the catch! The title of the game refers to the group as a whole and not to partners. The idea of the game is for the *group* to win as much money as possible. If all four sets of partners chose to be Stars for each round, the group total would be $100, plus. The group's success is judged by how close they come to a perfect game of plus $100.

After final scoring, discuss the groups' feelings and reactions to and during the game. Ask questions such as the following:

1. How could your group have achieved a higher score?
2. In what way was cooperation important to earn money?
3. Why didn't your group choose to be Stars each time?
4. How did you feel when you saw a set of partners in your group accumulating money—at *your* expense?
5. Why do we usually take for granted that we are expected to "beat" the other guy?
6. How might our day-to-day life be different if people did not always try to do better or win more than other people?
7. How well did you feel your group cooperated?

Evaluation: participation of each student in the game, teacher observation and evaluation of game scores as measures of competition or cooperation

Additional Activities:

1. This same activity can be done on a smaller scale, as a demonstration lesson to the class. Be prepared to lose a few pennies in the process! Ask for two volunteers who have some spare change with them, and who are willing to make a little more. Explain that you have six nickels that you will auction to them one at a time, the highest bidder getting the nickel. Allow no advice from the rest of the class. The two volunteers should alternate each time in making the first bid. Keep track of each final bid for accounting purposes. Discuss after the auctioning of the eighth nickel. Point out to the two volunteers that if they had cooperated, they could have received 16¢ each, purchasing four nickels for 4¢ if the first volunteer to bid each time bid one cent and the other refused to bid.
2. Have the children try to invent a game that would still be fun but would be based on cooperation instead of competition.

WHAT? A SAMPLER OF THEMATIC UNITS

Directions:
1. You will be playing ten different rounds in this game. The length of time each round will take is shown on your score sheet. During this time you and your partner will choose whether to be Stars or Heroes. *Both* of you, as a set, can only choose *one*.
2. The money earned in each round depends on the choices made by your partner and you plus the other three sets of partners in your group. Scoring will be according to the following:

DIAGRAM

4 Heroes	Lose 1 dollar each
3 Heroes 1 Star	Win 1 dollar each Lose 3 dollars
2 Heroes 2 Stars	Win 2 dollars each Lose 2 dollars each
1 Hero 3 Stars	Win 3 dollars Lose 1 dollar each
4 Stars	Win 1 dollar each

3. You can talk with your partner *once* each round in order to make a joint decision whether to be Stars or Heroes.
4. Before rounds 5, 8, and 10, you will be able to talk with the other members of the group, as to what choices to make together.
5. Secret signals are *not* allowed at any time during the gaming. Decisions are made *only* between you and your partner, except before rounds 5, 8, and 10.

Score Sheet

"WIN AS MUCH MONEY AS POSSIBLE"

ROUND	TIME	TALK WITH	CHOICE (HEROES/ STARS)	DOLLARS WON	DOLLARS LOST	
1	1 min.	partner				
2	30 sec.	partner				
3	30 sec.	partner				
4	30 sec.	partner				
5	2 min.	group				*BONUS ROUND DOUBLE SCORE
5	30 sec.	partner				
6	30 sec.	partner				
7	30 sec.	partner				
8	3 min.	group				*BONUS ROUND TRIPLE SCORE
8	30 sec.	partner				
9	30 sec.	partner				
10	3 min.	group				*BONUS ROUND MULTIPLY SCORE BY 5
10	30 sec.	partner				

Total

ACTIVITY EIGHT: GRADES SURVEY

Objective: to conduct a survey concerning grades and how students feel about them

Materials: survey sheets for every student
pencils

Procedure: Pass out copies of the survey sheet. Administer the questionnaire to your class, with each pupil writing responses to the questions, or divide the class into pairs so that one member interviews the other and then the interviewer is interviewed.

Tabulate the results on the board or a large piece of butcher paper. You might choose to pick out one question at a time to tabulate and analyze, or make a summary chart like the following:

FEELINGS ON GRADES	YES BOYS	YES GIRLS	TOTAL	NO BOYS	NO GIRLS	TOTAL
Important to them						
Wants the best grades						
Tries for better grades than friends						
Becomes jealous						
Compares grades						
Wouldn't cheat						
Knows people who cheat						

Analyze the data, having the children make observations and inferences about the charted data. You could have them predict how other intermediate grade children would respond to the same questionnaire. Then, if you wish, you could have your children interview pupils in other classrooms, taking just a sampling of three or four students from each class. Appoint interview teams of two: one person in each pair can read the questions while the other writes down the answers. When finished, tabulate and analyze the data as before. Discuss.

You might also have the children interview their junior high and high school brothers and sisters or neighbors for an interesting comparison of feelings on the subject.

Evaluation: successful completion of survey sheet by each student

Additional Activities:
1. Have the children discuss the results of their survey with their parents. Have feelings on this subject changed since their parents went to school?

2. Hold a debate—pro and con—on this topic: Should grades be abolished? The participants could use the results of their survey as evidence for their arguments.

3. Divide the class into committees. Have them discuss the problems of children who are uncomfortable and unhappy in a grading system that compares them to their peers. Have the children recommend what could be done to remedy this problem in terms of preventing children from suffering the unhappiness of competing with others.

How Do You Feel About Grades?

Survey Sheet

We are trying to find out how students of different ages feel about grades. Your name will not be used in our report, and we are not trying to decide what is good or bad. We are just trying to get a scientific record.

1. I am a ____boy____girl.

2. I am in____grade.

3. Good grades are important to me.

    ____yes____no

4. I would like the best grades in my class.

    ____yes____no

5. I always try to get better grades than my friends.

    ____yes____no

6. When I receive a lower grade than my best friend, I become jealous.

    ____yes____no

7. My classmates and I always compare grades on assignments and report cards.

    ____yes____no

8. I would rather receive a lower grade than cheat to get a higher one.

    ____yes____no

9. I know people who cheat to get a better grade on a test or an assignment.

    ____yes____no

10. How do you feel about a classmate who "brags" whenever he receives a better grade than you? Circle where your feelings would fall.

1	2	3	4	5	6
Doesn't bother me					Can't stand it

ACTIVITY NINE: SPORTS SURVEY

Objective: to conduct a survey concerning attitudes towards sports and games

Materials: survey sheets for every student

extra copies for administration of survey to other classrooms

Procedure: Pass out a copy of the provided survey sheet to each student. Once students have completed it, your class can, with your help, collect, tabulate, and analyze data as suggested in the survey, "How Do You and Your Classmates Get Along?" You may also wish to have your class interview students in other classrooms and compare that data with their own class's data.

Evaluation: successful completion of survey sheet and tabulation of results

Additional Activities:
1. Have the children create team cheers that emphasize playing the best you can.
2. Role play alternate ways of reacting to common argumentative game situations.
3. Play a favorite game without keeping score. At the completion of the game, take a poll of feelings about playing a game this way. Discuss likes and dislikes.
4. Select a "Player of the Week," chosen by classmates for demonstrating good sportsmanship and playing one's best in the class's daily games.

ACTIVITY TEN: BEHAVIOR SPECIMEN: "THE POSTER CONTEST"

Objective: to make observations concerning competitive behavior

Materials: copies of the story, "The Poster Contest," and the observation guide for every student

Procedure: The purpose of this behavior specimen is to provide an opportunity for the children to make observations of a situation involving competitive behavior. This exercise gives them an opportunity to act as social scientists in that they will be making a distinction between descriptions of behavior and inferences

Participating in Games & Sports

Survey Sheet

We are trying to find out more about how kids in this class and other classes feel about participating in games and sports. We'd like to ask you several questions about your feelings on the subject. Your name will not be used and we are not trying to decide what is right or wrong. We are trying to get a scientific record.

1. I am a ____boy____girl.
2. I am in ____grade.
3. I like to participate in team games.

    ____yes____no

4. It is important for me to be a better player than someone else on the team.

    ____yes____no

5. I am jealous of players who are better than I.

    ____yes____no

6. My best friend is a better player in most games than I am.

    ____yes____no

7. Winning a game is the most important part of playing.

    ____yes____no

8. When I am on the losing side of a game, I always become angry.

    ____yes____no

9. I would quit a team if it was losing most of its games.

    ____yes____no

10. The games in which I participate often end with everyone arguing.

    ____yes____no

about behavior. Their observations should describe the facts and are only *guesses* as to why the people behaved as they did.

To begin, pass out copies of the story and the observation guide. Explain to the children that today they will be acting as social scientists as they observe the behavior of two individuals. Explain the differences between descriptions and inferences. Have the children read the story silently to themselves or read it aloud together.

Once the story has been read, conduct a class discussion before having students fill in the observation guide. Ask for a description of what happened. Then ask students for inferences about David's behavior. At this point, have students individually complete the observation guide and share their answers in a group discussion.

In addition to discussing items in the observation guide, you may wish to carry on a follow-up discussion with a values focus. You may wish to use questions such as the following:

1. Do you wish the story had ended differently? Why?
2. Do you think anyone in the story should have behaved differently? Why and how?
3. Do you agree with this value judgement: "It was bad of David to tip the paint over on Joey's paper"? Why?

Evaluation: completion of observation guide, participation in class discussion

Additional Activities:

1. Role play the behavior specimen. Give only the people who are playing parts (David, Joey, and members of their class) the story. The rest of the class act as observers of the behavior specimen. Follow up the roleplaying with the observation guide and discussion.
2. Have the children make up their own behavior specimens. Let the rest of the class write down observations of, and inferences about, the behavior described.

THE POSTER CONTEST

Joey and David are classmates. They have been together in the same class since second grade. Even so, they are not close friends. Often they argue over who is smarter, who can run faster, or who can throw farther. This year they both have been working very hard in Mr. Peterson's fifth grade class on the Junior Fire Prevention program. Both are trying to become chief of the school's fire prevention program. A lot of children in the class think Joey should become chief since he has worked more carefully and done more outside work to earn the required points.

Both boys are presently involved in creating fire prevention posters for the contest that is sponsored by the city's fire department. David has worked hard on his poster, but Joey has been meticulous in completing the details on his, spending most of his free time at school as well as at home to create a poster which is perfect in every way. On the afternoon before the deadline, Mr. Peterson gave the children who were making posters an hour to work. Joey was putting finishing touches on his poster with tempera paint, at the table in the back of the room. David, who was working on his poster at his seat, rose to sharpen his pencil in the back of the room, and as he passed the table at which Joey was seated, jarred the table, causing Joey's container of paint to spill over most of his poster, ruining it.

Observation Guide

A. Write a sentence that describes David's behavior at the end of the behavior specimen. _____

_____

B. Check each item below that correctly describes what you *observed* in the story you just read.
   _____ 1. Joey and David are in Mr. Peterson's class.
   _____ 2. Joey and David are best friends.
   _____ 3. Joey and David argue quite a bit.
   _____ 4. Both boys want to become chief of the school's fire prevention program.
   _____ 5. A lot of the children think David should become chief because he has done more work.
   _____ 6. Both boys are writing stories for the fire department contest.
   _____ 7. David and Joey are making posters for the fire department contest.
   _____ 8. David tore Joey's poster.
   _____ 9. David jarred the table at which Joey was sitting, causing paint to spill over most of Joey's poster.

C. Check each item below that is an inference that you could draw from your observations.
   _____ 1. David felt angry when a lot of the children in the class thought Joey should become chief.
   _____ 2. David didn't care if a lot of the children in class wanted Joey to become chief.
   _____ 3. Joey was happy that many of the children thought he should become chief.
   _____ 4. Joey didn't care if David became chief instead of him.
   _____ 5. David was jealous when he saw how carefully Joey was working on his poster and heard about how much time he had spent on it.
   _____ 6. It was an accident that David caused paint to ruin Joey's poster.
   _____ 7. David jarred the table on purpose, in order that the paint would spill on Joey's poster.

ENVIRONMENTS

Environments: Land use and climatic influences on life styles along with map reading and map making are included in this theme. Logical inferences are encouraged by examining actual maps of the same area several years apart. Implications are discussed.

CURRENT CONCERNS
energy
pollution
overpopulation

BASIC NEEDS
clothing
food
shelter

INTERACTION
man with his natural and created surroundings

ENVIRONMENTS

AVAILABILITY OF GOODS AND SERVICES
effects of climate
natural resources

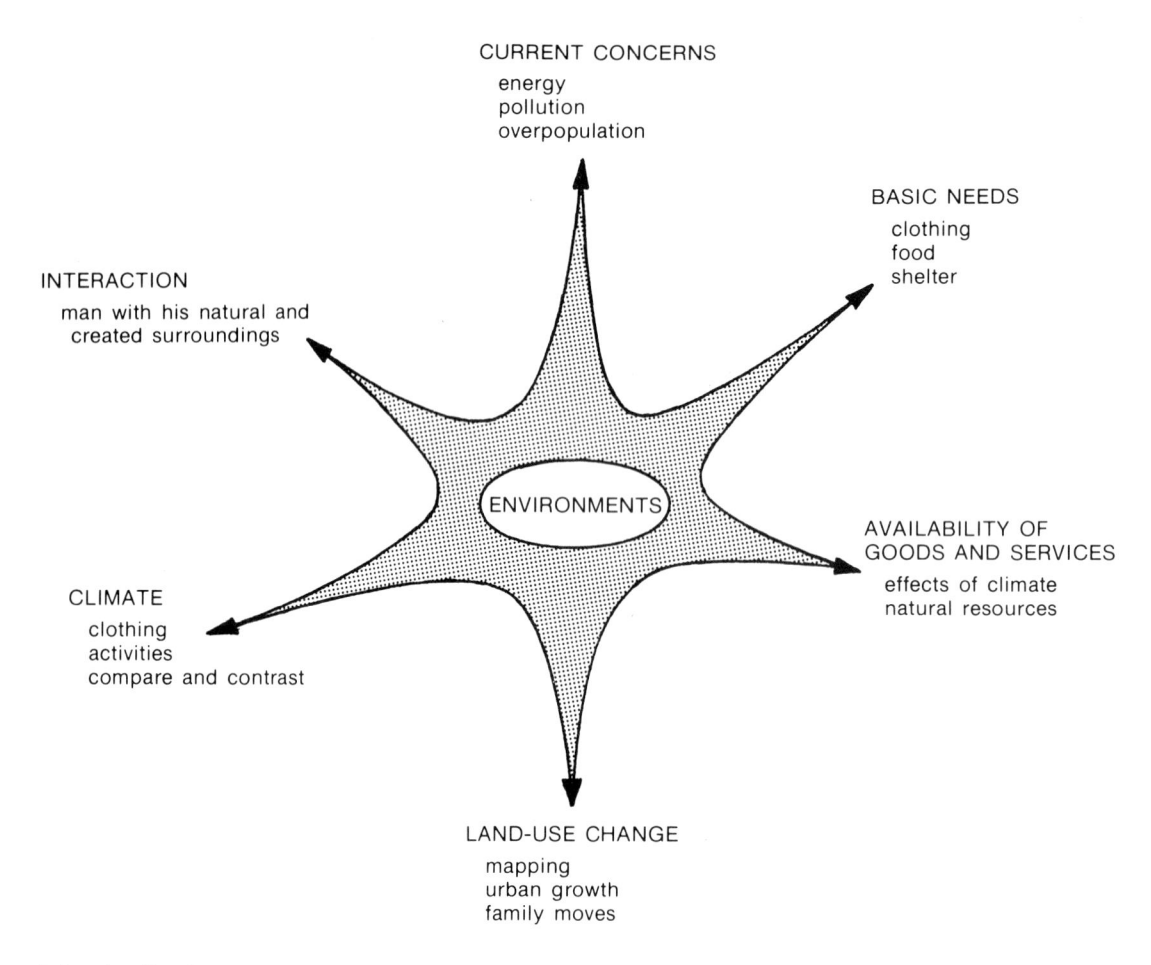

CLIMATE
clothing
activities
compare and contrast

LAND-USE CHANGE
mapping
urban growth
family moves

Introduction*

Since time began, the human race has been preoccupied with adaptation to its environment. In the early years this struggle was much less complex than it is today. The search for food, clothing, and shelter occupied most of one's time and effort. Today the interaction between an individual and the environment involves many other variables. For example, the issues of availability of energy, pollution, and world overpopulation reflect the complexity of the continuing struggle for adaptation to the environment.

This theme is of necessity restricted to a much smaller scale. It deals with the issue of children adapting to their environment. They are placed in situations designed to emphasize the impact that various aspects of the environment (climate, land use, availability of goods and services) have upon their daily lives. Activities stress group participation as well as individual interactions. This theme enables children to compare and reflect on the differences and similarities between the old and the new. Valuable insights into human nature can result from such reflection.

*Thanks to Ms. Rene Macomber, St. Paul Public Schools.

Unit Objectives:

The students will:

1. develop an awareness of the effects of climate on human life.
2. compare and contrast climates and make inferences about life in those climates.
3. recognize land-use changes and factors which influence them.
4. improve skills in reading and drawing maps.
5. learn how to construct, conduct, and evaluate the results of surveys.

Appropriate Grade Levels:

Three to Six (many activities are adaptable for lower grades as well)

ACTIVITY ONE: CLIMATE 1

Objective: to rank items on a worksheet and participate in a decision-making activity

Materials: picture worksheet for each child, or written worksheet for each child
pencils

Procedure: Read the following hypothetical situation to the class:

After living in Minnesota for seven years, your family has moved to California. Mark, a friend who now lives next door, is going to Minnesota to visit his grandfather and grandmother. This will be his first visit and he is going during wintertime. Mark has asked you and your brothers and sisters what he should take with him. (Note: Other states of similar climates can be substituted for those used in order to make the situation more directly related to your students' experiences.)

After reading the above story, pass out the worksheet with the seasonal items, either pictured or named, to each child. Ask each child to number the items in the order he would recommend them to Mark, a 1 by the first choice, a 2 by the second choice, and so on. If someone in the class is new to your environment, the sheet can be marked based on what he or she thinks the weather might be like during the winter.

After everyone has marked a list, put the children together in "family" groups of four or five. Then tell the class, "Mark has asked you and your brothers and sisters to recommend some clothes and toys to take with him. Now you must decide as a group what things you would suggest to him. You should have just one list when you are finished."

Have each group choose a recorder or appoint one yourself. Give each recorder an additional worksheet. Tell the children that they should not change the numbers on their own sheet even if the group list is not the same as theirs. Give the groups as much time as you feel is necessary for completion of this task.

Ask each recorder to read, in order, the list the group decided on. Ask the children, when the lists are shared, how they knew which things might be useful to Mark. Finally, ask how the choices would be different if Mark were going to Minnesota in the summer.

Evaluation: completion of ranking worksheet individually, and active participation in group rankings and discussions

ACTIVITY 1: WORKSHEET

Number the following toys and clothes in the order you would recommend them to Mark. Put a 1 by your first choice, a 2 by your second choice, and so on.

_____ a baseball glove	_____ a baseball
_____ an umbrella	_____ a beach towel
_____ earmuffs	_____ a tennis racket
_____ a baseball cap	_____ boots
_____ skis	_____ a fur-lined jacket
_____ baseball bat	_____ a hockey stick
_____ sunglasses	_____ a bathing suit
_____ mittens	_____ ice skates

WHAT? A SAMPLER OF THEMATIC UNITS

ACTIVITY 1:
WORKSHEET

Number the following toys and clothes in the order you would recommend them to Mark. Put a 1 by your first choice, a 2 by your second choice, and so on.

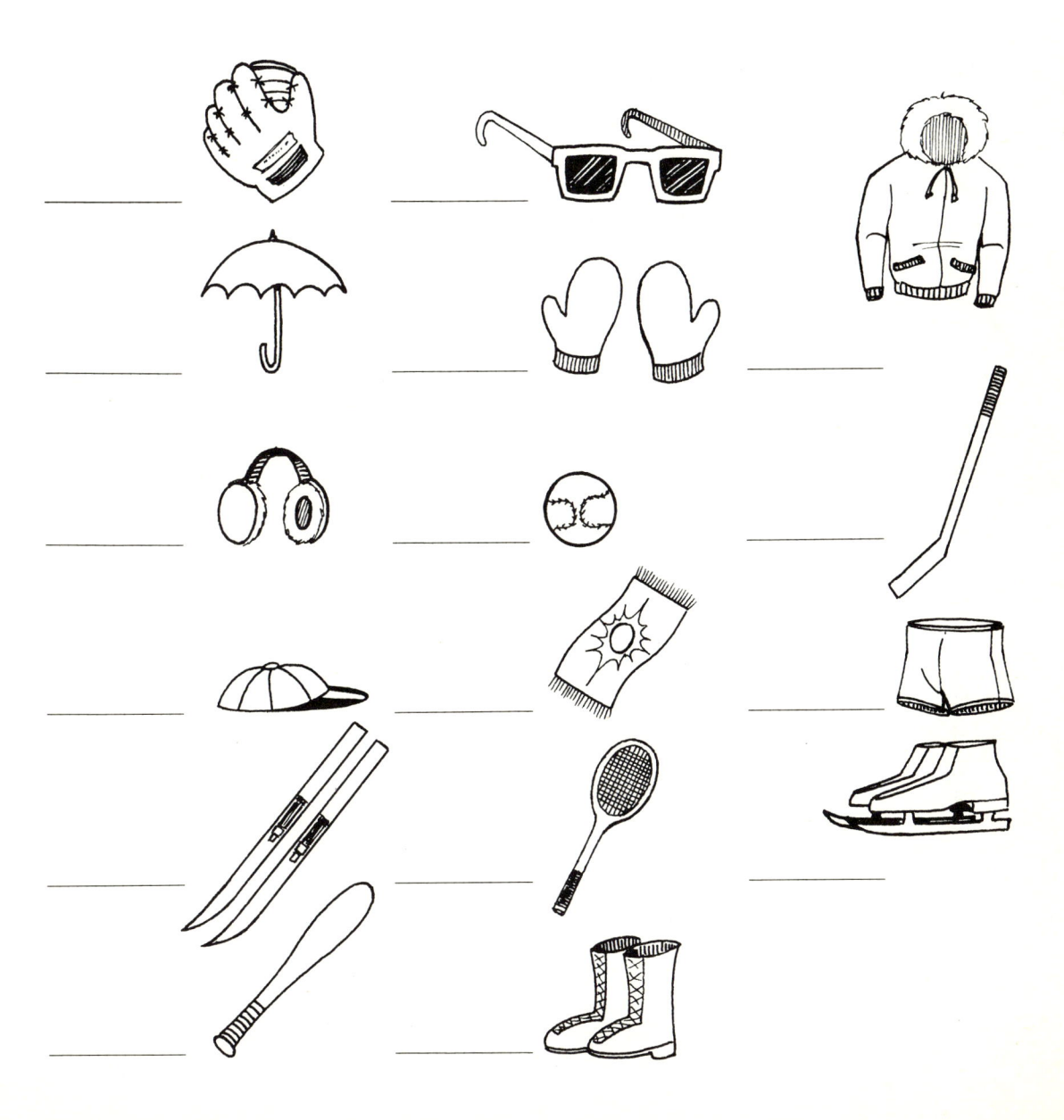

ACTIVITY TWO: CLIMATE 2

Objective: to conduct a survey of an adult and a teenager, to tally and summarize the results and hypothesize about how the results might change or vary

Materials: three survey sheets for each student
pencils

Procedure: Ask the class to recall some of the items on the sheet from Activity One. Ask if there are items which they use most in the summer or winter, or if they use the same items throughout the year.

Then ask the class how they could find out what activities other people like to do in the summer and winter or throughout the year if there is little seasonal change. After discussing how they might keep a record of their answers, suggest that each child survey two other people, if possible one teenager and one adult. Each of those surveyed should record the choices on a survey sheet. You may choose to use the survey sheet which follows or, if the items would be different due to the climate, have the children make up their own survey sheet. The survey should be conducted after school so that the results can be discussed prior to the next lesson, and each child in the class should also fill out a survey sheet.

Discuss the results of the survey prior to Activity Three. To begin the discussion, draw a large survey sheet on the board where the children can record their responses. The results can be tallied either by having the children record their responses during free time or by asking each child to come up and mark responses at the start of the discussion.

Now discuss the results of the survey by asking:

1. What activity do most of the adults like to do in the summer? In the winter?
2. What activity do most teenagers like to do in the summer? In the winter?
3. What activity do most of the children like to do in the summer? In the winter?
4. How might these results change if more people were surveyed?

Evaluation: completion of survey as directed, and participation in group discussion of the survey results

ACTIVITY TWO: SURVEY WORKSHEET

Child _____ Teenager _____ Adult _____

In the summer the outdoor activity I like best is:

Swimming	_____	Baseball	_____
Biking	_____	Golfing	_____
Camping	_____	Tennis	_____
Gardening	_____	Fishing	_____
Sleeping	_____	Other	_____
Walking	_____		

In the winter the outdoor activity I like best is:

Skiing	_____	Ice fishing	_____
Skating	_____	Hockey	_____
Sledding	_____	Snowball fights	_____
Snowshoeing	_____	Playing in the snow	_____
Tobogganing	_____	Other	_____

Please check whether you are a child, teenager, or an adult. Then put a check by your favorite activity in the summer and in the winter.

ACTIVITY THREE: COMPARING CLIMATES

Objective: to make inferences about the climates of two cities and to compare and contrast these two climates

Materials:
"Yellow Pages" worksheets (City A and City B)
pencils
climate worksheet for each child
United States map for each child

Procedure: Ask the children, "How is your house or apartment adapted to the climate in which you live? Would there be a difference if your home were located in another climate?" Then ask, "What are some sports that depend upon a certain kind of climate? Are there some sports that can't be played where we live?"

After discussing these questions, pass out to each student a copy of the adapted "Yellow Pages" from Cities A and B. These can be worked on individually or in pairs. Then pass out a copy of the climate worksheet to each child. Ask the class to look through the "Yellow Pages" from City A. From the goods and services listed, they should mark on the worksheet the kinds of weather they think City A has and a word or picture that helped them decide. Then have the class look at City B's "Yellow Pages" and follow the same procedure used for City A.

When the climate worksheet has been completed, ask the class the following questions:

1. What goods and services did both cities have? Which ones did one city have that the other did not?
2. What inferences can you make about City A's climate? City B's?

Now pass out a copy of the United States map to each student. Ask students where City A and City B might be located. Have them give reasons for their answers. After all have had a chance to respond, point out the location of City A (Tucson, Arizona) and City B (Saint Paul, Minnesota). Finish by comparing students' answers with the correct information and discussing any differences or similarities between the two. You might wish to set up a chart or graph to analyze the various answers given by the class.

Evaluation: completion of the climate worksheet and participation in group discussions.

YELLOW PAGES FOR CITY A

Air Conditioning Equipment
JOE'S AIR CONDITIONERS HAS ALL BRANDS. 

Garden Stores
CACTUSLAND — WE SELL CACTUS AND PALM TREES.

Awnings
COOL-RAY AWNINGS KEEP YOUR HOME <u>COOL</u>!

Sporting Goods
SPEEDWAY SPORTS — WE SELL SPORTING GOODS FOR FISHING, GOLF, BASEBALL & TENNIS.

Camping Equipment
THE BACKPACKER — WE SELL TENTS, SLEEPING BAGS, AND BACKPACKS.

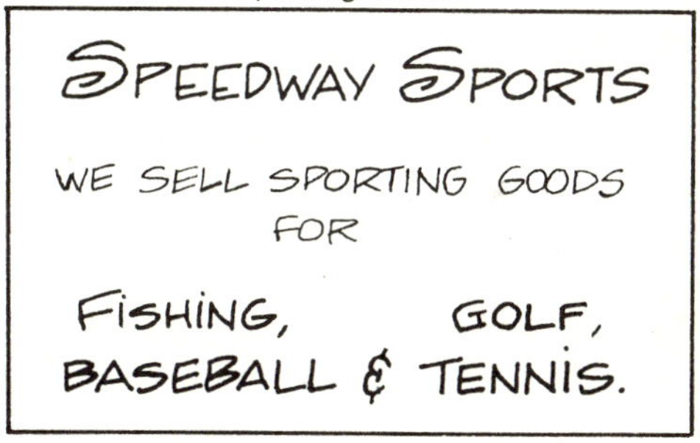

Swimming Pools
WILSON POOLS — WE BUILD POOLS ALL YEAR LONG!

Furnaces
DAY & NIGHT FURNACES — WE'VE SOLD FURNACES FOR **50** YEARS.

Garden and Lawn Sprinklers
LATHAM SPRINKLERS — WE INSTALL AUTOMATIC OR MANUAL SYSTEMS.

YELLOW PAGES FOR CITY B

Air Conditioning Equipment

WE SELL AIR CONDITIONERS FOR A ROOM OR A WHOLE HOUSE.

Awnings

AWNINGS, INC.

Camping Equipment

MR. OUTDOORS

SLEEPING BAGS
RAINWEAR
TENTS

Furnaces

ACE HEATING COMPANY

LET US HELP YOU KEEP YOUR HOUSE WARM THIS WINTER!

Garden Stores

WE SELL EVERYTHING FOR YOUR YARD!

Skating Equipment

SILVER SKATE SHOP

WE SELL NEW AND USED SKATES.

Snow Removal Services

PLOW·YOU·OUT

DRIVEWAYS AND PARKING LOTS CLEARED.

Snow Vehicles

SNOW KING

WE HAVE 6 KINDS OF SNOWMOBILES.

Sporting Goods

MIKE'S SPORTING GOODS

WE HAVE CLOTHES FOR HOCKEY, SKIING, GOLF, TENNIS AND BASEBALL.

Swimming Pools

POOL FUN

TOYS
PARTS

ACTIVITY THREE: CLIMATE WORKSHEET

Look at the goods and services for City A. Put a check by each of the kinds of weather you think that city might have. On the line, put the word or picture that helped you decide. Then do the same for City B.

CITY A'S CLIMATE   CITY B'S CLIMATE

Wet _____   Wet _____

Dry _____   Dry _____

Snowy _____   Snowy _____

Sunny _____   Sunny _____

Cloudy _____   Cloudy _____

Hot _____   Hot _____

Cold _____   Cold _____

Windy _____   Windy _____

ACTIVITY FOUR: LAND-USE CHANGE

Objective: to make inferences about land-use change after listening to a story and to hypothesize about environmental changes that may take place during the next fifty years.

Materials: the book *The Little House* by Virginia Lee Burton

Procedure: Before reading the book, ask the class to list some of the things that are around them (desks, chairs, etc.). Then ask them to name items that would be around them if they went outdoors (trees, grass, or snow, etc.). Ask if anyone knows the word for what surrounds a person. Whether a student knows or you tell them, print the word *environment* on the board. Then tell the class that you are going to read a story about a little house. They should listen carefully for the different kinds of environments in which the little house was found.

Read the story, *The Little House*, to the class. As you read, try to show as many of the pictures as possible. After you have finished the story, ask these questions:

1. Which part of the little house's environment stayed the same for many years?
2. Which part of its environment changed?
3. What kinds of things did the city add as it grew larger?
4. Why do you think the city grew?
5. Did the changes happen over a short or a long period of time? How do you know?
6. Why do you think no one wanted to live in the little house once other buildings were all around it? Would you have lived in it?
7. Think about the city in this story. How do you think your community looked fifty years ago?

Then ask the children what their environment might be like fifty years from now. Which parts of their environment will probably be the same as now? Which parts could change? Continue the discussion as long as the children seem interested and involved.

Evaluation: active participation in class discussion

ACTIVITY FIVE:
MAPS AND LAND-USE CHANGE

Objective: to hypothesize about the meanings of map symbols and, after looking at two maps, to hypothesize about the ages and areas represented by each

Materials: chalkboard and chalk

copies for each child of two maps showing land-use change

Procedure: Remind the class that the story *The Little House* talked about land-use change. Tell them that geographers can study changes in the land by looking at photographs taken from an airplane. They can make a map of a photograph and then compare maps of the same area taken a few years apart.

Tell the children that they are now going to look at two maps that have been drawn from airplane photographs. Explain that geographers use symbols for the features in the photograph and put these symbols on their maps. Put these symbols on the chalkboard and ask the class what features these symbols might stand for. After students have given their ideas, give them the correct names. The symbols used should be those shown on the student map sheets which follow.

After the discussion and symbol identification, assign the next activity to be done independently or in small groups. Pass out copies of the earlier map and the map of the same area thirty years later. Ask the children to study the two maps and look for some of the symbols that were discussed earlier. The map key will help them. After the children have had sufficient time to study the maps, ask the following questions:

1. What are some of the things you found on the maps?
2. Could these maps be of the same area? Why or why not?
3. After the children have decided that they could be of the same area, tell them that in fact they are and ask, "Which map is older? How can you tell?"
4. What might have caused the changes that you see in the newer map?

This same activity could be done using an area in your community. Draw a map showing the area thirty years ago and another showing the same area today. Have the students discuss symbols and land-use change. Slides could be taken of some of the features and the students could match the slides with the symbols on the newer map.

Evaluation: participation in discussions with answers indicating an understanding of the symbols and concepts presented

190   WHAT? A SAMPLER OF THEMATIC UNITS

ACTIVITY FIVE,
MAP 1

Map Key:

railroad ++++++++   bridge)——(marsh 🌾

street ═══════   lake 🌊

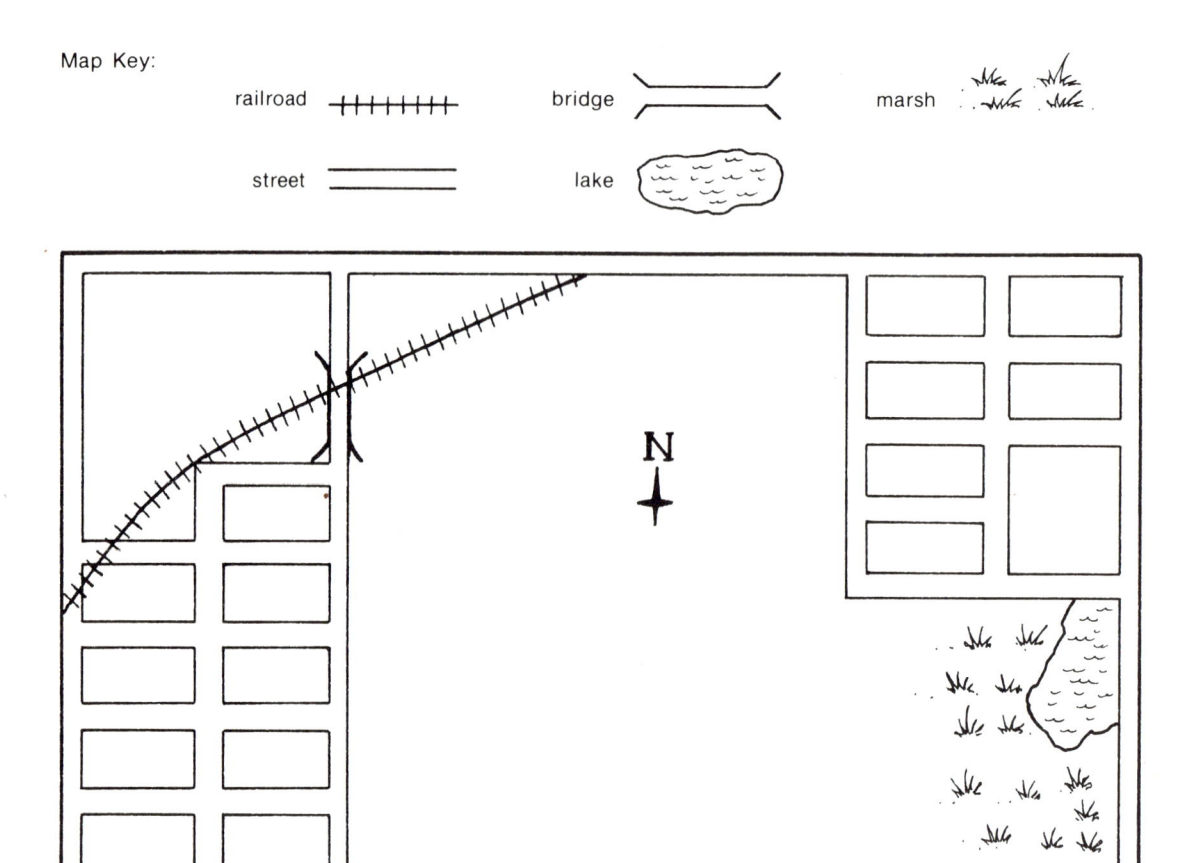

ACTIVITY FIVE, MAP 2

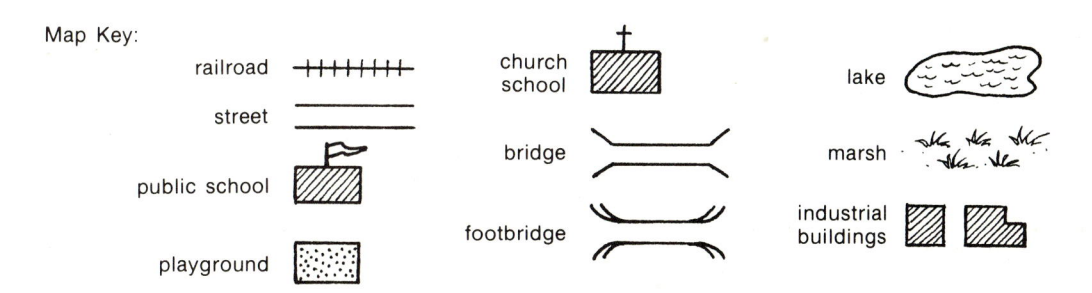

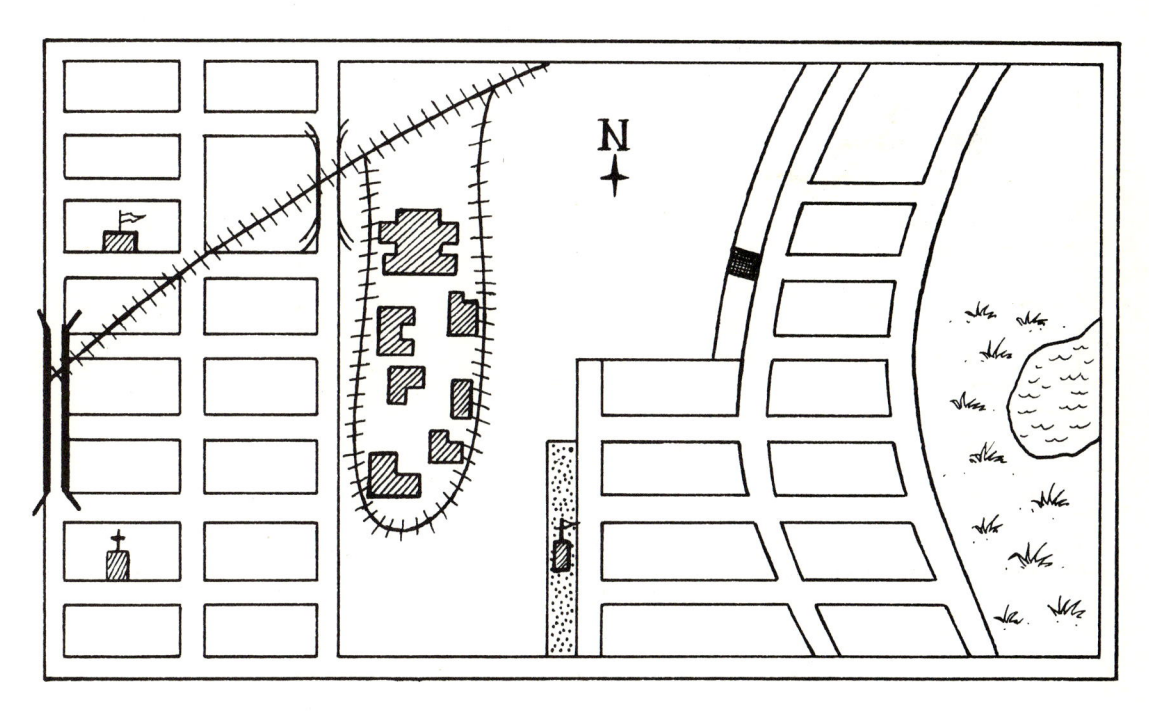

Map Key:

- railroad
- street
- public school
- playground
- church school
- bridge
- footbridge
- lake
- marsh
- industrial buildings

ACTIVITY SIX:
PLANNING LAND-USE

Objective: to complete a map of New City using the symbols presented in Activity Five and to compare their choices with a completed map.

Materials:
- map of New City for each student (page 193)
- completed map of New City as a transparency (page 194)
- pencils
- overhead projector

Procedure: Pass out a map of New City to each child. Tell them that this is a map of a city that is just being built, and that it is being built on farmland. Review the use of symbols and what these symbols stand for.

Now ask the children to fill in the rest of the map of New City, putting in houses, walking paths, churches, stores, and parks. Have them put their buildings, etc., wherever they think they should be located. Remind them to use the map key for their symbols. As the children are working on their maps, walk around and ask each child the reasons for his/her choices. If you are unable to talk to each child, try to see those you missed after the lesson has been completed.

After the children have finished their maps, show them a transparency of where things are actually located in New City. Ask how their choices were the same and how they were different. Ask the class what the advantages are of building a city on land where there are only a few houses. What might be some of the disadvantages? How many of them would like to live in New City?

Evaluation: completion of a New City map by each student

ACTIVITY SIX: STUDENT MAP

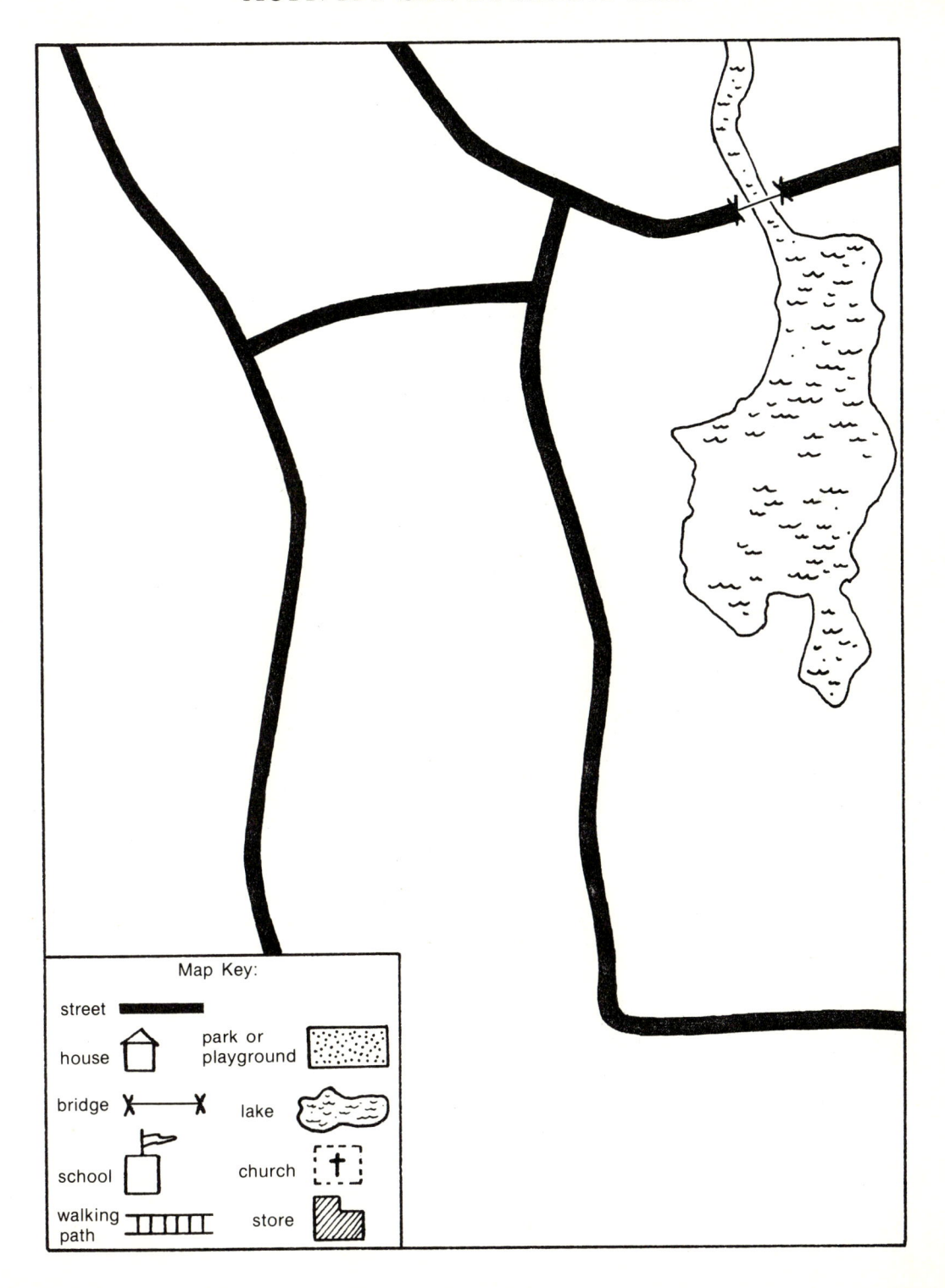

Map Key:
- street ━━━
- house ⌂
- park or playground ▓
- bridge ✕━━✕
- lake 〰️
- school 🚩
- church ✝
- walking path ⊞⊞⊞⊞
- store ▨

193

ACTIVITY SIX: TRANSPARENCY

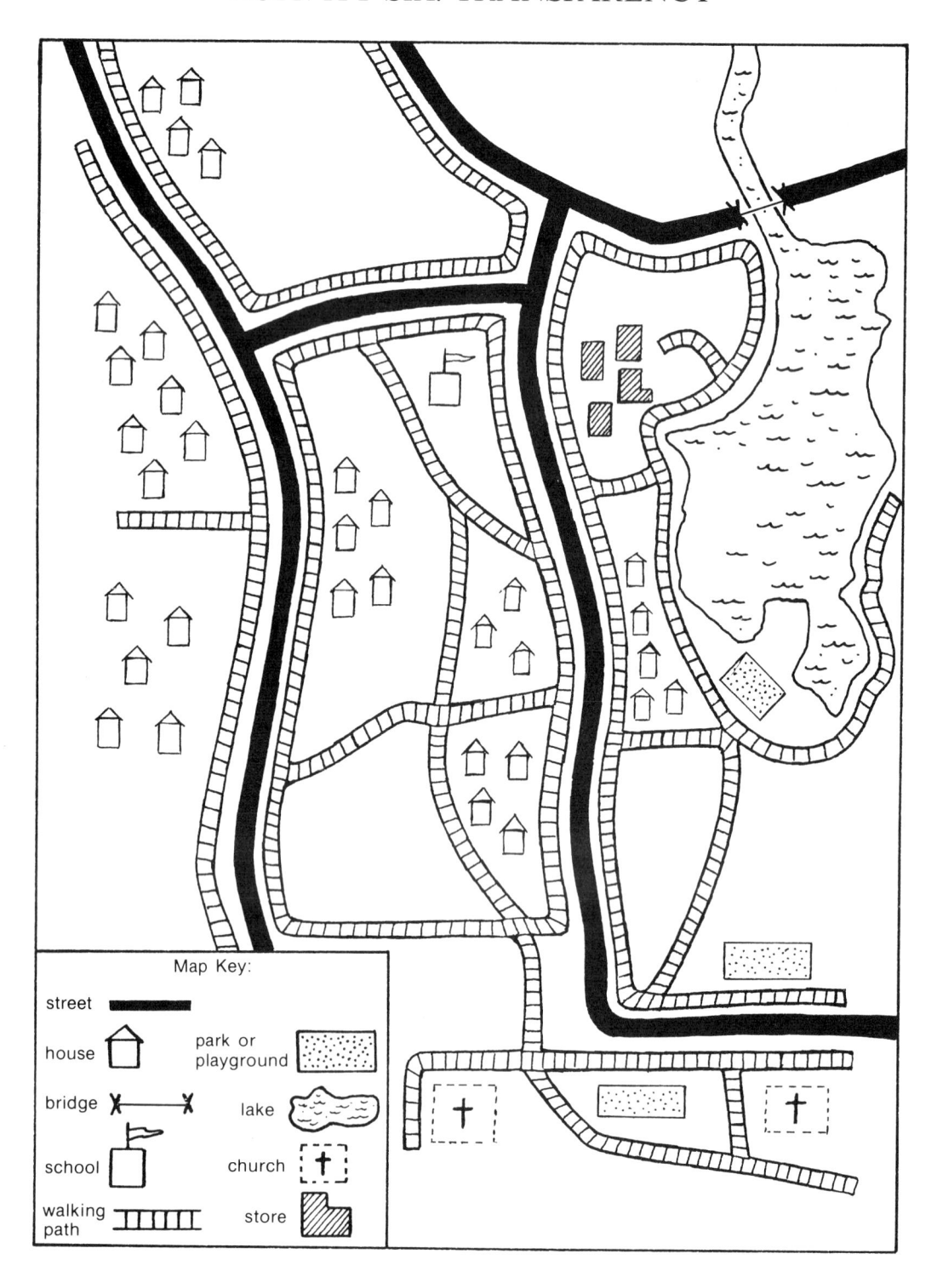

Map Key:
- street
- house
- bridge
- school
- walking path
- park or playground
- lake
- church
- store

WHAT? A SAMPLER OF THEMATIC UNITS

ACTIVITY SEVEN:
ROLE-PLAYING SKILLS

Objective: to participate in a role-playing situation concerning a family move decision

Materials: information sheet from New City for each student
role card for each family member (1 set of cards for each small group)

Procedure: Tell the students that in today's activity they are going to pretend to be someone else. The person they can choose to be is either a mother, father, sixteen-year-old brother, ten-year-old brother, or seven-year-old sister. After each child has chosen a "family role," place students in groups of five having one of each of the above-named members. The children should be seated so that it will be easy for them to communicate with the other members of their "family."

Tell the class, "Yesterday you learned a little bit about a city called New City. Today's lesson will also be about this city." Pass out information sheets to each member of each family, or have one child in each group read it aloud to the other members.

After the information sheet has been read, say, "Your family is thinking about moving out to New City from where you now live. Some of your family would like to move and others aren't sure. Here is the way the person you are pretending to be feels." Give each family member a role slip. Continue by saying, "Read your role sheet. Your family is going to discuss moving to New City and this sheet will help you in the discussion." Give the children plenty of time to read their sheets and ask any questions about their roles.

Ask one of the "parents" to start the discussion and then the others should join in, telling how they feel about moving to New City. Tell students that at the end of the discussion (ten minutes) they should, as a family, decide whether to move or stay where they live now. After the discussions, ask each father or mother what the family's decision is. If there is time, you can form a new set of families and have students role play different members of the family.

Evaluation: participation by each child in a role-playing group

ACTIVITY SEVEN: INFORMATION SHEET

COME TO NEW CITY!

THERE ARE PLACES TO WALK, FISH, SAIL, HORSEBACK RIDE, AND PLAY.

THERE ARE WALKING PATHS TO EVERY PLACE IN NEW CITY.

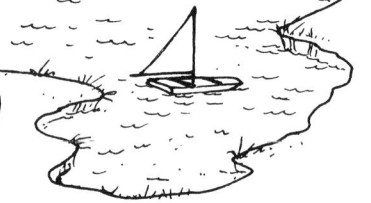

THE LAND HAS BEAUTIFUL HOUSES AND LAKES, WOODS, AND PARKS.

THERE ARE MANY KINDS OF HOUSES AT MANY DIFFERENT PRICES. THERE ARE HOUSES TO BUY AND HOUSES TO RENT.

CLOSE TO YOUR HOME WILL BE A PLACE TO SHOP.

THERE ARE LOTS OF JOBS AND THERE WILL BE MORE IN THE NEXT FEW YEARS.

ACTIVITY SEVEN: ROLE-PLAYING SLIPS

Cut the slips apart on the dotted lines and give one slip to each "family" member.

Mother- You like the neighborhood you live in now. Almost every morning, you take your children's grandmother shopping, to the doctor or out for a drive. In the afternoon you work at the school near your house. You have just heard about a good, full-time job nearby that you may be able to get.

Father- If you moved to New City, you are sure you could get a job in the Canning Company. Then it would take you only five minutes to drive to work and maybe you could walk. Now it takes you an hour to drive to work. You could fish in the lake at New City during your time off.

Older Brother- You are a junior in high school and have a lot of friends. You're not sure you would see them very often if you moved so far away. You like to go to movies and to bowl. The closest theaters and bowling alleys are in another town fifteen minutes away.

Younger Brother- You are in fifth grade and like to be outdoors all the time. Every weekend you go fishing with a friend or with your father. You'd like to move to New City because you could go horseback riding.

Sister- You are in third grade. You have a very good friend who lives next door to you. But, you like to be outdoors after school. When you drove to New City, you saw lots of children who looked your age. You also saw some houses that you'd like to live in.

ACTIVITY EIGHT:
LAND-USE CHANGE

Objective: to describe land-use around your school and to construct a map showing suggested land-use changes

Materials: drawing paper

crayons and pencils

Procedure: Discuss with the class how the land around their school is being used. If possible, take a walk around the area after raising the question, and continue the discussion after returning.

Ask if anyone knows of some changes in the area that have recently taken place, and if they know the reasons for the changes. If not, ask some children to try to find out. If some of the children do not live in the school's neighborhood, ask them how the land around their homes is being used and if there have been any recent changes.

Pass out a piece of drawing paper to each child. Ask them to think about some changes they would like to make in the use of the land in their own neighborhood, and then to draw a picture showing how the land would look after their changes. Some of the children might wish to make an aerial map of the changes. These children can use symbols for the features in their maps.

When the maps or pictures are completed, either ask each child to hold up and explain his or her product or put all of the drawings and maps on a bulletin board with the reasons for the land-use changes beside each picture. Be careful to praise students for the creativity of their suggestions rather than for the drawing itself.

Evaluation: completion of land-use change picture or map by each student

Additional Activities:

1. The National Wildlife Foundation publishes a variety of Environmental Discovery Units. You can obtain a complete list of available units by writing to the foundation's Department of Educational Services, 1412 16th Street NW, Washington, D.C. 20036.

2. An excellent guide for environmental exploration near or on school grounds is the book *Ten-Minute Field Trips* by Helen Ross Russell (Chicago: J. G. Ferguson Pub. Co., 1973). Every imaginable aspect of the environment can be explored through the activities packed into this very useful volume.

3. Winston Press (25 Groveland Terrace, Minneapolis, MN 55403) publishes a twelve-volume set of books titled, *Examining Your Environment*.

They deal specifically with such environmental topics as ecology, mini-climates, pollution, and trees.

4. Help your students to directly affect their school or community environment. Engage them in an active program to clean up litter, plant flowers or saplings, or otherwise enhance the inside or outside appearance of their school building. Your students could also measure the attitudes of their fellow students by surveying their feelings concerning the appearances of their school building and grounds before and after changes are made.

GROWING AND USING PLANTS

Growing and Using Plants: Weight, volume, length, temperature, and area are all incorporated in applied settings in this measurement-oriented theme. This unit will be of special interest to the amateur gardener and to those students who have a "green thumb."

GROWING AND USING PLANTS

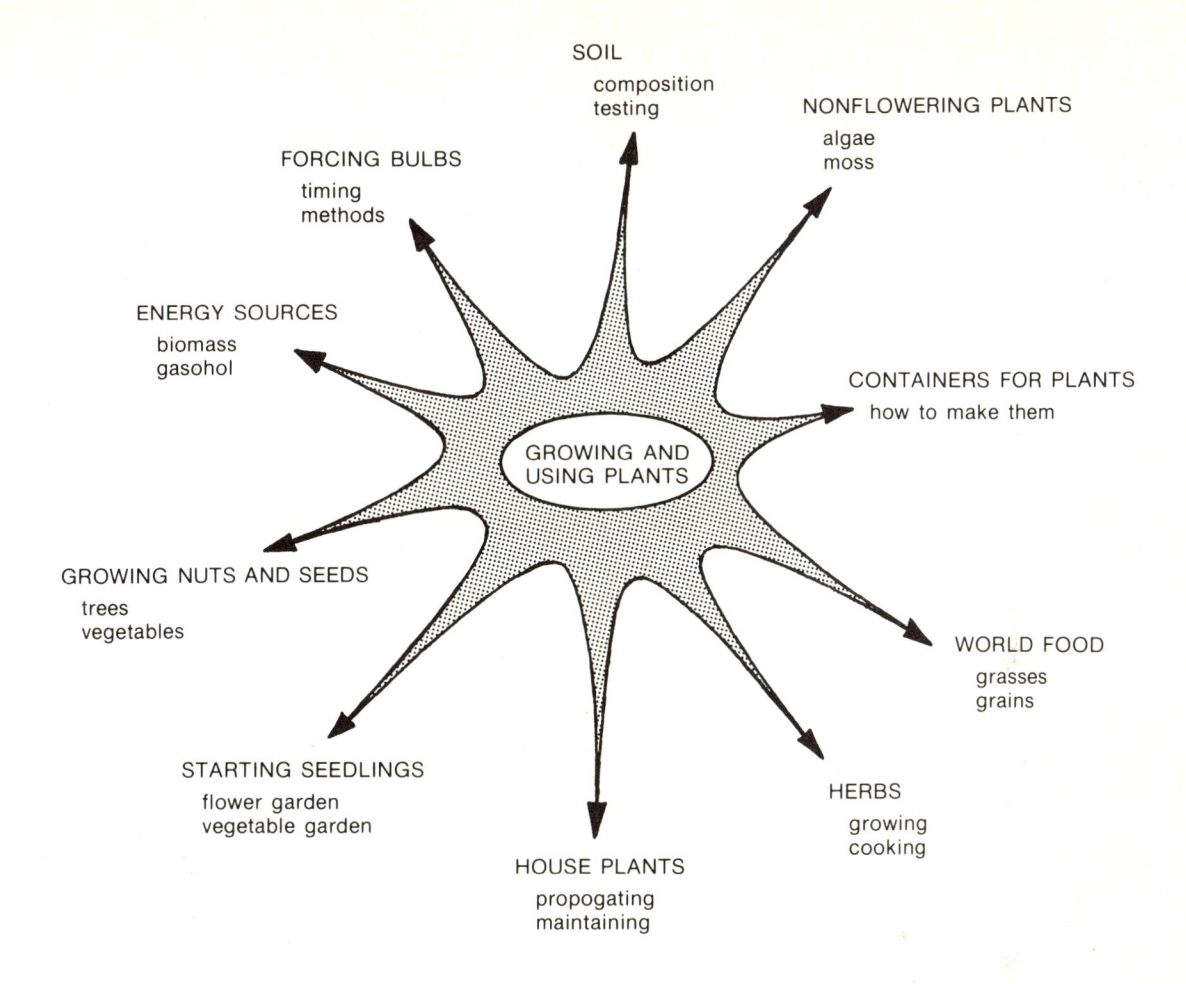

- **SOIL**: composition, testing
- **NONFLOWERING PLANTS**: algae, moss
- **FORCING BULBS**: timing, methods
- **ENERGY SOURCES**: biomass, gasohol
- **CONTAINERS FOR PLANTS**: how to make them
- **GROWING NUTS AND SEEDS**: trees, vegetables
- **WORLD FOOD**: grasses, grains
- **STARTING SEEDLINGS**: flower garden, vegetable garden
- **HOUSE PLANTS**: propagating, maintaining
- **HERBS**: growing, cooking

Introduction

This theme is planned to give children who have some knowledge of seed germination an opportunity to explore many ways that plants are propagated and used. The theme incorporates plant growth studies, record keeping, cooking activities, simple pottery making, container art, sugar fermentation studies, distillation procedures, and a variety of plant growth and propagation activities.

Plants and animals form a mutual support system, although most plants will grow in the absence of animals. The selection, hybridization, development, and cultivation of plants for man's use is the single most important resource-producing industry in the world. Agriculture makes us think of fields of wheat, corn, or alfalfa; but the process of cultivation applies to the growth of a wide variety of plants for shade and beauty as well as for forest and agricultural products.

This theme deals with a few of the many ways in which people can use plants. It can be easily expanded to include children developing a corner of the school grounds into an environmental center, setting up a small yard and garden sales center, constructing a window greenhouse in the classroom, or starting a houseplant boutique.

As the world's population increases, production of food must keep pace. Food plays a major role in the trade of products among nations. Whether children become commodity traders, grow food commercially, or just use their knowledge as a way of raising a backyard garden or beautifying their home, the theme is of immediate concern to them.

Unit Objectives:

The students will:

1. become aware of the many ways in which people use plants and plant products.
2. grow a variety of plants from seeds and cuttings.
3. be able to name some of the components of soil.
4. make pots and containers in which to grow plants.
5. learn about and grow both flowering and nonflowering plants.

Appropriate Grade Levels:

Three to Six

ACTIVITY ONE: INTRODUCING THE THEME

Objective: to introduce students to the theme of the unit

Materials: film or filmstrip of your choice

Procedure: Many fine films are available dealing with the production and use of plant products. Any one of them can be used to initiate a class discussion since most children have planted seeds, know of plant growth, and have some background information and interest. Ask children to brainstorm about the many kinds and uses of plants. Have them think of a day in their lives and what part plants and plant products play.

The webbing at the beginning of the unit is for your use, although it is likely that you will want to use it directly with your class as well. The activities presented in this unit are intended to provide suggestions, ideas, and guidance. As with other themes, encourage your children to identify and explore topics of high interest to them. Group sharing by means of reports, posters, and minibooks should be encouraged.

Evaluation: attention to, and participation in discussion of the film or filmstrip shown

WHAT? A SAMPLER OF THEMATIC UNITS 203

ACTIVITY TWO:
TESTING SOIL FOR ORGANISMS

Objective: to test garden soil for the presence of organisms

Materials:
funnel
light bulb
jar
garden soil
instant baby cereal
small plastic container
toothpicks

Procedure: Explain to your class that it is unwise to use soil directly from the garden because it may contain organisms that will eat or otherwise harm plants. Therefore, soil should be sterilized. Tell them that, before sterilizing, it might be interesting to test the soil for the presence of organisms. This is done using a funnel, a light bulb, and a jar.

Help your students follow these steps:

1. Place the garden soil in the funnel, set the funnel in the jar with a bit of water in the bottom (avoid using flammable liquids such as alcohol).

2. Hang a light bulb over the funnel as close to the soil as possible. Heat from the bulb will force the larger organisms out of the funnel and into the water where they can be observed.

3. Tiny soil organisms called nematodes can be cultured from a soil sample using instant baby cereal. Mix an individual serving-size package of cereal and add a teaspoon of soil to it. Place the mixture in a small plastic container with a cover. A shallow plastic box works very well.

4. In a day or two, condensation will form on the underside of the lid. Remove a drop of the liquid with a toothpick and examine it with a microscope. Nematodes are tiny, often nearly transparent worms that inhabit soil, water, and many other organisms.

Evaluation: successful completion of the tests described, with active participation observed of all students

ACTIVITY THREE:
PREPARING THE SOIL

Objective: to sterilize and otherwise prepare garden soil for indoor planting

Materials:
garden soil
cake pans
sand, humus, or vermiculite as desired

Procedure: An easy way to sterilize soil is to place it in a cake pan and bake it in an oven. Set the oven controls at 250°F and bake the soil for several hours or overnight. If an oven is available, you may choose to do this at school. Otherwise, you should bake the soil at home the evening before.

For successful planting, the soil should be soft and friable. Have your students test for proper consistency by taking handfuls of moist soil and squeezing them into balls. If, as they open their hands, the soil breaks apart, it is satisfactory. If it sticks together and packs, it can be loosened by adding sand, humus, or one of several soil conditioners such as vermiculite to it. You can use vermiculite, an insulation material made from mica, by itself for most planting needs as well if obtaining or sterilizing soil is not possible. Vermiculite is available in sacks at building material stores, as well as at garden stores. If you use vermiculite alone, you should add a bit of fertilizer (liquid or solid) occasionally.

Evaluation: completion of suitable planting soil mixture

ACTIVITY FOUR:
PLANTING FLATS

Objective: to make planting flats

Materials:
small cardboard boxes
plastic, preferably clear
vermiculite or sand

Procedure: Planting flats can be made from small cardboard boxes which have been cut down to about a 3" depth and lined with clear plastic. Flats are handy for starting seedlings and conducting investigations. Since the purpose of the plastic is to keep the cardboard dry, drainage can be a problem. If you put an inch of vermiculite, or sand, in the bottom of the flat before adding soil, and if you water only when the surface of the soil begins to dry out, the problem can be overcome.

Help your students prepare their flats following the suggestions given above. It is always wise to have more materials than needed for the finished products to allow room for errors. While any size and shape of box can be used, you may wish to have students save their empty milk cartons from lunch.

Evaluation: successful completion of planting flats by all students

ACTIVITY FIVE: POTS AND CONTAINERS

Objective: to make one or more pots or containers for planting

Materials: dependent upon type(s) of pots to be made (please see individual sections of the activity for specifics)

Procedure: Clay pots and plants go hand-in-hand. A ten-pound bag of clay from the local pottery supplier and many hands to pinch pots will produce an assortment of twenty to fifty containers, depending on size and wall thickness. If your school has a kiln, you are in business. If not, discuss the problem with the pottery supply person. Ask about clays that can be baked at low temperatures. In some cases, bisque, or low temperature firing, can be done in an ordinary oven.

Directions follow for making a variety of pots. As few or as many of these can be made as you desire. If more than one kind is made, several days will be needed to complete the activity.

Pinch Pots
Pinch pots are simple pots made without the help of a wheel or mold. Have students begin with a ball of clay about 2″ in diameter. Students should slowly fashion the clay into a pot shape. Tell them that pots that taper from the bottom to the top are easy to work and fine for plants. Encourage the children to keep pot walls uniform in thickness as much as possible. Note: clay should never be rinsed down a sink drain. Students should wipe off excess clay from their fingers before washing up.

Coil Pots
Long "snakes" of clay are used to fashion coil pots. Students should start with a one-inch ball of clay, rolling the clay carefully into a uniform snake about

12″ long. They should then wind and coil the snake, forming the bottom and then the sides of the pot. Once formed, they should carefully press the bottom and then the sides of the pot together using fingers and thumb. A lightly moistened sponge can be used to smooth and even the pot.

Charming pots can also be made from several separate coils of clay. Your students should start by making six coils, each about 2″ in diameter. Placing the first coil on a flat surface, they should then arrange the other coils to form the side walls. Tell them not to worry if a few small gaps remain between the coils. A long snake can be added to form the top of the pot. A bit of careful pinching and a light wipe with a moist sponge will ready the pot for drying and the kiln.

Containers from Sheets of Clay
Planting containers can also be made by using a rolling pin to form a sheet of clay. If the clay sticks to the pin, have students roll it out between two sheets of foil or plastic wrap. When they have an 8″ disc of clay, the edges can be slanted upward, forming a saucer or pan. A 10″ × 10″ rectangle can be formed into a tray by the same process.

Papier-mâché Pots
To begin making papier-mâché pots, have students mix torn newsprint and water in a bucket. They should then let the mixture soak for several days until the paper comes apart. At this point, they should be instructed to vigorously stir the mixture or work it with their hands. When the paper is almost all in fine shreds, help your students drain off some of the water and add a tablespoon of powdered wallpaper paste. Have each student select a glass jar that is a bit wider at the top than the bottom. They should take some of the papier-mâché and form it over the jar, squeezing out the water as they work. Once the mâché pot is formed, have students set their pots aside for several hours, but not long enough for them to dry completely. After some time, help them very carefully slide the mâché pot off the glass form. Later, additional mâché can be added once the pot has dried. A lip or raised designs can be added. Paint and varnish can be used to give the paper pot a moderate degree of water resistance. If desired, the inside of the pot can be coated with hot paraffin.

Small pots for transplanting can be made from a mâché base. In this case, try soft toweling or bathroom tissue. Have students completely shred the paper in the water, adding enough paper so the mixture is about the consistency of thin batter (slurry). Each student then needs to cut a piece of screen wire and form a small pot shape. He or she should pour the paper slurry through the screen pot form until the inside of the form is thinly coated with paper. When this is done, he or she should gently squeeze the moisture from the paper and allow it to dry. Once dry, a little spreading of the screen will make it possible to remove the light paper pot. Students should then trim the top and set the little pots aside to dry. Plants started in these containers can be planted directly in the garden, container and all.

WHAT? A SAMPLER OF THEMATIC UNITS

Other Containers

Many other containers can be made by children. Baby food jars can be painted or trimmed with paper. Cans can be cut with tin snips to form handles and curled edges. Containers can be "flocked" by painting them with glue, varnish, or shellac and rolling them in sand, vermiculite, or sawdust. Encourage creative and artistic expressions by children. Some may wish to make hanging pots, some animal-shaped pots, and some may wish to make animal heads with deep furrows in which rye grass can be planted.

Evaluation: successful completion of one or more pots by each student

ACTIVITY SIX: GROWING GRASSES AND GRAINS

Objective: to plant and grow grass or seed grains

Materials:
variety of grass and grain seeds
flats or pots filled with soil
opaque plastic
stick frame for plastic

Procedure: Arrange for your class to visit a farm or seed store where bulk seed is sold. Bring along a dozen little plastic bags with labels and purchase a tablespoon of each of a variety of seeds. Rye grass, oats, corn, millet, and alfalfa all grow vigorously and germinate in a hurry. Encourage children to try many kinds of seeds.

The seeds can be planted in flats or pots. Give your students this general seed depth planting rule: soil should cover the seed by no more than four times the seed's longest dimension. Tell them that very tiny seeds can be mixed with soil, with this mixture then sprinkled evenly over the soil in the flat and patted down. Tell the class that flats should never dry out during germination, but neither should they be overly moist. One of the better ways of keeping the soil surface moist is to cover the flat with thin opaque plastic until the seeds show signs of germination. Then build a frame over the flat with sticks or Tinkertoys and hang a clear plastic cover over the flat.

After germination has been checked, seeds can be planted in rows in the flats. Have students label each row carefully so that they can remember what was planted. It would be useful to make a class growth-rate chart for each variety.

Evaluation: successful growing of planted seeds, and completion of a growth chart marking their progress

ACTIVITY SEVEN:
GROWING AND COOKING WITH HERBS

Objective: to grow a variety of herbs and use them in cooking

Materials:
- variety of herb seeds
- flats or containers filled with soil
- cooking equipment and ingredients as desired
- plastic cups
- gauze
- aluminum foil

Procedure: Most hardware and seed stores carry collections of herb seeds. Included in the collection are packages such as rosemary, mint, chive, basil, thyme, and parsley. Have your children follow planting instructions on the packages. All will grow well in flats. Warn them that many herbs are slow to germinate, with some seeds taking as much as two weeks to sprout.

Collecting recipes using herbs can be an interesting library or resource activity to pursue while the class is waiting for the seeds to grow. Parents, grandparents, and neighbors can be consulted as well. Encourage your children to make a collection of herbs and spices and to find out about them: on what part of the plant they grow and which parts of the plant are edible. Have children make "fragrance boxes," which can be used to teach them to recognize many herbs and spices by their aroma. Such a box can be made from a small plastic cup, a bit of moist gauze, and a foil cover.

Evaluation: growth of herb seeds planted, cooking or collecting recipes for herbs, and correct identification of several herbs in a fragrance box

ACTIVITY EIGHT:
PROPAGATING HOUSE PLANTS BY CUTTINGS

Objective: to grow plants from houseplant cuttings

Materials:
- cuttings of common houseplants
- containers filled with sand or vermiculite
- pots filled with soil

WHAT? A SAMPLER OF THEMATIC UNITS

Procedure: Most varieties of green, vine-like houseplants can be snipped and rooted with comparative ease. Philodendrons, pothos, ivy and fleshy-leaved plants like Swedish ivy all root well. The trick is to root fairly short end cuttings. A good rule is to count leaves from the tip of the shoot and snip between the third and fifth leaf. We suggest that you make the cuttings at home and bring them to class. Cuttings can be put by students in well-drained pots with washed sand or can be rooted in vermiculite in paper or plastic cups with a hole in the bottom for drainage.

Several plants, including spider plants, air plants, begonia, and African violets, can be propagated from leaf cuttings. Have students start with a flat filled with clean sand or vermiculite. Have them place the leaf rib-side down slightly into the sand (some gardeners snip the middle rib in one or two places). Make sure they keep their flats moist and covered with plastic so the sand or vermiculite is always slightly moist. Tiny new plants will soon appear at the leaf margins. They can be removed by students and planted in pots when they have four leaves.

Evaluation: plant grown from rooted cutting by each student

ACTIVITY NINE: STARTING SEEDLINGS

Objective: to successfully start seedlings from seeds

Materials: variety of flower or vegetable seeds
flats filled with soil

Procedure: The success of the amateur gardener depends on his or her ability to start plants from seed early in the spring. Only through experience do children learn what plants can be started indoors, which ones to transplant to pots, and how to harden them before planting them in the garden. Seed packages provide general planting and growing information. Some packages suggest that seeds be sown indoors to start and others recommend that seeds be planted directly in the garden. Many seed companies will send seed catalogs free or for postage and handling costs.

Your children can start single rows of various vegetables and flowers in flats. When plants are up and four to six tiny leaves appear, they can be carefully transplanted into other flats or little pots. One of the common mistakes of the beginner is letting plants in flats grow too close together. If you don't want to transplant rows that are too thick, have students pull out plants (this is called thinning) so there is an inch between each plant left in the flat. Although the list of plants varies from region to region, here are a few that guarantee success and which children may wish to try.

Vegetables	Flowers
tomatoes, cabbage, broccoli, eggplant, hybrid bush melons, green peppers, cauliflower	petunias, portulaca, alyssum, verbena, calendula, snapdragons, marigolds

Large vegetables, root vegetables, most vines, corn, sunflowers, zinnias, sweet peas, and morning glories can be started indoors in pots. Encourage children to try any plant they wish since that is how one learns the skills of the amateur gardener.

Evaluation: successful growth of one or more plants started from seeds

ACTIVITY TEN:
STARTING PLANTS FROM NUTS AND FRUIT SEEDS

Objective: to start plants from fruit seeds or nuts, to learn that processed seeds will not grow

Materials:
variety of fruit seeds or nuts

variety of seed-containing processed foods

containers filled with soil

Procedure: Many interesting house plants and trees for a yard can be started from nuts or seeds taken from fruit. You may ask students to bring in seeds or you might bring them to school yourself. In the case of fruit, the seeds should be removed and washed carefully. They should be allowed to dry for a few days. Such fresh fruit as apricots, peaches, pears, apples, oranges, tangerines, lemons, limes, grapefruit, avocados, and grapes can be tried.

Nuts, too, will germinate but may pose some difficulties. Some must be frozen for a few weeks to induce germination, while others may require several months to germinate. Raw peanuts can be purchased from a health food store. Seeds from roasted peanuts, like those of cooked fruit, will not germinate.

You may also want to have your children plant seeds found in cans of fruits or vegetables. Let them try these seeds and discover that the preserving process and the associated heat kills seeds.

Well-drained, sandy soil seems to be the best choice for fruit seed germination. Once the little plants are up, they can be potted to make attractive houseplants. All of these plants need abundant sunlight. Be aware that the germination time for citrus seeds, avocados, and nuts may be as much as six weeks. For this reason, this activity might well be selected by a group that has another activity underway.

Evaluation: successful growing of plants from the seeds or nuts provided, knowledge gained of some conditions necessary for seed growth

ACTIVITY ELEVEN: BIOMASS AND GASOHOL

Objective: to learn about plant-produced energy sources, and to complete one or more activities producing gasohol

Materials:
seeds, as appropriate (see Procedure)
large pan
algae
fertilizer
instruments to measure weight
syrup or molasses
five-gallon bucket and cloth for cover
yeast
pressure cooker and hot plate
pan
rubber or plastic tubing

Procedure: As we approach the twenty-first century, we approach a time when world petroleum resources will be far below that of today and prices will be much higher. Many people have begun to search for alternative energy sources for home heating, vehicle propulsion, and the powering of some industries. Two interesting plant possibilities are biomass and gasohol.

Provide your class with the following background information. All parts of plants, roots, stems, and leaves, are made up of a high percentage of cellulose. Cellulose is a chemical in the same group with sugar and starch and will burn. Plants produce sugars, starches, and cellulose using sunlight as the powering source, and water from the soil and carbon dioxide from the air as basic raw materials. The process from plant to plant varies in efficiency. Many studies are underway to measure the amount of burnable material produced by plants per unit of growing area (such as an acre or hectare).

Children can conduct such studies by marking off areas and planting such high biomass producers as corn and sunflowers. Another simple plant to study, which under some conditions is an efficient biomass producer, is algae. To grow algae, fill a large pan with water, add a small amount of fertilizer, and set it in a sunny spot. A small amount of shredded algae should be added. In a week or ten days the algae should be strained from the water, dried, and weighed. Children can now, from their data, make estimates of what weight of biomass could be produced in a large pond or lake.

Gasohol is made by adding about ten percent alcohol to ninety percent gasoline. Though this does not seem like much of a gasoline saving, children can calculate how much gasoline could be saved in a year by their family, their community, and their state if gasohol were used in place of gasoline. Gasoline consumption figures are readily available from either state transportation or energy departments.

The alcohol that is added to gasoline is usually made from grain that has a high sugar content. Sugar cane, sugar beets, and corn can be used. Children can explore the fermentation process by using molasses or dark syrup. Help them mix about one cup of syrup or molasses with two quarts of water and put the mixture in a five-gallon bucket. Then add a package of yeast. Explain to your students that yeast is a plant that has no chlorophyll and cannot manufacture its food by photosynthesis. Yeast uses sugar for its growth energy and in the process gives off carbon dioxide, water, and alcohol (known as ethanol or grain alcohol). Make sure that they keep the bucket at room temperature and keep a damp cloth over the top of the bucket. In a short time, the children will see a froth of carbon dioxide bubbles forming over the liquid. Allow the yeast mixture to ferment for several days. Explain that the odor is not carbon dioxide but is other gasses and wastes produced by the yeast.

If you wish to have your class distill some alcohol from the mixture, an easy way is to use a small pressure cooker. Students should pour two inches of the liquid into the pressure cooker, which should then be covered and placed in a pan of water on an electric hot plate. Do not put the pressure gauge on, but instead attach a long rubber hose or plastic tube to the pipe on the top of the cooker. Use a candy thermometer and heat the water in the pan to about 160° to 180°F. Do not let the water in the pan boil. As soon as the liquid in the pressure cooker gets hot (about twenty to thirty minutes) alcohol will evaporate from the liquid, travel into the tubing, and condense. The drops coming from the tubing will contain a fairly high percent of alcohol.

Be sure, in following this last procedure, that you carefully follow these safety precautions:

1. Use an electric hot plate on low heat. Do not use an open flame since alcohol vapor burns.
2. Collect some alcohol in a container. Then turn off the heat. When the cooker is cool, open it. Dispose of the remaining liquid. Only then is it

safe to test and see if the collected alcohol will burn. Wrap a bit of cotton on a stick and moisten it with the distilled liquid. Ignite and observe how alcohol looks as it burns.

3. Carry out the activity in a well-ventilated place.
4. It is not a good idea to taste the alcohol. Because of the crude fermentation procedure, it will contain contaminants that often produce nausea and vomiting.

Evaluation: depends upon which activities are pursued; in general, participation in each activity used

ACTIVITY TWELVE: CULTIVATING NONFLOWERING PLANTS: ALGAE

Objective: to grow and learn about algae

Materials:
clumps of algae
containers
two goldfish tanks
one or two goldfish

Procedure: Begin by communicating the following information to your class. In the plant kingdom, the most noticeable phyla is that of the flowering plants. These include trees, shrubs, grasses, and leafy plants. There is a group of plants that have no flowers. Some produce new plants from spores and include mosses, ferns, fungi, and algae. The life cycle of these plants is different from flowering plants. Since they don't produce seed, propagation is usually done from spores or from parts of the plant.

Algae, a single-celled plant that usually grows in long filaments, is easy to propagate. Clumps of algae can be broken apart by your students and small bits should be started in new containers. People who study food growth processes have been interested in the relationship between plant-eating fish and algae. Common goldfish exhibit this relationship with algae. If two similar tanks are filled with water and "inoculated" with some shredded algae, an interesting experiment can be conducted. The only difference between the two tanks is that one or two goldfish are added to one of the tanks. Nothing more is added except a bit of water to replace the water that evaporates. Both tanks should be kept in a well-lighted place where they get a few hours of sun each day. Students should keep records for a month in the form shown.

	TANK 1 *Water and algae*	TANK 2 *Water, algae and goldfish*
	Weight of algae added to tank _____	Weight of algae and goldfish added to tank _____
	After one month	
	New weight of algae in tank _____	New weight of algae and goldfish in tank _____

Children will discover that the plant-animal tank shows a clearly different weight gain when compared with the tank with the algae alone.

Evaluation: successful completion of activities as directed, including the record described

ACTIVITY THIRTEEN:
NONFLOWERING PLANTS: MOSS

Objective: to grow and learn about moss as a nonflowering plant

Materials:
clumps of moss

cups of soil

flats

cheesecloth

plastic

Procedure: Moss can be grown from pieces of moss found in the garden or woods. Moss is often found in moist, shady places, growing on rocks or soil made up of decaying plant matter. Have your class prepare a flat with soil that is acidic. Soil can be acidified in several ways, although soil that is composed of humus or compost is usually acidic. An easy way to acidify soil is to add about one tablespoon full of powdered milk per pound of soil.

Have groups of students select a small clump of moss that has a slightly dried-out appearance and examine it carefully. They should find small, brown, spear-like projections on the top of the green moss shoots. This is the spore container. Instruct the groups to allow the moss to dry a bit and then pulverize it by rubbing it between their hands.

Have students remove a cup of soil from the top of their flats and mix this with the pulverized moss. They should smooth the soil in the flat and lay a single layer of cheesecloth over the flat. Next, have them sprinkle the moss-soil mixture over the cheesecloth and pat it gently. Instruct them that the flat must be kept moist, cool and out of direct sunlight. They should keep the flat covered with plastic and allow six weeks for a good layer of moss to form on the cheesecloth. The cheesecloth is used because it makes it possible to lift the moss from the flat. The moss can be used as a soil cover in a flower pot or in an ornamental dish arrangement. It makes a fine ground cover for a woodland terrarium.

Evaluation: successful growing of moss, individually or through active small-group participation

ACTIVITY FOURTEEN:
FORCED BULBS

Objective: to force bulbs to flower

Materials:
- variety of bulbs
- mesh container
- deep containers filled with sand or gravel and soil
- humus or ground moss
- pans for water

Procedure: Late in the fall, nurseries often sell remaining bulbs at reduced prices. This is the time to purchase bulbs for forcing. Forcing is the name of the process used to encourage bulbs to bloom at almost any time of the year. After purchase, store bulbs in a mesh container in a cool place. They can be kept on a shelf in the refrigerator. Since it takes about six weeks to bring a bulb to bloom, time the forcing procedure so you will have blossoms when you want them.

To force bulbs, first help students select containers having depths of about six times the diameter of the bulbs. Have them place one or two inches of clean sand or fine gravel in the bottom of the container, then add an inch of rich, sandy soil. The students can prepare the soil by mixing one part sand with one part humus or ground peat moss. Students should arrange several bulbs on this layer and cover the bulbs with more soil. They should then cover the bulbs to a depth of three or four times the diameter of the bulb.

The pots should next be set in pans of water for thirty minutes, then taken out and drained. Students should place the pots in a cool, dark, ventilated place for some time, the exact length of which depends on how quickly individual bulbs sprout (usually four to six weeks). Students should check the pots weekly for signs of life. As soon as they see the soil begin to crack and plant tips appear, or at the end of six weeks, they should place the pots on a warm, well-lighted windowsill. Many bulbs, including tulips, hyacinths, daffodils, and crocus, are suitable for forcing.

Evaluation: successful flowering of forced bulbs

Additional Activities:

1. Using a variety of seeds, have students make mosaic pictures. They should choose a subject, draw or outline their picture, then fill it in by gluing seeds to the paper. This project can be given an historical perspective by discussing the mosaics of such ancient civilizations as Greece and Rome.

2. Instead of relying solely on seeds, start new plants from vegetables. Sections of potatoes, carrots, and pineapples as well as avocado pits can be placed in containers filled with water, sand, or vermiculite to produce new plants. Start several at once and compare their rates of growth.

3. Many tasty activities can be pursued using seeds as the main or only ingredients. Cook with, or simply taste and compare, such items as peanuts, sunflower seeds, peas, baked beans, sesame seeds, and coconuts. Or explore the seeds and pits found in fruits. Cherries, grapes, peaches, apples, and oranges are delicious sources of easy-to-find, yet varied, seeds.

4. Help students create art objects from edible fruits and vegetables. Use toothpicks to combine various sized and shaped pieces of fruits and vegetables into sculptures. Encourage the students to taste bits of the various foods as they create the shapes desired for their final products. Or let them try their hands at carving stamps from potatoes, and then creating stamped pictures and designs.

5. Have students explore the effect of climate and environment on plant life. Create maps showing the locations of various types of vegetation throughout the world. Students can also learn from the selections of state trees and flowers. Have them plot these on a U.S. map, then look for patterns and similarities in various regions of the country. Have students speculate as to the reasons for states' choices.

6. Students can create lovely pictures by making leaf rubbings. Leaves are positioned under a piece of paper, then various shades of crayons are rubbed over the paper, creating on the paper the image of the leaf underneath. The beauty of autumn leaves can also be preserved by sealing them between sheets of waxed paper.

7. This theme contains numerous opportunities to involve students in measurement activities. A bit of reflection will indicate that children have made judgements about weight, volume, length, temperature, and area. This can be a very effective way to introduce or sustain the concept of measurement by embedding the concept in a series of activities that have something else (i.e., growing) as their primary focal point.

8. A great number and variety of plant-related activities can be found in the books *Growing Up Green* by Alice Skelsey and Gloria Huckaby, and *Snips and Snails and Walnut Whales* by Phyllis Fiarotta, both published by Workman Publishing Company, New York.

READ ALL ABOUT IT!

Read All About It: Headlines, sports, advertisements, polls, and comic strips are investigated and discussed for an in-depth consideration of the daily newspaper. The effective design of a newspaper-related learning station is illustrated.

ILLUSTRATIONS
- photos
- comics
- cartoons

SOURCES OF NEWS
- local
- state
- national
- international

CONTENTS
- scavenger hunt
- physical make-up

FACT AND OPINION
- sports
- hard news
- editorials
- reviews
- feature stories
- polls

NEWSPAPERS

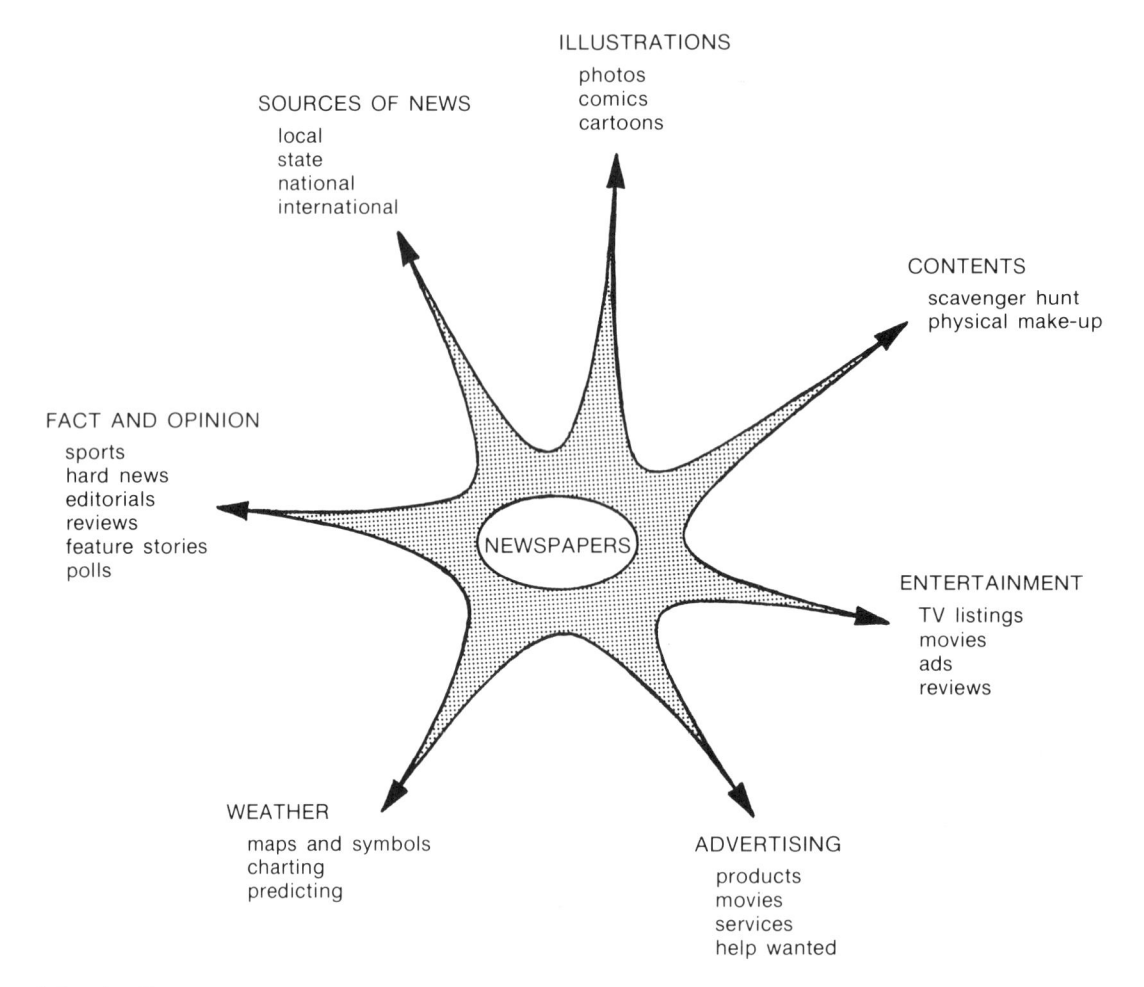

ENTERTAINMENT
- TV listings
- movies
- ads
- reviews

WEATHER
- maps and symbols
- charting
- predicting

ADVERTISING
- products
- movies
- services
- help wanted

Introduction

The daily newspaper represents a valuable but largely untapped source of materials and ideas for integrated studies. On a typical day, a newspaper contains science, math, language, social studies, and other areas of the curriculum waiting to be taught. Consider for a moment the photographs, maps, stories, advertisements, graphs, and statistical information found in the newspaper on any given day. You might be surprised to learn that the average daily newspaper contains approximately 150,000 words exclusive of want ads. That is the size of a small novel. Sunday papers, of course, are much larger and more varied in their content.

Perhaps you have thought of the newspaper as something for adults, or at most a possible current events source for senior high school students. There are, however, many possible educational uses of the newspaper with elementary, middle school, and junior high school students. In fact, the perception that the newspaper is for adults can add to the motivational aspect of learning once students find that they can achieve success using this tool.

In recent years, newspapers have lost readership. Declining circulation has been a fact of life for nearly every metropolitan daily. This has been the case for a number of reasons: rises in postage rates, increased costs of advertising, and the high cost of newsprint have no doubt contributed to the problems of marketing a newspaper. A recent survey determined four major reasons why people do not subscribe to a newspaper:

1. I don't have time to read it
2. I can't afford it
3. I already heard it on TV
4. There is nothing in there that interests me

These reasons, given by adults, are of significant interest to the teacher whose instructional objectives include basic literacy, the development of an informed citizenry, and awareness of technological, economic, and social developments. To help teachers meet the challenge of the encroachment of television and other competing factors as threats to literacy (for example, a half-hour television news broadcast has about 6,000 words, barely the equivalent of the newspaper's headlines) most major newspapers in the United States and Canada have developed newspaper-in-education programs. You can be quite sure that the major daily in your state or province has a program. Contact your newspaper for help with ideas for using the newspaper in your classroom.

In the next few pages, we will sample some ideas for using the newspaper as a learning tool in your classroom. The sample lessons will be drawn from language arts, social studies, math, and science. Although there are many kinds of things you can do educationally with the newspaper, we have tried to carefully select a limited number which will help you develop conceptual themes. You will note that the first five of these are presented for use with the class as a whole. The remaining eight are probably best reproduced for direct student use.

Unit Objectives:

The students will:

1. be able to differentiate correctly between fact and opinion, and learn the values of both in a newspaper.
2. learn about advertising techniques and appeals.
3. be able to identify various kinds of information found in newspapers and to locate them correctly.
4. be able to differentiate local, state, national, and international news.
5. be able to read weather symbols and maps.

Appropriate Grade Levels:

Four to Six

ACTIVITY ONE:
THE NEWSPAPER LEARNING STATION

Objective: to set up a learning center utilizing newspaper skills in the classroom (note that this is essentially a teacher goal, except for instructions to students concerning the use of the center)

Materials: will vary (see list in text for suggestions)

Procedure: This learning station is a self-contained activity center where one student, partners, or small groups may select independent learning activities. The center activities are those that follow although you can also include as many other activities as you choose. Activities can be duplicated on oak tag and used as activity cards, or on paper for individual consumption. Each activity uses the newspaper, and the activities presented are not sequenced in order or degree of difficulty, but are categorized as to the part of the newspaper used.

The learning station design includes a bulletin board for displays and for directions to the students. You might wish to identify particular areas of the display by labeling them with the words *information, interpretation, entertainment,* and *assistance,* and begin to define them with brief questions and graphics. Posted directions to students might read: "Choose an activity. Read the directions carefully. Ask for help if you need it. Put finished work in the proper box. Check off the titles of the finished work on the chart. Please keep things in their proper locations for the next person."

Post the numbered list of titles of activity cards near the class list so that students may record the numerals of completed cards. You might instead choose to individualize a bit more by having a record card prepared for and completed by each student. In any case, the record kept should look something like this:

PROGRESS CHART

| NAME | \multicolumn{10}{c}{ACTIVITY CARDS 1–10} |

NAME	1	2	3	4	5	6	7	8	9	10
1.										
2.										

All supplies and materials needed to use the learning station should be placed on a table in front of the bulletin board. These might include:

- stacks of newspapers
- reference books (dictionary, almanac)

WHAT? A SAMPLER OF THEMATIC UNITS

- blank outline maps
- paper (lined, graph, chart)
- glove
- tape recorder, blank tapes
- tools (scissors, rulers, markers, paste)
- basket or bin for completed work

The learning station will help the learner become familiar with the newspaper through varied activities using an interdisciplinary approach. It is designed to reinforce and extend the learner's academic skills and human understandings in relation to the variety of curriculum areas related to each activity. It is hoped that, as a result of these activities, learners will pursue special interests suggested under Additional Activities or as the result of independent thinking or research.

Evaluation: completion of center organization (teacher), participation of all students in center inservice

ACTIVITY TWO: PHYSICAL MAKEUP OF THE NEWSPAPER

Objective: to become familiar with the format of a newspaper, and to begin learning newspaper terminology

Materials: newspapers

paper and pencil

Procedure: To begin, hand out newspapers to all students and allow free reading time (ten to fifteen minutes). When finished, ask students to go back and count how many different sections and how many stories they read. This activity allows freedom of choice in their reading and makes them feel comfortable with the paper.

Next, lead a discussion based on their reading and viewing of TV, and ask them to consider these questions:

1. What conclusions can you reach concerning the amount of information received?
2. How does the media differ in the kinds of information it gives?
3. Why are both forms of the media important?

222   WHAT? A SAMPLER OF THEMATIC UNITS

You might also discuss radio and its place in communication. Ask if all three are needed to be well informed.

Spend the rest of the period taking students through the newspaper section by section. Explain the importance of each section. Show students the types of information they can find in each section. As you go through the paper, you may wish to identify terminology used by the newspaper world. You might want the students to begin a scrapbook containing specific examples of the terminology or types of writing as you continue the discussion.

Finally, explain to students that there are many different kinds of newspapers, some of which have different functions than a metropolitan daily. Ask them to bring an envelope stamped for mailing. Tell them that you want them to write a letter requesting a newspaper from another town. Have them bring in other newspapers they might receive in their homes and share them with the rest of the class. These can be tacked up for display.

Evaluation: completion of those activities carried out

Note:
You may wish to refer to the names and addresses of various leading newspapers given under Additional Activities.

ACTIVITY THREE:
SOURCES OF INFORMATION
AND FACT OR OPINION

Objective: to correctly identify stories as to the source of information, and as fact or opinion

Materials: newspapers

paper and pencils

Procedure: Begin by discussing the various ways in which news reaches the newspaper. Explain what a wire service is and how it feeds information to the newspaper. Ask students to look at the front page and see if they can determine the source of each story. Explain the importance of the dateline in determining the location of the story. Ask them why some stories have a byline and others do not.

Help your students begin to recognize fact and opinion. Tell them (unless they can tell you) that columnists and articles on the editorial and opinion pages usually contain some opinion, while news stories are supposed to be free of the writer's opinions and views. All news stories are written from the greatest objectivity that reporters can achieve, with more important stories carrying a byline. In comparison, news reviews are usually labelled opinion or analysis. They are written by columnists or appear on the editorial page. Finally, feature stories are not "hard news." The story is different from straight factual reporting in that it gives more background information and often opinion.

Once this information has been presented and discussed, have students select a straight news story. Ask them to list the facts in the order in which they are reported. Ask them where they think the story can be cut and still give all the pertinent facts needed. Discuss the importance of concise, factual, succinct writing in reporting the news. Explain pyramid construction and its value in editing news stories. Reporters use an inverted pyramid approach to writing news stories. In an inverted pyramid, "who," "what," "where," "when," and "why" are often incorporated into the story's lead paragraph.

Ask students to locate a straight news story and then a feature story about the same subject. Ask them to write down statements which they feel are the writers' opinions. Ask them to locate words which may color the reporting. Ask if they think there is a place in journalism for both kinds of news reporting. You might also wish to compare an editorial and a letter to an editor on the same topic. You can also use cartoons as a means by which opinions are expressed in the newspaper.

Finally, give the students a set of facts and ask them to write a straight news story, not expressing any opinion and using pyramid construction.

Evaluation: successful completion of activities assigned

ACTIVITY FOUR: ADVERTISING AND ITS IMPORTANCE

Objective: to identify and evaluate kinds of advertisements and to understand their economic importance to the publishing of newspapers as well as to consumers

Materials: newspapers

paper and pencils

Procedure: To begin, have students browse through the newspaper and tell you how many different kinds of advertising they can find: political, food, product, services, help wanted, or things to sell. Explain the difference between national advertising and local advertising, what display advertising is, and why the classified section is an important section to consumers. Ask the students why they think it is important for them to be able to read ads in the paper.

Discuss the economics of publishing the paper and why advertising is vital to the financial production of the newspaper. Ask students to consider whether or not papers use any guidelines for the type of advertising they carry.

Ask if they see any ads that they think are inappropriate for the newspaper to carry. This can provoke a lively discussion and you can draw on any previous discussions you may have had concerning freedom of the press and the people's right to know.

To find examples of different kinds of advertising, ask students to complete some or all of the following tasks:

1. Clip an ad showing how you can save money on something to buy.
2. Find an advertisement for something you would like to have at a price you would be willing to pay.
3. Find an ad about a service you might need.
4. Find an ad showing something the advertisers would like the public to do.
5. Find an advertisement for some place you would like to go.
6. Find an ad telling of something you can do or a place to go that won't cost you anything.
7. Find an advertisement for a job you might like.
8. Find a classified ad that is selling something you might like to have.
9. Find an ad for a contest you can enter free.

There are so many ways that a teacher can use the advertising sections to develop specific skills that you can choose your own activities once they find these ads. You might like to have them write an ad of their own. Certainly, your creativity and that of your students will guide you in selecting activities best suited for your class's needs.

Evaluation: successful completion of the activities assigned

ACTIVITY FIVE: PHOTOGRAPHS AND CARTOONING

Objective: to find and examine photos, cartoons, and comics in the newspaper

Materials: newspapers

paper and crayons or pencils

Procedure: Reading for entertainment is just as important as reading for fact. How do cartoons express opinions? Are all the captions serious under pictures found in the paper? Why do photographs add to any story in the paper?

Have the students go through the paper and examine the different kinds of photographs. Discuss how they add to the stories. Ask them to clip a few photographs and write their own captions.

Next, examine the comics and ask students to tell what each comic is expressing, for example, humor, irony, philosophy, telling a continuing story, or teaching a moral. Ask students to clip a comic that particularly appeals to them and write their own words for the comic strip.

Some students might like to draw their own comics and explain the purpose of their artwork. The students also might work in teams on this project, combining their skills and reinforcing each other in the learning process.

Finally, you might like students to do a photograph collage expressing an attitude, expressing one or different kinds of emotion, different kinds of action, or different kinds of people. Allowing the students to choose their own topics or themes gives them greater freedom in the learning process. However, you may wish to narrow the topic to your own subject goals. These can be displayed around the room and will create a great deal of interest in the school. Words cut from the newspaper can also be used in the collage.

Evaluation: successful completion of activities assigned or pursued

ACTIVITY SIX: A SCAVENGER HUNT

Objective: to find and identify various parts of a newspaper

Materials: newspapers
paper and pencils
scissors

Procedure: The purpose of this activity is to give students the opportunity to explore the newspaper and find and identify its many parts. Following is a list, in reproducible form, which you may use for this activity. You may choose instead to pull those items of interest to you and provide them to your students in some other format. In any case, it is suggested that you make it into a game or tape record some items for an individualized activity.

Evaluation: successful completion of the worksheet

A Scavenger Hunt

Use your newspaper to find the answers to the following questions. Find them as quickly as you can. Good luck!

1. What was the high temperature yesterday? _____
2. Give the headline of the article you feel was most important on the front page. _____
3. Where do you find information on the number of calendar days left in this year, and the time of sunrise and sunset? _____
4. How many sections does the paper have? _____
5. On what page do you find the first classified ad? _____
6. What telephone number do you call if you want to subscribe to the paper? _____
7. Name a person written up in a feature article. _____
8. Does this issue have a correction to an earlier issue? If so, what is it about? _____

9. Who drew the cartoon on the editorial page? _____
10. Who is managing editor of the paper? _____
11. How many letters from readers are there? _____
12. What is one subject of an advice column today? _____

13. How many couples applied for a marriage license? _____
14. How many baby girls were born? _____ baby boys? _____

WHAT? A SAMPLER OF THEMATIC UNITS

15. List four movies advertised. _____

16. What food item do you think is the best buy in a grocery ad? _____

17. Name one subject discussed in home repairs. _____

18. What was the high temperature in Boston yesterday? _____

19. What programs will be on TV at 6:30 tonight? _____

20. What teams are at the top of their leagues? _____

21. Name a prominent person written up in Sports. _____

22. Look for the miscellaneous section of the classified ads and copy the items to be sold in the first garage sale you find. _____

23. What does your horoscope say for today? _____

24. Articles on the front page sometimes come from different countries or cities. Find the article that came from farthest away. Name the place.

ACTIVITY SEVEN: TABOO FOR YOU?

Objective: to use movie titles and ads to classify, describe, and make value judgements

Materials:
newspapers
paper and pencils
reproduced worksheet, if desired

Procedure: The worksheet on page 229 can be reproduced and given to students for completion. If you choose to assign only some of the activities included, you may wish to present the assignment in a different format.

Evaluation: successful completion of at least the "Action" items

ACTIVITY EIGHT: SPORTS OPINIONS

Objective: to identify fact and opinion in sports stories and to make personal value judgements about various sports

Materials:
newspapers
paper and pencils

Procedure: Many of us persist in thinking of sports as being of interest only to the boys in our classes. In fact, more and more girls are both actively involved in sports as participants and avid followers of particular sports or teams. The worksheet on page 230 gives your students a chance to use this interest to differentiate fact from opinion, and to express personal preferences. As with the preceding activity, it may be reproduced and distributed or used in any other format desired.

Evaluation: successful completion of at least the "Action" items

TABOO FOR YOU?

Action

1. Skim through the newspaper to find the pages that show lists of theaters and movies.

2. Select the page that shows a theater in your neighborhood. Count and write down the number of theaters on this page that are showing films rated *X* (adults only), *R* (restricted to 17 or over unless accompanied by an adult), *PG* (parental guidance suggested) and *G* (general audiences). Write the rating symbols and show your tally like this:

    X_____   PG_____
    R_____   G_____

3. Compare the tallies. Copy and complete this sentence: "Most of the theaters on this page are showing ___ movies. I ___ (can/cannot) see these films."

More

1. Look over the movie titles and descriptions. List the titles that fit at least three of the following:
    a. comedy   e. animal
    b. horror   f. musical
    c. detective   g. cartoon
    d. western

2. Write the title of a movie that made you *sick*, or really *scared* or *embarrassed* you. Write a sentence that tells why you think such movies are made.

3. Conduct a survey to find out how people feel about film ratings that limit attendance on the basis of age.

SPORTS OPINIONS

Action

1. Find a sports column. Mark the name of the sports columnist and then read the column.
2. Locate and mark three facts in the column. (A fact is something that happened and can be checked out.) Use a color marker.
3. Locate and mark three opinions in the column. (An opinion is what someone thinks or feels about what happened.) Use a different color marker.
4. Decide which of the following sports you would like to be really good at:

archery	skiing
golf	swimming
fishing	stock car racing
hockey	tennis

5. List your choices in order from one to eight. Number one would be the sport you would like to be best at and number eight the sport you are least interested in.
6. Look at your list. Did you choose team sports or individual sports as your favorite? Think about your choices, then complete the following sentence: "I'm the kind of person who _____."

More

1. Find a news story about a sport you've never tried. Write your opinion.
2. Conduct an opinion survey about wrestling on TV. What did you find out?

ACTIVITY NINE:
WEATHER WATCH

Objective: to interpret symbols on a weather map correctly

Materials:
    newspapers
    paper and pencils
    chart paper and calendar

Procedure: Students are probably exposed daily to weather information and maps on television. Many, however, probably could not read the weather symbols on their own, since they are in the habit of listening to the information given rather than reading it. The worksheet on page 232 will give them practice in interpreting such maps on their own. The worksheet may be reproduced for student use if you desire.

Evaluation: successful completion of the worksheet activities

ACTIVITY TEN:
SUPER SERIOUS

Objective: to identify news stories as local, national, and international, and make value judgements concerning the seriousness of the news reported

Materials:
    newspapers
    pencils, glue, and paper

Procedure: It can be important to a student's understanding of the meaning and importance of news stories to be aware of the origin of that news. One part of this developing understanding is the ability to identify news as local, national, or international in scope. The worksheet on page 233 is designed to increase student awareness and understanding of that distinction. This set of activities could be easily included with, or expanded to, a regular current events activity in your classroom.

Evaluation: successful completion of the worksheet or assigned activities

WEATHER WATCH

Action
1. Find the weather map in today's newspaper.
2. Study the weather symbols that mean fair, cloudy, and partly cloudy.
3. Find the symbols that tell you if there will be rain, snow, or fog in your area today and tonight.
4. Draw all the symbols you find on a piece of chart paper. Make the symbols large. Show the chart to your class and talk about what the symbols mean.
5. Each day, put one of the symbols on a classroom calendar to show the day's weather.

More
1. Work with a small group. Using the weather map in the newspaper, make up questions to ask another group. For example: "Is it raining anywhere?", or "Does the southwest part of the US look as though it will get rain soon?"
2. Predict what the weather will be one week from today by thinking about what the weather has been. Write down your prediction. Next week, see if your prediction is correct.
3. Watch the evening news on TV. Do they use the same symbols as those in the newspaper?

SUPER SERIOUS

Action

1. Skim through the news section and check the datelines to find where the news happened.
2. Using color markers, mark local news stories with the letter *L,* national with the letter *N,* and international with the letter *I.*
3. Find local news stories that tell something about the following items:
   a. crime
   b. business or industry
   c. traffic or transportation
   d. environment
   e. housing

   Write the correct letter from the list near the headline of each of the local news stories. For example, a news article about a robbery would be marked with an *a.*
4. Decide which of the five marked articles tells about the *most serious* problem. Cut this article out, paste it on plain paper, and label it.

More

1. Look over the national news that you marked. Decide which news article tells about something that affects the most people. Cut it out, paste it on paper and label it *N.*
2. Look over the international news you marked. Decide which news article tells about something that affects our nation's government. Cut it out, paste it on paper, and label it *I.*
3. Pretend you are Superboy or Wondergirl (a wonder person who can take care of any problem). Which problem in the world would you work on? Why? Tell in writing or show in a cartoon or sketch.

ACTIVITY ELEVEN:
GALLOPING POLLS

Objective: to carry out a simple opinion poll

Materials: newspapers

paper and pencils

Procedure: We hear almost daily about the results of some recent poll. Once concerned primarily with politics, polls now report opinions on nearly every topic imaginable. In this activity, your students will first become familiar with an opinion poll published in the newspaper and will then design and carry out a poll themselves. (See page 235.) For those students who seek out advice on a topic for their own poll, you should have in mind a list of suitable subjects for their consideration.

Evaluation: successful completion of a survey

ACTIVITY TWELVE:
SUPER SUMMARIES AND SURVEYS

Objective: to view and review a television program

Materials: newspapers

paper and pencils

Procedure: This assignment requires some outside time for completion. Because students will need to view a television program before doing the exercises on page 236 such an assignment should be made ahead of class lesson time, or the activity sheet sent home for completion outside of school. You may wish to send a letter home to parents as well to inform them of the assignment and its purpose.

Evaluation: completion of a review of a TV program and of creative writing in connection with that show

GALLOPING POLL

Action

1. Find an opinion poll in the paper. Look it over and record the subject of the poll.

2. List some subjects that you think people could have a strong opinion about.

3. Go to your parents, a teacher, or an aide and have them help you plan a question you can ask others on the subject you choose. Your poll question should be one that can be answered yes or no. Example: "Do you think Beetle Bailey is an interesting comic?"

4. Ask your survey question of ten people. Be sure you ask males and females. Write down the results on a chart such as the one shown. When completed, share your results with the class.

Question _____

Men	Yes_____
	No_____
	No opinion_____
Women	Yes_____
	No_____
	No opinion_____
Boys	Yes_____
	No_____
	No opinion_____
Girls	Yes_____
	No_____
	No opinion_____

More

1. Make a list of the subjects of the opinion polls that other class members developed.

2. Find and clip news articles and pictures from the newspaper that relate to each of the mentioned subjects.

3. Divide a classroom bulletin board in half. Title one half of your bulletin board "We View With Alarm" and the other half "We View With Approval." Tack your news clippings under whichever heading you think they belong. Discuss the board with the class.

SUPER SUMMARIES AND SURVEYS

Action

1. Find the TV and radio highlights today. Notice what programs are being shown. Notice which ones have been chosen to have extra things written about them.
2. Choose a "situation comedy" (a comedy show in which the same characters appear in show after show and have funny things happen to them). Watch the program at home.
3. Write a short summary of the show you watched as it might appear in the paper.
4. Choose a series such as "Happy Days" or "Little House on the Prairie" and write a situation that could appear on that series.

More

1. Watch a game show on TV. Write a summary of the particular show you saw.
2. Think up a game that could be used for a new game show. Write a summary of it for a newspaper. Be sure to tell just enough about the rules of the game so the reader will be interested in seeing it played.

ACTIVITY THIRTEEN: COMICS

Objective: to read, analyze, and create various components of newspaper comics

Materials:
newspapers
paper and drawing or writing instruments

Procedure: The final activity of the unit concerns the section to which many students undoubtedly turn first—the comics. Because of this natural interest, you may wish to move this activity to an earlier point in the newspaper unit. However, it could serve as an enjoyable finale to your study of the newspaper as well. Be sure to allow sufficient time to encourage creative expression on the part of your students.

Evaluation: successful completion of "Action" items

COMICS

Action

1. Find a comic strip in the paper.
2. Find someone to work with.
3. List the names of as many characters as you can that appear in the comic strip.
4. Choose the two characters that interest you the most. Write words that describe these two.
5. Think of new words that could be used to describe each character that would change their personality (Sarge—tough, loud, shy, meek). Think of new names for the characters that would go with their new personalities.

More

1. Draw a new appearance for your characters to fit their new personalities.
2. Draw a three-box comic strip using your new characters.
3. Share your new comic strip with others. See if they find it funny.

Additional Activities:

1. Help your students create their own room newspaper. Set up a rotating staff to handle the various responsibilities related to writing and assembling a newspaper. Include all aspects of "real" newspapers felt to be appropriate for a room product. Students can also be responsible for the distribution of their newspapers to parents, teachers, and students.
2. A great number and variety of unusual items (150 to be exact) can be made from newspapers by following the directions in *The Newspaper Everything Book* by Vivienne Eisner and Adelle Weise (New York: E.P. Dutton & Co., Inc., 1975). With sufficient quantities of newspapers, students can create everything from baskets to book covers and tables to trays.
3. You may wish to involve your students in a recycling drive. Most communities now make arrangements for the periodic collection of newspapers. Your students could set up a newspaper drive at school and take care of collecting, bundling, and delivering the newspapers to the recycling collection site.
4. Most large newspaper publishers have put together lesson materials for

classroom use of their newspapers in a wide variety of ways. Some of the nation's major newspapers include the following:

The New York Times
229 W. 43 Street
New York, New York 10036

The Atlanta Constitution
Box 4689
Atlanta, Georgia 30302

The Chicago Tribune
Tribune Tower
Chicago, Illinois 60611

Louisville Courier Journal
525 W. Broadway
Louisville, Kentucky 40202

The Los Angeles Times
Times Mirror Square
Los Angeles, California 90053

The Houston Chronicle
801 Texas Street
Houston, Texas 77002

The St. Louis Post-Dispatch
900 N. 12 Street
St. Louis, Missouri 63101

Baltimore Sun
501 N. Calvert Street
Baltimore, Maryland 21203

Minneapolis Star and Tribune
425 Portland Avenue
Minneapolis, Minnesota 55488

Washington Post
1515 L. Street, N.W.
Washington, D.C. 20005

5. Other useful resources for the study and use of newspapers in the classroom follow:

BERNSTEIN, THEODORE, *Get More Out of Your Newspaper.* The New York Times School Service Department, 229 W. 43rd Street, New York, New York 10036, 1976.

CHEYNEY, ARNOLD B., *Teaching Reading Skills Through the Newspaper.* International Reading Association, Newark, Delaware, 1972.

DEROCHE, EDWARD F., *Project Update: The Newspaper in the Elementary and Junior High School Classroom.* International Media Press, Shorewood, Wisconsin, 1970.

EASTER, MARY B., *Remedial Reading and the Newspaper.* American Newspaper Publisher's Association, Dulles International Airport, Washington, D.C., 1975.

FIDELL, JEANETTE, AND HORN, VALERIE, *The New York Times for Reluctant Readers.* The New York Times School Services Department, 229 W. 43rd Street, New York, New York 10036, 1973.

MANONI, MARY H., *A Social Planetarium for the Now Curriculum.* The New York Times School Services Department, 229 W. 43rd Street, New York, New York 10036, 1975.

PIERCEY, DOROTHY, *A Daily Text for Thinking.* The Arizona Republic and Gazette, P.O. Box 1950, Phoenix, Arizona, 1971.

MNEMONICS

Mnemonics: This theme contains a wide variety of activities designed to assist in the memorization of school-related lists, names, arithmetic facts, capitals, spelling words, and rules. Special consideration is given to mnemonic devices for learning multiplication facts.

```
                    ASSOCIATION
                      memory
                      clothing          MATH GAMES
                      mannerisms          Contig
                                          Krypto

   ACRONYMS
   abbreviations
                                              MUSIC
                                              rhythm
                          ┌─────────┐         melody
                          │MNEMONIC │
                          │ DEVICES │
   CLASSIFICATION AND     └─────────┘
   GROUPING SCHEMES
   relationships

                                         STRATEGIES FOR LEARNING
                                         MULTIPLICATION FACTS
                                           fact chart
     REPETITION AND                        graph paper chart
     SPELLING WORDS    RULE LEARNING AND   circular slide rule
       written         PATTERN RECOGNITION
       oral              number sequence
                         pattern sequence
```

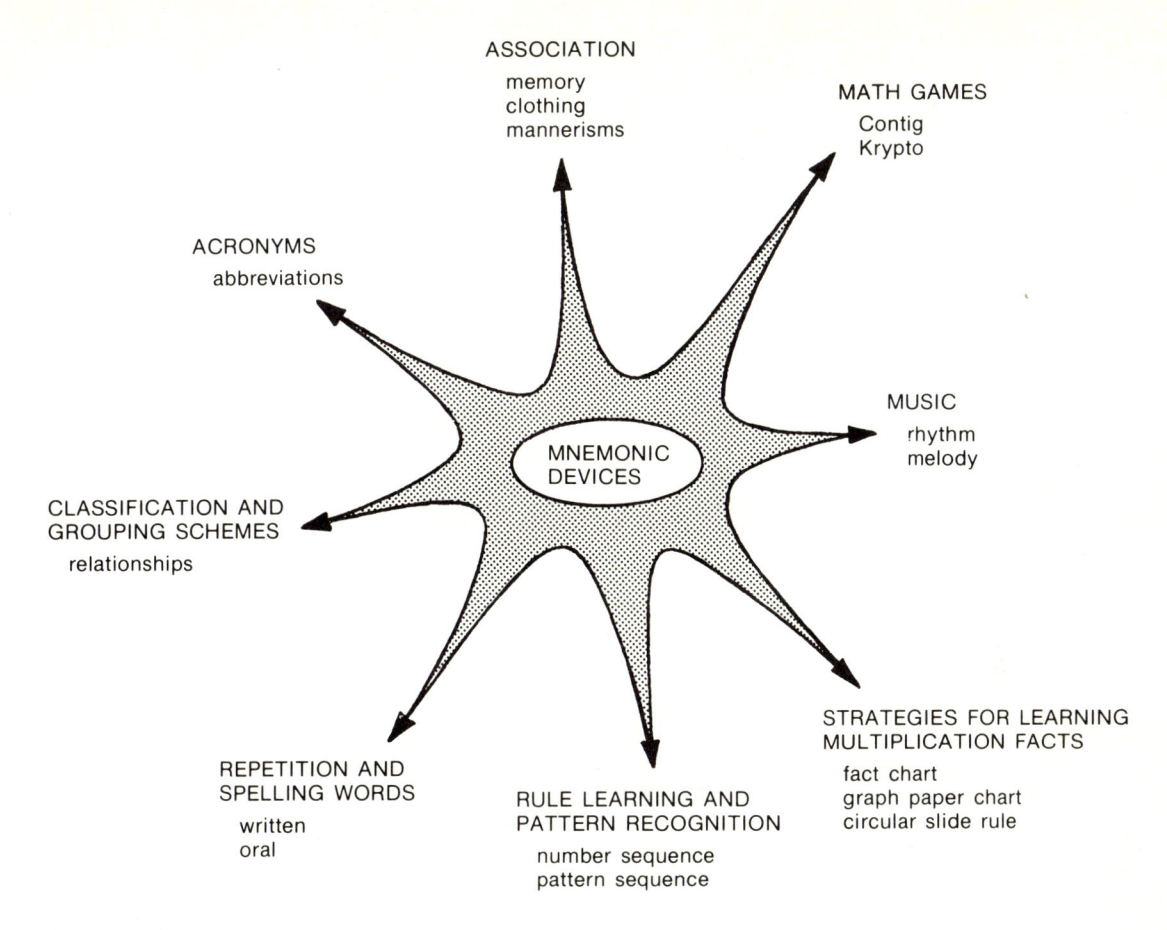

Introduction

Mnemonic (ni-'män-ik) adj.—assisting; intended to assist memory

It is useful to think about memory as relating to two different kinds of learning outcomes: 1. knowledge stating; and 2. rule application.* The former implies the preservation and retention of knowledge and meaning, and the ability to accurately relay such information to others. The latter, as its name implies, deals with the ability to use knowledge in an applied setting. This may require the individual to synthesize previously learned information and apply this to new problem situations. Both kinds of outcomes have an important place in the educational setting.

The activities here are designed to provide children with procedures that should simplify the task of memorizing specific information. Some of those items to be memorized will lack conceptual connections with previously learned information. This undoubtedly is the most difficult kind of material to memorize. Examples of these "free floating" bits of information are names of

---

*Gagne, R., and White, R., "Memory Structures and Learning Outcomes," *Review of Educational Research,* Spring 1978, pp. 189–222.

people, places, things, specific descriptive information about these, definitions, words of songs and poems, and *some* aspects of the interrelationships among elements in the real world (i.e., the fact that the bee is responsible for pollinating a wide variety of fruits and flowers).

The ability to recall is dependent upon the strength of the original association (implanting the item in memory), and by the interval between the time of learning and the time of revival. The strength of the original association usually determines whether an item is placed in long term or short term memory. The amount of forgetting is dependent upon these same two factors. These facts have tremendous implications for instruction.

If we expect children to remember things, then we must focus on the degree of impact that the material to be recalled has upon the individual at the time it is being encoded. Meaning, understanding, and self-construction are all factors that tend to accentuate the impact of the initial encoding.

Beyond these, there are mnemonic devices that can be utilized to aid students with memorization tasks. The sample lessons that follow are illustrative of the kind of things that can be done. You may enjoy developing other activities within each of the categories mentioned.

Unit Objective:

The students will learn a variety of procedures to simplify the memorization of specific information. These procedures will include rule learning, pattern recognition, repetition, and classification.

Appropriate Grade Levels:

Three to Six (adaptable for older and younger students as well)

ACTIVITY ONE:
REPETITION AND SPELLING WORDS: WRITTEN OR ORAL?

Objective: to learn an effective method for the memorization of spelling words

Materials: paper and pencils

Procedure: How do you learn? When asked this question, children aged seven to ten in Burnsville, Minnesota generated the following list*:

observing	writing
pictures and drawings	research

Ways to Learn/Teach, USMES Unit, Education Development Center, 55 Chapel Street, Newton, Mass., June 1975.

WHAT? A SAMPLER OF THEMATIC UNITS

TV	copying
experimenting	asking questions
survey	listening to teachers

In addition to these, memorization of isolated facts is often addressed through repetitive tasks of various kinds.

Focusing specifically on spelling words, a fourth grade class in Iowa City generated the following procedures for learning those words:

1. words flashed on a screen (flash cards)
2. write the word several times
3. read and study
4. make sentences using words
5. write definitions
6. write a story using words
7. practice test
8. have a spelling bee

This activity involves an experiment designed to test the relative effectiveness of two kinds of repetitive procedures on learning a list of spelling words. The two procedures are the use of flash cards with verbal repetition and the recopying of words in a notebook. A third procedure will combine both of these.

First, select an appropriate list of words to be learned. One such list used in a fourth grade class in Iowa City included these words:

escape	paralyze
luxuries	concern
mosquitos	stubborn
neighbor	across
occurrence	discuss

Second, select students who will be exposed to the three treatments. Pretest all subjects to be sure that they do not already know how to spell all the words on the spelling list used.

Next, make flash cards for each word, and then ask one group to view the flash cards and spell the words aloud. Repeat this procedure ten times. In the meantime, the second group should recopy each word in their notebooks ten times. Ask the third group to orally spell the word five times and then to recopy each word in their notebooks five times.

Your last step is to give all three treatment groups a post-test consisting of the ten words in random order. Record the results, figuring average scores for each group. It might be interesting to share and discuss the results with the whole class. You should also administer a retention test in three or four days, again recording and discussing the results with the class.

Evaluation: completion of tests, participation in class discussions and any activities associated with the group's study method

ACTIVITY TWO:
ASSOCIATION: WHAT WAS HIS NAME AGAIN?

Objective: to use associations by memorizing students' names

Materials: none needed

Procedure: Often memory can be assisted by forcing a mental association between the item to be remembered and some overt characteristic of that item. Such a technique is often used by persons credited with having outstanding memories. You have, no doubt, heard of the person who has been introduced to a room full of people and remembers everyone's name for the rest of the evening. An ability to remember in this way can enormously affect one's social poise and is obviously worth some attention. Such a feat is usually accomplished using mental associations.

Give your students a chance to practice associative memory techniques. When trying to remember the names of people, for example, urge them to make a conscious effort to mentally connect the person's name with some obvious property about that person, such as their clothing or their mannerisms. For example, <u>B</u>arbara might be wearing a <u>b</u>lue <u>b</u>louse. In addition to these associations, encourage children to use the individual's name in conversation whenever appropriate and initially to think of the name or some characteristic whenever looking at the person. You will be amazed at how much the students' ability to remember names will improve with a little practice.

A procedure that can be used to remember students' names on the first day of class deals with continuous repetition of ever-expanding sequences of names and faces. Using this procedure, it is possible to learn thirty names in about twenty to twenty-five minutes. The procedure is as follows. First, have all the students make and display name tags on their blouses or shirts. Next, select two or three students, mentally associating their names and faces, and do this until you feel quite comfortable with their names. Now expand the list by one name, repeating the above procedure. Continue until you can associate the names and faces of all the students. Order is not important after four or five names have been memorized.

The ability to recall people's names on Monday does not guarantee that you will be able to do it again on Tuesday. Explain to your class that steps must be taken to repeat the entire procedure once or twice more. The second and third times are obviously much easier. By the third time, you will probably only miss one or two names. Finally, to firmly plant these names in long term memory, you need only use them in normal activity as the opportunities arise.

One last point is worth noting. To conduct the above activity, it is obvious that the person doing the remembering must devote his or her full attention to the task. If that person is you, the teacher, engage children in group work or individual projects of some type while you conduct the activity. If the students are the ones involved, all class members can do it at the same time. Simply have them assemble in the center of the room in a group activity.

Evaluation: ability to name all the students in the class

ACTIVITY THREE:
A POCKET FULL OF . . .

Objective: to combine repetition and association to improve memory

Materials: set of cards, marked with the items to be memorized

two pockets or containers for each game

paper and pencils

Procedure: This activity utilizes both repetition and association. The general idea can be used to help students memorize basic factual information, such as names of people, places, and things, poetry, songs, or virtually any item of interest.

The first thing to do is to decide what is to be learned. As an example, you might use a word-picture association between the names of plants and their pictures. On one side of the card, you would print the name of the plant, and on the other paste its picture. Do this for all plants, or other items, on your list.

Now place the completed cards in one pocket. The object is for each student to transfer all cards to the second pocket and back again. A single card can be transferred only if the correct name of the plant is supplied. If not named correctly, the card is replaced in the same pocket at the back of the stack. When all cards have been moved to the second pocket, students repeat the procedure. By the time all cards are back where they started it is likely that the information has been memorized, since each card has been successfully reacted to on two different occasions. Note that this activity requires only a small period of spare time. As little as two or three minutes can be used to run through a small number of cards.

The game is solitary in nature and places one in competition only with oneself. The gimmick of moving cards from one pocket to another will motivate many children to learn the information.

If a large number of cards are involved, you may want to categorize the information first, asking pupils to react to smaller sections at a time. In addition, if long term memory is desired, this entire procedure will need to be repeated sporadically. The needed frequency of such repetition will be dependent upon the capabilities of the child involved.

Some of the types of items which could be learned using this procedure include:

1. names of animals and birds
2. facts about plants and animals
3. states and their capitals
4. number facts (addition, subtraction)
5. poetry and/or songs
6. specific facts about virtually anything

Evaluation: placement of all cards into the beginning pocket or container, indicating memorization of all items presented

ACTIVITY FOUR: RULE LEARNING AND PATTERN RECOGNITION

Objective: to use rules and patterns to improve memorization

Materials: paper and pencils, if desired

Procedure: Remembering rules and patterns is much more efficient than learning isolated numbers. This is true because in many cases (though not all) the isolated numbers can be thought of as being specific examples of a particular rule or pattern. For example, consider the following number sequence: 71421283542. It would be difficult to remember this sequence if the task were approached without attempting to find some structure or pattern. Further, it would be impossible to predict the next number in the sequence (which, incidentally, is a 4) unless some type of meaning was attached to it.

As soon as one realizes that any number in the sequence can be generated simply by adding seven to the previous number, i.e., 7 14 21 28, the pattern becomes clear and can be continued indefinitely. In this case, however, we are not remembering the sequence but rather the rule that generates that sequence.

The economy of this type of endeavor should be very clear. One rule or pattern permits immediate access to an infinite sequence of numbers. This is sometimes referred to as understanding, and has tremendous implications for what we do with children. Too often time is spent remembering isolated bits when that same time could be used more productively searching for the more general and more powerful rule or pattern.

The generation or the discovery of rules or patterns by children is an incredibly important intellectual endeavor and one most worthy of expanded attention in schools. In order to build skills of this type, provide opportunities for children to examine lists and search for patterns. When you begin, you may find yourself providing all of the answers. After several repetitions, however, at least some of your students will begin to be able to identify those rules or patterns themselves.

Evaluation: successful naming of sequences of numbers or items presented, and/or the ability to identify the rule or pattern in a sequence

*ACTIVITIES FIVE AND SIX:** MUSIC AND MEMORIZATION, AN INTRODUCTION

Activities that use melody, rhythm, or melody plus rhythm (music) may be structured to help students recall sequentially ordered numbers, letters, objects, or events. Some general ideas for combining musical elements and memorization are:

1. melody with telephone numbers
2. rhythm with spelling
3. rhythm with science facts (bones in the body, flower parts)
4. music with arithmetic facts (addition, subtraction)

The following two activities will look individually at these two musical components as they affect memory.

*The authors are indebted to their colleague in Music Therapy, Professor Judith Jellison, for her contributions to Activities Five and Six.

ACTIVITY FIVE:
RHYTHM AND MEMORIZATION

Objective: to use rhythm to aid memorization of the spelling of the names of states (or any other list)

Materials: simple rhythm instruments, if desired (tambourines, rhythm sticks)

Procedure: To illustrate this procedure, the spelling of states in the United States could be coupled with rhythm. While it may be that the use of rhythm is not necessary or appropriate to teach the spelling of all of the states, it may be helpful for learning those that tend to be the most difficult for many students.

Have the students look at a selected list of the states including Ohio. You will clap four slow and even beats. Ask students to select a state from the list that best "fits" the rhythm you have clapped. They will probably select Ohio since it has four letters. Now, both the students and you should clap while spelling Ohio in a slow and even four-beat rhythm. Note: When the entire class claps, students should use only two fingers to clap in the palm of the other hand. This enables the spelling of the states to be heard.

The students should then select another state from the list that they would like to hear spelled in rhythm. You will clap the new state's name in rhythm, making sure to keep the rhythm in a pattern that fits the four beats or repeated four beat patterns (8s, 12s) of Ohio. Examples would be as follows:

1	2	3	4	5	6	7	8
O	K	L	A	H	O	M	A
C	O	L	O	R	A	D	O
A	R	K	A	N	S	A	S

You and your students should clap and spell the new state rhythm together. Time should be spent with each rhythm in variations (clapping without spelling, spelling in rhythm without clapping, half the class, individuals) before introducing new rhythms.

Once a new rhythm is learned, combine that rhythm with the Ohio rhythm as indicated above. You may choose to use instruments after, and only after, the students do well with clapping. More difficult combinations may be attempted. In any case, be sure to keep a strong leader in front for each state rhythm group while you maintain the strong, four-beat Ohio rhythm.

Evaluation: correct clapping of rhythms presented, correct spelling of state names presented for learning

ACTIVITY SIX:
MELODY AND MEMORIZATION

Objective: to use melody to aid memorization of telephone numbers, or of any lists desired

Materials: melody instrument(s)

Procedure: The use of melody to assist in recall of an emergency telephone number is a further example of mnemonics. The telephone number used should be written on the board. Have students identify the direction of the notes in the melody from the numbers, with direction indicated by the magnitude of the number. For example: 633-1827 would result melodically in the starting note 6, down 3, same 3, down 1, up 8, down 2, up 7.

You should sing or play the starting note for the first number on a melody instrument. Students, following the melody pattern, then create melodies and present them to the class through singing or playing on melody instruments.

The class can determine the "best" melody and practice singing this newly created tune. In order to help the students retain this learning, have them sing the melody periodically throughout the year.

Evaluation: correct naming of numbers or items in sequence presented for memorization, correct use of melody system with identified items

ACTIVITY SEVEN:
ACRONYMS

Objective: to use acronyms to aid memorization

Materials: none needed

Procedure: As you may know, an acronym is a word formed from the initial letter or letters of each of the successive parts or major parts of a compound term. Both abbreviations and acronyms have been used as aids to memory for many years. Abbreviations, of which acronyms are a form, have been found on the earliest known tombs, monuments, and coins. Before the printing press was invented, when manuscripts were written by hand, many abbreviations were used to save time and space. Hundreds of Latin abbreviations are still used.

Some commonly used abbreviations and acronyms include the following:

AAA	American Automobile Association
CPA	Certified Public Accountant
NATO	North Atlantic Treaty Organization
VIP	Very Important Person

Others that probably have been a part of your past include:

HOMES	The names of the Great Lakes
ROYGBIV	The names and order of the colors of the spectrum
Every Good Boy Does Fine	The names of the lines of the musical staff

To make use of this memory technique, encourage children to construct their own acronyms and abbreviations for sequences which need to be memorized. Share these orally or by creating some type of room display. With a little encouragement, students can have a great deal of fun with this while also building their store of learned information.

Evaluation: correct recall of acronyms presented, sharing of created acronyms

ACTIVITIES EIGHT TO THIRTEEN: STRATEGIES FOR LEARNING BASIC FACTS

Although a balanced mathematics program must contain much more than mere calculations with whole numbers, fractions, and decimals, it is clear that such calculation is an important component of any program. Will it always be necessary for children to learn to compute by hand? While there are some who would suggest that students be taught instead to use small calculators, many parents are concerned that their children are not learning "the basics," including hand computation. The fact remains that the ability to calculate is a vital tool, required by those everyday occurrences that are quantitative in nature. Further, it facilitates problem solving for those who have mastered its finer points.

However, while the mastery of the basic facts has always been considered a worthwhile objective of a school mathematics program, it is also one which has caused grave consternation to teachers and pupils alike. Some students will never fully master these facts regardless of the methodology used, the amount of time spent, or the degree of pressure placed upon them to do so. Other students capable of such mastery find the process of learning these facts very distasteful.

WHAT? A SAMPLER OF THEMATIC UNITS

The activities that conclude this unit suggest alternate ways to learn these basics. We hope these activities will make the task more rewarding for both you and your children. Do keep in mind that the objective of mastery for all students needs to be questioned. Sometimes in our zealousness this simple fact can be forgotten, resulting in too much emphasis and too high a premium being placed upon it. If you remember that they are extremely useful tools but that many individuals have matured successfully and have become contributors to our society while never fully mastering all of the basic facts, you may be more apt to place the basics in the proper perspective.

ACTIVITY EIGHT: FACT CHART

Objective: to learn multiplication facts through the use of a fact chart

Materials: copy of chart for each student

pencils and scissors

Procedure: A very useful tool for pupils from the time they begin to develop an awareness of multiplication until all the basic facts are memorized (which can seem like forever) is the basic fact chart.

The chart is built as pupils progress. It should *not* be given to them already filled in to be memorized. In the early learning stages, the chart may be large enough to accomodate factors and products only through $5 \times 5 = 25$. As pupils develop the product relationships through various means (arrays, number lines, cross products), results are placed on the chart. It should be expanded to full size as the need for larger products arises.

Using the chart as a reference tool provides continuous reinforcement and will encourage retention of the facts. To use the chart to its best advantage, each pupil should make one. Individual charts may be mounted on tagboard and kept in the pupil's math book or taped to the top of his or her desk.

As pupils mature and are ready to be "weaned" from dependence upon the chart (be sure about this readiness) try this next step on an individual basis. Set goals with the children to commit the facts to memory. They will undoubtedly know half or more already. Determine this by administering a test on the facts. Those facts that are already known can be cut away from each chart. Be sure before cutting that a border is left around the chart so that it won't fall apart when it is cut.

Set a schedule with the children for the next testing. The interval used could be weekly, biweekly, etc. After each test, snip away the known facts. In this way, the pupils will be competing only against themselves. Individual progress will thus be very visible. The cut-up chart quickly shows that the number of facts requiring concentration is becoming fewer and fewer after each testing.

This process can also be extended by using a completed multiplication chart to find the corresponding division facts. The inverse relationship between multiplication and division is emphasized when the chart is used in this way. Example:

$48 \div 6 = ?$ Find 48 in the field of products. Find the 6 either at the left or at the top.
Find the missing factor in the corresponding top or left row.

Evaluation: correct naming of all multiplication facts, same for division facts if extended to these facts

ACTIVITY NINE: GRAPH PAPER CHART

Objective: to complete graph paper chart for multiplication facts

Materials: graph paper
crayons

Procedure: When graph paper squares are colored in, a vivid pattern of multiplication facts appears. Have pupils color in the second row of squares to show the product of 1×1, 1×2, and 1×3. Have them leave one square blank around each product. Next, have them color blocks to show 2×1, 2×2, and 2×3. Be sure that one row is left blank between each product. The pattern will look like this:

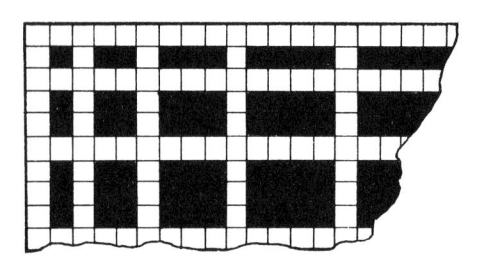

Examination of the colored blocks reveals multiplication facts as regions of various sizes. Special regions are along the major diagonal starting with the

WHAT? A SAMPLER OF THEMATIC UNITS **253**

1 × 1 block, these regions all being square in shape. By looking at the two halves of the chart when a diagonal line is drawn from corner to corner, students can see pairings of regions to illustrate the commutative property.

To make other discoveries, have students extend the paper and complete blocks beyond 6 × 6. If this activity is done on larger scale graph paper, it can become a good group project for class display.

Evaluation: correct completion of graph paper chart, ability to correctly answer questions concerning the patterns it shows

ACTIVITY TEN:
USING A CIRCULAR SLIDE RULE FOR MULTIPLICATION AND DIVISION

Objective: to construct and correctly use a circular slide rule for multiplication and division computations

Materials:
copies of two slide rule components for each child
thumbtacks
corks, tape, or small pieces of soft wood

Procedure: This particular rule has been modified slightly (numbers through 100 added) from the engineer's rule. It was developed as part of the Minnesota Mathematics and Science Teaching Project (Minnemast), Unit #27, *Numbers and Their Properties,* published by the University of Minnesota Press, 1970.

In this activity, it is used to generate products to 100, although its use can be extended further. The circular rule illustrated can be reproduced for student use. Before proceeding, have students cut out both circles, place a thumbtack (point up) precisely through the cross hairs in the center of each rule and place a cork, piece of tape, or small piece of soft wood on top of the tack. The inner rule should rotate smoothly within the layer.

When this is completed, instruct students on the use of this device. For example, show them how to multiply 6 × 8 (a similar procedure is used for all problems of the form a × b = n where a and b are known). Explain orally, or provide in written form, the following steps:

1. Locate the first factor on the outside rule. (6)
2. Place 1 of the inside rule directly under the number identified in Step 1. (6)
3. Locate the second factor on the inside scale. (8)

4. Read product on outside scale directly opposite the second factor on the inside scale. (48)

Provide many similar problems to the class so that each student can practice and learn this technique.

This circular rule can also help to show that division is the operational inverse of multiplication. Thus, to divide 48 by 8, students should be instructed to first align 8 on the inside scale under 48 on the outside scale, then to find 1 on the inside scale and read the answer directly opposite it on the outside scale (in this case, 6). Again, repeated opportunities for practice should be provided.

Activities with the circular slide rule can also be extended to calculation with multidigit numbers. The procedure always remains the same (i.e., steps 1–4), but the slide rule can be used to approximate products through 1000. For example, the same placement of the rule as explained above could be used to illustrate $60 \times 8 = 480$.

It should be noted, however, that the precise answer is not always forthcoming when multiplying larger numbers because of the inaccuracy in this particular slide rule, and the adjustments which the student must make. Still, use of this rule forces children to estimate answers and to consider the reasonableness of their conclusions.

Multiplication slide rules use a logarithmic scale. For a detailed explanation, see *Computing Devices* by Donavan Johnson and William Glenn, Webster Publishing Company, 1961.

Evaluation: correct answers given to multiplication and division problems with the aid of the circular slide rule

ACTIVITY ELEVEN:
HOW MANY BASIC FACTS MUST ONE LEARN?

Objective: to complete multiplication computations using either or both of the two finger methods

Materials: none needed

Procedure: The prospect of memorizing 100 multiplication facts is overwhelming for some students. Fortunately, by applying one or two mathematical principles and number tricks, that number can be reduced considerably. There really are not 100 distinct basic facts to learn. Refer to a multiplication chart and consider these points:

255

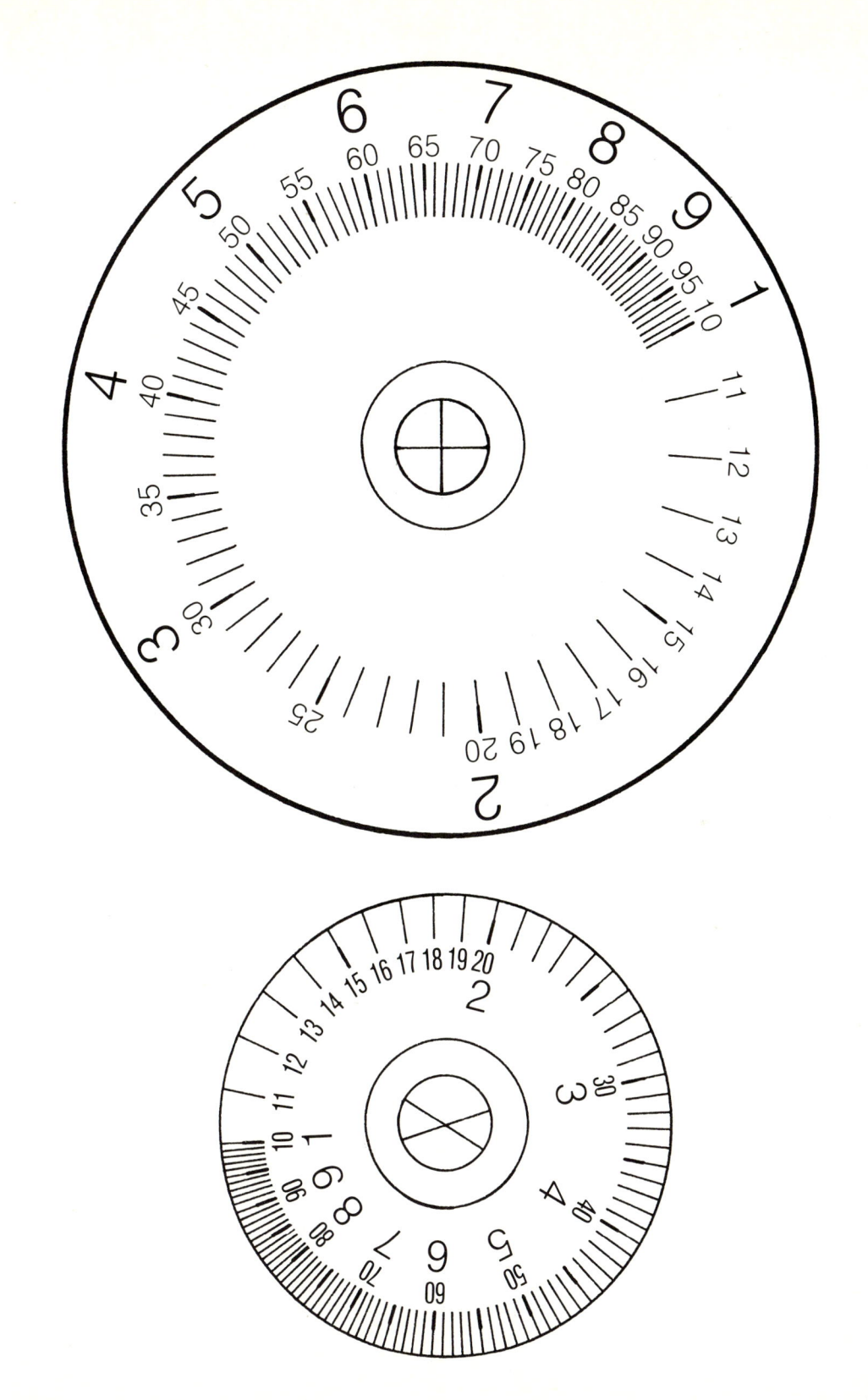

TOTAL NUMBER LEFT	
100 −45 ――― 55	1. Application of the commutative property of multiplication reduces the number from 100 to 55. This principle states that for all real numbers, a × b = b × a. It is thus necessary for the child to learn only about half of the total number of facts.
−9 ――― 45	2. The zeros are easy.
	3. The ones are easy.
−8 ――― 36	4. The twos are also easy—children don't multiply by twos, but double instead.
−7 ――― 31	5. There are now 31 left, and ten of these are doubles (5 × 5, 8 × 8).

Children will need to spend some time practicing the remaining rules. Here are two number tricks that may help to ease the burden. Both are forms of finger multiplication. Please note that such "tricks" as these do not promote true understanding and therefore are not to be confused with basic developmental activities. It is assumed that such work has preceeded the use of these methods.

The first method uses fingers to represent specific numbers as shown here.

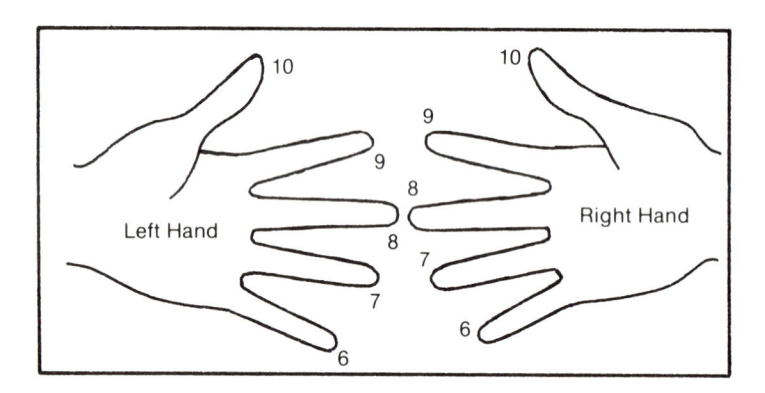

For the multiplication of two numbers, give your students the following directions.

1. Touch together the two fingers that represent the numbers you wish to multiply. For example, to multiply 8 × 7 the hands should be positioned as in the diagram.

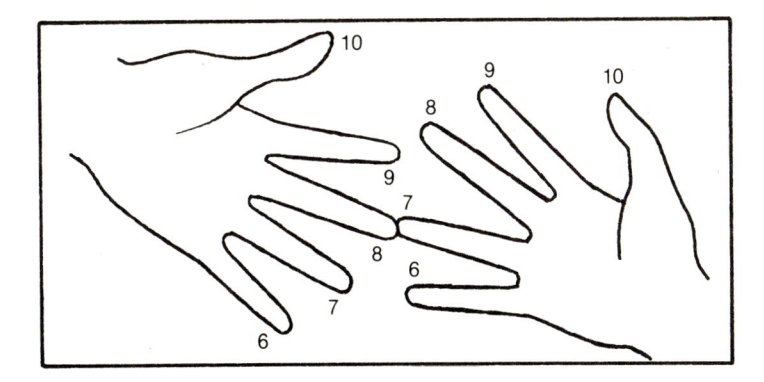

2. Count the number of fingers touching and below. This is the number of tens (in this problem, 5 tens or 50).

3. Multiply the number of fingers (including thumbs) above those touching on the left hand by those above on the right hand (here, 2 × 3 = 6).

4. To find the product, add the results of steps 2 and 3 (50 + 6 = 56; therefore, 8 × 7 = 56).

Students should be given more opportunities to calculate in this way until they can do this process quickly.

The second method is based on residuals over five. Using the same example of 8 × 7, students should be instructed to:

1. Raise three fingers on the left hand (5 + 3 = 8) and two on the right hand (5 + 2 = 7). The total of the raised fingers is thus 5, representing the number of tens.

2. The number of fingers not raised on the left hand is 2, and on the right hand is 3. These represent the ones.

3. The product of these "down" fingers is six (2 × 3). This is added to the 50 generated above. The product of 8 and 7 is therefore 50 + 6 or 56.

Evaluation: correct answers to multiplication or division problems through use of either or both of the methods taught

ACTIVITY TWELVE: CONTIG

Objective: to apply basic arithmetic facts in a game situation

Materials:
Contig game board (see page 259)
3 dice
playing chips

Procedure: Contig is a math facts game that can be used by two or more players. It is suggested that you make a printed copy of the rules available to players along with the game board. This is a good game for your students to play independently when work is finished. The rules of the game are as follows.

The first player shakes the three dice. That player may add, subtract, multiply, or divide using each die only once. A chip is placed on that number. Each player, in turn, repeats this procedure. The objective is to generate, using three dice, a number that appears next to a number which is already covered by a chip. A player earns one point for each chip the new number is touching. The person with the highest number of points wins the game.

Evaluation: participation in the game by each student

ACTIVITY THIRTEEN: KRYPTO

Objective: to correctly use computation skills to play the Krypto game

Materials: 52 cards, marked as directed in Procedure

Procedure: Krypto is played with a deck of 52 cards, numbered from 1 to 25. There are:

- 3 cards each of the numbers from 1 to 10
- 2 cards each of the numbers from 11 to 17
- 1 card each of the numbers from 18 to 25

The object of the game is to combine five cards (the hand) to equal the sixth card (the objective, or Krypto card) by using only the rules of simple arithmetic. Any number from 2 to 8 can play. The rules of the game are as follows.

\multicolumn{8}{c	}{**CONTIG**}
1	2	3	4	5	6	7	8
9	10	11	12	13	14	15	16
17	18	19	20	21	22	23	24
25	26	27	28	29	30	31	32
33	34	35	36	37	38	39	40
41	42	44	45	48	50	54	55
60	64	66	72	75	80	90	96
100	108	120	125	144	150	180	216

A dealer is selected by having each player draw a card from the deck, with the player having the highest card dealing first. Thereafter, as the hands are dealt, the winner of each previous hand is the next dealer. Five cards are dealt to each player, numbered side down. The cards remain down until the dealer turns up the Krypto card (the next card in the deck). As this is done, all players pick up their hands and begin to play. The aim of each player is to use the numbers on each card in his or her hand to equal the Krypto card by using addition, subtraction, multiplication, or division. *Each card must be used once and only once.* The first player to use all five cards to match the Krypto card says "Krypto" and verifies how his or her cards were combined to get that number. One point is scored for each correct solution. A new hand is then dealt and the play continues.

Evaluation: participation in Krypto game, ability to perform correctly the computations required in the game

PATTERNS AND CHANGES

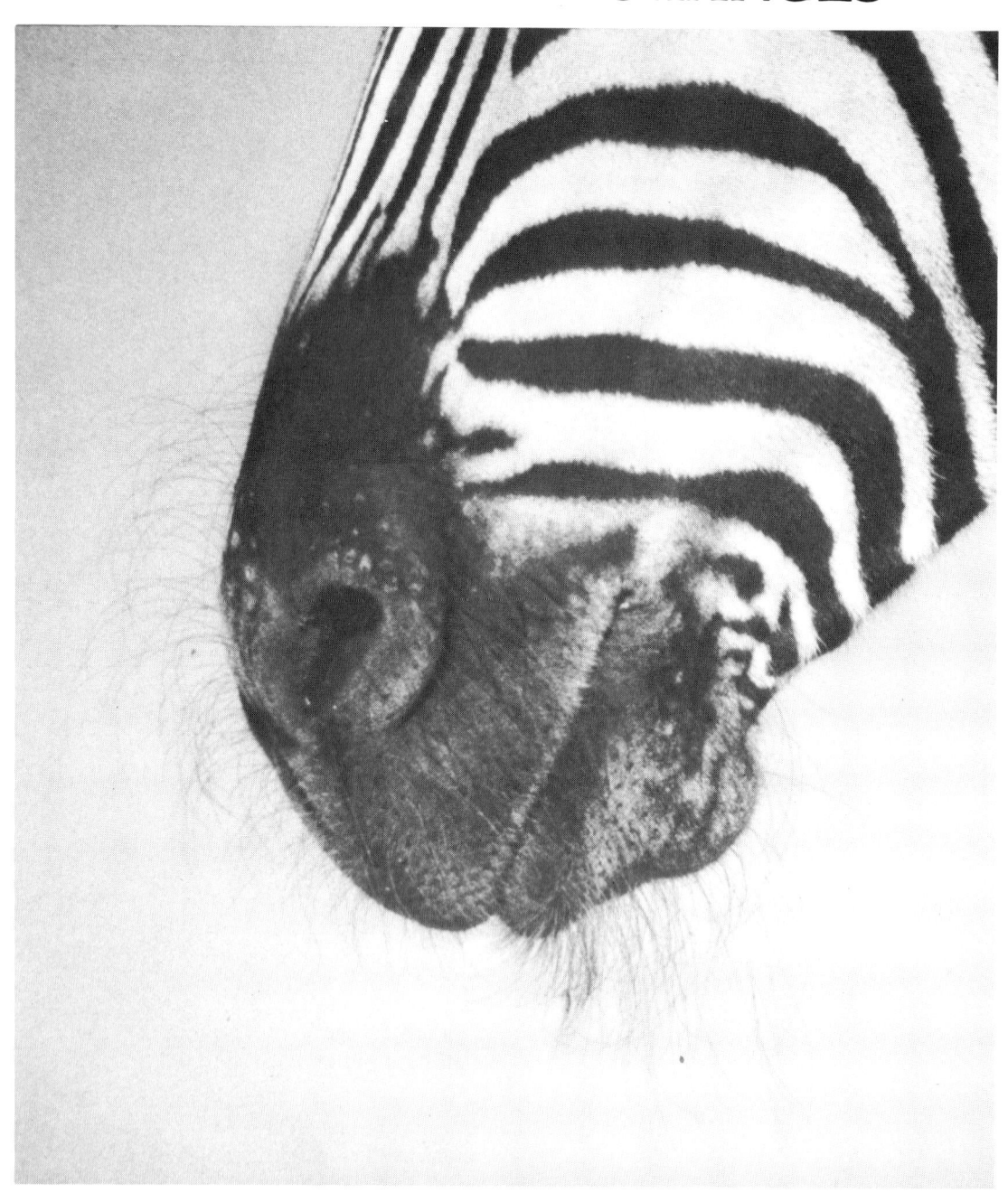

Patterns and Changes: Prediction of regularity and patterns through experimentation and systematic data collection permit the student to deduce several fundamental principles of the physical sciences.

WEATHER PATTERNS
temperature
barometric pressure

CENTER OF GRAVITY
balance

PATTERNS AND CHANGES

SEASONS
sun, moon and earth systems
daily, weekly and
 monthly changes

PENDULUMS
sand
connected
long-arm

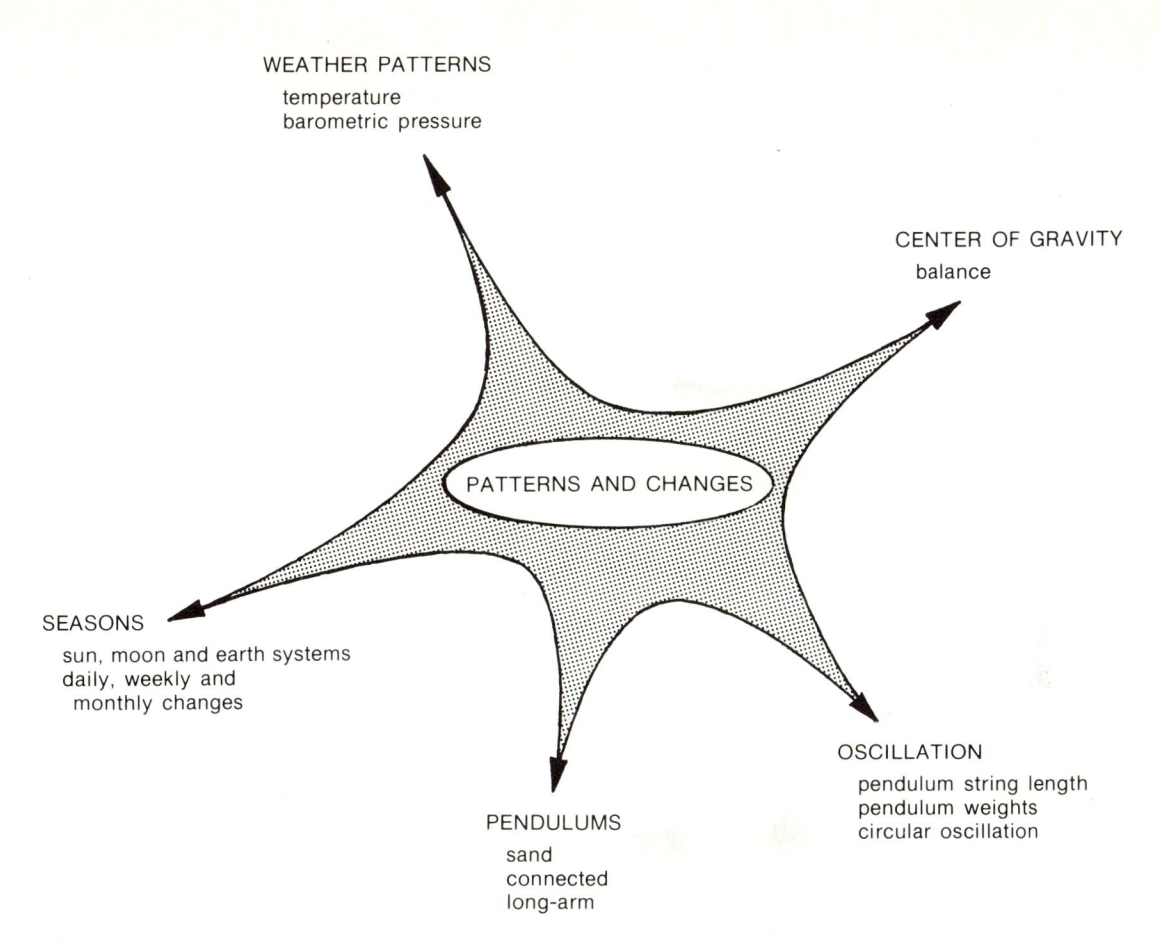

OSCILLATION
pendulum string length
pendulum weights
circular oscillation

Introduction

All of the systems we observe display changes. Many systems change from a first state to a second and then back to the first. A pendulum is a classic example of a system that displays regular oscillations. To list all systems is beyond the scope of this unit. A few systems that children know of or can easily understand include:

1. *The sun/moon/earth system.* The sun's apparent position changes but the change repeats itself every twenty-four hours. The moon's position changes but it goes through one change from full moon to new to full every twenty-nine and a half days and exhibits thirteen of these phases per year.

2. *The climate of a region.* Climate changes during the seasons but repeats itself every year. Short-range weather patterns are very complex but variations from sunny periods to cloudy periods often show a cycle of about seven days.

3. *The rise and fall of rivers.* Rivers respond to a variety of climatic conditions. Seasonal snow melts and monsoon rains are but two of the causes.

4. *The growth of plants*. Growth is a function of climate and most plants in temperate zones emerge in the spring, flourish during the summer, and go into a resting or dormant stage during dry and cold periods.

In this unit, you should introduce the concept of systems that change in a predictable way. You may wish to show how a pendulum swings and retraces the same path over and over. Through discussion about the motion of the sun, the polar angle of the earth, the path of the earth, and the resulting seasonal phenomenon, expand the children's awareness of the many oscillating systems that exist. Describe how seasons are related to a host of naturally reoccurring changes, such as the rising and falling of rivers, plant growth cycles, and seasonal bird migrations.

You will also want to point out that, often, an oscillating system will "force" oscillation in a new system. As an example, explain that the vibrating strings of a guitar force the sounding box to vibrate, generating audible sound waves in the air. There are also systems that resonate with each other. Just as a pendulum has a particular period, so does the back-and-forth motion of the springs of a car. Almost everyone has at one time or another driven over a dirt road with "washboards." The washboarding or arranging of piles of dirt across the road is generated by many cars. Each car's springs are resonant with the others. Each oscillating set of springs builds the washboards that in turn set the next car's springs into rhythmical oscillations.

As in other units, you can use a film or book about seasons, pendulums, weather, or even bird migration to introduce the unit theme and begin to expand the children's understanding of cycles and oscillations. After viewing and discussing the book or film, you may wish to develop a web, starting, if desired, with the webbing presented at the beginning of this unit.

Following that introduction, you may begin to use some or all of the eight activities that follow. The first six of these activities deal with several kinds and arrangements of pendulums. Throughout these activities, be sure to give your students ample time to play with the different pendulums they construct, and a large space like a gym or open stairwell to work in. The remaining two activities concern balance and weather patterns.

All of these activities can be used as guides and need not be followed in any order. After some basic understandings have been developed, encourage groups of children to go beyond the suggestions and explore other systems that change from one state to another in a regular, predictable way. You may, in particular, want to work with those systems with which children are most familiar, such as the seasons of the year. No matter what or how many patterns and systems you investigate, your students are sure to benefit from their new understandings of the order that exists in the world around them.

Unit Objectives:

The students will:

1. learn about some common systems, such as the seasons of the year and the sun/moon/earth system, and how they bring about changes.

2. learn about different kinds and characteristics of pendulums.
3. build an understanding of the effects of systems on their lives and those of others around them.

Appropriate Grade Levels:

Three to Six

ACTIVITY ONE:
MAKING A SIMPLE PENDULUM

Objective: to make and use a simple pendulum, and to explore how to change its period

Materials:
- small pieces of cardboard
- string
- masking tape
- weights (washers, fishing sinkers, nuts or bolts, etc.)

Procedure: Give your students the following directions, either orally or in writing:

1. Take a piece of string and push it through the hole in your piece of cardboard. Tie a knot, and then fasten the cardboard to the underside of your desk with masking tape. In this way, your desk is supporting your pendulum. Now tie a weight to the loose end of your string.
2. You may instead fasten a stick between two desks and fasten the string to the stick if you prefer. This may give your pendulum more room in which to swing, and you could share it with a friend.

Be sure to allow sufficient time for students to assemble and mount their pendulums, repeating directions or giving assistance as needed.

Once the pendulums are ready, explain to students that the period of a pendulum is the time duration for a complete back-and-forth swing or oscillation. Allow students a minute or two to set their pendulums in motion and to time their periods. Then explain that they are to try to find out how they can change the period of the pendulum. To get them started, tell them that one way they might change the period is to start the swing in different places.

Next, ask students to try to think of three changes they could make with their pendulums that might change the period, and write those possibilities down. Then divide the class into several small groups in which students will share their ideas with each other. You may want to appoint a recorder to write down some of the suggestions of the group members. Finally, have students test each of the suggestions. When finished, they should circle those suggestions that did change the period of the pendulum. End with a discussion time during which the findings of each group are shared.

Evaluation: completion of pendulum and ability to name ways in which a pendulum's period can be changed

ACTIVITY TWO:
PENDULUM STRING LENGTHS AND OSCILLATIONS

Objective: to measure and graph the relationship between changes in the arm lengths of pendulums and their periods of oscillation

Materials:
- string
- weights
- tape
- cardboard
- chart and graph forms

Procedure: Review the findings of Activity One by pointing out that the students probably found out that the length of the string is related to the pendulum's oscillation period. Tell them that, while they have no way of testing it, a change in the pull of gravity would change the period. The period would, in fact, get longer as the pull of gravity decreased. Because of the effects of gravity, ask if students think that a pendulum would work in a space ship or a space laboratory, or on the moon.

Ask for volunteers to complete this sentence. The longer the string, the _____ the period of the pendulum. Then tell your class that their next investigation will be to find out whether a pendulum with a twenty-one cm string, making ten oscillations in ten seconds, will make ten oscillations in twenty seconds if changed so that the string is forty-two cm long.

Before they begin, explain to them that all relationships are not linear. That is, when one variable (such as pendulum length) changes, the other variable (period) changes, too, but that if you plot length versus period, the points on the grid do not lie in a straight line. After eliciting some guesses as to the kind of a pattern or curve several such points (length of pendulum arm vs. period) would make, have students carry out the experiment. While doing so, have them collect some data and plot it on graph and chart forms like those printed below. Note that they will be making several variations of string length to complete the experiment.

When they are finished, tell them to look carefully at their curves and predict the answer to the following questions.

1. If you make a pendulum with a three meter-long string, how many swings would you predict this pendulum would make in ten seconds?
2. How long would the pendulum string have to be if the pendulum were to make ten swings in one minute?

Evaluation: completion of pendulum experiment and the chart and graph recordings of the results

Length of arm in cm	Number of seconds per 10 swings

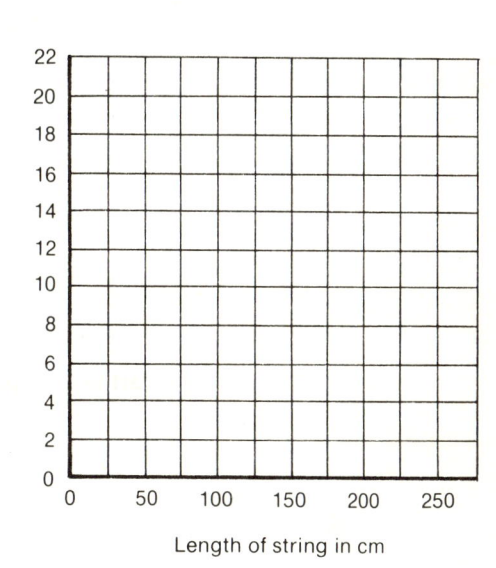

ACTIVITY THREE:
PENDULUM WEIGHTS AND OSCILLATIONS

Objective: to make paper cup pendulums and to measure and record the effects of varying weights on the period of oscillation

Materials: Slinky spring, or several rubber bands tied together

paper cups with sand in them

Procedure: If students have completed Activities One and Two, they have by now discovered that the period of a pendulum is related to the string, or arm, length. They are now going to need to determine how long the string should be so that their pendulums oscillate once in one second. They will again need to each use a short piece of stick, string, and a small weight to set up the pendulum under their desks. Because this pendulum needs to be an accurate minute-measuring device and will be used for several other activities, it should be made with care.

Once this "timing" pendulum has been completed by each student, you are ready to begin the next step of the experiment. To do so, you will need a Slinky spring or a chain of rubber bands, a cup, and some sand. If you don't have a Slinky, tie the rubber bands together instead. Then have the oscillating slinky set up as shown. Note that the paper cup is fastened to the slinky or rubber bands by using three bent paper clips.

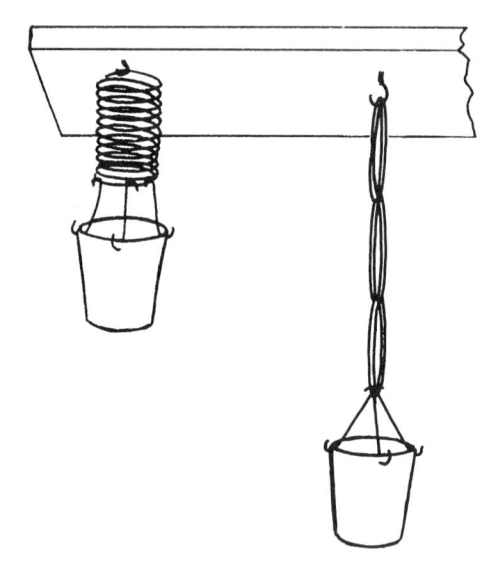

Point out that the oscillation in this case consists of an up and down, rather than a back and forth, motion. Remind students that when, in Activity One, they added weights to their pendulum, the addition did not seem to change the period. They should now place a few weights in the cup so that the slinky is stretched to about twenty-four inches (about sixty-one cm). Someone should then start it oscillating up and down, keeping in mind that now one oscillation or period is the time it takes for the cup to move to the down position, up, and back down again. Have students start their pendulum second counters to find out how many times the Slinky oscillates in ten seconds. Once this information is recorded, some weights should be removed or added, and the new period measured and recorded. Have students complete these sentences, which could be written on the board while they are conducting their experiment:

1. When the cup was lighter, the spring oscillated _____ times in ten seconds.
2. When the cup was heavier, the spring oscillated _____ times in ten seconds.

If students are surprised by their findings, point out that this kind of an oscillating system *does* change its period as the bob weight is changed. Ask what else they think could be changed that would change the period of the Slinky system, and list all of the ideas expressed on the board. Have students then select one idea that interests them or their group and change their Slinky system accordingly to find out if making this one change does change the period of their system. Remind them to use their pendulum second timers and to check their results carefully.

Finally, ask this question: "Does the period of the Slinky system versus weight in the cup generate a set of points that are linear? What would you guess?" Have students, individually or within small groups, guess whether this would be a linear set of points or a nonlinear set of points. Have them follow their guesses by collecting data and checking their results, using forms like those shown.

Evaluation: completion of paper cup pendulums, the experiments described using them, and the records to be kept of the results of those experiments

Weight (number of same-sized washers in cup)	Number of oscillations in 10 seconds

Weight or number of same-sized washers

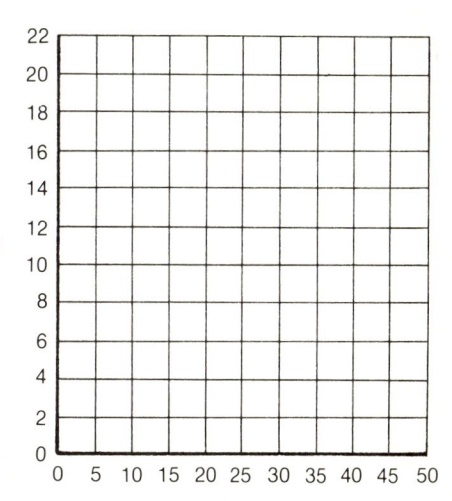

Number of oscillations in 10 seconds

ACTIVITY FOUR:
PENDULUM STRING LENGTH AND NUMBER OF OSCILLATIONS

Objective: to vary the string length of a pendulum and measure the corresponding changes in the number of oscillations

Materials: Tinkertoys

string pendulums, two per child

paper clips

Procedure: To carry out this experiment, each student will again need a minute measuring pendulum. Each student will also need to make a simple Tinkertoy frame from which a single pendulum is suspended. Once all "equipment" is set up and ready to use, give the following directions.

1. Using your one-second timing pendulum, swing this pendulum and record the number of times it oscillates in ten seconds.
2. Make a second pendulum but make the string two inches shorter (about five cm) and suspend it from the same frame. Swing only the first pendulum. Record what happens to the second one.
3. Now swing both at the same time. Which one stops first? Did anything else happen to the one that stopped? Record.
4. Change the strings so that both pendulums supported from the frame are the same length. Now swing them together, and record what happens.

Tell your students that this strange effect can be seen even more clearly if two very long pendulums are suspended from a string stretched across the top of a doorway or between two light fixtures. The two pendulum strings should be fastened, about a foot apart from each other, to the cross-string. Once this is set up (you will probably want to do this activity with the whole class at once because of space requirements), one student should start one pendulum swinging, while the others count the number of oscillations it makes before stopping completely. Now have someone shorten the string so that it is one inch shorter. The modified pendulum should be swung again and the number of oscillations again counted and recorded. The string should continue to be shortened in one inch intervals, with the counting and recording repeated each time, using charts like those shown.

Complete the activity by having the class discuss how the second pendulum could be changed so that the first would stop when its bob makes forty oscillations. Finish by having students check their ideas for accuracy.

Evaluation: completion of the experiments described and the recording of the results of those experiments

Amount shortened on 2nd pendulum	Number swings first pendulum makes before stopping

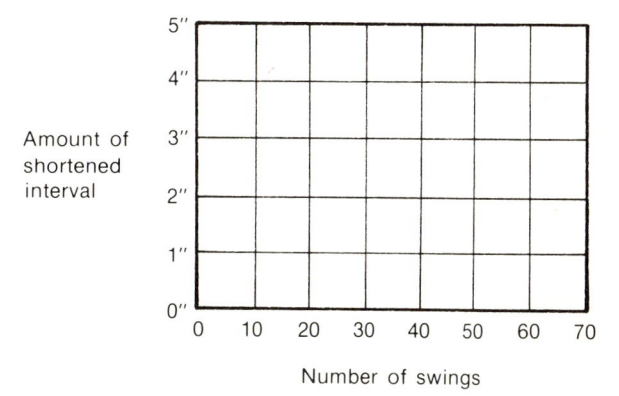

Amount of shortened interval

Number of swings

ACTIVITY FIVE:
OSCILLATIONS OF COUPLED PENDULUMS

Objective: to observe the effects of a coupling rod on the oscillations of two pendulums

Materials:
- ten rubber bands
- two thumbtacks
- a light stick about fifteen inches long
- two paper cups about half full of sand
- six paper clips
- two white paper "targets"
- paper and pencils

Procedure: For this activity, students will need to make two chains of rubber bands as shown and fasten them to the underside of a desk with thumbtacks. The stick, which will serve as a coupling rod, can be slid between any of the rubber band loops and moved from one to another as desired. Each cup should be fastened to the lower end of a rubber band chain using paper clips. When completed, your apparatus should look like the illustration shown on the next page.

When everything is ready to use, instruct students to remove the coupling rod and pull down on one cup, starting it oscillating. They should then observe whether or not the second cup begins to oscillate. Next, they should insert the coupling rod and repeat the procedure, observing what happens. Bring out, through discussion if possible, that the force needed to start the motionless pendulum comes from the one that is moving, with the force carried from one pendulum to the other through the coupling.

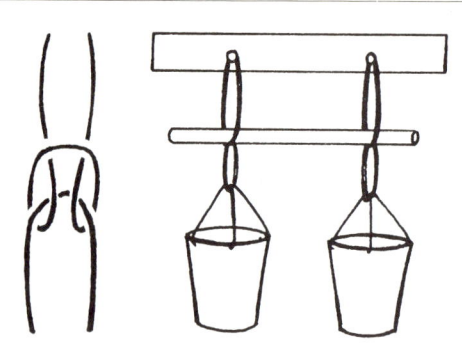

Now ask students to consider why one pendulum stops completely and then starts again. Why doesn't the system come to a "balance" (when both pendulums are oscillating uniformly) and just keep going? The final part of the activity involves fastening two white paper "targets" to the ends of the coupling rod. These targets will help students focus on the motion of the coupling rod. They should try various combinations of weights in the cups and various placements of the rod in the rubber band loops. As always in experiments, they should keep a record of what happens as the system is changed.

Finish with a class discussion in which the following questions are considered.

1. What things determine whether the targets move up and down together, or whether one moves up and the other moves down?
2. What determines the time duration from when both ends of the coupling rod are moving up and down together until, after moving in opposite directions, they again move together?

Evaluation: completion of the outlined experiments, participation in class discussions

ACTIVITY SIX:
CIRCULAR OSCILLATIONS

Objective: to observe and record the movements of circular oscillations of a pendulum

Materials:
    pendulum support (a board laid across a table will work)
    sifted sand or table salt
    a paper cone
    string

Procedure: Begin the activity by reminding the class that the pendulums made up to this point have oscillated back and forth or up and down. In working with these pendulums, they have found something out about the factors that determine the oscillation period. In contrast, the pendulum that they will now make, which will also be suspended from a string, can be swung in a circular pattern.

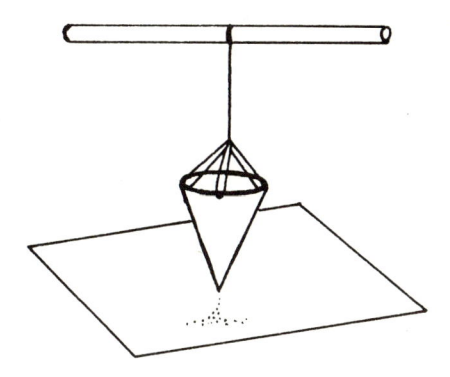

Help your students set the equipment up as illustrated, and fill the cone with the sand or salt. Lay a large sheet of brown paper under the cone where it is hanging. When you are ready to begin, cut a hole in the bottom of the cone and swing it in a circle. It won't always follow a circle, but try!

If you wish to keep a record of the patterns, use salt on black paper and photograph it from above, or trace the pattern with pencils of different colors. Ask students to look and see how well you did at swinging the cone in a perfect circle. Point out that, as the salt or sand came from the cone, the ridge that built up was thicker in some places than others. Ask if anyone can explain this. Ask students to come up with a rule for it by filling in the blanks in these sentences:

1. The faster the cone travels, the _____ salt there is in the ridge.
2. The slower the cone travels, the _____ salt there is in the ridge.

Now ask students to look carefully at the patterns. Ask them to find the part of the pattern that has thin ridges and the part that has thick ridges. You may now want to repeat the procedure several times, involving students directly in the experiment and comparing the results. After several patterns have been made and recorded, draw on the board three pictures of patterns that a cone might make. They should look something like those shown on page 272. Ask students to mark an X where they think the ridge would be the thickest and an O where they think the cone was travelling the fastest.

Evaluation: completion of described experiment, participation in group discussions

ACTIVITY SEVEN:
FINDING THE CENTER OF GRAVITY

Objective: to balance objects or shapes by finding their centers of gravity

Materials:
construction paper cut-outs
string
two corks
a bottle
two forks
two straight pins

Procedure: Ask students if any of them has ever watched a circus high wire or tightrope walker. Bring out in your discussion that most performers use an umbrella or a long pole to help them keep their balance. Discuss why this might be so.

Now discuss how an object on a string could be balanced. Instruct each student to cut out objects from construction paper. Suggest symmetrical shapes, such as butterflies or leaves, or circus items or performers. Stretch several strings across the room so that everyone will have room in which to work. Students should now try to get their shapes to balance on the string. An on-going discussion of students' experiences and discoveries should be helpful.

Whether or not students have difficulty, you may wish to carry out the following activity. Take two corks, a bottle, two forks, and two pins. Push one cork into the opening of the bottle and stick one of the pins into the center of the cork. Stick the remaining pin into the unused cork. Now see if anyone can get the other cork and the two forks to balance on the pin in the bottle. Discuss successes and failures and try to conclude by coming up with an explanation of how and why objects in both activities balanced as they did.

Evaluation: completion of balancing activities, participation in class discussions

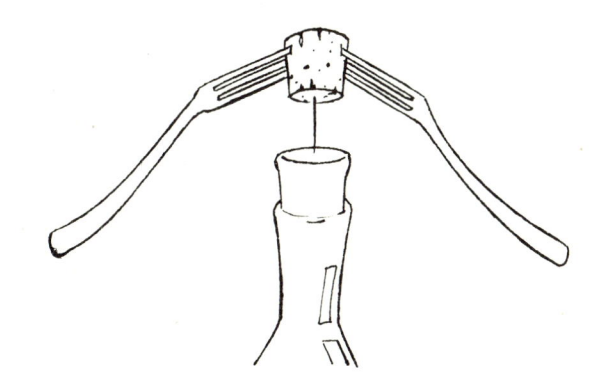

ACTIVITY EIGHT: DISCOVERING WEATHER PATTERNS

Objective: to record and examine temperature and barometric pressure patterns for various U.S. locations

Materials: daily newspapers

paper and pencils (graph paper, although not essential, is advisable)

Procedure: With your class, select several locations in the United States. Using the daily paper, look up and record the temperatures (and barometric pressure if available) at these locations. After about two weeks, plot the temperatures and pressures on a graph. In most cases, a rhythmic change pattern will show up. Ask students if it is possible to predict weather from the graph.

You might wish to first conduct, or at least begin, this activity with the class as a whole. Once students understand the procedures of the activity, have each student choose a city of his or her own on which to focus. Individual students will now look up and record daily temperatures and plot the points on a graph. In either case, guide selection so that your class is considering weather in all parts of the country.

Now you might want to look at the "larger picture" of weather. Most weather bureaus keep yearly records of weather which are available in publications describing seasonal weather changes. Ask your school librarian to secure such a record. From these, help your students develop graphs showing yearly fluctuations in temperature, sunshine, precipitation, and air pressure. Point out to them that such information is important in making estimates of heating costs, needed fuel supplies, and even water costs for keeping a lawn green during the summer. In light of recent developments, ask why designers of solar-heated houses need this kind of information.

Note: You may want at this point to refer to the energy unit in this book and move naturally into another interdisciplinary theme.

Evaluation: completion of group and/or individual weather graphs

Additional Activities:

1. If you can locate one, bring in a roquet (pendulum) game, for your students to enjoy. Or, make one of your own, building a wooden frame containing six parallel rungs from which an equal number of string-attached balls are suspended. Have students note the effects of one swinging ball upon the others.

2. Several additional activities related to pendulums are contained in the book *The Great Perpetual Learning Machine* by Jim Blake and Barbara Ernst (Boston: Little Brown & Co., 1976). Also included is a list of useful resources that will be well worth your time to locate. Another useful source, notable for the pendulum games that it describes, is *The Whole Cosmos Catalog of Science Activities* by Joe Abruscato and Jack Hassard (Santa Monica, CA: Goodyear Publishing Co., 1977).

3. In order to explore any or all of the four seasons of the year, you may wish to pursue some of the many activities outlined in *The Reasons for Seasons* by Linda Allison (Covelo, CA: Yolla Bolly Press, 1975). As a group or independently, students can explore animal and plant growth in the spring, summer, fall, or winter, learn about the systematic changes in the universe, and study seasonal weather changes throughout the year.

INVENTIONS

Inventions: The activities vary widely as to content and level, identifying thirteen areas within which children can invent and discover. There is something here for everyone!

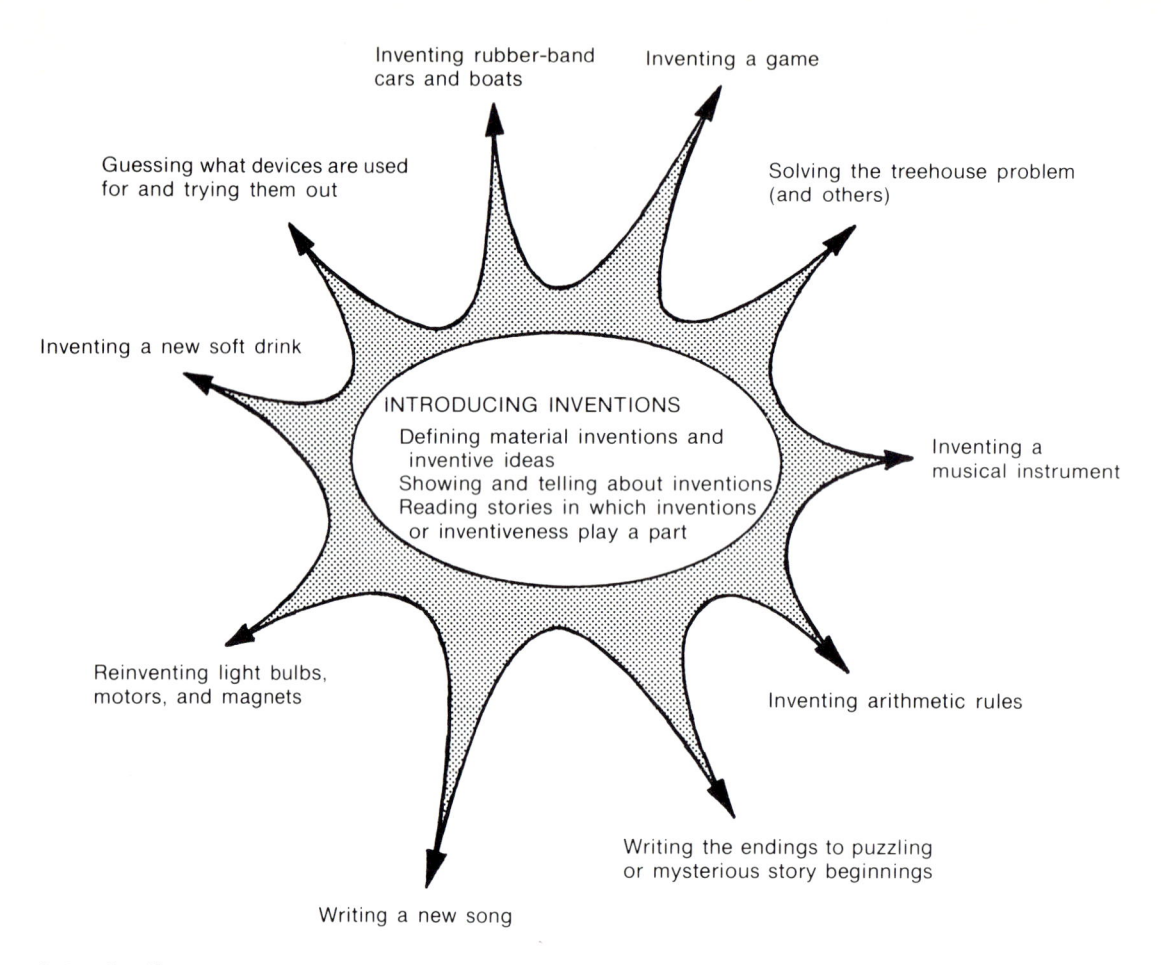

Diagram: "INTRODUCING INVENTIONS" central node with rays pointing to:
- Inventing rubber-band cars and boats
- Inventing a game
- Guessing what devices are used for and trying them out
- Solving the treehouse problem (and others)
- Inventing a new soft drink
- Inventing a musical instrument
- Reinventing light bulbs, motors, and magnets
- Inventing arithmetic rules
- Writing a new song
- Writing the endings to puzzling or mysterious story beginnings

Central node contents:
INTRODUCING INVENTIONS
Defining material inventions and inventive ideas
Showing and telling about inventions
Reading stories in which inventions or inventiveness play a part

Introduction

Children at play discover many things. They find that wagons will coast downhill but must be pushed up. They find that a yo-yo will come back if it is spinning, but will not return if it is motionless. They find that water poured onto sand at the beach soaks in rapidly, but water poured on the sidewalk forms puddles or runs off.

This unit suggests several ways of helping children learn to pose and solve problems through invention. More specifically, the unit explores some of the hows and whys of fabrications, fiction, devices, and substances, and then presents a variety of problem situations in which children are challenged to complete a story, devise an explanation, or create something that is needed.

As teachers, we know that it is difficult to structure learning situations for children in which creativity and inventiveness occur. Since it is very difficult to create or invent on order, we are tempted to build learning situations in which each child succeeds at a simple task. That is part of the intent of this unit. For that reason, its structure is somewhat looser than that of previous units. Through this more open-ended organization, we hope to free you to allow your students' interests and creativity to determine the time given to each activity of the unit, and the number of activities pursued and completed.

Therefore, on the pages that follow you will find first three general activities to begin to get your class involved in this unit. These are followed by twelve invention and discovery areas that small groups can explore or follow. Undoubtedly, your students' investigations will turn up other equally workable areas of exploration and should be encouraged. Please remember that all of the units in this book are intended as starting points, and not completed plans. All unit planning should be based largely on the characteristics and interests of your students, time, and resources available, as well as on your own areas of expertise.

Unit Objectives:

The students will:

1. find out about many of the inventions and creations we enjoy and use.
2. discover that objects can have many functions.
3. understand what "to invent" means in the broad context.
4. have the freedom to create ideas, stories, poems, new objects, and new things from existing objects.

Appropriate Grade Levels:

Three to Six

ACTIVITY ONE:
PRETEST AND UNIT INTRODUCTION

Objective: to measure general inventiveness before beginning the unit, and to introduce the unit theme (Note: this is essentially a teacher's objective)

Materials: paper
pencils, and crayons if desired

Procedure: To begin the inventions unit, give your students the following directions.

Pretend that your neighbors cleaned out their garage and piled up things for the garbage man to haul away. In the pile were a pair of old roller skates, a tire, some boards, several cardboard boxes, a plastic bucket, a box of mixed nails, screws and tacks, a broken tricycle, a leaky hose, and a coil of rope. You can have any of the things in the pile. Write a paragraph describing an item you could make using several of the throw-aways. Then draw a picture of it.

Next, select one or two simple inventions (a board for carding wool, a spinning wheel, a butter churn, a rolling pin) and present them to your class explaining that these items were used when the related tasks were done by hand. Mention some tasks that are still done by hand (folding letters to go into envelopes, tying shoe laces, peeling oranges) and ask if there is an invention or device that might do these tasks.

However, be sure to explain to children that inventions aren't just limited to devices that perform particular tasks. Inventions in a broad context include verbal fabrications, fiction, new art forms, new solutions to problems, and new songs as well as new devices and substances. To conclude this unit introduction, you may wish to present stories without endings or puzzles for students to complete or solve as a beginning to being inventive.

Evaluation: completion of written and drawn assignments, participation in group activities and discussions

ACTIVITY TWO: BEGINNING RESEARCH

Objective: to find and use resource materials related to inventing

Materials: a variety of resource materials in your school library

Procedure: As further preparation for the unit, send your class to the school resource center. Ask the librarian or media specialist to set up a cart of books, games, puzzles, etc. that could be kept in your classroom for a few days. You might also want to simply have your students given directions that will help them locate appropriate resource materials for themselves.

Upon returning to your classroom, put the webbing diagram from the opening page of this unit on the board or have your students create a web of their own. From this, allow students time during which they can explore their resources and begin to identify possible projects.

Evaluation: successful location and perusal of library materials related to inventions

ACTIVITY THREE:
PROJECT PLANNING

Objective: to begin planning group projects and to collect related materials

Materials: variable, depending upon projects identified

Procedure: At this point, all of your students should have had time to seek out and look through a variety of resource materials. They now need to divide into small groups, each of which can identify an invention or category of inventions on which they, as a group, wish to work. Perhaps the best way to divide the class is to have students contribute project ideas to a class list, and then have the children organize according to their project choice. Another method would be to set up groups first and then allow time for each group to choose one project to be completed.

Once groups have identified the "invention" on which they wish to work, your task will be to help children with suggestions, ideas, sources of information, and materials needed for construction. However, be sure to encourage groups to plan their investigations before you make suggestions. When help is sought from you, suggestions in the form of questions can help direct thoughts and encourage alternative approaches so that the students are ultimately finding their own answers and solutions.

Once each group of students has selected a project idea or area, suggest that they consider several related investigations. For example, if the children in one group choose "Inventing a Soft Drink," one of the general areas listed for exploration in subsequent pages of this unit, they could find out about two or more of these:

1. soft drink flavors
2. carbonation and CO_2
3. history of the development of the soft drink industry
4. natural and artificial flavors
5. bottles, cans, and recycling
6. trademarks
7. inventing a new flavor

Help each group to first choose a few themes of high interest for study and then develop daily plans for the following two or three days. Discuss with them the nature of the final report on the invention or discovery that you will expect from each group. You will find it helpful to have each group submit a set of plans and a description of their proposed report in advance. Such plans will not only help you keep track of progress made, but will also be useful guides for the students themselves. In addition, these written plans should be useful evaluation guides for both you and your students.

You may also want to make some related assignments, such as the development of a report or minibook describing their experiences or discussing other inventions which fit into the same category as the item they have developed. For example, a group making rubber-band cars could make a collage of auto pictures and describe a variety of cars and their histories.

Finally, if possible, the children's completed inventions should be displayed in a central location of the school so their ideas and creations can be shared with other students.

Evaluation: project plan submitted by each group

ACTIVITY FOUR AND BEYOND: TWELVE INVENTION AND DISCOVERY AREAS

The following pages contain activity suggestions in a variety of general areas of invention and discovery. As explained in the unit introduction, this list is certainly not complete or all-inclusive of possible fields of exploration. Rather, it is intended to be used by you as a set of examples of how students can branch out within a general area of interest and study.

The general planning and implementation procedures for these twelve activities have been outlined within Activity Three. The areas for investigation included here are:

1. cars
2. games
3. music
4. numbers
5. stories
6. songs
7. light bulbs and motors
8. soft drinks
9. inventions needed
10. fortresses, castles, and hideaways
11. steam engines
12. airplanes

In each area, the objective of the activities will be the completion of the identified projects, and materials will be dependent upon the project undertaken. Evaluation would then be based on completion of the project, and perhaps on the planning that precedes it.

ACTIVITY FOUR: AUTOMOBILES

1. Set up a toy auto display showing the make and year of several cars.
2. Make posters or drawings of automobiles, dream cars, racing cars, modified cars, dune buggies, and others.
3. Find out what makes automobiles go, including information on gasoline, diesel, and battery-powered cars.
4. Research what percent of a newspaper is devoted to autos by measuring the space used by articles, feature advertisements, classified advertisements, and parts ads.
5. Write and/or read stories about autos.
6. Write and/or sing songs about autos.
7. Do research on foreign automobiles, their makes and history.
8. Find out about automobile racing and stunt driving.
9. Build scale model autos from kits.
10. Construct rubber-band-driven autos or create vehicles using Tinkertoys. Solve problems related to connecting rubber bands, wheel friction, axle construction, and so on.
11. Hold auto races and measure the speed of travel of the cars used. One way to do this is to lay out a marked track on the floor. Using a clock, watch, or one-second pendulum, the speed of cars can be measured.

$$speed = \frac{distance\ travelled}{time}$$

EXAMPLE:

$$speed = \frac{6\ meters}{4\ seconds} = 1.5\ meters\ per\ second$$

ACTIVITY FIVE: GAMES

1. Find as many kinds of puzzles and games as possible. Find out what the difference is between a game and a puzzle.

2. Research a wide variety of games, finding out kinds and rules of:
   card games
   board games
   playground games

3. Look into a variety of puzzles, including interlocking and number combinations such as magic squares and many others.

4. Create and play games and puzzles intended for one or two players or for teams.

5. Compare games of strategy (checkers, Chinese checkers, chess) and games of chance (using spinners, card turning, or dice).

6. Learn about the psychology of games. For example, try to answer the question, "Can you play a game better if you practice? Can you flip a coin or roll a die better with practice?" Plan a study to find out if practice improves one's ability in both chance and skill games.

7. Study the mathematics of chance. In particular, dice offer some interesting investigations. Some examples follow:
   a. Roll a single die (six sides numbered one through six). Keep a record of the number of times each face is up in ten, fifty, and seventy-five rolls. Predict the number of times each face will be up in 100 rolls.
   b. Roll two dice. Keep a record of the number of times twos, threes, fours, through twelves are rolled. Make a histogram of 100 rolls.
   c. Devise a chance table for two dice showing how many times each sum (two–twelve) can be expected to appear in seventy-two rolls.

8. Invent a game. First complete a description table indicating the game's use, chance or skill, number of players, card, board, or other, what other game it is like, how many minutes it takes to play, and what you will learn by playing the game.

9. Invent a puzzle involving a maze or pieces. Find out what skills are needed (i.e., fitting parts) and what puzzle it is like.

ACTIVITY SIX: MAKING A MUSICAL INSTRUMENT

1. Make a list of as many musical instruments as you know. Divide the instruments according to how they make sounds. Find out what is needed to play each group.
2. Find out how sirens work. Make one using a piece of cardboard, a hole punch, and a straw. Use a Tinkertoy support. Find out what makes the siren loud or soft, and high or low in pitch.
3. Make three lists of instruments. First, list instruments that make mostly low sounds. Second, group those making mostly high-pitched sounds. Third, find instruments that produce both low and high sounds.
4. Make a bottle xylophone. Tune bottles by partly filling them with water, each to a different level. Try creating a variety of tones by tapping the bottles with a wooden mallet and a metal spoon, or blowing over the tops of the bottles.
5. Make a one-string guitar, using a board, two eye screws, and a piece of fine wire stretched between the screws. The wire can be tightened by twisting one of the eye screws. Cut strips of wood for frets and set them in place so you can shorten the string and play different notes.
6. Make a tub bass, using a large metal can, an old bucket, or an old washtub. You will need a strong piece of cord, two pieces of wood, and a nail. Fasten the cord to the center of the tub using a short stick. The cord can be tightened by pressing down on the stick.
7. Make a bazooka from a piece of one-inch plastic pipe and two round pieces of wood.
8. Invent a new instrument that will play several notes.

ACTIVITY SEVEN: INVENTING NUMBER PATTERNS AND ARITHMETIC RULES

1. Design magic squares. Here is an example. In this square, the numbers in each row and the numbers in each column add to twelve. But the diagonal numbers add to seven and seventeen. Can you substitute numbers so the diagonals, too, will add to twelve? Can you now use the numbers 1, 2, 3, 4, 5, 6, 7, 8, and 9 in each of the cells so that the rows,

columns, and diagonals will all add to fifteen? Is it possible to so arrange the numbers so that the four corners, too, add to fifteen? Try the numbers 10, 11, 12, 13, 14, 15, 16, 17, 18. How about 11 through 19? Invent a new magic square with a five by five matrix. When you are an expert, try a four by four magic square using the numbers 1–16. Warning: This can be very difficult!

2	4	6
3	4	5
7	4	1

2. Make discoveries using a hand-held calculator. Construct a matrix to generate fractions to decimals and write the answers in the matrix. Can you see any patterns? Before the matrix is complete, can you predict some of the decimals?

NUMERATOR

DENOMINATOR

	6	7	8	9
6	$\frac{6}{6}$ 1	$\frac{6}{7}$ .8571	$\frac{6}{8}$ .75	$\frac{6}{9}$ .6666
5	$\frac{5}{6}$ .8333	$\frac{5}{7}$ .7412	$\frac{5}{8}$ .625	$\frac{5}{9}$
4	$\frac{4}{6}$ .6666	$\frac{4}{7}$ .5714	$\frac{4}{8}$ .5	$\frac{4}{9}$
3	$\frac{3}{6}$ .5	$\frac{3}{7}$ .4286	$\frac{3}{8}$	$\frac{3}{9}$
2	$\frac{2}{6}$ .3333	$\frac{2}{7}$ .2857	$\frac{2}{8}$	$\frac{2}{9}$
1	$\frac{1}{6}$ .16666	$\frac{1}{7}$	$\frac{1}{8}$	$\frac{1}{9}$

Try several other matrices using different numerators and denominators.

3. Make some more hand-held calculator discoveries. Once you think you see a pattern, guess the answer before you press the = button.

1 × 11 = _____   10 × 11 = _____

2 × 11 = _____   11 × 11 = _____

3 × 11 = _____   100 × 11 = _____

4 × 11 = _____   101 × 11 = _____

5 × 11 = _____

Without using your calculator, predict the decimal equivalents of:

	Guess	**Press**
5/11	_____	_____
6/11	_____	_____
7/11	_____	_____
8/11	_____	_____
9/11	_____	_____
10/11	_____	_____

4. Complete calculator sevenths. Use your calculator to find decimal equivalence to six places for these fractions:

1/7 = _____   4/7 = _____

2/7 = _____   5/7 = _____

3/7 = _____   6/7 = _____

Can you find a sequence of digits and a pattern that would help you write the decimal for any seventh?

Can you find a rule that will help you predict the equivalents for:

8/7 = _____   How about: 15/7 = _____

9/7 = _____   16/7 = _____

10/7 = _____   17/7 = _____

11/7 = _____   18/7 = _____

5. Complete more calculator fraction patterns. Work these problems with your calculator. Write the first six digits of each answer in the corresponding row in the Table.

	FIRST	SECOND	THIRD	FOURTH	FIFTH	SIXTH
1 ÷ 13						
2 ÷ 13						
3 ÷ 13						
4 ÷ 13						
5 ÷ 13						
6 ÷ 13						

Look at the first and fourth columns. What pattern do you see? Compare the second and fifth columns. What do you notice? Compare the third and sixth columns.

Can you guess what numbers would be in the seventh column? Check your guesses using your calculator.
What is the sum of the numbers in the first row? The last row?
What about the other rows?
Expand the table to include 7 ÷ 13, 8 ÷ 13, etc. Are the patterns the same? Can you predict the decimal equivalent for 12 ÷ 13, and so on?

6. Collect at least six discs. Jar lids, plates, can tops, and wheels can be used. Measure the distance across each and the distance around each in cm. Chart this data:

Distance around						
Distance across						
Distance around ÷ distance across						

7. Count out 100 toothpicks. Draw parallel lines on a large sheet of paper. The lines should be exactly one toothpick length apart. Hold the toothpicks about one meter above the center of the paper and drop them one at a time. Keep a record of the number of toothpicks that touch one of the parallel lines. How many touched a line? How many did you drop? What number do you get when you divide the number that touched a line into the number dropped? Try again and see if you get about the same number. Can you tell why you get this number each time?

ACTIVITY EIGHT: WRITING ENDINGS TO STORIES

1. Collect comic strips from several newspapers. Cut and paste white paper over the word boxes. Then, reorder the pictures and write new dialogue. They can be used for announcements, bulletin boards, funny or sad stories.

2. Collect magazine pictures and mount them on one side of a page. Arrange them so they tell a story. Across from each picture, write one or two paragraphs of the story.

3. Cut full-page advertisements from magazines. Cut and paste white paper over the captions and writing. Write new captions and descriptions. Some can be funny, some mysterious, some ridiculous.

4. Collect several old "throw away" readers. Carefully cut out the pages

and separate the short stories. Rewrite parts of the story or the end of the story. Cut out paragraphs that are changed or not needed. Staple the new story together with a construction-paper cover.

5. Work with add-on stories. Have each person in a group write the first paragraph of a story. Then exchange papers and have each person read his or her paper and write a second paragraph. Continue until each story is complete. Hang up the stories so everyone can read them.

6. Have your teacher select an interesting story and read about half of it to you. Then, in a group, plan the remainder of the story and have each one in your group select a paragraph of the second half to write. When finished, the story can be read aloud or placed conveniently so everyone can read it.

7. Select one of the short super 8 mm film cartridges provided by your teacher and watch it on a projector. Then write a narrative and devise sound effects for appropriate parts of the film. When ready, use a tape recorder and make the sound track for the film. Share your final production with the entire class.

ACTIVITY NINE:
SONGS

1. Work with a partner. Write out the words to a simple song you both know, one line at a time. Then sing the song and underline each word or part of a word that corresponds with a beat of the music. Now, using the same beat pattern, write a new verse to the melody.

2. This time, start with an unknown verse. Now, underline the beats in the verse and try several melodies until one is discovered that matches the beat. If you can, record it on a cassette and teach it during music class.

3. Write your own music and match it with a poem. Or write both the words and music for a new song. Teach it to a friend.

ACTIVITY TEN:
INVENTING A NEW SOFT DRINK

1. How often have you wished for a new soft drink flavor? Create a new flavor by mixing two or more soft drinks together, keeping careful records of proportions used. You may choose from orange, strawberry,

grape, lemon-lime, and cola. You will need several paper cups and a measuring cup. Once you have invented several new drink flavors, have other students taste each and record preferences. You might also like to create names for your new beverages and draw posters to advertise them.

2. What makes the "fizz" in soft drinks? Learn about carbonation and CO_2.

3. Find out about and compare artificial and natural flavors and sweeteners.

4. Conduct a survey of soft drink flavor preferences, comparing choices according to age and sex.

5. Study the history and development of the soft drink industry. Find out how long people have been drinking soft drinks, where they were first manufactured, and so on.

6. Find out about soft drink packaging and recycling of bottles and cans. Plan and carry out a recycling program in your class, school, home, or neighborhood.

ACTIVITY ELEVEN: SURVEYING FOR NEEDED INVENTIONS

Categorize the things you do during the day, and write these on a recording sheet. Ask other children and adults what item, thing, or device that they do not have or that needs to be improved, they would find helpful in each category. Some category headings you may wish to use include:

clothing

toys and sports equipment

transportation

food

beverages

cooking equipment

home items

containers

Now reduce the list to those items that were mentioned several times. Select one suggested or needed item and design such an item. Your design should include a drawing and a description.

WHAT? A SAMPLER OF THEMATIC UNITS 289

ACTIVITY TWELVE:
FORTRESSES, CASTLES AND HIDEAWAYS

Cardboard boxes are thrown away daily. Yet they can be cut apart, fastened together, stacked, and in general used for building projects. A good fastening agent is liquid contact cement (water base). To use it, brush the cement on the surfaces to be joined and allow it to dry until the gloss disappears. Then press the surfaces together. The bond is instantaneous.

You can build such things as puppet stages, reading hideaways, towers, tunnels, rockets, and geodomes. Cardboard is easy to cut with a pair of stout scissors or light tin snips. The finished product can have holes cut for windows and can be painted with leftover interior wall paint.

Before you start, you will need to do some planning. First, create a satisfactory design. Next, assemble all needed materials and equipment. While building, be sure to cut safely and follow the gluing directions carefully. Finally, check your finished product for any modifications needed or desired.

Additional Activities:

1. Have your students explore the lives of famous inventors. Written or oral reports or pictorial displays can be created from their findings. Later in the unit, have them create a similar item by interviewing their fellow classroom inventors about what they invented and why.

2. Ask students to create lists of the most important inventions ever created. Have each student choose one of these inventions and explore its effect on mankind. Direct them to predict how civilization might have developed differently had that item not been invented.

3. An exploration of science fiction literature can turn up a wide array of imagined inventions. Your students might search older science fiction books to find devices that have now been built, or predict which of those from current literature may, in the future, become actual objects. Finally, encourage them to create, in drawings, writings, or three-dimensional representations, possible future inventions.

4. Many inventive projects can be found in Steven Caney's *Play Book* (New York: Workman Publishing Co., 1975). These can be followed by your students as directed or used as inspirations for original creations.

GO FLY A KITE!

Go Fly a Kite: Children design and test a variety of kites. Kite-related literature, music, and poetry are suggested as possible extensions.

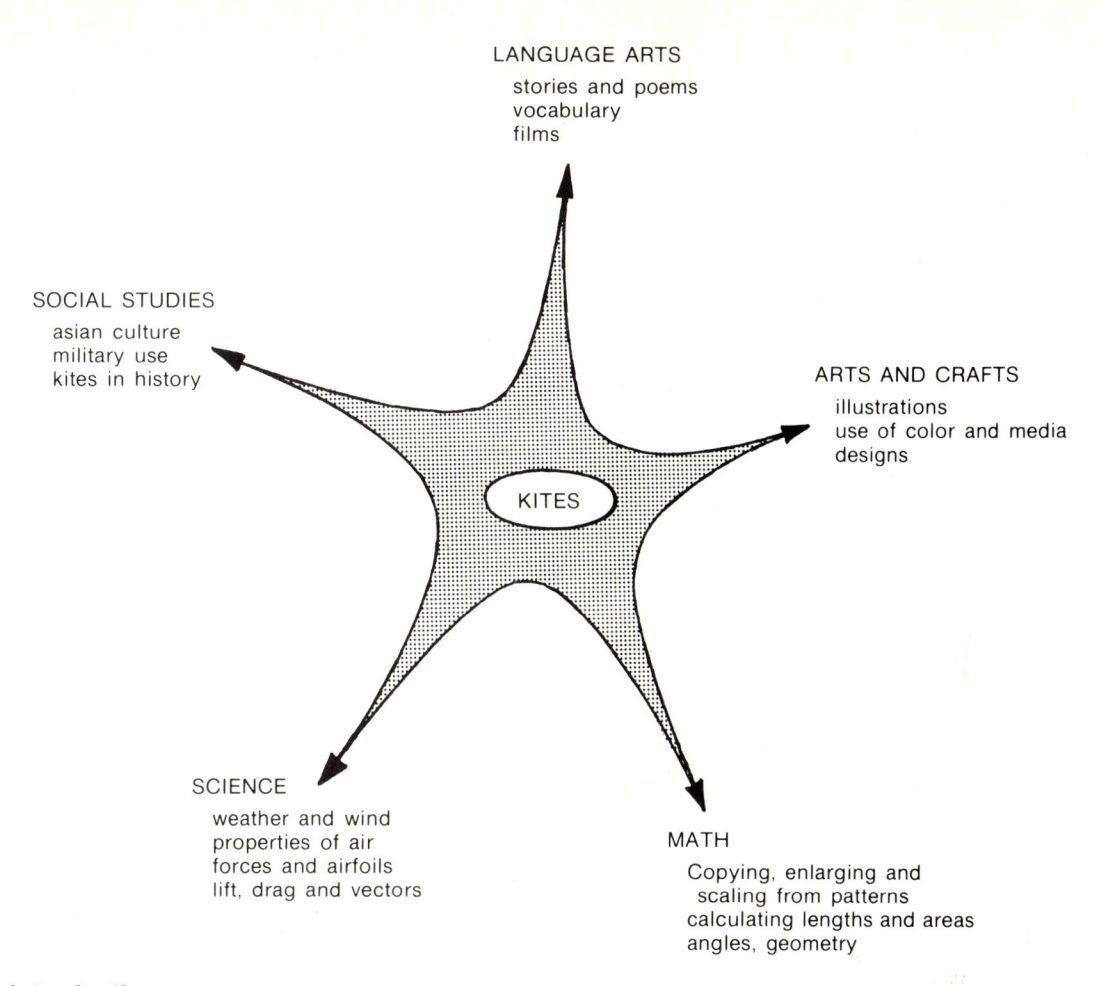

LANGUAGE ARTS
  stories and poems
  vocabulary
  films

SOCIAL STUDIES
  asian culture
  military use
  kites in history

ARTS AND CRAFTS
  illustrations
  use of color and media
  designs

KITES

SCIENCE
  weather and wind
  properties of air
  forces and airfoils
  lift, drag and vectors

MATH
  Copying, enlarging and
   scaling from patterns
  calculating lengths and areas
  angles, geometry

Introduction

Kites seem to hold a strong fascination for both young and old. There is something almost magical about a simple construction of paper, sticks, and string being able to soar high into the atmosphere. Windy March and April skies are dotted regularly with kites of all sizes, shapes, and colors, and many students anxiously await the ringing of the bell at the end of the school day so that they, too, can send their kites flying.

This unit is designed to build from the almost universal appeal of kites towards an understanding of some basic principles of flight. Along the way, it touches on history, cultural awareness, creative expression, mathematical figuring, decisionmaking, problem solving, and cooperation.

Although it contains only ten activities, it could stretch over a longer time period than that list implies. Many activities could, in fact, require several days for satisfactory completion. In addition, student interest and enthusiasm could lead to the inclusion of activities not even listed. For example, the sharing of one of Charlie Brown's kite experiences in the *Peanuts* cartoons could lead to a variety of investigations and creations of comics, newspapers, and interpersonal relationships.

Because several activities depend largely on the success of scientific experiments, it is advisable that you, the teacher, prepare for those experiments by trying them yourself before you attempt to present them to your class. They are not difficult, but your students can't be expected to learn much from a frustrating class period during which an experiment fails. While even the best planned activities can fizzle, a little preparation can usually prevent such disappointments.

In the midst of all your lofty educational planning, don't lose sight of the recreational and creative possibilities of this unit. The activities included in this theme allow for lots of fun and relaxation. If properly handled, this unit could leave your students with not only a store of new knowledge but also with better feelings about themselves and their classmates. And that's a combination of outcomes that's tough to beat!

Unit Objectives:

The students will:

1. learn about basic concepts of flight (force, lift, drag, center of gravity).
2. develop recording skills.
3. gain basic air information (pressure, motion, velocity, airfoil, and associated pressure differences).
4. increase his or her knowledge of the history of kites.
5. develop a greater appreciation of color and design.
6. improve arithmetic and measurement skills (copying, enlarging, measuring).
7. participate in creative language arts and music activities.

Appropriate Grade Levels:

Second to Fourth (could be usable for upper grades as well in most cases)

ACTIVITY ONE:
UNIT INTRODUCTION

Objective: to introduce the unit and conduct a pre-test (note that this is a teacher's objective)

Materials: books, films, and/or pictures about kites
chalkboard and chalk
paper and pencils

Procedure: Select several books about kites. Familiarity with the introductory sections of the books will be very helpful. Through discussion, film, or pictures, present the following information to the class.

> *Kites have been around for many hundreds of years. They were used by the Chinese to communicate long before telephone or mail service was available. Instead of passing out a cigar, a proud father flew a kite high into the air so that all the neighbors for miles around would know that the baby had arrived. Kites have even served the military. Giant box kites that would carry a person as a passenger were flown high above the enemy lines in World War I. Benjamin Franklin is reported to have used a kite to investigate static electricity in low storm clouds.*

Show your children pictures of a variety of kites, both simple and complex. Inform them that a simple cross kite can be built in an hour, while it may take a professional kite builder several days to make an elaborate flying ship-kite complete with hull, sails, and riggings.

Work with your children in developing a thematic web. Start by writing the word kites on the board. Ask children to suggest things that relate to kites. When completed, it may look something like the webbing at the beginning of this unit.

You may also wish at this time to assign children to do some individual reading and research about kites and prepare reports on their findings. Or you may want to have children draw pictures of kites they would like to build, listing materials needed for constructing the kite.

Finally, as a kind of pretest, ask each student to write a paragraph telling some of the things they know about kites, including an explanation of why they think kites fly. Save these for use at the end of the unit to measure individual growth. The information contained in these paragraphs can also guide unit development.

Evaluation: completion of pretest paragraphs, participation in other class discussions and activities

ACTIVITY TWO:
SMALL FORCES PRODUCING A LARGE FORCE

Objective: to learn that small forces together can produce a large or greater force

Materials: small plastic bags (at least twenty)

books
two tables

Procedure: To demonstrate that small forces acting together produce a large force, begin by having the children slip small plastic bags under books. The bags should then be inflated by having the students blow into them. The children will discover that, by doing so, they can lift heavy books.

Next, turn a table upside down and place it on another table. Have children insert bags between the two tables all around the edges. At least twenty bags are needed. Have a child lie on the top, or inverted, table. At the signal "Go," all the children should blow into the bags. If they don't succeed the first time in lifting the child, encourage them to try again. Then ask them if this helps explain how large kites are able to lift people into the air.

Evaluation: participation in group activity

ACTIVITY THREE: TETHERED AIRFOILS

Objective: to learn the meanings of the terms, "lift," "drag," and "attack angle"

Materials: electric fan
10 × 20 cm pieces of tagboard
twelve cm-long sticks

Procedure: Have your children attach approximately 10 × 20 cm pieces of tagboard to light sticks about twelve cm long. When they have finished, turn on the fan and instruct the students to hold their cardboard in the stream of air coming from the fan. Through questioning, help them discover what such terms as "lift," "drag," and "attack angle" mean.

Following this activity, ask children to find pictures of birds, airplanes, gliders, frisbees and other objects in flight. Ask them to describe how these objects fly using the new words which they learned using the "tethered" aircraft (tagboard and stick apparatus).

Evaluation: completion of tethered airfoil activity, correct application of terms learned to related situations

WHAT? A SAMPLER OF THEMATIC UNITS 295

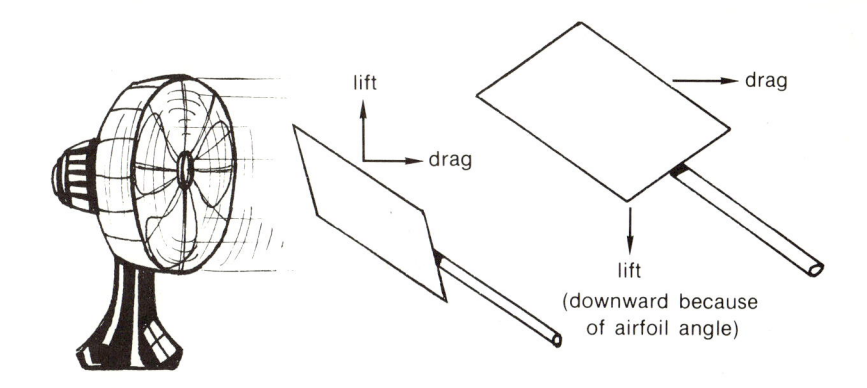

ACTIVITY FOUR:
EGG IN THE BOTTLE

Objective: to learn about the force exerted by air as its pressure changes

Materials: small-necked bottle
peeled, hard-boiled egg
paper
matches

Procedure: You will need a bottle whose neck is smooth and slightly smaller in diameter (about five mm) than that of a peeled, hard-boiled egg. Make a twist of paper and light it with a match. Drop the lighted paper into the bottle and quickly set the egg onto the bottle's mouth. If everything goes according to plan, the egg will squeeze together and slide into the bottle with a loud plop. Have children try to guess why this happens. If they can't explain it, tell them that the flame heats the air, causing the air in the bottle to expand. If the egg is sitting on the bottle, it may bounce a bit as the warm air escapes. When the flame goes out, the air in the bottle cools and contracts, and the air pressure in the bottle drops. The greater outside air pressure then pushes the egg into the bottle.

You can remove the egg by inverting the bottle and blowing air past the egg. If you force enough air into the bottle, its pressure will push the egg back out. When doing this, be very careful not to swallow the egg as it comes out of the bottle.

Children can feel the pressure change in the bottle by placing a hand, which has been moistened to insure a good seal, over the bottle just as a small scrap of burning paper is dropped into the bottle. The bottle will "magically" stick to their hands! Discuss how "invisible" air can exert considerable force as its pressure changes.

Evaluation: participation in class activities described

ACTIVITY FIVE:
THE BERNOULLI EFFECT

Objective: to learn about the pressure exerted by air in motion (the Bernoulli Effect)

Materials:
ping pong balls (two or more)
string
plastic straws
vacuum cleaner
beach ball, or other lightweight ball
thread spools
tagboard discs
straight pins

Procedure: According to Daniel Bernoulli, the pressure of air in motion is less than the pressure of motionless air. You can set up several interesting demonstrations to prove this. The first one requires two ping pong balls, some string, and a plastic straw. Fasten the balls to a piece of string about 75 cm in length, with one ball at each end. Hang the string over a support so that the balls hang loosely about one cm apart. Blow air between the ping pong balls using the straw to produce a strong jet. The balls will move together. Although these and other experiment directions are written as if you are performing for your children to watch, you may wish to involve them more directly in carrying out the steps involved.

A second demonstration is one often used in stores to attract customers' attention to vacuum cleaner displays. Using a vacuum cleaner and a hose attachment, blow a jet of air upward. Toss a light ball into the stream of air. The ball will bob from one side of the stream to the other but will not leave the stream and will appear to be suspended in midair.

A third demonstration involves the use of a thread spool and a disc cut from tagboard which has been pierced through the center with a common pin. Have several students each fasten a plastic hose into the hole of a spool. Then have them each insert a pin with a disc of tagboard on it into the opposite end of the spool. Have them try to blow the disc off the spool. If someone keeps a continuous stream of air flowing through the spool, the cardboard cannot be blown off even if the spool is turned over and the cardboard hangs without apparent support.

After these demonstrations are completed, discuss the fact that, in each case, the fast moving air has a lower pressure than the surrounding air. The air surrounding the ping pong balls exerted greater pressure, pushing them together. The air outside of the air jet from the vacuum cleaner pushed the ball back into the lower pressure area in the stream. The air pressure on the side of the tagboard away from the spool was greater than the fast moving air between the spool and the tagboard. Extend this by explaining that, when a curved surface is moved through the air or forced into moving air, the air moves faster over the curved side than the flat side. Thus, the air on the flat, underside of a curved wing or curved kite body exerts greater pressure and lifts the wing or the kite.

Evaluation: participation in class activities, ability to explain or describe the Bernoulli Effect

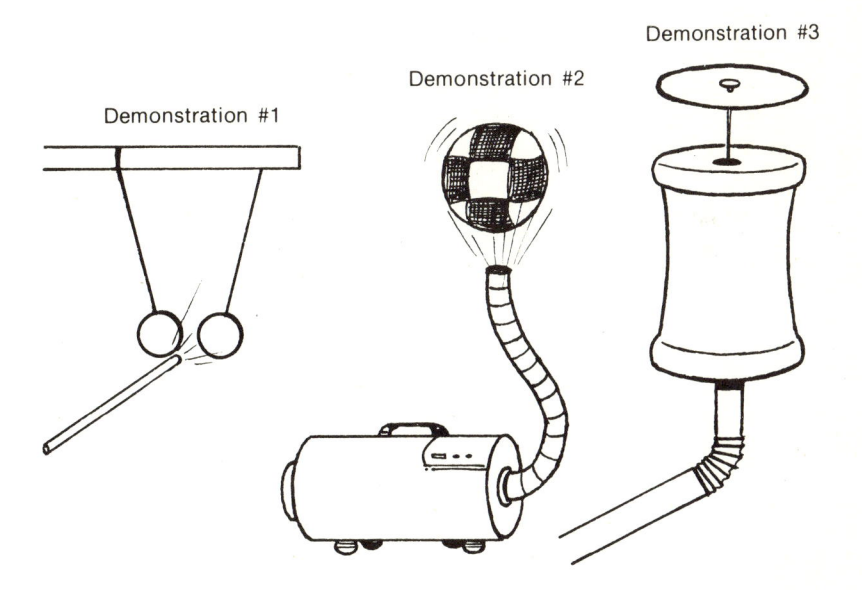

Demonstration #1

Demonstration #2

Demonstration #3

ACTIVITY SIX:
BACK TO KITES

Objective: to learn about the effect of lift, drag, and angle of attack on kites

Materials:
- electric fan
- cardboard kites of three different sizes, with string and tails
- sticks

Procedure: Have your children investigate the behavior of a small kite in the stream of air produced by a fan. Here are a few questions for investigation.

1. Does the area of the kite relate to lift and drag? To answer this, have your students cut three different sized kites from cardboard and fasten them each to a stick. These then can be held in the air stream, one at a time. When doing this, the distance from the fan and the angle of the kite to the air stream should not change.

2. If you change the angle of attack of the kite, how do lift and drag change? The children will have to devise a way of rotating the kite in the air stream, measuring its attack angle, and measuring (or carefully estimating) lift and drag.

3. Does the angle of attack relate to how high the kite will fly? Students will have to devise a way to measure the height of the kite. In each test, the string length should be held constant, with only the bridle connections being changed.

4. Does the length of the tail and the attack angle relate to the stability of the kite? Make clear to your students that, in the case of two-variable problems, only one variable at a time should be changed. By the time this investigation is completed, your students should have learned that a stable kite flies in a vertical position with little or no bobbing and swooping.

Evaluation: participation in group activities, understanding of modifications needed to make kites fly better evidenced by the making of those modifications

ACTIVITY SEVEN:
INVESTIGATING THE CENTER OF GRAVITY
(A TIPPING CONTEST)

Objective: to measure the center of gravity of a toy tower

Materials:
- Tinkertoys
- sheets of cardboard
- string
- weights
- protractors

Procedure: Divide your class into several small groups. Each group should be given a set of Tinkertoy pieces and given fifteen minutes in which to build a tower. The towers must each be fifteen inches tall. When the fifteen minutes have elapsed, each group should place its tower on a sheet of cardboard and slowly tilt the cardboard. The tower that can be tilted the most without falling determines the winner.

One way to measure the amount of tilt is to use a device called a clinometer. You can make a clinometer from a piece of cardboard, a string, a weight, and a protractor. As the clinometer tips, the string and the weight cross the number line of the protractor, marked off as it is in degrees. The point at which the clinometer line rests represents the tilt of the board in degrees.

After the contest is over, line up the towers from most to least stable. Discuss the differences and see if you can come to some conclusion as to what it is about one tower that makes it more stable than another.

Evaluation: completion of clinometers, toy towers, and measurement of center of gravity of the tower

ACTIVITY EIGHT:
KITE BUILDING

Objective: to select a kite design and begin kite construction

Materials:
- kite-building materials (paper, sticks, string, etc., with specifics dependent on kites chosen to be built)
- kite plans, printed separately or in books

Procedure: Your students have by now learned about some scientific principles that relate to flight. Now it is time for them to put these findings into practice.

Distribute plans for several kites, or allow time for students to select plans from printed sheets or resource books. Provide the children with rulers and meter sticks. Supply sheets of newsprint or wrapping paper. Have children enlarge the plans for the kite of their choice to full scale. Have them check their materials list against their plans.

Once students are ready to begin making their kites, you should hold short skill sessions as needed, showing all children or small groups of children how to carry out some of the construction operations (stick cutting and fastening, paper covering, coloring, decorating, attachment of bridle, construction and attachment of tails). You will also need to give aid and assistance to individuals throughout the building of the kites. Note: This activity may take several days to complete.

Evaluation: kite construction begun from selected kite plans or patterns

ACTIVITY NINE: KITE TESTING

Objective: to test the ability of the kites to fly and make any final adjustments needed

Materials: none needed, unless extensive modifications are required

Procedure: Each child's kite should now be nearly or fully completed and ready for a preliminary flight. Have students take their kites onto the playground and fly them. Observe carefully and keep records of each kite's performance. Have students consider these questions:

1. Did my kite rise? How fast? How high?
2. Was it stable?
3. What other problems, if any, were encountered?
4. What could be done to improve my kite's flight?

Once you're back in your classroom, hold small group problem-solving sessions. These should deal with reviews of those concepts that the children may need to keep in mind in order to solve their kite problems. These sessions may be devoted to problems such as wind force, kite lift, bridle attachment, balance, and stability. Provide time in which the children can make whatever modifications they have determined to be needed.

Evaluation: correct identification of any flight problems and completion of these corrections and/or modifications

ACTIVITY TEN: KITE FLYING DAY

Objective: to fly individual kites and evaluate the flights of all kites made

Materials: none needed

Procedure: This is the big day! By now, at least the major "bugs" should have been ironed out, and all kites should be decorated and ready to go. You may wish before the event to make and display posters in your school describing the event and inviting others in the school to attend. Since weather is important, your plans should include several alternate dates.

On kite day, begin by flying all of the kites together, making individual adjustments as needed. When all of the problems have been solved, have students fly kites one at a time. Discuss how each kite behaves and how it could be improved. When everyone has had his or her turn, you may wish to finish by again flying all kites at once. You may wish to end the unit by drawing pictures or writing stories about the kite flying and displaying the kites in the school where everyone can enjoy them. One or more photos of the kites would also be a nice record of the event. However, it is doubtful that *any* record will be needed to help your students remember the culmination of the unit!

Evaluation: flight of all kites

Additional Activities:

1. Help your students investigate aerial photography. Have them try to answer these questions: Can you send a small camera up with a kite? How could you trip the camera shutter? Suggest that they could perhaps do it with a tug on the kite string. Point out that some people have used a piece of slow-burning string as a timing device. Encourage research and careful experimentation.

2. Contact a sports store to see if you can locate a person who knows about hang gliding. Perhaps that person would be willing to talk to the class and be interviewed, or give a demonstration.

3. See if there is a kite store in your neighborhood or city. Contact the owner. Perhaps you can take the class to the shop, or he or she will bring some kites to your class. Oriental stores or museum shops might also be located nearby, with kites for sale or on display.

4. Your library, school or public, is likely to contain some or all of the following resource books. They contain directions for creating, flying, and understanding the flight principles of kites. And don't forget, for comic relief, the *Peanuts* books by Charles Schultz. Your students may not feel as badly about lost or broken kites once they share the experiences of poor old Charlie Brown!

   BRUMMITT, WYATT, *Kites*. Golden Press, 1971.

   DAWNER, MARIAN, *Kites, How to Make and Fly Them*. Lathrop, Lee, and Shepard Co., Inc., 1968.

   Elementary Science Study, "Gases and Airs." Webster Division, McGraw-Hill, 1967.

   Environmental Education, "Air Movement." State Department of Education, St. Paul, Mn., 1972.

   HONE, ELIZABETH B., and others, *A Sourcebook for Elementary Science, Second Edition,* Harcourt Brace Jovanovich, 1971.

   Minnesota Mathematics and Science Teaching Project, "Angles and Space," Unit 21. University of Minnesota, 1970.

   MOUVIER, JEAN-PAUL, *Kites!* Franklin Watts, Inc., 1974.

   National Geographic, "Kite-Fighting Warriors of Japan." April 1977.

   NELSON, LESLIE and LORBEER, GEORGE, *Science Activities for Elementary Children*. William C. Brown Co., 1952.

   NEWMAN, LEE SCOTT and JAY HARTLEY, *Kite Craft*. Crown Publishers, 1974.

   PELHAM, DAVID, *The Penguin Book of Kites*. Penguin Books, 1976.

Epilogue

Singer Peggy Lee a few years back recorded a song entitled "Is That All There Is?" You might very well be asking that question at this point. Is that all there is to an integrated approach? The answer is an emphatic yes and no. Yes, because conceptually this approach is fairly simplistic, it does make sense and it can be ably defended from a number of perspectives. We have attempted to do just that in this book. No, because there are literally an infinite number of permutations that this approach can take, and one can never really master all of the whats, whys, and wherefores. There will always be that simple investigation that could have been carried out and for one reason or another never was, or those general directions not pursued that might have improved the overall quality of the theme.

Teaching involves a great deal of judgment. Good teachers make good judgments more often than they make bad ones. As you become more comfortable with this approach you will undoubtedly begin to routinely make better judgments. This will be an exciting time for you intellectually, one that will be forever changing and one that will be as much (or more) of a challenge for you as it is for the kids.

As a parting thought, we would like to suggest some things about teacher behaviors that have proven effective in the past and that are worth remembering as you embark on this new teaching and learning adventure.

1. Introduce the theme in a flexible manner that not only allows the children to relate it to their particular situation but also opens up various avenues of potential investigation.
2. Serve as a coordinator and collaborator. Assist, rather than direct, individuals or groups of students as they investigate different aspects of the problem.

3. Involve students regularly in project or theme activities. This regularity will allow the children to have a chance to become involved in the challenge and carry out comprehensive investigations.

4. Provide the tools and supplies necessary for initial hands-on work in the classroom. Later on, children can become partially responsible for the location, procurement, and development of needed materials.

5. Be patient. Allow the children to make their own mistakes and to find their own way. But do offer assistance and point out sources of help if the children become frustrated in their approach to the problem.

6. Provide frequent opportunities for group reports and student exchanges of ideas in class discussions. In most cases, students will, by their own critical examination of the procedures they have used, improve or set new directions in their investigations.

7. Ask higher level questions (questions not answerable with a single word or fact) to stimulate thinking.

8. Make sure that groups are appropriately constituted and that the criteria for group involvement are continually varied. This will ensure the broadest possible set of experiences for each individual.

9. Remember that success is defined differently. It is not simply the mastery of specific bits of knowledge, although this is sure to occur. It is not only the following of a particular line of investigation predetermined by the teacher. Success in a integrated study is defined by the progress that students make toward the solution of a particular problem or concern. Success is defined in terms of process as much as it is defined in terms of specific product outcomes. Evaluate accordingly!

APPENDIX

Useful Instructional Resources

Earlier in this book we discussed the fact that the development and maintenance of an integrated study requires the availability of instructional resources beyond those normally found in textbooks. You will be pleased to know that literally tens of thousands of activities in mathematics, science, social studies, and other areas are already in existence. The task of the teacher, then, need not be to continually develop new activities but rather to adapt existing materials to fit the particular setting whenever possible.

This appendix is designed as a brief overview to some of the materials and references that are available for your use. In the classroom materials and activities sections we have tried to include the price and address for ordering these materials for your own classroom use. The teacher's guides and references should be available at your local library.

GENERAL INTERDISCIPLINARY RESOURCES

Classroom Materials and Activities

Architecture: A Shelter World, Patton Pending, 565 Hamilton Avenue, Palo Alto, CA 94301, $11.

The Cemetery Box, Good Apple, Inc., Box 299, Carthage, IL 62321, $10.

The Center Solution (Ideas for Classroom Learning Centers), The Learning Works, P.O. Box 6187, Santa Barbara, CA 93111, $5.

Detective Box, The Coal Bin Inc., P.O. Box 2051, Kalamazoo, MI 49003, $13.

Essence I and *Essence II,* Addison-Wesley Publishing Co., 2725 Sand Hill Road, Menlo Park, CA 94025, $21 and $35.

Expressions, Harcourt, Brace, and Jovanovich, Inc., 757 Third Avenue, New York, NY 10017, $50.

Game-Sim Series 1, California Learning Simulations, 750 Lurline Drive, Foster City, CA 94404, $250.

Man Creates: Philosophers, Patton Pending, 565 Hamilton Avenue, Palo Alto, CA 94301, $15.

Monster Box, The Coal Bin Inc., P.O. Box 2051, Kalamazoo, MI 49003, $13.

Think Box (Special Projects for Creative Thinking), The Learning Works, P.O. Box 6187, Santa Barbara, CA 93111, $5.

Teacher's Guides and References

BAKER, JUDITH L. "Shh! Discussion Time," *Grade Teacher,* January 1971, pp. 89–90.

BINGHAM, ALMA. *Improving Children's Facility in Problem Solving.* Teachers College Press, 1958.

BURNS, MARILYN. *The Book of Think.* Little, Brown and Co., 1976.

CANEY, STEVEN. *Kids' America.* Workman Publishing Co., 1978.

CARDOZO, P., and MENTEN, T. *The Whole Kid's Catalog.* Bantam Books, 1975.

DEMILLE, R. *Put Your Mother on the Ceiling.* Viking Press, 1973.

GOLDBERG, EDWARD D. and GOLDBERG, ANN T. "Teaching Problem-Solving Skills," *Instructor,* November 1971, pp. 88–9.

HARMIN, M., KIRSCHENBAUM, H., and SIMON, S. *Clarifying Values Through Subject Matter: Applications for the Classroom.* Winston Press, 1973.

JACOBS, GABRIEL. *When Children Think.* Teachers College Press, 1970.

KAHL, DAVID H. and GAST, BARBARA J. *Learning Centers in the Open Classroom.* International Center for Educational Development, 1974.

KAPLAN, SANDRA, KAPLAN, JO ANN, MADSEN, SHEILA, and GOULD, BETTE. *A Young Child Experiences.* Goodyear Publishing Co., Inc., 1975.

KATCHEN, CAROLE. "Give a Child a Camera," *Scholastic Teacher,* January 1973, pp. 14–15.

MASSIALAS, B., and ZEVIN, J. *Creative Encounters in the Classroom: Teaching and Learning Through Discovery.* John Wiley, 1967.

SHULMAN, L., and KEISLAR, E. *Learning by Discovery: A Critical Appraisal.* Rand McNally, 1966.

SMITH, J. *Setting Conditions for Creative Teaching in the Elementary School.* Allyn and Bacon, 1966.

TORRANCE, E. P. and MYERS, R. *Creative Learning and Teaching.* Harper and Row, 1970.

"Visual Education: Give a Child a Camera and . . ." *Grade Teacher,* November 1969, pp. 81–91.

WURMAN, R. (ED.). *Yellow Pages of Learning Resources.* M.I.T. Press, 1972.

YANES, SAMUEL, and HOLDORF, CIA. *Big Rock Candy Mountain: Resources for Our Education.* Delacorte Press, 1971.

YARDLEY, ALICE. *Young Children Thinking.* Citation Press, 1973.

LANGUAGE ARTS

Classroom Materials and Activities

The Big Book of Independent Study, Goodyear Publishing Company, Inc., 1640 Fifth Street, Santa Monica, CA 90401, $17.

Caption Cards: Current Events, Educational Design Associates, P.O. Box 915, East Lansing, MI 48823, $4.

Creative Expression Books, Scholastic Book Service, 904 Sylvan Avenue, Englewood Cliffs, NJ 07632, $1 each (titles include *Dinosaur Bones, Ghost Ships, Jungle Sounds,* and *Cook-up Tales*).

Creative Learning Centers: Set II, Mass Media, Creative Teaching Press, Inc., 5305 Production Drive, Huntington Beach, CA 92649, $6 and $8.

Interact, P.O. Box 262, Lakeside, CA 92040, publishes materials, at $5 each, with such titles as *Claim, Detective, Persuasion,* and *Television,* which are stimulating for use in connection with language arts activities.

Let's Write a Poem: A Poetry Workshop, Guidance Associates, 757 Third Avenue, New York, NY 10016, $53.

Mankind (Open-Ended Reading Task Cards), from *Keys to Understanding* by Creative Teaching Press, Inc., $6.

Origins of Words, Curriculum Associates, Inc., 6 Henshaw Street, Woburn, MA 01801, $1.

A Pocketful of Poetry, Guidance Associates, $53.

The Productive Thinking Program, Charles E. Merrill Publishing Co., 1300 Alum Creek Drive, Columbus, OH 43216, $150.

Propaganda Game, WFF'N Proof Learning Games Assoc., 1490 South Boulevard, Ann Arbor, MI 48104, $10.

The Stop, Look, and Write Series, Bantam Books, 666 Fifth Avenue, New York, NY 10022, $7.

Teacher's Guides and References

APPLEGATE, MAUREE. *Helping Children Write: A Thinking Together about Children's Creative Writing.* Row, Peterson, 1954.

ASHTON-WARNER, SYLVIA. *Teacher.* Bantam Books, 1963.

BARNEY, LEROY. "Writing about the Out-of-Doors," *Grade Teacher,* April 1971, pp. 104–5.

BLACKBURN, JACK E. and POWELL, W. CONRAD. *One at a Time All at Once: The Creative Teacher's Guide to Individualized Instruction Without Anarchy,* Goodyear Publishing Company, Inc., 1976.

CULLUM, ALBERT. *Push Back the Desks.* Citation Press, 1967.

DIFFIN, LESLYE. "Opening the Door to Poetry," *The Instructor,* October 1966, pp. 3–4.

Drama with and for Children (OE 33007). U.S. Department of Health, Education and Welfare, 1960.

FORTE, IMOGENE, PANGLE, MARY ANN, and TUPA, ROBBIE. *Center Stuff for Nooks, Crannies and Corners.* Incentive Publications, Inc., 1973.

HENNINGS, DOROTHY GRANT, and GRANT, BARBARA M. *Content and Craft: Written Expression in the Elementary School.* Prentice-Hall, 1973.

HENRY, MABEL WRIGHT. *Creative Experiences in Oral Language.* National Council of Teachers of English, 1967.

HOPKINS, LEE BENNETT. *Let Them Be Themselves: Language Arts for Children in Elementary Schools.* Citation Press, 1974.

KOCH, KENNETH. *Wishes, Lies and Dreams: Teaching Children to Write Poetry.* Vintage Books, 1970.

LIVINGSTON, MYRA COHN. *When You Are Alone/It Leaves You Capone: An Approach to Creative Writing with Children.* Atheneum, 1973.

NELSON, R. M. "Getting Children into Reference Books," *Elementary English,* September 1973, pp. 884–7.

PAUL, GRACE. "Pestiferous Letters," *Grade Teacher,* November 1973, pp. 22, 24, 26.

PILON, B. *Teaching Language Arts Creatively in the Elementary Grades.* John Wiley and Sons, Inc., 1978.

RICE, SUSAN, ED. *Films Kids Like.* American Library Association, 1973.

SANDERS, SANDRA. *Creating Plays with Children.* Citation Press, 1970.

SCHAFF, JOANNE. *The Language Arts Idea Book: Classroom Activities for Children.* Goodyear Publishing Company, Inc., 1976.

SIMON, SIDNEY B., and LIEBERMAN, PHYLLIS. "Analyzing Advertising: An Approach to Critical Thinking," *National Elementary Principal,* September 1966, pp. 16–18.

SMITH, J. *Creative Teaching of Language Arts in the Elementary School.* Allyn and Bacon, 1973.

STANFORD, G., and STANFORD, B. *Learning Discussion Skills Through Games.* Citation Press, 1969.

SWYERS, BETTY J. "Get It on Tape," *Grade Teacher,* November 1971, pp. 4, 6.

WOLFE, EVELYN. "Advertising and the Elementary Language Arts," *Elementary English,* January 1965, pp. 42–49.

GENERAL SCIENCE REFERENCES

Magazines

T means "teacher-oriented"; C means "child-oriented." The publications listed are helpful in keeping abreast of changes in science.

Audubon, National Audubon Society, Harrisburg, PA. (Published bimonthly.)

Cornell Rural School Leaflets, New York State College of Agriculture, Ithaca, NY 14850. (Quarterly; T)

Junior Natural History, American Museum of Natural History, New York, NY 10024. (Monthly; C and T)

My Weekly Reader, American Education Publications, Education Center, Columbus, Ohio 43216. (Weekly during the school year)

National Geographic, National Geographic Society, 1146 Sixteenth St. N.W., Washington, D.C. (Monthly; C and T)

Natural History, American Museum of Natural History, 79 St. and Central Park West, New York, NY 10024 (Monthly; C and T)

APPENDIX

Ranger Rick's Nature Magazine, National Wildlife Federation, Washington, D.C. (Eight times yearly)

Science Newsletter, Science Service, Inc., 1719 N. Street N.W., Washington, D.C. 20036. (Weekly; T)

Science and Children, National Science Teachers Association, Washington, D.C. 20036. (Eight times a year; C and T)

Sky and Telescope, Sky Publishing Corp., Cambridge, MA. (Monthly)

Tomorrow's Scientists, National Science Teachers Association, Washington, D.C. 20036. (Eight issues a year; T)

Weatherwise, American Meteorological Society, 3 Joy St., Boston, MA 02108 (Monthly; T)

Books

ALTHOUSE, ROSEMARY and MAIN, CECIL JR., *Science Experiences for Young Children,* Teachers College Press, Columbia University, New York, 1975. A box of ten teacher booklets containing activities for primary-level children on colors, food, magnets, wheels, pets, water, seeds, air, senses, and human growth.

ANDERSON, RONALD, and others, *Developing Children's Thinking through Science,* Prentice-Hall, Inc., Englewood Cliffs, N.J., 1970, 370 pp. A methods book.

BERGER, MELVIN, and CLARK, FRANK, *Science and Music,* Whittlesey House, New York, 1971.

BRUNER, JEROME S., *The Process of Education,* Random House, Inc., New York, 1960, 97 pp. The paperback edition of a provocative book.

BUSCH, PHYLLIS, *Exploring as You Walk in the Meadow,* J. B. Lippincott Company, Philadelphia, PA, 1972, 40 pp. Suggestions about exploring and finding.

CARIN, ARTHUR A., and SUND, ROBERT B., *Teaching Modern Science,* Charles E. Merrill Books, Inc., Columbus, OH, 1970, 625 pp. Methods of using the discovery approach.

COBB, VICKI, *Science Experiments You Can Eat,* Lippincott, Philadelphia, 1972. Teaches simple chemistry and other science areas through food preparation.

COOPER, ELIZABETH K., *Science on the Shores and Banks,* Harcourt Brace Jovanovich, New York, 1960; *Science in Your Own Back Yard,* Harcourt Brace Jovanovich, New York, 1960.

DE VITO, ALFRED and KROCKOVER, GERALD H., *Creative Sciencing,* Little, Brown, and Company, Boston, 1976. A wide variety of teaching ideas and activities to stimulate creativity in elementary school and junior high school children.

The ESS Reader, Education Development Center Inc., Newton, MA, 1970, 236 pp. A collection of articles on science teaching.

FRIEDL, ALFRED E., *Teaching Science to Children, The Inquiry Approach,* Random House, New York, 1972. Features a large array of hands-on science activities for elementary-school children.

GOLDBERG, LAZER, *Children and Science,* Charles Scribner's Sons, New York, 1970, 146 pp. A guide for parents and teachers to a program of science based on children's curiosity.

GOOD, DONALD G., *Science and Children Readings in Elementary Science Education,* William C. Brown Company, Publishers, Dubuque, Iowa, 1972, 422 pp. Collected readings.

HERBERT, DON, *Mr. Wizard's Science Secrets,* Popular Mechanics, New York, 1953; *Mr. Wizard's Experiments for Young Scientists,* Random House, Inc., New York.

HONE, ELIZABETH B., and others, *A Sourcebook for Elementary Science,* Harcourt Brace Jovanovich, New York, 1971, 475 pp. Techniques and procedures for teaching science.

LANSDOWN, BRENDA, and others, *Teaching Elementary Science through Investigation and Colloquium,* Harcourt Brace Jovanovich, Inc., New York, 1971, 433 pp. A science teaching methods book.

LEWIS, JUNE E., and POTTER, IRENE, *The Teaching of Science in the Elementary School,* Prentice-Hall, Inc., Englewood Cliffs, NJ, 1970, 574 pp. Teaching suggestions and subject matter.

LYNDE, CARLTON J., *Science Experiences With Home Equipment* 1955, *Science Experiences With Inexpensive Equipment* 1956, *Science Experiences With Ten-Cent Store Equipment* 1955, D. Van Nostrand Co., Inc., New York.

MILGROM, HARRY, *Explorations in Science: A Book of Basic Experiments,* E. P. Dutton & Co., Inc., New York, 1961, 128 pp. Exciting experiences that help children understand their world.

PIAGET, JEAN, *Six Psychological Studies,* Random House, New York, 1967. Perhaps the most readable account of Piaget's contribution to an understanding of the thought development of the child.

PODENDORF, ILLA, *Discovering Science on Your Own,* Children's Press, Chicago, 1962. A book to accompany *101 Science Experiments.* For good readers.

PODENDORF, ILLA, *101 Science Experiments,* Grosset and Dunlap, New York, 1960. Simple experiments on a wide variety of science principles.

PODENDORF, ILLA, *The True Book of Science Experiments,* Children's Press, Chicago, 1954.

SCHMIDT, VICTOR E., and ROCKCASTLE, VERNE, *Teaching Science with Everyday Things,* McGraw-Hill, Inc., New York, 1968, 167 pp. Experiments and experiences in many areas of science.

SCHNEIDER, HERMAN, and SCHNEIDER, NINA, *Let's Find Out,* Young Scott Publications, Inc., New York, 1946, 39 pp. A science picture book with simple experiments.

STONE, A. HARRIS, *Science Projects That Make Sense,* McCalls, New York, 1971. Leads children to probe simple problems through use of the five senses.

TANNENBAUM, HAROLD E., and A. PILTZ, *Evaluation in Elementary School Science,* Office of Education Circular N 575, U.S. Government Printing Office, Washington, D.C., 1964.

UNESCO Source Book for Science Teaching, UNESCO Publications Center, 801 Third Avenue, New York, 1973. This is especially useful for work in settings where materials have to be constructed.

U.S. Department of Agriculture, Yearbooks: *Soils and Man* 1938, *Climate and Man* 1941, *Grass* 1948, *Trees* 1949, *Insects* 1952, *Plant Diseases* 1953, *Water* 1955, *Soil* 1957, *Land* 1958, *Food* 1959, *A Place to Live* 1964, *Outdoors, U.S.A.* 1967, *A Good Life for More People: Landscape for Living* 1972, U.S. Government Printing Office, Washington, D.C. 20402.

VICTOR, EDWARD, *Science for the Elementary School,* The Macmillan Company, New York, 1970, 785 pp. Methods and subject matter.

VYGOTSKY, L. S. (translated by Eungenia Hanfmann and Gertrude Vakar), *Thought and Language,* M.I.T. Press, Cambridge, 1962. Although most people find this book an effort to read, a further elaboration of the concept levels we have used for our analyses may be valuable to some teachers.

WHITE, LAURENCE B., *Investigating Science With Rubber Bands,* Addison-Wesley, Reading, MA, 1969. Activities that use rubber bands as the basic material.

WHITE, LAURENCE B., *Investigating Science With Paper,* Addison-Wesley, Reading, MA, 1970. Activities that use paper as the basic material.

WHITE, LAURENCE B., *Investigating Science With Nails,* Addison-Wesley, Reading, MA, 1970. Activities that use nails as the basic material.

World Almanac, Newspaper Enterprises Association, New York. A useful book of facts, which is published annually.

Organizations

American Forestry Association
919 Seventeenth Street N.W.
Washington, D.C. 20006

Friends of the Earth
30 East 42 Street
New York, NY 10017

Izaak Walton League
1326 Waukegan Road
Glenview, IL 60025

League of Women Voters
1730 M Street N.W.
Washington, D.C. 20036

National Geographic Society
17 and M Streets N.W.
Washington, D.C. 20036

National Parks Association
Washington, D.C. 20009

National Wildlife Federation
1412 Sixteenth Street N.W.
Washington, D.C. 20036

Planned Parenthood—World Population
515 Madison Avenue
New York, NY 10022

Population Reference Bureau
1755 Massachusetts Avenue, N.W.
Washington, D.C. 20036

MATHEMATICS RESOURCES

Activity Resources Company, Inc. (1977–78)

Materials may be obtained through: P.O. Box 4875, Hayward, CA 94540 (415) 782-1300

1. *Colored Cube Activity Cards* (K–5) 50 cards #1138 $2.95

Children build sequences with colored cubes from the fifty activity cards contained in the book. Either the colored squares on the book covers or the colored cubes from the ESS kit can be used for these activities.

2. *Metric Fun Activity Cards*
Set A: Primary (K–3) #8256 $5.00
Set B: Intermediate (3–7) #8257 $5.00

3. *Metric Cooking Cards* (2–7) #8417 $5.00
Students have an opportunity to investigate, estimate, measure, and discover metric relationships using these cards.

4. *Task Cards* (K–6) #3500-5 for K through #3506-5 for 6 $3.75 each
The same selections of twenty math puzzles contained in the targetmath duplicating masters, available here in task card form. Students can write on these plastic coated cards which can then be wiped clean and used again and again. Teacher's guide included.

Addison Wesley Publishing Company School Division (1978)

Materials may be obtained through: 2725 Sand Hill Road, Menlo Park, CA 94025

1. *Management Cards* (K 6)
#03071 for Grade K–1, #03072 for Grade 2, #03076 for Grade 6, $10.89 for each
Each package listed above contains thirty-five cards. This set is designed for use with the *Investigating School Mathematics 1973* series.

2. *Management Cards* (K–6)
#02491 for Grade K–1, #02492 for Grade 2, #02496 for Grade 6, $10.89 for each
Each package listed above contains fifty cards. This set is designed for use with the *Elementary School Mathematics 1971* series.

3. *Developmental Math Cards* (1–6)
#00527 (Kit A–Grade 1), #00528 (Kit B–Grade 1), #00529 (C–2), #00530 (D–2), #00531 (E–3), #00532 (F–3), #00533 (G–4), #00534 (H–4), #00535 (I–5), #00536 (J–5), #00537 (K–6), #00538 (L–6) $5.57 for each #00540 Primary Set (Kits A–F), #00541 Junior Set (Kits G–L) $31.26 for each
These are open-ended activity cards to supplement any basal math program with their colorful and motivating art work. They provide lots of active involvement, fun, and good mathematics for children.

4. *Cuisenaire Rods Student Activity Cards* #01173 $11.95
These 126 cards provide for the investigation and exploration of math concepts through active involvement with Cuisenaire rods.

5. *The Calculator Work Box* 1977 (7–9) #06771 $45.00
This set contains two copies each of eighty assignment cards. Topics include the calculator, numbers, measurement, real life math, and extra points. Each group of eight cards ends with a self-test. Two teacher's guides and a pad of student record charts are included.

6. *Metric Activity Cards* 1975 (1–6) #02760 Complete Set—$35.20
#02761 Kit A, Length (thirty cards and Teacher's manual)—$16.00 #02762 Kit B, Area and Temperature (twenty-four cards and Teacher's manual)—$12.80 #02763 Kit C, Volume, Capacity, and Mass (twenty-two cards and manual)—$9.12

These cards are classified into six topic groups; the first half of the cards in each group is designed for primary grades, the second half for intermediate grades.

APPENDIX

Creative Teaching Associates (1974)

Materials may be obtained through: P.O. Box 293, Fresno, CA 93708 (209) 251-9410

Pattern Blocks Task Cards (K–6) #4150 $4.95

These multi-colored cards are designed to provide manipulative experiences with concepts including symmetry, area, shape recognition, and fractions.

Creative Publications (1978)

Materials may be obtained through: 3977 E. Bayshore Road, P.O. Box 10328, Palo Alto, CA 94303

1. *Color Cube Activities* #36621 $17.95

   Over 130 math activities, printed on colorful cards, invite independent work. Some of the activities described include number patterns, basic operations, place value, magic squares, and metric measurement. The activities are ungraded and useful for students in grades K–8.

2. *Student Activity Cards For Cuisenaire Rods* #30502 $12.95 (1–6)

   Students use these cards with the Cuisenaire rods to reinforce skills in addition, subtraction, multiplication, division, fractions, and some geometry. Ten topic areas include: matching rods, stories about rods, equalities and inequalities, families of rods, and factors and multiples.

3. *Math Balance Activity Cards* #33103 $4.25

   Set of twenty cards which complement the teacher guide. Includes work on addition, subtraction, multiplication, division, and relations.

4. *Fraction Bars Introductory Card Set* #32020 $4.50

   Over twenty-five enjoyable games and activities that students play with only a knowledge of whole numbers. This concrete, visual approach develops positive attitudes and readiness for fractions and their operations. Pictorial, spiral bound, printed in five colors.

5. *Fraction Bars Card Set I* #32021 $4.50

   Over twenty-five games and activities in which playing cards with fractions supplement fraction bars. These stimulating games are designed to teach specific objectives for fractions and their operations.

6. *Fraction Bars Card Set II* #32022 $4.50

   Over twenty-five games and activities featuring twelve-sided dice which generate 144 fractions. These challenging games extend the fraction bar model to provide conceptual development and motivated practice for the four operations.

7. *Loop Activity Cards* #30416 $13.00

   Set of eighty four-color activity cards to accompany the book, *Attribute Games and Activities*. Includes one-, two-, and three-loop cards, and puzzle cards for both A-blocks and People Pieces. Use the cards with the book or design your own games to suit your needs.

8. *Geoboard Activity Cards—Primary Set* #34051 $13.95

   One hundred fifteen cards encourage the student to work independently as he or she explores, compares, makes shapes and designs, counts, and works with coordinates, perimeter, and areas. Organized in twelve sections by topic, cards are large and durable and attractively packaged in their own storage box with teacher instructions.

9. *Geoboard Activity Cards—Intermediate Set* #34052 $13.95 (3–6)

   Suitable for learning centers and independent work, these 121 cards include developmental activities, games, and exercises using the geoboard in elementary mathematics. The student begins with exploring, counting, and moves on to area, perimeter, symmetry, fractions, coordinates. Instructions for teacher included.

Cuisenaire Co. of America, Inc.

Materials can be obtained through: 12 Church Street, New Rochelle, N.Y. 10805

1. *Student Activity Cards for Cuisenaire Rods* (1–6) #20020 $12.95
   This is a set of 126 activity cards for Cuisenaire rods, with fun games and challenging activities to introduce and practice the basic operations of arithmetic. It is divided into ten topic areas and can be used by students to reinforce their understanding of addition, subtraction, multiplication, division, and fractions, as well as some geometric relations.
2. *Introducing Geoboards* (K–3) #20380 $7.95
   Many fun games and activities introduce squares, rectangles, triangles and other polygons, as well as such concepts as symmetry, rotation, and reflection. The author's rich use of illustrations makes this set of sixty cards particularly valuable.
3. *Geoboard Activity Cards* (4–8) #20040 $11.95
   This set includes ninety-six cards for investigating geometric concepts.

Didax Incorporated (1978)

Materials may be obtained through: P.O. Box 2258, Peabody, Mass. 01960
Unifix Activity Cards Kit #N 42-73 $29.50
   The kit contains forty-eight double-sided assignment cards (ninety-six sides), subdivided into six sets of eight double-sided cards. The activities and assignments are self-evident even to children of poor reading ability. Accessory materials, in the form of *Number Name Tiles, Mapping Arrows,* etc., are included, together with six small labelled boxes designed as containers for these various components. There is also an additional envelope containing eight *Mapping Cards* and eight *Vocabulary Cards*.

Educational Materials Catalogs (1978)

Materials may be obtained through: P.O. Box 2158, Berkeley, CA 94702

1. *A Guide to Adventure in Mathematics* (4–8) $10.95
   These 144 multi-colored activity cards provide for shared experiences and resulting discussions which deepen student understanding.
      Available through: Activity Resources Company, Inc.
            P.O. Box 4875, 20655 Hathaway Ave.
            Hayward, CA 94540
2. *Metric Activity Cards* $4.95
   A set of forty activity cards that instantly creates ten learning centers in your classroom.
      Available through: Modern Math Materials
            1658 Albemarle Way
            Burlingame, CA 94010

Educational Teaching Aids (1978)

Materials may be obtained through: 159 W. Kinzie Street, Chicago, IL 60610

1. *ETA Math Activity Card Programs* #4310 $67.50 for a set of 5
   A series of five different Math Activity Cards Sets, providing exercises for reg-

APPENDIX

ular, remedial, or enrichment use. Answers are found on the back of the answer booklet.
- *ETA Beginning Math Program I* (K–3) $13.50 #4305
This set covers simple addition, subtraction, multiplication, and some elementary fractions through experiences with manipulatives. Sixty cards. Teacher's guide.
- *ETA Math Program II* (3–5) $13.50 #4306
This set contains work with number sentences involving all basic operations plus some work with single fractions.
- *ETA Math Program III* (5–8) $13.50 #4308
This set concentrates on experiences leading towards mastery of multiplication, but incorporates topics of order, grouping, and the distributive property.
- *ETA Math Program IV* (3–6) $13.50 #4309
For reinforcement and enrichment a variety of math concepts including metric measurement, time, fractions, graphing, and geometry are taught.
- *ETA Math Program V* (5–8) $13.50 #4307
This is a collection of stimulating math puzzlers including both arithmetic and geometric problems.
2. *Activity Cards* (1–6) #5832-Series 1, #5836-Series 2, #5840-Series 3, #5844-Series 4 $5.95 for each
These include activity cards on five topics: length, weight, capacity, time, and looking around us. Thirty-two per set.
3. *ETA Metric Activity Cards* #550AX (K–3), #550BX (4–6) $5.95 per set
Forty reproducible cards on linear measurement, area, mass, volume/capacity, and temperature are included. There are answer sheets and a record chart.
4. *Daigger Base 10 Block Activity Card Set* #5590 $9.95
This set provides a variety of reproducible games and activities for use with the Daigger Base 10 Block Sets. You also get a 36 × 48 cm place value mat, two dice, an area grid, answer cards and teacher's guide.
5. *ETA Unifix Card Sets 1 and 2* #120-A (K–2), #120-B (2–5) $32.95 for each set
Set 1 includes 114 cards covering sorting, matching, classifying, counting, number recognition, addition, and subtraction. Set 2 has 116 cards on place value, multiplication, division, fractions, percent and bases.
6. *ETA Discovery Blocks and Activity Cards* #1500 $19.95
This set consists of 140 blocks in seventeen shapes. The blocks are made of thick, select hardwood. Fifteen activity cards lead the student to self-discovery of area, fractions, and spatial relationships. The cards are graduated in difficulty.
7. *Activity Cards for Attribute Blocks* #4376 $4.75
The cards provide an introduction to grouping, sequencing, sets, and logic.
8. *ETA Geoboard Activity Cards* #9562 (K–3), #9662 (3–8) $13.95 per set
Each set of over 110 cards shows creative and fundamental ways of using geoboards in a classroom. Teacher's guide is included.
9. *Color Cube Activity Cards* #9502 $17.95
This set includes over 130 math games and activities in number patterns, basic operations, place value, prime and composite numbers, metric measurement, etc. It should be used with color cubes.

Great Ideas, Inc. (1978)

Materials may be obtained through: 40 Oser Ave., Hauppauge, NY 11787
Arithmablocks Activity Cards (3–6) #128 $8.50

These are activity cards specifically designed for use with Arithmablocks. Each activity involves the student in investigating an important math concept. The set includes seventy-eight activities.

Harcourt Brace Jovanovich (1975)

Materials may be obtained through: 757 Third Avenue, New York, NY 10017
Supercube (4–6) #354030-3 $75.00
Supercube is a collection of activity cards that intrigue pupils with games, puzzles, riddles, cartoons, photographs, and drawings. Each card presents and develops a single, simple mathematical concept, and then provides for open-ended activity. It includes sixty-four six-page activity folders and twelve single cards.

LaPine Scientific Company (1978–79)

Materials may be obtained through: Dept. D4, 6009 S. Knox Ave., Chicago, IL 60629
1. *Metric Measurement Poster and Activity Cards* #Z-12475E $12.30 per set
   The twenty-four activity cards supply directions for converting measurements, for finding the distances between cities, and for converting degrees Fahrenheit to Celsius. A teacher's guide and answer card are included.
2. *Activity Cards Kit* #Z11913E $34.25
   This kit contains forty-eight doublesided assignment cards in a durable box designed for storage of the graded envelopes. Also included is a teacher's guide, number name titles, mapping cards, and eight vocabulary cards.
3. *Student Activity Cards* #Z-11063E $11.95
   These are 126 activity cards for Cuisenaire rods with fun games and challenging activities to introduce and reinforce children's understanding of addition, subtraction, multiplication, division, fractions, and geometric relations. Teacher's notes and answers included.
4. *Geoboard Activity Cards* #Z-11273E (K–3), #Z-11274E (3–6) $13.95 per set
   In the primary unit over twenty cards provide developmental skills using the geoboard. The set is organized in twelve sections by topic. Each of the sections is introduced with a teacher direction card followed by nonverbal student activity cards. The intermediate set of 120 cards includes activities and games using the geoboard. Teacher's guides included.

Mafex Media Aids, Inc.

Materials may be obtained through: 90 Cherry Street, Johnstown, PA 15902 (814) 535-3597
1. *Math Activity Cards* #377900 $5.50
   These elementary math cards provide stimulating exercises that include number lines, sets, addition-subtraction facts. The write-on, wipe-off surface is reusable for years.
2. *Activity Cards* #467300 (2–6), #467200 (1–4), #467400 (3–8) $4.95 for each
   Each packet contains forty-eight reusable cards. There is an emphasis on reinforcement of specific skills. The cards are multi-graded and self-directing.
3. *Task Cards* Primary: #955300 (Time), #955400 (Measurement), #955500 (Metric) Intermediate: #955700 (Metric) $12.95 for each
   These self-directed task cards cover seventeen basic areas (K–8). They may be used to teach basic skills, reinforce or enrich a basic curricular area.
4. *Activity Cards Sets 1 thru 5* #456400(Set 1), #456500(Set 2), #456800(Set 5) $5.95 for each set

APPENDIX   **317**

These five sets of fifty-two cards each are designed to provide an excellent foundation in basic math skills. Topics included are: introduction to addition and subtraction; basic addition and subtraction operations with an introduction to regrouping; addition and subtraction facts with regrouping in ones, tens, and hundreds places; introduction to multiplication; and multiplication facts with products to 90.

5. *Motivator Activity Cards* #672300 $35.75

    Plastic laminated activity cards provide an exciting method for developing mathematical skills. Dark wax markers are used to write on the cards, which can be wiped clean and used over and over. Answer sheets are provided. Topics included are: number readiness, multiplication/division, fractions, mathematics review, addition and subtraction.

6. *Geometric Shapes Activity Cards* #377600 $5.50

    These cards are designed for independent student activities in learning concepts concerning triangles, squares, rectangles, and line segments. The cards in a set of eight have write-on, wipe-off surfaces.

7. *Metric Measure Activity Cards* #457600(Set 1), #457700(Set 2) $5.95 for each

    Set 1 introduces linear metric units with correct spellings and abbreviations, the use of metric tapes and calipers, and perimeter. Set 2 covers area, capacity, volume, mass/weight, and temperature.

8. *Metric Masters and Task Cards* #533100 $13.29

    Metric task cards offer thirty-two progressive metric tasks, using a pure metric approach. The teacher's guide serves as a resource book.

Midwest Publications Company, Inc.

Materials may be obtained through: P.O. Box 129, Troy, MI 48084

No Read Math Activities Vol. 1-Lower Elementary, Vol. 2-Upper Elementary, Vol. 3-Junior High $35.00 for each 198 card set

These activity cards are in key sort card form following the same table of contents. The cards from either set may appropriately be used in junior or senior high if necessary. Since no reading is involved, the cards can be used in a multi-lingual classroom.

Math Shop, Inc. (1974–75)

Materials may be obtained through: 5 Bridge Street, Watertown, MA 02172

1. *Attribute Guide Cards* #4031 $3.25

    These forty assignment cards on Carroll and Venn diagrams, etc., are useful when planning coordinated programs which demand an individualized assignment card approach.

2. *Multibase Arithmetic Blocks Work Cards* #5076 $28.50

    One set of cards for each of the four basic operations are included here along with the manuals *The Arithmetic and Algebra of Natural Numbers* and *A Manual of Practical Considerations*.

3. *Math Balance Activity Cards* #4004 $2.30

    This set of twenty work cards includes work on the four basic operations and relations. Topics are introduced through number as a property of a set.

4. *Geoboard Activity Cards* (Primary) #33009 $12.95

    Here are 120 cards that promote high interest activities which develop basic geometric concepts. The set includes a teacher's guide.

5. *Geoboard Activity Cards* (Intermediate) #33010 $9.95
   These 120 cards include developmental activities, games, and exercises for elementary mathematics.
6. *Willbrook Discovery Mathematics Work Cards* #5162 $60.50
   This box of 174 work cards is indexed according to subject. Cards are packed in a durable vinyl-covered box and they have a varnished dirt-resistant finish.

Scott Resources, Inc. (1975), (1977)

Materials may be obtained through: 1900 E. Lincoln, Ft. Collins, CO 80522
1. *Geo-Area Activity Cards* #601-Activities Kit ($6.95), #606-Playing Cards ($2.80), #689-Set of 5 Geoboards ($12.00)
   The kit includes twenty geoboard activity cards, ten game rule cards, and a deck of fifty-one Geo-Area playing cards. It provides exciting card games that reinforce the different methods of computing area on the geoboard.
2. *Color Cube Activity Cards-Math Lab Set* #0501 $16.95
   Here are over 130 exciting math activity and game cards packaged in an attractive, durable box. They are designed for Grades K–9.
3. *Geoboard Activity Cards* #0562-Primary, #0662-Intermediate $13.95 for each
   The primary set of over 120 cards provides developmental and perceptual activities and games using the geoboard. It is organized in twelve sections by topic for grades K–3. The intermediate set includes 120 cards which offer developmental activities, games, and exercises using the geoboard. It is designed for grades 3–8. Instructions for the teacher are included with each set.
4. *Chip Trading Activity Cards* #0675-Set I, #0676-Set II, #0677-Set III, #0678-Set IV, #0679-Set V, #0685-Teacher's Guide
   Each set contains twenty-eight cards and is designed to be used with the corresponding Chip Trading Set.

Selective Educational Equipment, Inc. (1978)

Materials may be obtained through: 3 Bridge St., Newton, MA 02195
1. *AIM Interest Area Activity Cards* #AIM001 through #AIM010 $4.85 for each
   These sets include sixteen activity cards and two answer cards each. The topics included are: people and events, places, environment, health, games, science, sport, design, communication, and enrichment.
2. *Unifix Activity Cards Kit* #UNICDS $27.50
   The set includes ninety-six individualized activities on forty-eight cards. Also included with the cards are separate envelopes containing accessory materials such as numeral, operational, and mapping arrow plaques with storage container for each of the plaques, and teacher's notes.
3. *Student Activity Cards for Cuisenaire Rods* #CUISAC $11.95
   This set of 126 activity cards for cuisenaire rods introduces and reinforces the basic operations of arithmetic with games and challenging activities. It is designed for grades 1–6.
4. *Color Cube Activity Cards* #CCARDS $17.95
   This set includes over 130 exciting math activities on cards and teacher's notes. Two sets of color cubes are recommended for use with these cards.
5. *SAM Activity Cards* #XSGBCK-SAM cards and set of 335 geoblocks $41.00 #XSAMGO-SAM cards for geoblocks
   These geoblock activity cards involve the child in: measurement; shape names and properties; construction; perimeter; area and volume; classification; obser-

APPENDIX

vation, duplication, and analyses of patterns; problem posing and problem solving. The cards are usable independently from the entire SAM unit.

6. *SAM Activity Cards* #XSPBCK-SAM activity cards, pattern blocks, mirrors $25.40 #XSAMPB-SAM cards for pattern blocks $8.00
   These forty-four cards may be used independently of the SAM kit and involve activities with: counting; addition and subtraction; equations and open sentences; fractions; linear measurement; shape properties and construction; symmetry; classification; duplication and analyses of patterns; problem posing and problem solving.

7. *SAM Activity Cards for Soma Cubes* #XSAM33 $1.85
   The activities on these cards add significant rationale for the use of soma cubes in the classroom; e.g., some cards challenge the student to determine the surface area and/or volumes of his or her structures. Cards are designed for grades 2–12+.

8. *Primary Shapes with Activity Cards* #INV354 $15.75
   Each of the twenty-four activity cards has from ten to twenty activities and provides for practical and written work with shape nomenclature and relationships, practical measuring, value of fractions, simple area and perimeter, and attacking and interpreting related problems. The manipulative materials consist of forty-six large, colored plastic shapes (squares, rectangles, triangles) of various related sizes ranging from 5 cm × 5 cm to 20 cm × 20 cm. Cards are designed for grades 1–4.

9. *SAM Activity Cards for Tangrams* #XSSRO4-SAM activity cards and 2 tangram puzzles $6.50, #XSAMTA-SAM activity cards for Tangrams $5.25
   These cards, which can be used independently of SAM, provide activities involving: counting; equations and open sentences; fractions; shape names; properties, and construction; symmetry; area; classification of attributes; observation, duplication, and analyses of patterns; problem posing and problem solving. There are twenty-eight cards in all. Cards are designed for grades 1–5.

10. *SAM Activity Cards for Geoboards* #XS3GEO-SAM activity cards and equipment for geoboards $11.75, #XSAMGB-SAM activity cards for geoboards $8.50
    These fifty-six activity cards (including an evaluation card) call for the use of two types of geoboards—regular 6×6 (pin) and a circular board resembling a clockface.

11. *Cube-o-gram Volume and Area Activity Cards* #CUBECD $4.95
    These twenty-four activities, from easy to complex, help build student counting, measuring, and perception skills. Each activity requires the student to transform the flat views shown on the card into a 3-dimensional cube-o-gram object whose mass and surface area can be determined easily. A teacher's guide comes with the twenty-four cards.

12. *Triangle Cards* #XKIT02 $13.75 (K–12+)
    This see-kit contains a wide variety of activities, challenges, and puzzles for preschoolers to adults. The complete kit contains: two sets of thirty-six triangle cards, fifty-nine activity cards, a set of label cards, a pair of steel mirrors, and a teacher's guide.

Spectrum Educational Supplies Limited

Materials may be obtained through: 8 Denison Street, Markham, Ontario
1. *Centicube Number Experience Cards #1* #3-910 $16.75 (K–3)
   This set of fifty-six illustrated cards is designed for use with the centicube and

covers basic number experience from counting and matching to simple ideas of addition and subtraction. It is complete with teacher notes and answers.

2. *Centicube Number Experience Cards #2* #3-912 $17.95
   This set of sixty-four cards progresses from the first set. Here, more advanced addition and subtraction is exercised leading on to multiplication, division, fractions, and decimals with teacher's notes and answers.
3. *Centicube Metrication and Measurement Cards* #3-911 $32.00
   Metrication and measurement through structured experiments in length, area, volume, and mass utilizing the centicube is provided in this set of 107 cards. They are divided into three broad age ranges—forty-three cards for primary, thirty-seven cards for junior, twenty-seven cards for intermediate. Teachers' notes and answers are included.
4. *Discovering Metric Activity Cards* #3-970(Mass), #3-972(Capacity), #3-974 (Area), #3-971(Linear), #3-973(Volume) $2.95 for each
   These are five sets of twelve each of metric activity cards which are designed for grades 1–4.
5. *Measure and Observe Activity Cards* #4-798 $10.50
   This is a full set of forty-eight illustrated learning cards designed to convey a full understanding of measurement from nonstandard units to the confident use of measuring tools.

St. Paul Book and Stationery (1977–78)

Materials may be obtained through: 1233 W. County Road "E", St. Paul, MN 55112

1. *Unifix Task Cards* #LC251 (K–2), #LC256 (2–4) $3.95 for each
   The K–2 set contains twenty-seven Unifix games and activities. The 2–4 set contains twenty-four Unifix games and activities.
2. *Unifix Activity Cards Kit* #TY4273 $28.00
   Forty-eight double-sided task cards are categorized into six graded sets demonstrating simple to more complex Unifix early math concepts. The kit includes teacher's guide, vocabulary cards, and label cards.
3. *Attribute Block Task Cards* #TH4423 $8.50
   These cards are to be used with the Invicta Desk Top Attribute Block Set. Thirty-four cards with graded activities are provided.
4. *Cuisenaire Activity Cards* #CX20020 $11.95 (1–6)
   This set of 126 cards provides games and activities for individualized or group use.
5. *High-interest Math Task Cards* #ED2120-Set 1, #ED2121-Set 2 $2.95 for each
   These individualized math task cards motivate students with subjects ranging from sports to food. The sets contain twelve cards each. They deal with multiplication and division skills.
   #ED2122-Set 3, #ED2123-Set 4 $2.95 for each
   These cards involve activities with fractions and decimals.
6. *Money Matters Activity Cards* #WZ221 $4.95
   These forty-two reproducible task cards provide a range of individualized activities for money learning.
7. *Geoboard Task Cards* #SF107 $1.75

APPENDIX

This set of nineteen double-sided task cards provides for individualized learning of perimeter, area, coordinates, and basic geometric concepts.

8. *Pattern Blocks Task Cards* #TH4150 $7.95
   This is a series of twenty-four colorful, laminated activity cards for learning geometric concepts through manipulation of pattern blocks. It includes a pad of reproducible sheets for recording discoveries.

9. *Tangram Task Cards* #SF104 $1.35
   Thirty challenging puzzles are included on fifteen cards for use with tangram shapes.

10. *Metric Task Cards* #TP160-Set 1 (Gr. 2–4), #TP161-Set 2 (Gr. 4–6) $4.95 for each
    These reproducible cards provide for activities and games for teaching metric measure. Set 1 contains forty-five cards. Set 2 has forty-six cards.

11. *Metric Fun Activity Cards* #TS150 (Gr. 1–4), #TS130 (Gr. 3–6) $4.95 for each
    Sets A and B each contain forty-four reproducible tasks and games.

12. *Math Games Box* #ED9110 $6.95
    This set contains 150 cards with individualized games and activities for a wide range of skill levels.

13. *Addition and Subtraction Activity Cards* (1–4) #FK233 $4.95
    These forty-four cards provide high-interest, basic math tasks.

14. *Super Math Activity Cards* (3–6) #FK259 $4.95
    These forty-five cards provide for practice with whole numbers, fractions, and decimals.

15. *Computation Game Cards* (2–6) #FK235 $4.95
    These forty-six cards reinforce basic skills.

Science Research Associates, Inc. (SRA) (1978)

Materials may be obtained through: 259 E. Erie Street, Chicago, IL 60611

1. *Metric Activity Cards* #88-118 (Complete program) $229.50 (1–3) #3-1001 (Primary activity cards) $95.75 #88-119 (Complete program) $229.50 (4–6) # 3-1002 (Intermediate activity cards) $95.75
   The complete programs include activity cards, spirit masters, and a manipulative kit. There are 105 four-page activity cards in each set. The cards are coded by grade level and skill area. Hands-on activities develop measurement concepts and skills.

2. *Mathematics: An Activity Approach* #3-2975 (Complete kit) Write for price.
   188 activity cards are included in this kit. These cards contain all necessary information for hands-on math experiences.

3. *Math Applications Kit* #3-545 $87.50 (4–8)
   270 activity cards require students to collect and use data to derive conclusions. The teacher's handbook contains evaluation questions, critiques, and correlation charts. Ten reference cards, a student handbook, and an almanac are also included.

4. *Metric Math Applications Kit* #3-400020 $110.00 (4–8)
   This kit offers practice in metrics. 200 activity cards require students to collect and use data to derive conclusions.
   2 centimeter grids, a teacher's handbook, and thirty student workbooks are also included.

John Wiley and Sons, Inc. (1975)

Materials may be obtained through: 605 Third Ave., New York, NY 10016

1. *Nuffield Mathematics Project Work Cards* #ISBN65193-1 (Speed1) $3.19, #ISBN65201-6 (Decimals 1) $3.57, #ISBN65202-4 (Number Patterns) $3.75, #ISBN65195-8 (Symmetry) $3.75, #ISBN65194-X (Angles) $3.75, #ISBN65230-X (Similarity 1), #ISBN65229-6 (Decimals 2), #ISBN65232-6 (Number Patterns 2), #ISBN65221-O (Co-ordinates 2), #ISBN65193-1 (Area) $4.15 for each

   These carefully graded work cards provide modules of work devoted to a single math topic. They are designed to be used by students in grades 6–9.

2. *Nuffield Mathematics Problem Cards* #ISBN65208-3 (Green Set) $3.57, #ISBN65209-1 (Green Set Cards) $2.25, #ISBN65184-2 (Purple Set) $3.57, #ISBN65183-4 (Red Set) $3.57

   These cards provide sets of problems with solutions and material for follow-up work.

Photo Credits

Cover photo: Curtis Cooper
Photo taken at John Muir Elementary School, Mrs. Herman's fourth-grade class, courtesy of Santa Monica Unified School District

Thematic unit photos:

    Parkland, p. 65: U.S. Forest Service
    Flight, p. 70: Marshall Licht
    Consumerism, p. 77: Ken Johnson
    What Time Is It?, p. 90: Herbert Petermann
    Sailboats, p. 102: Herbert Petermann
    Energy, p. 112: Ken Johnson
    Cooperation/Competition, p. 149: Curtis Cooper
    Environments, p. 177: Steven McBrady
    Growing and Using Plants, p. 200: Steven McBrady
    Read All About It!, p. 217: Steven McBrady
    Mnemonics, p. 240: Herbert Petermann
    Patterns and Changes, p. 260: Herbert Petermann
    Inventions, p. 275: Herbert Petermann
    Go Fly a Kite!, p. 290: Times photo by Ken Dare

Index

A

Abbreviations, 249–250
Abruscato, Joe, 97, 148, 274
Abstract reasoning, 9
Abstraction, 12
Accomodation, 8
Acronyms, 249–250
Add-on stories, 287
Administrators, 16–17, 43
Advertising, 77, 79–83, 87–89, 217–219, 223–224, 228, 286
Advertising appeals, 87–89
Aerial photography, 73, 189, 301
Affective domain objectives, 47–48
Agriculture, 201
Aircraft, 73, 274
Airfoils, 294–295
Air pressure, 295–297
Algae, 212–214
Allison, Linda, 274
Anachronisms, 92
Analysis questions, 37
Analytic thinkers, 12
Animals, 41, 274

Application questions, 37
Apollo II, 76
Archeology, 101
Aristotle, 16
Arithmetic rules, 283–286
Assessment, 41, 43–48, 51–52
Assimilation, 8
Association, 242, 244–245
Association Montessori Internationale, 40
Astronauts, 76
Attack angle, 294, 298
Attitudes, 152–154, 172–173
Attractiveness, 88
Ausubel, David, 49
Automobiles, 281
Awareness statements, 51

B

Balloons, 73, 75
Bean jar problem, 152, 164–165
"Beat the Clock," 101
"Beauty Contest," 154–157

325

INDEX

Behavior specimen, 172, 174
Behavioral statements, 46–48, 51
Bernoulli, Daniel, 296
Bernoulli effect, 296–297
Bernstein, Theodore, 239
Big Dipper, 101
Biomass, 211–213
Birds, 70, 73, 75, 294
Blake, Jim, 97, 148, 274
Blindfold activity, 152, 157–159
Boats, 102–111
Boelcke, Oswald, 74
Boston whaler, 103
Brainstorming, 6, 28, 83, 160, 202
Brand loyalty, 88
"Bridle for Pegasus, A," 73
British Nuffield projects, 26
Brown, Robin, 41
Brummitt, Wyatt, 302
Bruner, Jerome, 16–17, 21, 54
BuBois, William Père, 73
Building projects, 289
Bulbs, 215
"Bulbs and Batteries," 33–36
Bulletin boards, 41, 75, 220
Burton, Virginia Lee, 188

C

Calculation, 250–259
Calculators, 284–286
Calendar time, 100–101
Caney, Steven, 289
Captain Ahab, 103
Captain Bligh, 103
Car racing, 100
Carbonation, 288
Careers, 70, 73, 76, 110
Cartoons, 224–225
Carver, George Washington, 39, 55, 59
Causal terms, 39
Causality, 32
Cayley, 75
Cellulose, 211

Center of gravity, 272–273, 299
Center Stuff for Nooks, Crannies, and Corners, 89
Change for Children, 89
Charts, 51, 251–253
Chemicals, 41
Cheyney, Arnold B., 239
Chinese junk, 103
Circuits, 33–34
Circular slide rule, 253–255
Classified advertising, 223–224
Clay projects, 204–206
Climate, 177, 179–187, 216, 261
Clinometer, 299
Clipper ships, 103
Clocks, 90, 98–99
    "built-in," 94–95
    making and using, 95–96
Cognitive domain objectives, 47–48
Coil pots, 205–206
Comic strips, 217, 224–225, 237–238, 286, 291
Community, as a resource, 3
Comparison shopping, 89
Competitive behavior, 172, 174–176
Computing Devices, 254
Concept development, 33, 46
Conceptual structures, 1, 12
Concrete operations, 9
Concrete thinking, 17
Conformity, 88
Conservation, 115
Conservation of matter, 8–9
Constellations, 101
Constructivity principle, 12
Consumer research, 84–86
"Consumerism," 77–89, 223–224
Consumption, energy, 116–120
Container art, 201, 204–207
Content, 39
Content accountability, 2
Content outline, 2
CONTIG, 258–259
Contract, 71, 74–76
Convenience, 88
Cooking, 201, 208, 216

INDEX

"Cooperation/Competition," 149–176
"Cooperation Day," 153
Cooperative groups, 48, 157–158, 162–163, 164–165
Cooperative learning, 13, 43
Cooperation Squares game, 152, 162–163
Cooperative stories, 163
Creative writing, 10
Creativity, 88
Critical thinking, 9
Cultivation, 201
Cultural awareness, 291
Current events, 231
Cuttings, 208–209

D

Data collection, 77, 260, 264–265
DaVinci, Leonardo, 75
Dawner, Marian, 302
Day and night, 97–98
Decimals, 284–285
Decision-making, 57–58, 179–181, 195, 290
Deductive reasoning, 3
Definition questions, 36
DeRoche, Edward F., 239
Deschooling Society, 14
Describing, 172, 174
Desired behavior statements, 47–48
Devices, 276
Dewey, John, 17, 21, 23
Diagnosis, 48–51
Diaries, 67
Dienes, Zoltan P., 12, 21
Direct answers, 38
Discipline-centered teaching, 21
Discovery, 33, 49
Discussions, 105–106, 114, 159, 162–163
Disney, Walt, 73
Display advertising, 223–224

Displays, 13, 39–41, 110–111, 125, 301
Distillation, 201, 212–213
Division, 253–259, 285–286
Double Eagle II, 74
Draftometer, 129
Drag, 294, 298
Drawing inferences, 3
Dynamic principle, 12

E

Earhart, Amelia, 73, 76
Early childhood education, 40
Easter, Mary B., 239
Economic stability, 77
Economy, 88
Editorials, 222–223
Egyptian kuffa, 103
Einstein, Albert, 5
Eisner, Vivienne, 238
Electrical appliances, 128
Electrical energy, 112, 117–119, 143–148
Electricity, 33–35
Enactive learning, 17
"Energy," 112–148
    conservation, 114–116, 120, 124, 130–135
    consumption, 114
    crisis, 113–114
    sources, 114, 211–213
Environmental Study Units, 198
"Environments," 177–199, 216
Equilibrium, 8
Ernst, Barbara, 97, 148, 274
Escapement, 101
ESS, 26
Estimating, 59
Evaluation, 43–46, 51–53, 57, 150–151
Examining Your Environment, 198–199
Extrapolating, 3

F

Fabrications, 276, 278
Facilitating learning, 32
Fact and opinion, 218–219, 222–223, 228, 230
Fact charts, 251–253
Feature stories, 222–223
Feeling statements, 50
Fermentation, 212–213
Ferns, 213
Fiarotta, Phyllis, 216
Fiction, 276, 278
Fidell, Jeanette, 239
Finger multiplication, 256–257
Five Weeks in a Balloon, 75
Fizzies, 100–101
"Flight," 70–76
Flowering plants, 213
Flowers, 67, 209–210
Fokker, Anthony, 74
Food production, 202
Forced bulbs, 215
Forced Choices Activity, 152, 159–161
Forces, 293–294
Formal logic, 9
Formal operations, 9
Forte, Imogene, 89
"Fortresses, Castles and Hideaways," 289
"Four Networks" thesis, 14
Fractions, 284–285
Fragrance boxes, 208
Freedom, 54–55
Freedom of the press, 224
Fruits, 210–211, 216
Fungi, 213

G

Gagne, Robert, 42, 241
Games, 282
Gandhi, 4
Gas, use of, 118–119
Gasohol, 211–213
Gasoline Pump Problem, 10–11
Generator, 146–147
Geography, 69, 189
Germination, 67, 207–208
Getzels, J. W., 8
Glenn, William, 254
Gliders, 75, 294
Global goals, 44
Globes, 97
Goddard, Robert, 75
"Go Fly a Kite!," 43
Goldstein, Kurt, 27
Goods and services, 184–187
Grades survey, 169–171
Graphs, 68, 94–95, 142, 145, 147, 265, 267, 269, 274
Grasses and grains, 207
Gravity, 261, 264, 272–273, 299
Great Perpetual Learning Machine, The, 97, 148, 274
Group status, 151
"Growing and Using Plants," 200–216
Growing Up Green, 216

H

Hang gliding, 301
Hartley, Jay, 302
Hassard, Jack, 97, 148, 274
Headlines, 217
Heat containment, 133
Heat energy, 112, 130–135, 138
Heat loss, 129, 134–135
Helicopters, 75
Herbs, 208
Hero worship, 88
Hierarchical theory of motivation, 27
Holistic-dynamic theory of motivation, 27
Hone, Elizabeth, 302
Horatio Hornblower, 103
Horn, Valerie, 239
Horology, 101

Horse-trading Problem, 9–10
Houseplants, 208–209
Howe, Kathy, 150
Huckaby, Gloria, 216
Hull designs, 106–107
Humanistic psychology, 27
Humor, 88
Hunt, J. McV., 40
Hypotheses, 9
Hypothesizing, 47–48, 182, 188, 189

I

"I learned" statements, 51, 159
Iconic learning, 17
Illich, Ivan, 14
Independence, 58
Inductive reasoning, 3
Inferences, 172, 174, 177, 184, 189
Information questions, 36
Inquiry, 33, 151
Insects, 68, 73
Instructional themes, 1
Insulators, 131
Integrated studies, 11, 13, 21, 58
Integrated themes, 2, 3, 19
Integration, 54–55
Intellectual development, 16–17
Interdisciplinary connections, 2
Interviews, 58, 76, 160, 169
Intuitive thinking, 17
Intuitive thought stage, 8
"Inventing a Soft Drink," 279, 287–288
Inventions, 275–289
Inventors, 289
Investigation, 33
Itard, Jean, 40

J

Jason of the "Argonaut," 103
Johnson, Dick, 41
Johnson, Donavan, 254

K

Kaplan, 89
Kilowatt meter, 127, 128
Kites, 41, 43–44, 46, 73, 75, 290–302
Knowledge stating, 241
Kon Tiki, 104
KRYPTO, 258–259
Kurth, Dawn, 79–81

L

Land use, 177, 188–194, 198
Language development, 32, 46
Lapsed time, 92
Law of Rational Skepticism, 18
Learning hierarchy, 42
Learning station, 220–221
Leaves, 67–68, 209, 216
Lee, Peggy, 303
Library, use of, 3
Life cycles, 68
Lift, 294, 298
Light, 143–148
Lillienthal, 75
Lindbergh, Charles, 73, 76
Little House, The, 188–189
LORAN, 111
Lorbier, George, 302
Luxury, 88

M

Macomber, Renee, 178
MACOS, 16
Magic Squares, 283–284
Magnifying glass, 137, 139
"Man in Flight," 73
Manoni, Mary H., 239
Maps, 111, 177, 184, 189–194, 198, 216, 219, 231–232
Marshall, Sylvia, 54
Maslow, Abraham, 27

INDEX

Math facts, 250–259
Mathematical Variable theory, 12
Mathephobes, 22
McGree, Kathy, 41, 52, 64
Meaningful learning set, 49
Measurement, 38–39, 68, 73, 91, 216
Mechanical energy, 112, 142
Melody and memorization, 247, 249
Memorization, 240–259
Memory, 241–242, 244
Minnemast, 26, 253, 302
"Mnemonics," 240–259
Moby Dick, 104
Models, 73–74
Money, 89
Montessori, Maria, 40
Montessori Method, The, 40
Montgolfier, 75
Mosaic pictures, 216
Moss, Senator Frank E., 82
Mosses, 213–215
Motivation, 17, 42
Motor domain, 48
Mouvier, Jean-Paul, 302
Multiple Embodiment principle, 12
Multiplication, 251–259, 284
Music and memorization, 247–250
Musical instruments, 283

N

NASA, 73
National Geographic, 74, 302
National Wildlife Foundation, 198
Naval history, 104
Navigation, 110–111
Nelson, Leslie, 302
Nematodes, 203
Newman, Lee Scott, 302
News sources, 218, 231, 233
News stories, 222–223, 231, 233
Newspapers, 84, 89, 217–239, 273–274, 291

format, 221–222, 225–227
terminology, 221–222
Newspaper Everything Book, The, 238
Non-flowering plants, 213–215
Number lines, 99
Number patterns, 283–286
Nuts, 210–211

O

Object permanence, 8
Objectives, higher order, 3, 33, 57
Observatory, 101
Observing, 47–48, 57–58, 172, 174, 176
Operational definition, 39
Order of happenings, 39
Organisms in soil, 203
Oscillation, 261–271
Outcome questions, 36

P

Pangle, Mary Ann, 89
Papier-mâché, 206
Parachutes, 75
Parents, 16, 41, 43, 208, 234
"Parkland," 65–69
Pattern recognition, 246–247
"Patterns and Changes," 97, 260–274
Peanut butter, 39, 41, 52, 54–61
Peanuts, 55, 291, 302
Peer perception statements, 68
Pelham, David, 302
Pendula, 90, 96–97, 101, 108, 261–271
Perceptual Variability principle, 12
Peter Pan, 104
Phoenician galley, 63
Photographs, 224–225
Piaget, Jean, 8–9, 16–17, 21, 32, 54
Piercey, Dorothy, 239

INDEX

Pinch pots, 205
Planting, 204–205, 207, 213–215
Plant-produced energy, 211–213
Plants, 200–216, 262, 274
Plaster casts, 67
Play Book, The, 289
"Player of the Week," 172
Poe, Edgar Allen, 76
Pole star, 101
Political activities, 83
Polls, 217, 234–235
Ports-of-call, 104
"Poster Contest, The," 152, 172, 174–176
Pottery making, 201, 205–206
Predicting, 47–48, 169, 232, 260, 263
Pre-operational stage of development, 8
Preschools, 40
Pressure changes, 295–297
Priority statements, 49–50
Problem finders, 2, 5, 10–11
Problem solving, 2–4, 6–11, 164–165, 276, 291, 300
Problems in teaching, 4–6
Process, 49
Process approach, 16
Process objectives, 39
Process of Education, The, 16
Product, 49
Product promotion, 77, 87
Product testing, 86
Progress, 54
Project planning, 279–280
Propagation, 201
Purpose questions, 36
Puzzles, 278, 282
Pyramid construction, 223

Q

Questioning, 32–39
Questionnaires, 80–82

R

Radio, 111
Radio compasses, 111
Readiness, 16–17
Reasons for Seasons, The, 274
Recall, 242
Reception learning, 49
Record keeping, 201
Recording, 47–48, 57, 68
Reference answers, 38
Reflectors, 137, 139
Regatta, 106, 109, 110–111
Relationship questions, 36
Relevance, 54
Repetition, 245–246
Reporting, 57
Representational thought, 17
Research skills, 3, 105
Reversibility, 9
Reviews, 234, 236
Rhythm and memorization, 247–248
Richtofen, Baron von, 74
Rivers, 261
"Roatsy Oatsies," 89
Rockets, 73, 75
Role playing, 174, 195–197
Room newspaper, 238
Roquet game, 274
Rotation, 90, 97
Rubbings, 216
Rule application, 241
Rule learning, 246–247
Russell, Bertrand, 18
Russell, Helen Ross, 198

S

"Sailboats," 102–111
Satellites, 73, 111
Scarcity, 79
Schrank, Jeffrey, 165
Schultz, Charles, 55, 302
Schumacher, E. F., 4

INDEX

Science fiction literature, 289
Sea navigation, 110–111
Seasonal change, 182–183, 261–262, 274
Security, 88
Seedlings, 209–210
Seeds, 67, 201, 207–211, 216
Seguin, Edouard, 40
Self-actualization, 27
Selsam, Millicent, 57
Senate Subcommittee for Consumers, 82
Sensorimotor stage of development, 8
Sex in advertising, 88
Shadows, 97–98
Shippen, K., 73
Sidereal time, 101
Simulation games, 149
Sirens, 283
Skelsey, Alice, 216
Skills mastery, 3, 42
Skimming, 89
Slinky spring, 265–267
Small Is Beautiful, 4
Snips and Snails and Walnut Whales, 216
Sociograms, 48
Sociometric survey, 151, 152–154
Soil, 202–205, 214
Solar energy, 112, 136–141
Songs, 73, 76, 287
Sources of information, 222–223
Space exploration, 73
Speed, measuring, 108
Spores, 213, 214
Sports, 228, 230
Sports survey, 172–173
Spring scale, 106
Sputnick, 75
Stangl, John, 41
Status, 88
Stimulus-bound interpretation, 11
Stimulus-free interpretation, 11
Story endings, 286–287

Structure, 16
Style changes, 88
Sugar fermentation, 201, 212
Sundials, 90, 98, 101
Sun time, 91
Supply and demand, 77–79
Support systems, 201
Surveys, 59, 79–82, 115, 120–121, 151–154, 169–171, 172–173, 182–183, 234–235, 288
Symbolic language, 8
Symbolic learning, 17
Synthesis questions, 37
Synthesizing, 241
Systems, 261–263

T

Taba, Hilda, 23
Tank table, 106–108
Task analysis, 42
Teacher role, traditional, 2
Teaching Human Beings, 165
Television, 79–83, 89
Ten-Minute Field Trips, 198
Testing, 41, 43, 74
Tethered airfoils, 294–295
Thematic approach, 2, 3, 19, 22
Theme clarification, 30
Thought and Language, 32
"Three R's," 2, 14
Tilt, 299
Timbers, 68
Time, 60–61, 90–101
Time line, 75
Tinkertoys, 268, 299
Treasure Island, 104
Trees, 28–32, 66–69
"TV Center," 89
Twenty-one Balloons, The, 73
Twigs, 68–69
Two-way chart, 51–53
Typa, Robbie, 89

INDEX

U

"Unparalleled Adventure of One Hans Pfall, The," 76
USMES, 26, 242

V

Values clarification, 152
Value judgements, 228–231, 233
Vanity, 88
Vector forces, 104
Vegetables, 209–210, 216
Vermiculite, 204
Verne, Jules, 75
Vygotsky, Lev. S., 31, 46

W

Wastebasket archeology, 101
Water clock, 101
Weather, 43, 69, 218, 219, 231–232, 261–262, 273–274
Webbing diagram, 63–64
Weise, Adelle, 238
"What Time Is It?," 90–101
White, R., 241
Whole Cosmos Catalog of Science Activities, 97, 148, 274
"Win as Much Money as Possible,"152, 165–168
Wind, 43, 68, 104
Wood, 69
World War I, 74
World War II, 74
Wright, Orville and Wilbur, 73–74

Y

Yeast, 212

Z

Zeppelin, Count, 74
Zodiacal constellations, 101